War, the American State, and Politics since 1898

This book examines major international conflicts from the Spanish-American War through Vietnam, arguing that foreign wars have strong effects on American state development, policymaking, political parties, and elections. First, major wars expose and highlight problems requiring governmental solutions or necessitating emergency action. Second, despite well-known curtailments of civil liberties, wars often enhance democracy by drawing attention to the contributions of previously marginalized groups and facilitating the extension of fuller citizenship rights to them. Finally, wars affect the party system. Foreign conflicts create crises – many of which are unanticipated – that require immediate attention, supplant prior issues on the policy agenda, and engender shifts in party ideology. These new issues and redefinitions of party ideology frequently influence elections by shaping both elite and mass behavior.

Robert P. Saldin is Assistant Professor of Political Science at the University of Montana. From 2010 to 2012, he is a Robert Wood Johnson Scholar at Harvard University. Previously, he was the Patrick Henry Postdoctoral Fellow at Johns Hopkins University, a Miller Center Dissertation Fellow in Politics and History, and a Visiting Scholar at the University of California at Berkeley's Institute of Governmental Studies. In 2008, Saldin received his Ph.D. from the University of Virginia. His refereed articles have appeared in *Journal of Politics*, *Political Research Quarterly*, and *The Journal of Policy History*, among others.

War, the American State, and Politics since 1898

ROBERT P. SALDIN

University of Montana

CAMBRIDGE
UNIVERSITY PRESS

CAMBRIDGE
UNIVERSITY PRESS

32 Avenue of the Americas, New York NY 10013-2473, USA

Cambridge University Press is part of the University of Cambridge.

It furthers the University's mission by disseminating knowledge in the pursuit of education, learning and research at the highest international levels of excellence.

www.cambridge.org
Information on this title: www.cambridge.org/9781107690981

© Robert P. Saldin 2011

Portions of this book appeared previously in the following articles: "Foreign Affairs and Party Ideology: The Case of Democrats and World War II," *Journal of Policy History* 22:4 (Fall 2010); "World War I and the 'System of 1896,'" *The Journal of Politics* 72:3 (July 2010); "Foreign Affairs and the 2008 Election," *The Forum*, 6:4 (Dec. 2008).

First published 2011
First paperback edition 2013

A catalogue record for this publication is available from the British Library

Library of Congress Cataloguing in Publication data

Saldin, Robert P., 1977–
War, the American state, and politics since 1898 / Robert P. Saldin.
  p. cm.
Includes bibliographical references and index.
ISBN 978-0-521-11915-3 (hardback)
1. Politics and war – United States – History – 20th century.   2. United States – Politics and government – 20th century.   3. United States – History, Military – 20th century.
4. Political culture – United States – History – 20th century.   5. Political parties – United States – History – 20th century.   6. Spanish-American War, 1898 – Political aspects – United States.   7. WorldWar, 1914–1918 – Political aspects – United States.   8. WorldWar, 1939–1945 – Political aspects – United States.   9. Korean War, 1950–1953 – Political aspects – United States.   10. Vietnam War, 1961–1975 – Political aspects – United States.   I. Title.
E743.S244   2010
973.9–dc22   2010018293

ISBN 978-0-521-11915-3 Hardback
ISBN 978-1-107-69098-1 Paperback

For My Family

Contents

Acknowledgments

In writing this book, I have been the happy beneficiary of generous assistance on many fronts. The project began as a doctoral dissertation at the University of Virginia. My greatest intellectual debt is to my thesis advisor, Jim Ceaser. From the day I arrived in Charlottesville, he has been a consistent source of guidance, encouragement, and inspiration. Sid Milkis, with his passion for politics and history, has likewise been an important influence from my earliest days in graduate school. Both are constant reminders of what initially drew me toward academia and the intellectual life in the first place. In the summer of 2005, as I transitioned from the relatively formulaic stages of planning and proposing my dissertation to the more nebulous process of actually writing it, I had the good fortune of meeting David Mayhew. Without knowing what he was getting himself into, David offered to read whatever I produced. His generosity and extensive comments on multiple readings of the manuscript have been absolutely invaluable. John Owen brought the insights of an international relations scholar to the project. Finally, Russell Riley, an eleventh-hour addition to the committee, got up to speed quickly and provided excellent suggestions for strengthening the manuscript as it transitioned from dissertation to book.

Numerous friends and colleagues supplied helpful feedback on various parts of the manuscript, including Nitu Bagchi, Brian Balogh, Robert Eisinger, Shamira Gelbman, Larycia Hawkins, Steve Knott, Gregg Lindskog, Rob Mickey, Nelson Polsby, Adam Sheingate, Gordon Silverstein, and George Thomas. Dan DiSalvo, Patrick Roberts, and Sid Tarrow read the entire manuscript at critical junctures and provided extensive commentary. Dylan Laslovich was a reliable research assistant.

This book could not have been completed without generous institutional and financial backing. The Institute of Governmental Studies at the University of California, Berkeley, offered me an engaging home as a Visiting Scholar for two years. I am especially indebted to the late Nelson Polsby – founder of, and longtime officiant over, IGS's famous afternoon tea sessions – for fostering and welcoming me into Berkeley's dynamic community of scholars. Another vital source of support came from the Miller Center of Public Affairs. For more than a decade, the Miller Center's Fellowship Program in Politics and History, run by Brian Balogh and Sid Milkis, has played a central role in the growth of the American political development subfield. I was fortunate to spend a year in the program. Following graduate school, Johns Hopkins University's Patrick Henry Postdoctoral Fellowship allowed me to focus on turning the dissertation into a book. Special thanks go to Adam Sheingate and Matt Crenson. My position at Hopkins also permitted me to complete the political scientist's requisite tour of duty in Washington. The American Political Science Association's Centennial Center and its Warren E. Miller Fellowship in Electoral Politics provided a base of operations in the heart of the American state. For the past two years, the University of Montana's Political Science Department has been an ideal place to put the finishing touches on this project. Along the way, critical financial assistance came from the Dean's Dissertation Fellowship in the College of Arts and Sciences at the University of Virginia, the Earhart Foundation, and the University of Montana's Office of the Vice President for Research and Development. I also thank Lew Bateman and his team at Cambridge University Press for believing in this project and shepherding it into print.

Most importantly, I thank my family, to whom I dedicate this book. I am particularly grateful for the support of my parents, my sister Kate, and my love, Erin. As skilled writers, readers, and educators, each of them has also contributed intellectually to this project. For years, my mom and dad have served as dedicated sounding boards and editors of my work. I simply could not have done this without their help. Finally, a heartfelt expression of gratitude goes to Erin. Her love, patience, and confidence mean more to me than anything.

RPS
Missoula, Montana
Summer 2010

1

Introduction

In the years following the terrorist attacks of September 11, 2001, and the invasion of Iraq by the United States in 2003, an old question has received new attention: How does war affect the state and its citizens? This line of inquiry has been pursued by thoughtful citizens and thinkers for most of human history, and it counts Thucydides and Aristotle among the many who have contributed to the discussion. The book that follows is an attempt to shed new light on this ancient and universal question in the American context.

This question is particularly timely to consider in the United States, not only because events of the last decade have (once again) thrust it to the forefront of the nation's consciousness, but also because political scientists – ideally, a source to which today's thoughtful citizens and thinkers might turn for insights into these kinds of perennial concerns – have largely avoided it. Political scientists studying the United States usually limit their causal variables to those that can be found within the nation's borders. Regrettably, this narrow approach leaves out an enormous explanatory factor: foreign wars. The under appreciation of major U.S. wars as a causal variable in the domestic realm limits our understanding of American politics and government. A few leading scholars have recently pointed out this deficiency. As David R. Mayhew contends:

Wars have been underexamined as causal factors in American political history.... Political scientists who study American domestic politics have underappreciated [their] effects.... In general, the study of elections, parties, issues, programs, ideologies, and policy making has centered on peacetime narratives and causation.[1]

Similarly, Ira Katznelson has noted this omission in the American political development (APD) literature, arguing that "the neglect of international forces is pronounced in the subfield of APD.... APD scholars have been attuned

[1] David R. Mayhew, "War and American Politics," *Perspectives on Politics* 3:3 (Sept. 2005), 473. See also: Mayhew, *Electoral Realignments: A Critique of an American Genre* (New Haven, CT: Yale University Press, 2002), 156–8.

almost exclusively to internal processes and developments.... [The resulting] loss to intellectual vibrancy has been considerable.... None of the subfield's landmark books... has made international subjects integral to its analysis."[2] Mayhew and Katznelson zero in on a blind spot that is all too common among political scientists studying the United States. The domestic and international realms are generally treated as separate entities, existing independently of one another. Like brief thunderstorms, international events are cast as temporary distractions that can make the lights flicker on Capitol Hill; once the storms pass, however, normal business resumes unperturbed and in accordance with previously scheduled events.

John Gerring's otherwise fine treatment of party ideologies is representative of the problem. To his credit, he directly explains his domestic focus, arguing that "because foreign policy has rarely played a significant role in American electoral politics, I focus primarily on domestic policies." He continues in a footnote:

Foreign policy issues have entered debate at infrequent intervals (generally under conditions of open or imminent military conflict) after which politics has resumed its normal pace and usual domestic preoccupations.... [P]arty views on foreign policy have not corresponded neatly with the historical development of party views on domestic policy matters; which is to say, foreign policy ideologies have changed at different times and (often) for different reasons than domestic policy ideologies. Therefore, foreign policy provides a somewhat misleading guide to the public political identities of the American parties, and is best analyzed separately.[3]

This explanation raises some questions. First, exactly how rare and infrequent are major foreign policy issues? In its approximately 220 years as a country, the United States fought "hot wars" for more than 40 of those years, was immersed in the Cold War for decades, and has been involved in numerous smaller international conflicts. So, not all that rare. Second, how can domestic and foreign policy ideologies be considered in total separation? In reality, far from existing in isolation, each interacts with and influences the other. Third, why then are foreign wars virtually absent in the American political science literature? The short answer, it seems, is that addressing foreign *and* domestic policy is hard. As Gerring says, wars and other international events have not always "corresponded neatly" with the standard domestic-based accounts of American political history. That is, major international events throw a kink into academic narratives. Grand theories get undermined by these ornery wars.

---

[2] Ira Katznelson, "Rewriting the Epic of America," *Shaped By War and Trade: International Influences on American Political Development*, eds., Katznelson and Martin Shefter, (Princeton, NJ: Princeton University Press, 2002), 7–8. This book is an early response to this problem, offering an edited collection of "exploratory" essays probing the ways international forces influence domestic politics. Theda Skocpol issued an earlier and unheeded call for more research in this area: Skocpol, "Bringing the State Back In: Strategies of Analysis in Current Research," *Bringing the State Back In*, eds., Peter Evans, Dietrich Rueschemeyer, and Skocpol (New York: Cambridge University Press, 1985).

[3] John Gerring, *Party Ideologies in America, 1828–1996* (New York: Cambridge University Press, 1998), 7.

Perhaps as a result, wars and other foreign irritants get ignored. The obvious problem with this approach is that it overlooks what any reasonable observer would have to acknowledge: Wars have had a major and ongoing influence on domestic American politics.

In short, what is missing from typical political science accounts of American politics is an understanding of how domestic and international factors relate to one another. To the extent scholars of American politics recognize that international factors might play a role in domestic politics, they seem to view them as side issues that temporarily help or hurt a rigid, preexisting domestic agenda. Lost is the possibility that international influences might alter or upset domestic politics in a meaningful and lasting manner.

War and American Political Development

The broad, historically based American political development (APD) subfield within the larger American politics literature would be a natural home for this kind of scholarship. Skeptical of the adequacy of rational choice modeling and comprehensive theoretical systems to effectively address core political questions, APD embraces historical analysis to explain how certain factors contribute to specific outcomes and constitute patterns.[4] In contrast to political history, though, APD is more rooted in political thought and maintains the political scientist's tendency to categorize and make connections across time. Four main approaches can be seen in APD work. In one approach, scholars, including Stephen Skowronek, Richard Bensel, and Elizabeth Sanders, study key periods of state development in American history and the set of causal factors that defined them.[5] A second approach, typified by Theda Skocpol, Rogers Smith, Daniel Kryder, Jacob Hacker, and James Morone, examines a crucial subject such as race, religion, or social policy over the course of American history or at particularly important junctures.[6] A third segment of APD scholarship addresses institutional development, as seen in the writings of Nelson

---

[4] On APD, see: Karen Orren and Stephen Skowronek, *The Search for American Political Development* (New York: Cambridge University Press, 2004).

[5] These works (far from an exhaustive list) concern development of the American state in particular eras or with reference to particular movements: Progressive Era: Stephen Skowronek, *Building a New American State: The Expansion of National Administrative Capacities, 1877–1920* (New York: Cambridge University Press, 1982). The Civil War and Reconstruction: Richard Bensel, *Yankee Leviathan: The Origins of Central State Authority in America, 1859–1877* (New York: Cambridge University Press, 1990). Populism: Elizabeth Sanders, *Roots of Reform: Farmers, Workers and the American State* (Chicago: University of Chicago Press, 1999).

[6] Theda Skocpol, *Protecting Soldiers and Mothers: The Political Origins of Social Policy in the United States* (Cambridge, MA: Harvard University Press, 1992); Rogers M. Smith, *Civic Ideals: Conflicting Visions of Citizenship in US History* (New Haven, CT: Yale University Press, 1997); Daniel Kryder, *Divided Arsenal: Race and the American State During World War II* (New York: Cambridge University Press, 2000); Jacob Hacker, *The Divided Welfare State: The Battle Over Public and Private Social Benefits in the United States* (New York: Cambridge University Press, 2002); James Morone, *Hellfire Nation: The Politics of Sin in American History* (New Haven, CT: Yale University Press, 2003).

Polsby, Jeffrey K. Tulis, Sidney Milkis, Skowronek, Gerring, Eric Schickler, and Daniel Carpenter.[7] A final portion of the APD field, represented by scholars such as Theodore Lowi, Samuel Beer, Michael Sandel, and James W. Ceaser, is dedicated to political ideas.[8]

Clearly, this APD subfield – with its emphasis on critical historical periods and the American state's development – is tailor-made for scholarship concerning war's influence on domestic politics. This is particularly true of the first and second approaches (the study of critical periods of change and the study of a crucial topic over time). Yet, like the larger American politics literature, the APD subfield has generally overlooked foreign affairs.

Segmentation: International and Domestic Events

The failure to address these matters in the broader American politics literature (and the APD subfield) is partially due to academic boundaries. Wars have typically fallen within the ambit of international relations. Because of this subfield segmentation, American politics scholars have tended to ignore international origins of domestic politics, while international relations experts avoid explicit study of the United States. As a result, the American politics and international relations literatures have been constrained by an artificially restricted universe of variables.

International relations scholars have addressed the relationship between international politics and domestic politics theoretically, if not in direct relation to the American case. In the 1960s and 1970s, scholars emphasized how domestic politics affects foreign policy via interest groups, class, and national goals.[9] And in 1978, Peter Gourevitch, influenced by the Primat der Aussenpolitik school, focused on the flip side by suggesting that international events

---

[7] Nelson W. Polsby, "The Institutionalization of the U.S. House of Representatives," *American Political Science Review* 62:1 (1968), 144–68; Jeffrey K. Tulis, *The Rhetorical Presidency* (Princeton, NJ: Princeton University Press, 1997); Sidney M. Milkis, *The President and the Parties: The Transformation of the American Party System since the New Deal* (New York: Oxford University Press, 1993); Skowronek, *The Politics Presidents Make: Leadership from John Adams to Bill Clinton* (Cambridge, MA: Belknap Press of Harvard University Press, 1997); Gerring, *Party Ideologies in America: 1828–1996*; Eric Schickler, *Disjointed Pluralism: Institutional Innovation and the Development of the U.S. Congress* (Princeton, NJ: Princeton University Press, 2001); Daniel P. Carpenter, *The Forging of Bureaucratic Autonomy: Reputations, Networks, and Policy Innovation in Executive Agencies, 1862–1928* (Princeton, NJ: Princeton University Press, 2001).

[8] Theodore Lowi, "The Public Philosophy: Interest Group Liberalism," *American Political Science Review* 61 (1967). Lowi, *The End of Liberalism* (New York: Norton, 1969); Samuel Beer, "In Search of a New Public Philosophy," *The New American Political System*, ed., Anthony King (Washington, DC: American Enterprise Institute, 1978); Michael Sandel, *Democracy's Discontent: American in Search of a Public Philosophy* (Cambridge, MA: Harvard University Press, 1996); James W. Ceaser, *Nature and History in American Political Development* (Cambridge, MA: Harvard University Press, 2006).

[9] Prominent works include: Richard H. Snyder, H. W. Bruck, and Burtin Sapin, *Foreign Policy Decision-Making* (New York: Free Press, 1962); Gabriel Kolko, *The Politics of War* (New York:

can also affect domestic politics.[10] In essence, his "second image reversed" argument holds that the causal arrow points both ways. Although some maintained that domestic events were the prevailing causal factor,[11] momentum had shifted by the late 1980s. Stressing the work following Gourevitch's pivotal piece, Robert D. Putnam concluded that international events exert far greater influence on domestic politics than vice versa.[12] Currently, however, the tide has shifted again, with the dominant strain in the international relations literature now suggesting that domestic politics affects decisions in the international realm. These scholars examine national politics to discern influences on a wide range of international political issues varying from war to trade policies.[13] In sum, while American politics scholars generally look only at domestic factors, international relations scholars have been much more prone to explore the relationship between international and domestic events, albeit with varying and

Random House, 1968); Stephen D. Krasner, *Defending the National Interest: Raw Materials Investments and U.S. Foreign Policy* (Princeton, NJ: Princeton University Press, 1978).

[10] Peter Gourevitch, "The Second Image Reversed: The International Sources of Domestic Politics," *International Organization* 32:4 (Autumn 1978). The Primat der Aussenpolitik school, led by Otto Hintze and Leopold von Ranke, argued that wars and external pressures, as opposed to national character (Innenpolitik), shape states. See: Otto Hintze, "Military Organization and the Organization of the State," *The Historical Essays of Otto Hintze*, ed., Felix Gilbert (New York: Oxford University Press, 1975), 178–215; Theodore von Laue and Leopold von Ranke, *The Formative Years* (Princeton, NJ: Princeton University Press, 1970). Also relevant here is *Between Power and Plenty: Foreign Economic Policies of Advanced Industrial States*, ed., Peter J. Katzenstein (Madison: University of Wisconsin Press, 1978).

[11] For example: Aristide Zolberg, "Origins of the Modern World System: A Missing Link," *World Politics* 33 (January 1981); Zolberg, "Beyond the Nation-State: Comparative Politics in Global Perspective," *Beyond Progress and Development*, eds., J. Berting, W. Blockmans, and U. Rosenthal (Rotterdam, Netherlands: Erasmus Universiteit, 1986); Ronald Rogowski, *Commerce and Coalitions* (Princeton, NJ: Princeton University Press, 1989); Kurt Taylor Gaubatz, "Election Cycles and War," *The Journal of Conflict Resolution* 35:2 (June 1991), 212–44.

[12] Robert D. Putnam, "Diplomacy and Domestic Politics: The Logic of Two-Level Games," *International Organization* 42 (Summer 1988). See also: James E. Alt, "Crude Politics: Oil and the Political Economy of Unemployment in Britain and Norway, 1970–1985," *British Journal of Political Science* 17 (April 1987), 149–99; Peter B. Evans, *Dependent Development: The Alliance of Multinational, State, and Local Capital in Brazil* (Princeton, NJ: Princeton University Press, 1979); Katzenstein, *Small States in World Markets: Industrial Policy in Europe* (Ithaca, NY: Cornell University Press, 1985); Gourevitch, *Politics in Hard Times: Comparative Responses to International Economic Crises* (Ithaca, NY: Cornell University Press, 1986).

[13] See, for example: Peter Trubowitz, *Defining the National Interest: Conflict and Change in American Foreign Policy* (Chicago: University of Chicago Press, 1998); James D. Fearon, "Domestic Politics, Foreign Policy, and Theories of International Relations," *Annual Review of Political Science* 1 (1998), 289–313; Susan Peterson, *Crisis Bargaining and the State: The Domestic Politics of International Conflict* (Ann Arbor, MI: University of Michigan Press, 1996); Richard N. Rosencrance and Arthur A. Stein, *The Domestic Bases of Grand Strategy* (Ithaca, NY: Cornell University Press, 1993); Bruce Bueno de Mesquita and David Lalman, *War and Reason: Domestic and International Imperatives* (New Haven, CT: Yale University Press, 1992); Bruce Russett, *Grasping the Democratic Peace* (Princeton, NJ: Princeton University Press, 1992). Jack Snyder, *Myths of Empire: Domestic Politics and International Ambition* (Ithaca, NY: Cornell University Press, 1991).

conflicting conclusions being favored during different eras. This book relies on the theoretical work of these international relations scholars in assessing how international events affect domestic U.S. politics.

This book also speaks to another key international relations debate over the role war plays in state building and political development.[14] Bruce D. Porter and Charles Tilly, following Otto Hintze and Leopold von Ranke, argue that war and external pressures shape states; are often key catalysts for political development, centralization, and bureaucratization; and can create fault lines within states.[15] Indeed, Tilly goes so far as to suggest that wars have "made" states because they require states to meet significant institutional and logistical challenges. Porter argues that in the case of these war-induced state expansions, "what goes up seldom comes down."[16] In other words, state expansion only moves in one direction. Citizens acquiesce to a larger role for government even after the crisis that brought about the "ratchet effect" has passed. Similarly, politicians and bureaucrats find new ways to spend the money and have their own interests in maintaining an expanded government footprint.[17] Most of this work has centered on countries other than the United States.[18] In general, this body of work has not substantially informed American politics research, at least so far as it is considered by political scientists.[19] One exception is

---

[14] Other relevant work not mentioned in this paragraph includes: Matthew Kroenig and Jay Stowsky, "War Makes the State, but Not as It Pleases: Homeland Security and American Anti-Statism," *Security Studies* 15:2 (2006), 225–70; Brian M. Downing, *The Military Revolution and Political Change: Origins of Democracy and Autocracy in Early Modern Europe* (Princeton, NJ: Princeton University Press, 1992); Karen A. Rasler and William R. Thompson, "War Making and State Making: Government Expenditures, Tax Revenues, and Global Wars," *American Political Science Review* 75 (1985), 491–507.

[15] Bruce D. Porter, *War and the Rise of the State: The Military Foundations of Modern Politics* (New York: Free Press, 1994); Charles Tilly, *Coercion, Capital, and European States, AD 990–1990* (Oxford, England: Blackwell, 1990); Hintze, "Military Organization and the Organization of the State;" Laue and Ranke, *The Formative Years*. See also: Karen A. Rasler and William R. Thompson, *War and State Making* (Boston: Unwin, Hyman, 1989).

[16] Porter, 14.

[17] On the "ratchet effect," see: Porter. Alan T. Peacock and Jack Wiseman, *The Growth of Public Expenditure in the United Kingdom* (Princeton, NJ: Princeton University Press, 1961).

[18] Tilly. Porter. Jeffrey Herbst, *States and Power in Africa* (Princeton, NJ: Princeton University Press, 2000); Fernando Lopez-Alves, "The Transatlantic Bridge: Mirros, Charles Tilly, and State Formation in the River Plate," *The Other Mirror: Grand Theory through the Lens of Latin America*, ed., Miguel Angel Centeno and Lopez-Alves (Princeton, NJ: Princeton University Press, 2000). In contrast to Tilly and Porter, Herbst and Lopez-Alves contend that the "war makes the state" process has generally not occurred in Africa and Latin America.

[19] One partial exception is the early presidency literature, which places considerable emphasis on the importance of war and the U.S. role in foreign affairs as an explanation for the increased importance of the presidency. See, for instance: Aaron Wildavsky, "The Two Presidencies," *Transaction* 4 (Dec. 1966), 7–14; Clinton Rossiter, *Constitutional Dictatorship: Crisis Government in the Modern Democracies* (Princeton, NJ: Princeton University Press, 1948); Edward S. Corwin, *The President's Control of Foreign Relations* (Princeton, NJ: Princeton University Press, 1917). For a more recent exception see: Andrew J. Polsky, "The Presidency at War," *The Presidency and the Party System*, ed., Michael Nelson (Washington, DC: CQ Press, 2006), 557–75.

Aaron L. Friedberg, who argues that in the American case, war is not necessarily the mother of the state. Rather, he argues that the United States's geographical isolation, combined with its founding antistatist principle, has created a "rollback effect" at the point other countries experience a ratchet effect. This uniquely American impulse to resist centralization and to protect unfettered liberty helps explain the comparatively weak connection between war and state growth in the United States – particularly during the Cold War, Friedberg's focus.[20] In any event, taken as a whole, this work serves to frame a critical debate for consideration of the American state. Amid much work on war-induced ratchet effects, the most prominent American political development accounts of the state tend to overlook wars, whereas Friedberg emphasizes U.S. antistatism, even during wartime. What follows is, in part, a study of the wartime American state. One aim is to assess the extent to which the American state has been "made" by war.

THE ARGUMENT

The rise and fall of political regimes has been a central focus for American politics scholars, especially those studying institutions and American political development. Political regimes, or orders, refer to periods in which a political coalition creates, consolidates, maintains, and eventually loses control over the nation's political agenda.[21] Commonly identified regimes include the post-1800 Jeffersonian Democrats, Jacksonian democracy, the Civil War and Reconstruction, the "System of 1896," the Progressive Era, the New Deal, the 1960s (usually taken to mean the late 1960s and early 1970s), and, perhaps, the rise of various types of conservatives in the 1980s. Scholars have frequently centered regime analysis on a particular institution. Skowronek, for instance, traces the primacy of the presidency in the rise and fall of regimes throughout American history.[22] Other work focuses on one particular regime or, as an offshoot of this concept, a policy regime.[23]

---

[20] Aaron L. Friedberg, *In the Shadow of the Garrison State: America's Anti-Statism and Its Cold War Grand Strategy* (Princeton, NJ: Princeton University Press, 2000).

[21] Polsky offers careful definitions of regimes. See: Polsky, "The 1996 Elections and the Logic of Regime Politics," *Polity* 30:1 (1997), 153–4. Polsky, "A Theory of American Partisan Regimes," Philadelphia American Politics Research Seminar, University of Pennsylvania, Philadelphia, 1 November 2002, http://urban.hunter.cuny.edu/~apolsky/REGIMETHEORY .htm, last accessed 23 April 2009.

[22] Skowronek, *The Politics Presidents Make*. Significant work has also placed Congress or parties at the center of regimes: Keith T. Poole and Howard Rosenthal, *Congress: A Politico-Economic History of Roll-Call Voting* (New York: Oxford University Press, 1997); Elaine K. Swift, *The Making of an American Senate: 1787–1841* (Ann Arbor, MI: University of Michigan Press, 1996); Gerring, *Party Ideologies in America, 1828–1996*.

[23] For the New Deal, see: John J. Coleman, *Party Decline in America: Policy, Politics, and the Fiscal State* (Princeton, NJ: Princeton University Press, 1996); Gary Gerstle and Steve Fraser, eds., *The Rise and Fall of the New Deal Order, 1930–1980* (Princeton, NJ: Princeton University Press, 1989); Milkis, *The President and the Parties*. For the Progressives: Daniel T. Rogers, *Atlantic Crossings: Social Politics in a Progressive Age* (Cambridge, MA: Harvard

Yet what stands out most in the regime scholarship is the central role played by political parties. The party realignment literature has produced perhaps the most influential and acclaimed work assessing political regimes.[24] Indeed, it is no stretch to say that realignment theory has long offered the primary framework for understanding American political history, particularly as it relates to the party system. It suggests that important "realigning" or "critical elections" result in major shifts in the parties' relative electoral strength and upset each party's internal composition. The dominant party falls into minority status, while the opposition party (or a new party, like the Republicans in 1860) takes power in Washington. This shift is accompanied by a new policy agenda reflecting the new majority party's ideology. The realignment genre's widely identified critical elections include 1800, 1828, 1860, 1896, and 1932. However, Mayhew's recent broadside attack on realignment theory has called its key assumptions into serious question. Finding that it fails to satisfy its own requirements when confronted with empirical evidence, Mayhew concludes that realignment theory "does not come close to working."[25] Other work has, to one degree or another, questioned the whole enterprise of periodization.[26]

With his critique of realignment theory, critics worry that Mayhew has done to the political scientist what Frederick Nietzsche did to modern man – that is,

---

University Press, 1998). For policy regimes, see, for instance: Skocpol, *Protecting Soldiers and Mothers*; Martha Derthick, *Policymaking for Social Security* (Washington, DC: Brookings, 1979); Jonathan Oberlander, *The Political Life of Medicare* (Chicago: University of Chicago Press, 2003); W. Elliot Brownlee, "Tax Regimes, National Crises, and State-Building in America," *Funding the Modern American State, 1941–1995*, ed., Brownlee (New York: Cambridge University Press, 1996).

[24] There is a vast realignment literature. Among the most important works are: V.O. Key, "A Theory of Critical Elections," *Journal of Politics* 17 (1955), 3–18; Key, "Secular Realignment and the Party System," *Journal of Politics* 21 (1959), 198–210; E.E. Schattschneider, "United States: The Functional Approach to Party Government," ed., Sigmund Neumann, *Modern Political Parties: Approaches to Comparative Politics* (Chicago: University of Chicago Press, 1956), 194–215; Schattschneider, *The Semisovereign People: A Realist's View of Democracy in America* (New York: Holt, Rinehart, and Winston, 1960); James L. Sundquist, *The Dynamics of the Party System: Alignment and Realignment of Political Parties in the United States* (Washington, D.C.: Brookings Institution, 1973); Walter Dean Burnham, "The Changing Shape of the American Political Universe," *American Political Science Review* 59 (1965), 7–28; Burnham, "Party Systems and the Political Process," eds., William N. Chambers and Burnham, *The American Party System: Stages of Political Development* (New York: Oxford University Press, 1967); Burnham, *Critical Elections and the Mainsprings of American Politics* (New York: Norton, 1970).

[25] Mayhew, *Electoral Realignments*, 156. There were also earlier critics of realignment theory; see especially, *The End of Realignment? Interpreting American Electoral Eras*, ed., Byron E. Shafer, (Madison, WI: University of Wisconsin Press, 1991).

[26] Mayhew, "Suggested Guidelines for Periodization," *Polity* 37 (2005), 531–5; Orren and Skowronek, *In Search of American Political Development*; Orren and Skowronek, "Beyond the Iconography of Order: Notes for a New Institutionalism," *Dynamics of American Politics: Approaches and Interpretations*, eds., Lawrence C. Dodd and Calvin Jillson (Boulder, CO: Westview Press, 1994), 311–30; Robert C. Lieberman, "Ideas, Institutions, and Political Order: Explaining Political Change," *American Political Science Review* 96:4 (2002), 697–712.

undercut crucial foundational pillars for the entire basis of society (or, in Mayhew's case, the discipline).[27] Thus, political scientists are left collectively grasping for a firm foundational theory upon which to rest their regressions. Yet while Mayhew undeniably knocked down a pillar of the political science literature, he suggested three alternative ways of understanding American political history. They may be less unified and ultimately less satisfying than the neat and tidy realignments you can set your watch by, but Mayhew's hypotheses offer some hope to the disoriented political scientist teetering on the edge of theoretical abyss. The first such alternative to explain "long stretches of American history, in drawing together elections, parties, and policy making" – and the one explored here – is "bellicosity," or wars.[28] Mayhew notes that the five major wars fought between the 1750s and the 1860s create a compelling explanatory framework for the first third of American political history.

This book examines how major wars affect American domestic politics, arguing that they provide an explanatory framework that ties together American state building, democratic rights policy making, and the political party system. I suggest that American domestic politics is inevitably intertwined with international events and that foreign wars influence domestic politics in three important areas. First, government responses to the crises arising from wars engender alterations to the American state. Second, wars have frequently brought about the extension of full citizenship and civil rights to previously marginalized minority groups that contribute to a war effort. Finally, because wars are such disrupting events that have the ability to fundamentally upset the political landscape, they have frequently influenced the party system.

It is also worth noting that by better understanding the past we should be better positioned to intelligently grapple with current international conflicts and their domestic ramifications. Thus, while striving to advance our understanding of American political history, this book also seeks to utilize that knowledge as a resource in coming to terms with the contemporary political situation. In sum, to overlook wars in the study of domestic American politics is to miss a key causal variable.

War and the American State

According to political philosophers Thomas Hobbes and John Locke, the primary reason governments are formed is to provide security.[29] Individuals

---

[27] Ceaser and Andrew E. Busch, *Red Over Blue: The 2004 Elections and American Politics* (Lanham, MD: Rowman & Littlefield, 2005), 21–30.

[28] Mayhew, *Electoral Realignments*, 156. The other possibilities he suggests are race and economic growth. Mayhew notes: " . . . the elections figuring in these stories have not necessarily exhibited lasting wrenches, or indeed sometimes any wrenches at all, in voter alignments. Instead, conventional historical evidence about what seems to have happened when and why is the guide. Policy themes and an eye for electoral verdicts, irrespective of their statistical properties, are the starting points" (156–7).

[29] Thomas Hobbes, *Leviathan* (1651); John Locke, *Two Treatises of Government* (1689).

willingly forfeit the benefits inherent in the "state of nature" in order to gain a basic level of security for their lives and property in a state of law and order. Although modern states play a much larger and influential role in society than Locke imagined – and a far different one than Hobbes anticipated – protecting its citizenry remains the most basic and essential role of the state.

Drawing on Max Weber and Otto Hintze, a government, or state, is generally thought to encompass those institutions that exercise control over a specified region and its inhabitants.[30] For Theda Skocpol, the state includes "the administrative, judicial, and policing organizations that collect and dispense revenues, enforce the constitutive rules of the state and society, and maintain some modicum of domestic order."[31] Especially central to a state, according to Skowronek, are its bureaucracy, its military, and its economic regulation.[32] State building, then, can be thought of as an organizational process in which new governing institutions are created, existing institutions are expanded or strengthened, or the relationship between government and society is altered. It should be noted that, although state building has received extensive attention, it is also possible for the state to undergo changes that decrease its power, influence, or array of responsibilities.

Work on the American state has generally centered on two expansionary periods. The first encompasses those decades between the Civil War and the Great Depression during which the national government expanded its authority and created a professionalized bureaucracy. With regard to this period, Skowronek details the development of national administrative capacities, Skocpol explains the emergence of new benefit programs for veterans and poor mothers, and Bensel and Sanders establish the importance of regional conflicts and reform movements.[33] The second widely studied period of state building is the New Deal. This body of work argues that Franklin Roosevelt and the Democratic Congress responded to the economic calamities of the Great Depression by establishing new programs overseen by new agencies within the federal government.[34] Still other accounts put political parties, the bureaucracy, Congress, the presidency, or professionals at the center of state building.[35]

---

[30] Max Weber, *Economy and Society*, eds., Guenther Roth and Claus Wittich (Berkeley, CA: University of California Press, 1992); Hintze, *The Historical Essays of Otto Hintze*.

[31] Skocpol, *Protecting Soldiers and Mothers*, 43.

[32] Skowronek, *Building a New American State*, 4.

[33] Skowronek, *Building a New American State*; Skocpol, *Protecting Soldiers and Mothers*; Bensel, *Sectionalism and American Political Development, 1880–1980*; Sanders, *Roots of Reform*.

[34] See, for instance: Edwin Amenta, *Bold Relief* (Princeton, NJ: Princeton University Press, 1998).

[35] Martin Shefter, *Political Parties and the State: The American Historical Experience* (Princeton, NJ: Princeton University Press, 1994); Milkis, *Political Parties and Constitutional Government: Remaking American Democracy* (Baltimore, MD: Johns Hopkins University Press, 1999); Scott C. James, "A Party System Perspective on the Interstate Commerce Act of 1887," *Studies in American Political Development* 6 (1992), 163–210; James, "Building a Democratic Majority: The Progressive Party Vote and the Federal Trade Commission," *Studies in American Political Development* 9 (1995), 331–85; James, *Presidents, Parties and the State: A Party System Perspective on Democratic Regulatory Choice, 1884–1936* (New York: Cambridge

What is largely absent from all of this work, however, is a systematic connection between the American state and international events. There are a few exceptions to this general rule. One is political scientist Bartholomew H. Sparrow's account of World War II-induced state building.[36] While effective in rounding out and adding nuance to the typical account of a New Deal-spawned state, Sparrow's work speaks only to that particular era. Similarly, Suzanne Mettler focuses on the same time period in demonstrating the importance of the G.I. Bill.[37] Certain historians and economists provide other exceptions. W. Elliot Brownlee argues that crises (the Civil War, World War I, the Great Depression, World War II, and the "Reagan Revolution") spurred state building by creating financing "systems."[38] In a similar but broader vein, Robert Higgs posits that wars and economic depressions lead to expansions of state capacities. "Governmental expansion," argues Higgs, "historically has been highly concentrated in a few dramatic episodes, especially the world wars and the Great Depression."[39] However, like the post-Civil War and New Deal accounts of state development, Higgs's account is narrowly focused on World War I, the Great Depression, and World War II. There is much more to this story.

I argue that major American wars exert an enormous influence on the American state. For the most part, wars have provided the critical jolts needed to enact policies that had long been considered but not acted upon. In considering

University Press, 2000); Derthick, *Policymaking for Social Security*; Carpenter, *The Forging of Bureaucratic Autonomy*; Carpenter, "State Building Through Reputation Building: Coalitions of Esteem and Program Innovation in the National Postal System, 1883–1913," *Studies in American Political Development* 14 (2000), 121–55; Louis Galambos, *The New American State: Bureaucracies and Policies since World War II* (Baltimore, MD: Johns Hopkins University Press, 1987); Schickler, Disjointed Pluralism; Julian E. Zelizer, *Taxing America: Wilbur D. Mills, Congress, and the State, 1945–1975* (New York: Cambridge University Press, 1999); Skowronek, The Politics Presidents Make; Milkis, *The President and the Parties*; Brian Balogh, *Chain Reaction: Expert Debate and Public Participation in American Commercial Nuclear Power, 1945–1975* (New York: Cambridge University Press, 1991).

36 Bartholomew H. Sparrow, *From the Outside In: World War II and the American State* (Princeton: Princeton University Press, 1996). Historian Steven Watts provides a similar account of war and its influence on America in the country's early history, especially the period surrounding the War of 1812: Watts, *The Republic Reborn: War and the Making of Liberal America, 1790–1820* (Baltimore, MD: Johns Hopkins University Press, 1987). Marc Allen Eisner does the same for World War I: Eisner, *From Warfare State to Welfare State: World War I, Compensatory State-Building, and the Limits of the Modern Order* (State College, PA: Pennsylvania State University Press, 2000).

37 Suzanne Mettler, *Soldiers to Citizens: The G.I. Bill and the Making of the Greatest Generation* (New York: Oxford University Press, 2005); Mettler, "Bringing the State Back In to Civic Engagement: Policy Feedback Effects of the G.I. Bill for World War II Veterans," *American Political Science Review* 96 (June 2002), 351–65.

38 W. Elliot Brownlee, "Tax Regimes, National Crisis, and State-Building in America," *Funding the Modern American State, 1941–1995*, ed., Brownlee (New York: Cambridge University Press, 1996).

39 Robert Higgs, *Crisis and Leviathan: Critical Episodes in the Growth of American Government*, (New York: Oxford University Press, 1987), 18.

wars and the American state, a general pattern emerges: Preceding a war, a small minority has proposed and promoted shifts in state activities but seen their initiatives stall in the face of limited interest and appeal; the shock of a war then provides new and compelling reasons for adopting the languishing policy and it is implemented, often in short order. In this manner, war-wrought alterations to the American state are generally undertaken as a response to crisis. Because wars are crises of the first order and expose serious problems requiring governmental solutions, they generate rare consensus for fundamental changes to the American state. Wars act as "focusing events" and create "windows" of opportunity.[40] John Kingdon argues that major policy shifts occur infrequently and only when "changes in the political stream" or new problems garner attention and briefly open a "policy window."[41] The same principle influences the state during war. Major wars not only open such windows of opportunity but, in fact, frequently compel responses from the federal government that have the effect of creating new policies, layers, and institutions within the federal government.

While altering state capacities during times of war is required due to the immediate crisis, the fundamental institutional alterations frequently endure long after the emergency has passed, as path dependency theorists would expect. Political scientist Margaret Levi argues: "Path dependency has to mean, if it is to mean anything, that once a country or region has started down a track, the costs of reversal are very high. There will be other choice points, but the entrenchments of certain institutional arrangements obstruct an easy reversal of the initial choice."[42] Among other things, then, path dependency suggests that once a certain course of action has been taken, it becomes ingrained and exceedingly difficult to reverse. Yet not all new wartime initiatives endure. Although many remain in place largely without change, others fall by the wayside once the war is over or remain in place but are reduced in scope.

The following chapters explore the relationship between war and the American state by way of numerous cases. The Spanish-American War led to a

---

[40] John W. Kingdon, *Agendas, Alternatives, and Public Policies* (Boston: Little, Brown, 1984). See also: Frank R. Baumgartner and Bryan D. Jones, *Agendas and Instability in American Politics* (Chicago: University of Chicago Press, 1993). On focusing events, see also: Thomas A. Birkland, "Focusing Events, Mobilization, and Agenda Setting," *Journal of Public Policy* 18:1 (1998), 53–74.

[41] Kingdon, 166–9.

[42] Margaret Levi, "A Model, a Method, and a Map: Rational Choice in Comparative and Historical Analysis," *Comparative Politics: Rationality, Culture, and Structure*, eds., Mark I. Lichbach and Alan S. Zuckerman (New York: Cambridge University Press, 1997), 28. See also: Paul Pierson, *Politics in Time: History, Institutions, and Social Analysis* (Princeton, NJ: Princeton University Press, 2003); Pierson, "Increasing Returns, Path Dependence, and the Study of Politics," *American Political Science Review* 94:2 (2000), 251–67; Gerard Alexander, "Institutions, Path Dependence, and Democratic Consolidation," *Journal of Theoretical Politics* 13:3 (2001), 249–69. For a critique of path dependency, see: Herman Schwartz, "Down the Wrong Path: Path Dependence, Increasing Returns, and Historical Institutionalism," unpublished manuscript, http://www.people.virginia.edu/~hms2f/Path.pdf, last accessed 24 April 2009.

vast overhaul of the national security system and the professionalization of the armed forces and saw the United States emerge as an imperial power. World War I expenditures required increased revenue, leading to the permanent establishment of the income tax. In World War II, similar economic constraints ushered in the mass-based, progressive income tax, and the governing administrative institutions familiar to today's workforce. The Korean War saw the federal government establish a massive national security state and new bureaucracies to oversee it. Additionally, the military draft regimented American society for some twenty years after the war was over, and Congress ceded key powers to the office of the presidency. At first glance, Vietnam appears to be an unusual case because, though it occurred at the same time as the Great Society, it did not produce any lasting increases in state capacities. On the contrary, America's first clear defeat in a major war brought about the end of the peacetime military draft and little else. Clearly, the kinds of effects wars have on the state are diverse and vary widely. Yet all of the effects explored here influence what the federal government does and how it goes about doing it. The catalog of war-wrought state influence is by no means exhausted in the analysis that follows. An effort is made to both highlight some of the most important and enduring war effects, while also taking stock of some of the idiosyncratic and less obvious kinds of state-related ramifications wars produce. This analysis, then, seeks to be illustrative rather than to offer a comprehensive account of all the cases in which war has influenced the state.

War and Democratic Rights Policy

Wars' democratizing power was recognized by ancient Greek philosophers. Thucydides observed that when oligarchs enlisted commoners to fight in wars, the latter demanded increased equality.[43] Similarly, Aristotle recognized that in wartime, oligarchies frequently allowed democratic and participatory reforms in exchange for military service.[44] Several decades ago, some sociologists and historians studied this relationship and came to similar conclusions. Arthur Marwick argued in the 1960s and early 1970s that "those who participate in the war effort have to be rewarded."[45] The extreme strains that institutions endure during wars force adaptation to meet the challenge. As a result, Marwick maintains, marginalized groups are often required to bolster the effort, which, in turn, leads to social gains.[46]

These accounts diverge from the standard view of democratization in America. A large literature maintains that the extension of democratic rights

---

[43] Thucydides, *History of the Peloponnesian War*, 3–27.

[44] Aristotle, *The Politics*, Book 6, Chapters 6–7.

[45] Arthur Marwick, *Britain in the Century of Total War: War, Peace and Social Change* (Boston: Little, Brown, 1968), 12. See also: Stanislaw Andrezejowski, *Military Organization and Society* (London: Routledge and K. Paul, 1954).

[46] Marwick, *War and Social Change in the Twentieth Century* (London: Macmillan, 1974), 6–14.

in the United States played out through an inevitable, progressive process.[47] Scholars have also emphasized the role of social movements, notably the Civil Rights Movement.[48] Others have more pointedly examined the relationship between wars and rights, but have focused on the way in which wars can weaken democracy. They argue that, because dissent is less tolerated when national security is at stake, democratic principles are frequently sacrificed. In Geoffrey Stone's words, "the United States has a long and unfortunate history of overreacting to the perceived dangers of wartime. Time and time again, Americans have allowed fear and fury to get the better of them. Time and time again, Americans have suppressed dissent, imprisoned and deported dissenters, and then – later – regretted their actions."[49] Metaphorically, these critics tend to see a civil rights pendulum that swings toward security – and against rights – during wartime and in the opposite direction during periods of peace.

Recently, though, some scholars have offered a different view of democratization in the United States that overlaps with that suggested by the ancient philosophers and the midcentury sociologists and historians.[50] Political scientists Philip A. Klinkner and Rogers M. Smith, for instance, emphasize wars' historic importance in fostering racial progress for African Americans.[51] Similarly,

[47] Schattschneider, *A Semisovereign People*; Key, *Politics, Parties, and Pressure Groups* (New York: Crowell, 1964); Sidney Verba, Norman H. Nie, and Jaeon Kim, *Participation and Political Equality* (New York: Cambridge University Press, 1978).

[48] For an overview of this literature, see: Stephen F. Lawson, "Freedom Then, Freedom Now: The Historiography of the Civil Rights Movement," *The American Historical Review* 96:2 (1991), 456–71.

[49] Geoffrey R. Stone, *Perilous Times: Free Speech in Wartime, From the Sedition Act to the War on Terror* (New York: W.W. Norton, 2004), 5. See also: David Rabban, *Free Speech in its Forgotten Years, 1870–1920* (New York: Cambridge University Press, 1997); Paul Murphy, *World War I and the Origins of Civil Liberties in the United States* (New York: W.W. Norton, 1979); William H. Rehnquist, *All the Laws but One: Civil Liberties in Wartime* (New York: Vintage, 1998); Corwin, *Total War and the Constitution* (New York: Ayer Co. Publishers, 1947). Specifically on World War II Japanese internment, see: Greg Robinson, *By Order of the President: FDR and the Internment of Japanese Americans* (Cambridge, MA: Harvard University Press, 2001); Eric L. Muller, *Free to Die for Their Country: The Story of the Japanese American Draft Resisters in World War II* (Chicago: University of Chicago Press, 2001); Peter Irons, *Justice at War: The Story of the Japanese-American Internment Cases* (New York: Oxford University Press, 1983); Jacobus tenBroek, Edward Norton Barnhart, and Floyd W. Matson, *Prejudice, War and the Constitution: Causes and Consequences of the Evacuation of the Japanese Americans in World War II* (Berkeley, CA: University of California Press, 1970); Roger Daniels, *The Politics of Prejudice: The Anti-Japanese Movement in California and the Struggle for Japanese Exclusion* (Berkeley, CA: University of California Press, 1962).

[50] For example: Ronald R. Krebs, *Fighting for Rights: Military Service and the Politics of Citizenship* (Ithaca, NY: Cornell University Press, 2006); Mettler, *Soldiers to Citizens*; Mettler, "Bringing the State Back In to Civic Engagement: Policy Feedback Effects of the G.I. Bill for World War II Veterans"; Mettler and Eric Welch, "Civic Generation: Policy Feedback Effects of the G.I. Bill On Political Involvement Over the Life Course," *British Journal of Political Science* 34:3 (July 2004), 497–522; John David Skrentny, *The Minority Rights Revolution* (Cambridge, MA: Harvard University Press, 2002); Skrentny, *The Ironies of Affirmative Action* (Chicago: University of Chicago Press, 1996).

[51] Philip A. Klinkner and Rogers M. Smith, *The Unsteady March* (Chicago: University of Chicago Press, 1999).

political scientist Azza Salama Layton and legal historian Mary L. Dudziak contend that leaders within the Civil Rights Movement used the international context of the Cold War to successfully advance their agenda – a point overlooked, Layton notes, in the domestically oriented social movements literature.[52] This perspective on democratization in the U.S. complements John Jay who, writing under the pen name Publius, asserted in *The Federalist* that "fighting side by side throughout a long and bloody war" for independence united Americans as a single people.[53]

Building on this diverse and dispersed literature, I highlight the role wars have played in the extension of new rights to women, African Americans, and youths. Major American wars have ultimately enhanced and improved democracy by rewarding marginalized groups with fuller citizenship rights after they have contributed to a war effort. In these instances, minority groups have – often for years – had forces pushing for expanded rights. But they were only successful when a war provided the final, necessary push toward adoption. This process plays out in two ways. First, it is a personnel issue. Wars typically require the mobilization of labor forces, both military and civilian, which are not required in peacetime. As a result, the state is forced to tap into previously under-utilized segments of the population. Second, it is a moral issue. Wartime service and sacrifice have highlighted group marginalization and discrimination, and created new and compelling moral reasons to extend full citizenship rights to these groups. In other words, wars create new covenants between the people and the state, and become the anvil on which new contracts are forged between citizens and their government. Wars, then, have been an important part of what makes Americans a single people.

Of course, there have been well known instances of civil rights' violations *during* wars, including the forced relocation of Native Americans, the Civil War-era suspensions of *habeas corpus*, the outlawing and imprisoning of political dissidents during World War I, and World War II's internment of Japanese descendants. This legacy has been extensively treated by other scholars and, as such, will not be part of this study.[54] But it is certainly clear that these miscarriages of justice seem to go hand-in-hand with wars, and that at least some

---

[52] Azza Salama Layton, *International Politics and Civil Rights Policies in the United States, 1941–1960* (New York: Cambridge University Press, 2000), see especially Chapter 2 and pg. 150; Mary L. Dudziak, *Cold War Civil Rights: Race and the Image of American Democracy* (Princeton, NJ: Princeton University Press, 2000). See also: Francisco E. Gonzalez and Desmond King, "The State and Democratization: The United States in Comparative Perspective," *British Journal of Political Science* 33:1 (2004), 193–210.

[53] John Jay, "No. 2: Concerning Dangers from Foreign Force and Influence," *The Federalist Papers*, ed., Rossiter (New York: Mentor, 1999), 6. During the American Revolution Alexander Hamilton, in a letter to Jay, suggested giving slaves their freedom in exchange for their wartime military service. Hamilton, "Alexander Hamilton to John Jay," *The Papers of Alexander Hamilton*, ed., Harold C. Syrett, Vol. 1, Ch. 15, Document 24 (New York: Columbia University Press, 1979).

[54] See, for instance: Stone. Rabban; Robinson; Muller; Irons; Daniels.

aspects of these rights abuses live on after wars end. Future presidents may, for instance, find it advantageous to cite prior episodes of rights retractions to justify their own retrenchments.

Nonetheless, marginalized minority groups that contribute to a war effort – be it on the homefront or abroad on the frontlines – have been consistently rewarded for their participation. In this manner, wars have played a crucial, if inadvertent, role in extending democracy to previously excluded groups. Comparatively, these advances are a bigger story than the isolated and largely temporary, if inexcusable and disgraceful, civil rights abuses that often occur in the midst of war.

There is a clear pattern of wartime contributions leading to democratic extensions. World War I galvanized the women's suffrage movement; African Americans gained new voting rights during World War II and laid crucial foundations for the Civil Rights Movement; Korea was crucial to the military's racial integration; and the Vietnam War was the pivotal factor in extending the franchise to 18–20 year olds through the Twenty-Sixth Amendment. Even in those cases where certain gains were not fully realized immediately upon implementation, the war-induced change was still undeniable and, in any event, the enactment of new laws and regulations was a critical step in eventual practical realization.

War and the American Party System

Two categories of party change are explored here: elections and party ideologies. Because major wars are such profound and unpredictable social, cultural, and political events, they have introduced new, long-lasting issues and policy concerns. In short, wars create crises – many of which are unanticipated – that require immediate attention and supplant prior issues on the policy agenda. These kinds of effects are akin to seismic shifts in the nation's political landscape and, in response, political parties are forced to reassess their public philosophies. These new issues and redefinitions of party ideology frequently influence elections by shaping both elite and mass behavior.

Elections. The notion that wars profoundly affect elections stands in stark contrast with generally accepted understandings of voter behavior. This disparity is partially attributable to differing research purposes. The voting behavior literature traces ongoing developments whereas the current project focuses on the influence of events. Although the elections literature comprises some of the best political science research, its effort to identify the general and consistent factors that motivate vote choice has obscured the important role events frequently play. While there is significant disagreement over what factor or factors shape voters' choices, the overwhelming academic consensus is that foreign affairs have little or no influence on elections. The public is thought to possess scant information, hold few opinions, and be generally indifferent to international issues.

One major faction of election studies maintains that timely issues of any sort are relatively unimportant. The "Michigan School" holds that voters have long-standing judgments about the parties based on issues, events, and candidates from previous elections, and that these long-term factors – as opposed to specific campaign issues – determine voters' partisan identification and decisions in the ballot booth.[55] The rival "Columbia School" contends that social characteristics, including race, gender, religion, and marital status, are the most reliable determinants of the vote.[56] Incumbency is also often cited as an important factor in voter choice, particularly in congressional elections.[57]

A second major grouping within the election studies literature argues that certain domestic issues, primarily related to economics, determine the vote. Proponents of this position hold that voter assessments regarding the state of the economy swing election outcomes.[58] While the economy as an issue dominates this branch of the literature, other domestic issues like abortion or gays in the military occasionally receive some attention.[59] Richard G. Niemi and Herbert

[55] See, for instance: Angus Campbell, Philip E. Converse, Warren E. Miller, and Donald E. Stokes, *The American Voter* (New York: Wiley, 1960); Larry M. Bartels, "Partisanship and Voting Behavior, 1952–1996," *American Journal of Political Science* 44 (2000), 35–50; Donald Green, Bradley Palmquist, and Eric Schickler, *Partisan Hearts and Minds: Political Parties and the Social Identities of Voters* (New Haven, CT: Yale University Press, 2002).

[56] Bernard R. Berelson, Paul F. Lazarsfeld, and William N. McPhee, *Voting: A Study of Opinion Formation in a Presidential Campaign* (Chicago: University of Chicago Press, 1954); Katherine Tate, *From Protest to Politics: The New Black Voters in American Elections* (Cambridge, MA: Harvard University Press, 1994); Barbara Norrander, "The Evolution of the Gender Gap," *Public Opinion Quarterly* 54 (1990), 566–76; Miller and J. Merrill Shanks, *The New American Voter* (Cambridge, MA: Harvard University Press, 1996); Geoffrey C. Layman, "Religion and Political Behavior in the United States: The Impact of Beliefs, Affiliations, and Commitment from 1980 to 1994," *Public Opinion Quarterly* 61 (1997), 288–316; Herbert F. Weisberg, "The Demographics of a New Voting Gap: Marital Differences in American Voting," *Public Opinion Quarterly* 51 (1987), 335–43.

[57] Gary C. Jacobson, *The Politics of Congressional Elections*, 4th ed. (Boston: Addison-Wesley, 1997).

[58] Morris P. Fiorina, *Retrospective Voting in American National Elections* (New Haven, CT: Yale University Press, 1981); Helmut Norpoth, "Presidents and the Prospective Voter," *Journal of Politics* 58 (1996a), 776–92; Norpoth, "Rejoinder," *Journal of Politics* 58 (1996c), 802–6; Richard Nadeau and Michael Lewis-Beck, "National Economic Voting in U.S. Presidential Elections," *Journal of Politics* 63 (2001), 159–81; Dean Lacy and J. Tobin Grant, "The Impact of the Economy on the 1996 Election," *Reelection 1996: How Americans Voted*, eds., Weisberg and Janet M. Box-Steffensmeier (Chatham, NJ: Chatham House, 1999); Michael B. MacKuen, Robert S. Erikson, and James A. Stimson, "Question Wording and Macropartisanship," *American Political Science Review* 86 (1992), 475–86; MacKuen, et al., "Comment on [Presidents and the Prospective Voter]," *Journal of Politics* 58 (1996), 793–801; Lewis-Beck, *Economics and Elections: The Major Western Democracies* (Ann Arbor, MI: University of Michigan Press, 1988); Harold D. Clarke and Marianne C. Stewart, "Prospections, Retrospections, and Rationality: The 'Bankers' Model of Presidential Approval Reconsidered," *American Journal of Political Science* 38 (1994), 1104–23.

[59] Alan I. Abramowitz, "It's Abortion, Stupid: Policy Voting in the 1992 Presidential Election," *Journal of Politics* 57 (1995), 176–86; R. Michael Alvarez and Jonathan Nagler, "Economics, Issues, and the Perot Candidacy: Voter Choice in the 1992 Presidential Election," *American*

F. Weisberg summarize this body of work as follows: "many economic voting models include little else in the way of candidate or noneconomic issue factors, as if they were of little importance. When other variables... are included, it is sometimes pointed out that those 'control' variables are themselves influenced by economic factors."[60] This election literature has only occasionally given passing attention to foreign affairs, usually with reference to Korea or Vietnam.[61] Yet even in these rare cases, foreign affairs play a minor and idiosyncratic role and do not challenge the general consensus that the international realm is unimportant in the voting booth.

This conclusion raises the question of why presidential and congressional candidates spend a great deal of time and money addressing foreign affairs issues in campaigns. One possible answer is that candidates and campaign workers need to immerse themselves in the ivory tower where street-smart political scientists can teach them what ordinary Americans really care about. Another possibility is that professional politicos understand something the academics do not – namely that, at least under certain circumstances, the American voter does indeed care about something other than the state of the economy. One of the few exceptions to the previously asserted academic consensus makes this argument. John H. Aldrich, John L. Sullivan, and Eugene Borgida examine a wide range of empirical evidence from 1952 to 1984 and conclude that the voting public holds identifiable views on foreign policy, can differentiate between candidates on these issues, and that these assessments affect individual vote choice.[62] This project builds on this scholarship and demonstrates how the process works in practice.

Journal of Political Science 39 (1995), 714–44; Alvarez and Nagler, "Economics, Entitlements, and Social Issues: Voter Choice in the 1996 Presidential Election," *American Journal of Political Science* 42 (1998), 1349–63; Miller and Shanks, *The New American Voter*.

[60] Richard G. Niemi and Weisberg, "What Determines the Vote," *Controversies in Voting Behavior*, eds., Niemi and Weisberg (Washington, DC: CQ Press, 2001), 185.

[61] John Kenneth White, *Still Seeing Red: How the Cold War Shapes the New American Politics* (Boulder, CO: Westview Press, 1997); Steven J. Rosenstone, *Forecasting Presidential Elections* (New Haven, CT: Yale University Press, 1983); C.W. Ostrom, Jr. and D.M. Simon, "Promise and Performance: A Dynamic Model of Presidential Popularity," *American Political Science Review* 79 (1985), 334–58; Stephen Hess and Michael Nelson, "Foreign Policy: Dominance and Decisiveness in Presidential Elections," *The Elections of 1984*, ed., Nelson (Washington, DC: Congressional Quarterly Press, 1985); Miller and Shanks, "Policy Directions and Presidential Leadership: Alternative Interpretations of the 1980 Presidential Elections," *British Journal of Political Science* 12 (1982), 266–356; Nie, Verba, and John R. Petrocik, *The Changing American Voter* (Cambridge, MA: Harvard University Press, 1976); Benjamin I. Page and Robert Y. Shapiro, "Effects of Public Opinion on Policy," *American Political Science Review* 77 (1983), 175–90; Gerald M. Pomper, "From Confusion to Clarity: Issues and American Voters, 1956–1968," *American Political Science Review* 66 (1972), 415–28.

[62] John H. Aldrich, John L. Sullivan, and Eugene Borgida, "Foreign Affairs and Issue Voting: Do Presidential Candidates 'Waltz Before a Blind Audience'?," *American Political Science Review* 83:1 (1989), 123–41. For similar findings about the 2000 presidential election, see: Sowmya Anand and Jon A. Krosnick, "The Impact of Attitudes toward Foreign Policy Goals on Public Preferences among Presidential Candidates: A Study of Issue Publics and the Attentive Public in the 2000 U.S. Presidential Election," *Presidential Studies Quarterly* 33:1 (2003), 31–71. For

I examine seven elections that occurred during or shortly after major wars and argue that the general thrust of the political science elections literature is incomplete in its assertion that party identification, social characteristics, or the state of the economy more or less single handedly drives American elections. Because the purpose of the elections literature is to track ongoing developments and patterns in voting behavior, it has at times missed the episodic. At both the elite and mass level, wars change expectations, values, beliefs, and aspirations, thereby altering the psychological state of the citizenry in crucial respects. In a liberal democracy, this process has repercussions in the voting booth. The American political science elections literature, then, is too deterministic in its emphasis on party identification, social characteristics, and the state of the economy. Events shape elections too. This study's primary focus – like that of the elections literature – is on presidential elections, though two midterms are also considered. Clearly, wars do not influence every election. But of the nineteen presidential elections held during the time frame explored here (1900–1972), five – more than a quarter – were heavily influenced by war and cannot be properly understood outside of that context.

Many political scientists are wary of exploring contingent events, preferring instead to focus on underlying or long-term factors. This approach is, of course, perfectly appropriate to address many questions. Yet as Mayhew argues, it can also at times lead to "blinkered explanation[s]. . . . We pay a considerable price as would-be explainers of politics by ignoring . . . events as causes . . . [and] contingency. Many events are contingent, and in the real world unexpected happenings are powerful engines of political change."[63]

Wars' effects on elections also add weight to critiques of realignment theory.[64] One problem is that, like much of the American politics literature, this influential body of work exclusively focuses on domestic issues. Additionally, wars are contingent events that come and go on a schedule of their own and are not timed every thirty-two to thirty-six years.[65] Realignment theory appears to have been born of an effort in political science to try to escape the political reality of contingent events.

Party Ideology. While running for president in 1968, George Wallace frequently said that "there ain't a dime's worth of difference between the two parties." The American party system, he suggested, was rigged to offer the voters two versions of the same thing; voters simply were not given real alternatives. Though it seems doubtful that Wallace surveyed the literature before

1980 and 1984: Miroslav Nincic and Barbara Hinckley, "Foreign Policy and the Evaluation of Presidential Candidates," *Journal of Conflict Resolution* 35:2 (1991), 333–55.

[63] Mayhew, "Events as Causes: The Case of American Politics," *Political Contingency: Studying the Unexpected, the Accidental, and the Unforeseen*, eds., Ian Shapiro and Sonu Bedi (New York: New York University Press, 2007), 100, 120.

[64] Mayhew, *Electoral Realignments.*

[65] Burnham, *Critical Elections and the Mainsprings of American Politics.*

opining, his argument was in fact essentially supported by a vast and time-tested literature. Scholars have often found that ideological differences – at least any of a serious or fundamental nature – are lacking in the American political tradition. Political scientist Louis Hartz argued that, in stark contrast to Europe, a classical liberal consensus was firmly planted in American culture, and that any party differences were minor and played out within the narrow confines of that ideological box.[66] Historians such as Richard Hofstadter and Daniel Boorstin led the "consensus school," which articulated a similar lack of ideological conflict.[67] Hofstadter touched on political parties in making his broader consensus argument: "It is in the nature of politics that conflict stands in the foreground," he wrote. But the "fierceness of the political struggles has often been misleading; for the range of vision embraced by the primary contestants in the major parties has always been bounded by the horizons of property and enterprise."[68]

In keeping with Hofstadter's argument, American political parties have frequently been said to lack ideology.[69] Visiting in the 1830s, Alexis de Tocqueville observed that "great political parties are those that are attached more to principles than to their consequences; to generalities and not to particular cases; to ideas and not to men.... America has had great parties; today they no longer exist." And even when they did exist, Tocqueville thought "the two parties were in agreement on the most essential points."[70] Fifty years later, a young Woodrow Wilson denounced the lack of "principles" in America's political parties, criticizing these organizations for failing to live up to the "responsible party" ideal.[71] The Progressive movement brought ideological leaders

---

[66] Louis Hartz, *The Liberal Tradition in America* (New York: Harcourt, Brace & World, 1955).

[67] Richard Hofstadter, *The American Political Tradition and the Men Who Made It* (New York: Knopf, 1948); Daniel Boorstin, *The Genius of American Politics* (Chicago: University of Chicago Press, 1953). More recently, but prior to September 11, 2001, Francis Fukuyama suggested the American consensus surrounding classical liberalism and democracy had become a worldwide phenomenon. Francis Fukuyama, *The End of History and the Last Man* (New York: Free Press, 1992).

[68] Hofstadter, ix, viii.

[69] For an extensive discourse on defining ideology, see: John Gerring, "Ideology: A Definitional Analysis," *Political Research Quarterly* 50:4 (Dec. 1997), 957–94. I adopt Gerring's conclusion that "the definitional core of the concept consists of three intertwined attributes – coherence, differentiation, and stability.... One might note that this core definition of ideology takes no cognizance of whether a party's views on political matters are distorting, dogmatic, repressive, self-interested, or reflective of a particular social class or social order." Gerring, *Party Ideologies in America, 1828–1996*, 6.

[70] Alexis de Tocqueville, *Democracy in America*, trans., Harvey C. Mansfield and Delba Winthrop (Chicago: University of Chicago Press, 2000), 167.

[71] Woodrow Wilson, *Congressional Government*, (Boston: Houghton Mifflin, 1885); Wilson, "Cabinet Government in the United States," *International Review* 7 (Aug. 1879). Also available in: Wilson, *The Political Thought of Woodrow Wilson*, ed., E. David Cronon (Indianapolis, IN: Bobbs-Merrill), 29–53. William Y. Elliott picked up where Wilson left off: Elliott, *The Need for Constitutional Reform* (New York: Whittlesey House, McGraw-Hill, 1935).

including William Jennings Bryan, Theodore Roosevelt, and Wilson to the fore
and generated a scholarly enthusiasm in the "Philosophy of History." Yet the
movement's partisan influence was blunted because progressivism amounted to
a square peg next to the Democrats' and Republicans' round holes and failed
to map directly onto either party's political thought.[72]

Contemporary studies have noted the lack of ideological conflict in the post-
World War II era, emphasizing the absence of intraparty ideological cohesion.
The Democratic Party was, at least until recently, composed of conservative
"Southern Democrats" and liberals based in the Northeast, Midwest, and far
West.[73] Similarly, the Grand Old Party had its Goldwater conservatives as well
as its more moderate "Rockefeller Republicans."[74] Additionally, the Hartzian
conception of a severely constrained ideological sphere has enjoyed a long life
in the political science literature addressing the party system.[75] Realignment
theory partially challenged this conventional wisdom by arguing that sharp
ideological conflict has marked the several "critical" or "realigning" elections in

---

[72] This era's historians – predecessors to the consensus school – emphasized political conflict and
the inevitable progressive force of History. See, for instance: Herbert Croly, *The Promise of
American Life* (New York: E.P. Dutton, 1909); Croly, *Progressive Democracy* (New Brunswick,
NJ: Transaction Publishers, 1998 [1914]); Charles Beard, *An Economic Interpretation of the
Constitution of the United States* (Toronto, Canada: Collier-Macmillan, 1913); Beard, *The
American Party Battle* (New York: Macmillan Company, 1929); John Dewey, *Reconstruction
in Philosophy* (Boston: Beacon Press, 1957 [1920]); Dewey, *Political Writings*, eds., Debra
Morris and Ian Shapiro (Indianapolis, IN: Hackett Publishing, 1993). See also: Ceaser, *Nature
and History in American Political Development*. Robert Nisbet, *History of the Idea of Progress*
(New York: Basic Books, 1980); Michael McGerr, *A Fierce Discontent: The Rise and Fall of the
Progressive Movement in America, 1870–1920* (New York: Oxford University Press, 2005).

[73] Nicol C. Rae, *Southern Democrats* (New York: Oxford University Press, 1994); Edward G.
Carmines and Michael Berkman, "Ethos, Ideology, and Partisanship: Exploring the Paradox
of Conservative Democrats," *Political Behavior* 16:2 (June 1994), 203–18; Shafer, *Quiet Rev-
olution: The Struggle for the Democratic Party and the Shaping of Post-Reform Politics* (New
York: Russell Sage Foundation, 1983); Shafer and Richard Johnston, *The End of Southern
Exceptionalism: Class, Race, and Partisan Change in the Postwar South* (Cambridge, MA:
Harvard University Press, 2006).

[74] Rae, *The Decline and Fall of the Liberal Republicans from 1952 to the Present* (New York:
Oxford University Press, 1989).

[75] Austin Ranney and Willmoore Kendall, *Democracy and the American Party System* (New York:
Harcourt, 1956); Anthony Downs, *An Economic Theory of Democracy* (New York: Harper &
Row, 1957); Clinton Rossiter, *Parties and Politics in America* (New York: Cornell University
Press, 1960); Beer, "Liberalism and the National Idea," *Left, Right and Center: Essays on
Liberalism and Conservatism in the U.S.*, ed., Robert A. Goldwin (Chicago: Rand McNally,
1965). Robert E. Lane, "The Politics of Consensus in an Age of Affluence," *American Political
Science Review* 59:4 (1965), 874–95; *Political Oppositions in Western Democracies*, ed., Robert
Dahl (New Haven: Yale University Press, 1966); Everett C. Ladd, *American Political Parties:
Social Change and Political Response* (New York: W.W. Norton, 1970); Lowi, "Party, Policy,
and Constitution in America," *The American Party System*, eds., Chambers and Burnham (New
York: Oxford University Press, 1975); Burnham, "The System of 1896: An Analysis," *The
Evolution of the American Electoral Systems*, ed., Paul Kleppner (Westport, CT: Greenwood
Press, 1981), 147–202.

U.S. history. But after the once-a-generation critical electoral is over, American politics reverts back to non-ideological tranquility.

Only in the postreform era have scholars consistently focused on ideology as a central component of political parties. Research shows that the parties have become more ideologically cohesive internally and more polarized comparatively in this post-1968–1972 period.[76] Congressional studies are paying more attention to ideology, many noting the increasing ideological cohesion of the caucuses.[77] The elections and voting literature notes a revival in parties, partisanship, and ideological voting at the individual level.[78] Other studies explore ideology and parties at the state level.[79] Scholars are also addressing

[76] See, for example: Shafer and Johnston; Abramowitz and Kyle L. Saunders, "Ideological Realignment in the U.S. Electorate," *Journal of Politics* 60:3 (Aug. 1998), 634–52; John Aldrich, *Why Parties? The Origin and Transformation of Political Parties in America* (Chicago: University of Chicago Press, 1995); Miller and M. Kent Jennings, with Barbara G. Farah, *Parties in Transition: A Longitudinal Study of Party Elites and Party Supporters* (New York: Russell Sage Foundation, 1986).

[77] See, for instance: Polsby, *How Congress Evolves* (New York: Oxford University Press, 2004); Gregory L. Hager and Jeffery C. Talbert, "Look for the Party Label: Party Influences on Voting in the U.S. House," *Legislative Studies Quarterly* 25:1 (2000), 75–99; Kim Quaile Hill, Stephen Hanna, and Sahar Shafqat, "The Liberal-Conservative Ideology of U.S. Senators: A New Measure," *American Journal of Political Science* 41:4 (1997), 1395–413; David W. Rohde, *Parties and Leaders in the Postreform House* (Chicago: University of Chicago Press, 1991); Keith T. Poole and R. Steven Daniels, "Ideology, Party, and Voting in the U.S. Congress, 1959–1980," *American Political Science Review* 79:2 (1985), 373–99; Steven S. Smith, "The Consistency and Ideological Structure of U.S. Senate Voting Alignments, 1957–1976," *American Journal of Political Science* 25:4 (1981), 780–95.

[78] Larry Bartels, "Partisanship and Voting Behavior, 1952–1996," *American Journal of Political Science* 44:1 (2000), 35–50; Abramowitz and Saunders; William D. Berry, Evan J. Ringquist, Richard C. Fording, Russell L. Hanson, "Measuring Citizen and Government Ideology in the American States, 1960–93," *American Journal of Political Science* 42:1 (1998), 327–48; Edmond Costantini and Linda O. Valenty, "The Motives: Ideology Connection among Political Party Activists," *Political Psychology* 17:3 (1996), 497–524; Edward G. Carmines and Harold W. Stanley, "The Transformation of the New Deal Party System: Social Groups, Political Ideology, and Changing Partisanship among Northern Whites, 1972–1988," *Political Behavior* 14:3 (1992), 213–37; Norrander, "Ideological Representativeness of Presidential Primary Voters," *American Journal of Political Science* 33:3 (1989), 570–87; Elinor Scarbrough, *Political Ideology and Voting, an Exploratory Study* (New York: Oxford University Press, 1984); Teresa L. Levitin and Warren E. Miller, "Ideological Interpretations of Presidential Elections," *American Political Science Review* 73:3 (1979), 751–71.

[79] Joel Paddock, "Explaining State Variation in Interparty Ideological Differences," *Political Research Quarterly* 51:3 (1998), 765–80; Robert S. Erikson, Gerald C. Wright, Jr., and John McIver, *Statehouse Democracy* (New York: Cambridge University Press, 1993); Hill and Jan E. Leighley, "Party Ideology, Organization, and Competitiveness as Mobilizing Forces in Gubernatorial Elections," *American Journal of Political Science* 37:4 (1993), 1158–78; Paddock, "Inter-Party Ideological Differences in Eleven State Parties: 1956–1980," *Western Political Quarterly* 45:3 (1992), 751–60; Paddock, "Beyond the New Deal: Ideological Differences between Eleven State Democratic Parties, 1956–1980," *Western Political Quarterly* 43:1 (1990), 181–90; Robert M. Entman, "The Impact of Ideology on Legislative Behavior and Public Policy in the States," *Journal of Politics* 45:1 (1983), 163–82.

the role of intraparty factions, considering, among other things, their ideological influences on the larger parties.[80] Several factors have been cited as drivers of party ideology, including economics and social class, ethnicity and culture, critical realignments, and elite-led responses to various domestic events.[81] John Gerring aptly summarizes this literature: "To put it baldly, the premise of non-ideological parties no longer seems to fit the facts as we know them. Indeed, contemporary work by political scientists and historians points toward a new understanding of ideology's involvement in American party politics."[82]

The most prominent and comprehensive account of party ideologies comes from Gerring.[83] He focuses on "presidential parties," or those elements of a party that "select (or endorse) a party's national platform and presidential nominee," and examines only the parties' "public ideology–the words and actions by which leaders represented their party before the general electorate"

---

[80] Howard Reiter, "Party Factionalism: National Conventions in the New Era," *American Politics Quarterly* 8:2 (1980); Reiter, "Intra-Party Cleavages in the United States Today," *Western Political Quarterly* 34:3 (1981); Reiter, "Why Did the Whigs Die (and Why Didn't the Democrats)? Evidence from National Nominating Conventions," *Studies in American Political Development* 19 (Fall 1996), 185–222; Reiter, "Bases of Progressivism Within the Major Parties: Evidence from the National Conventions," *Social Science History* 22:2 (1998); Reiter, "Creating a Bifactional Structure: The Democrats in the 1940s," *Political Science Quarterly* 116:1 (2001), 107–29; Reiter, "Factional Persistence within Parties in the United States," *Party Politics* (May 2004); Daniel DiSalvo, "The Death and Life of the New Democrats," *The Forum* 6:2 (2008); DiSalvo, "Party Factions in Congress," *Congress & the Presidency: A Journal of Capital Studies* 36:1 (2009), 27–57.

[81] Beard, *The American Party Battle*; Arthur M. Schlesinger, Jr., *The Age of Jackson* (New York: Book Find Club, 1945); Ladd, *American Political Parties: Social Change and Political Response* (New York: W.W. Norton, 1970); Burnham, *Critical Elections and the Mainsprings of American Politics*; Raymond E. Wolfinger, "The Development and Persistence of Ethnic Voting," *American Political Science Review* 59:4 (1965), 896–908; Michael Parenti, "Ethnic Politics and the Persistence of Ethnic Identification," *American Political Science Review* 61:3 (1967), 717–26; Robert Kelley, *The Cultural Pattern in American Politics: The First Century* (New York: Alfred A. Knopf, 1977); Kleppner, "Ideology and Political Culture from Jefferson to Nixon," *American Historical Review* 82:3 (June 1977), 531–62; Michael Barone, *Our Country: The Shaping of America from Roosevelt to Reagan* (New York: The Free Press, 1990); Rae, "Class and Culture: American Political Cleavages in the Twentieth Century," *Western Political Quarterly* 45:3 (Sept. 1992), 629–50; Key, "A Theory of Critical Elections"; Key, "Secular Realignment and the Party System"; Schattschneider, *The Semisovereign People*; Burnham, "The Changing Shape of the American Political Universe"; Burnham, "Party Systems and the Political Process"; Sundquist; Gerring, *Party Ideologies in America, 1828–1996*.

[82] Gerring, *Party Ideologies in America, 1828–1996*, 6. See also: Gerring, "Continuities of Democratic Ideology in the 1996 Campaign," *Polity* 30:1 (Autumn 1997), 167–86; Gerring, "Party Ideology in America: The National-Republican Chapter (1928–1924)," *Studies in American Political Development* 11:1 (Spring 1997); Gerring, "A Chapter in the History of American Party Ideology: The Nineteenth-Century Democratic Party (1828–1892)," *Polity* 26:4 (Summer, 1994), 729–68.

[83] Gerring, *Party Ideologies in America: 1828–1996*; Abramowitz and Saunders; Aldrich, *Why Parties?*; Miller and M. Kent Jennings, with Barbara G. Farah, *Parties in Transition: A Longitudinal Study of Party Elites and Party Supporters* (New York: Russell Sage Foundation, 1986).

(to the exclusion of "private communications, motivations, and interests").[84] One limitation of this method is that by emphasizing only the dominant ideological strain within a party, the important role played by internal factions, such as Southern Democrats, is minimized. Nonetheless, Gerring's approach is perfectly appropriate for his purpose of presenting an historical synthesis of American party ideology.

Challenging the consensus school (that is, a lack of ideological distinction between parties), Gerring argues that from 1828 onward the Republicans (or their Whig precursors prior to 1860) and the Democrats have offered coherent, identifiable, and changing ideologies in opposition to one another. The "National" Republicans through 1924 emphasized Protestantism, moral reform, free labor, social harmony, and statism before transitioning in 1928 to a "Neoliberal" party rooted in antistatism, free markets, capitalism, right-wing populism, and individualism. Meanwhile "Jeffersonian" Democrats from 1828 to 1892 embraced white supremacy, antistatism, and civic republicanism prior to the party's "Populist" epoch, which was characterized by egalitarianism, majoritarianism, and Christian humanism. Democrats experienced an additional transition to "Universalism" in the late 1940s with the adoption of civil rights, social welfare, economic redistribution, and inclusion. Gerring's thorough account of the parties' ideological development concludes with a consideration of the factors that drive this change. Ultimately, he finds there "is no general factor" and that "lots of things" drive ideological shifts.[85]

Yet international influences are notably absent from Gerring's extensive list of "lots of things." I argue here that events in the form of foreign wars alter party ideologies because they reshape the political landscape, thereby compelling political parties to alter their governing philosophies. In other words, wars force the dimension of international relations into the ideological package.

In making these arguments, I adopt Gerring's approach to ideologies. The primary focus here is on a party's dominant ideological strain as seen in "presidential parties": their national platforms, presidents, and presidential nominees.[86] Little attention is given to minority factions unless they came to represent the dominant ideological strain. While some nuance and historical detail may be lost in this approach, it follows Gerring's well-reasoned lead, highlights the dominant and most important ideological thread, and constitutes the most reasonable approach for developing an overall, historical synthesis of party ideology in America. The value added here is not in establishing a grand theory of party ideology in this historical context, but rather in building upon the leading interpretation and in identifying a central source of party ideology overlooked in previous scholarship.

This book explores ideological change in the Democratic Party at two critical points: following World War II and during the Vietnam War. While Gerring is

---

[84] Gerring, *Party Ideologies in America: 1828–1996*, 6. See also: 22–7.
[85] Ibid., 274–5.
[86] Ibid., 6.

certainly correct that no single factor can account for all instances of ideological change, these wars are intimately tied to enduring shifts in the Democrats' public philosophy. In addition, this project breaks with Gerring to suggest the Democratic Party entered a fourth ideological epoch during the Vietnam era when the liberal wing of the party, inspired by the New Left, took control of the organization. Although only two of the five wars explored here led to major shifts in party ideology, two shifts are significant. Major ideological repositioning is rare. Gerring's analysis of the entire history of both American parties only identifies three points of ideological transition (and only two in the years included in this study). The shifts identified here are also important because the question of America's role in the world became a central component of the party's ideological makeup.

ORGANIZATION, APPROACH, AND RATIONALE

This book is an attempt to understand the domestic ramifications of war in American politics. It examines the major "hot wars" the United States has been involved in since it emerged as a world power and foreign policy became a more consistently important feature of American politics, namely: the Spanish-American War, World War I, World War II, the Korean War, and the Vietnam War. Each case constitutes a chapter. The book begins with the Spanish-American War because this was the conflict that launched the United States into the realm of imperial, world powers. These cases were selected because each involved a significant sacrifice of American lives and a significant financial hardship.[87] Smaller conflicts such as the Persian Gulf War did not entail the high commitment and losses of these major wars. Similarly, although the Cold War (broadly construed) was a constant backdrop in American life for several decades, there was no sustained military conflict or loss of American lives.[88] Korea and Vietnam – the two most important conflicts within the Cold War era – are, of course, included in the study.

Each case study includes a brief historical introduction to the war in question and is then broken up into three parts. The "War in Brief" introductions serve only to convey basic information and dates that are helpful for understanding

---

[87] A small literature exists on the interplay of war, casualties, public opinion, and elections. See, for instance: David Karol and Edward Miguel, "The Electoral Cost of War: Iraq Casualties and the 2004 U.S. Presidential Election," *Journal of Politics* 69:3 (Aug. 2007), 633–48; Scott S. Gartner and Gary M. Segura, "Race, Casualties, and Opinion in the Vietnam War," *Journal of Politics* 62 (2000), 115–46; Gartner and Segura, "War, Casualties, and Public Opinion," *Journal of Conflict Resolution* 42 (1998), 278–300; Gartner, Segura, and Bethany A. Barratt, "War Casualties, Policy Positions, and the Fate of Legislators," *Political Research Quarterly* 57:3 (2004), 467–77; Zeev Maoz, "Normative and Structural Causes of Democratic Peace 1946–1986," *American Political Science Review* 87:3 (1993), 624–38.

[88] In addition, as Friedberg demonstrates, America's anti-statist origins and ideology prevented the U.S. from becoming a highly militarized state during the Cold War. Friedberg, *In the Shadow of the Garrison State.*

each chapter. The first substantive portion of each chapter describes important influences on the American state. The second section of each chapter (with the exception of the Spanish-American War) concerns the expansion of democracy for previously marginalized groups. The third part of each chapter concerns political parties and, in most cases, each war's influence on ensuing elections. The Spanish-American War, for instance, elevated the issue of imperialism to the forefront of the 1898 and 1900 elections and colored those campaigns. The chapter on World War I notes the failure of the "System of 1896" in explaining the 1920 election, which halted a long period of Democratic dominance and ushered in an era of Republican control. The World War II chapter, in contrast, is less focused on parties as they relate to election results, emphasizing instead war-wrought alterations in the Democratic Party's ideology. Korea then returns to an elections focus, whereas Vietnam considers both the era's elections and the altered and enduring ideology of the Democratic Party.

It is important to say a bit about what the book does not do. This book is not intended to document and detail all of the domestic effects wrought by major wars in the United States. It is simply not feasible to comprehensively address the full range of effects. I chose to examine the effects described above for four reasons. First, there are several consistent themes this project attempts to draw out that are, for the most part, consistent across major wars. Those effects that are characteristic of major wars in general were selected for focused attention. Second, the effects considered here are critically important in and of themselves and are significant features of American politics and society. Third, these effects were chosen for their relevance to, but frequent absence in, the political science literature. The three key touchstones of this project speak to important debates in the discipline. Yet, the relationship between these debates and major U.S. wars has been overlooked and is in need of consideration. Finally, I also made an attempt to demonstrate the broad range of possible effects wars can have. In addition to highlighting key thematic effects typically present in all wars, this project simultaneously attempts to illuminate the peculiar idiosyncratic effects instigated by wars as a means of emphasizing the diverse and far-reaching array of possible implications.

Additionally, this book does not directly address the post-9/11 wars in Afghanistan and Iraq. As of this writing, these conflicts are still ongoing. Both have already seen their share of twists and turns, and there is certainly no guarantee that the final chapter has been written. The relative lack of perspective we have on Afghanistan and Iraq severely undercuts one's ability to reach the kind of definitive conclusions that are possible with the wars included in this study. An analysis of Afghanistan and Iraq at this time simply cannot be informed by either the amount of evidence or the level of theorizing that are available in the cases where the outcome is known. I leave it to others in the coming years and decades to address the legacy of Afghanistan and Iraq on American politics.

As a final point on the book's organization and approach, a question that arises in making the arguments presented here is whether one can understand the effects of war without studying periods of peace. That is, it may be problematic to attribute particular effects to war if that factor alone is being studied. Thus, there is also a need to consider variance during peacetime to definitively attribute certain effects to war. I address this concern in two ways. First, although the American politics literature is lacking with regard to the impact of international influences, it is quite robust in terms of explaining peacetime politics and development. This book relies heavily on that excellent body of work – especially that in the American political development subfield. Additionally, in examining the effects of wars on domestic politics, I attempt to engage my topics at three different points: prewar (with a broad, long-term focus); contemporaneously (in detail); and postwar (again, with a broad, long-term focus).

For millennia, citizens, statesmen, and intellectuals have sought to understand the ways in which wars can shape and transform society. In many respects, this ancient question is as relevant today as it was when it was considered by Thucydides, Aristotle, or Publius. This book is an attempt to address this question in a systematic manner with respect to the United States. And to the extent this project is successful in generating insight into the relationship between war, the state, and politics in America's past, it will also hopefully provide additional context for understanding our current period.

2

The "Splendid Little War"

"Was there ever before such a war with such great results, so short in duration, such wonderful successes, with no reverses?" asked Vermont Senator Redfield Proctor shortly after the Spanish-American War's conclusion in the summer of 1898. For the United States, at least, the answer is assuredly no. Nonetheless, as Lewis L. Gould notes, "the war has not received very much attention as a force for social change at the end of the nineteenth century."[1] Rather, scholarly attention has focused on the 1896 presidential election and the Progressive movement that followed as purported turning points in American political history.

The 1896 election has played a prominent role in the realignment literature since the theory's inception, and its prominence as a "critical election" that produced a "sharp and durable" realignment has endured through the literature's development. Following on the heels of the panic of 1893, as V.O. Key initially argued, the 1896 election brought the Republican Party to power and the "Democratic defeat was so demoralizing and so thorough that the party could make little headway in regrouping its forces until 1916."[2] Similarly, James L. Sundquist has asserted that this 1896 realignment set the stage for American politics until World War I.[3] Meanwhile, American political development (APD) scholars have written about the myriad formal and informal changes the political system underwent during the Progressive years.[4]

While the importance of these developments should not be dismissed, the legacy of the Spanish-American War has been unjustly overlooked. Even those

---

[1] Lewis L. Gould, *The Spanish-American War and President McKinley* (Lawrence, KS: University Press of Kansas, 1980), 55.

[2] V.O. Key, Jr., "A Theory of Critical Elections," *Journal of Politics* 17:1 (Feb. 1955) 11.

[3] James L. Sundquist, *Dynamics of the Party System*, revised edition (Washington, DC: Brookings Institution Press, 1983), 170.

[4] See, for instance: Jeffrey K. Tulis, *The Rhetorical Presidency* (Princeton, NJ: Princeton University Press, 1987); John Gerring, *Party Ideologies in America, 1828–1996* (New York: Cambridge University Press, 1998).

few political scientists who have examined the role of wars on American domestic politics have skipped this conflict.[5] In a sense, this is understandable because the conflict with Spain did not include the widespread societal upheaval of, say, the world wars. Nonetheless, the Spanish-American War did influence American politics in important and unexpected ways. First, the war had a demonstrable effect on the American state. It exposed and highlighted national security problems that required an overhaul of the armed services and the establishment of a professional army to replace the decentralized, state-run militia system. This instance of state development was a key indication that the United States had emerged as a world super power. In addition, the Spanish-American War led to a new role for the American state as an imperial power with the acquisition of the Philippines.[6] Indeed, the U.S. occupation of the Philippines for a half century was a difficult and costly encounter that resembles America's experience in Vietnam, Iraq, and Afghanistan.

For the two major political parties, the Spanish-American War also brought profound change. Imperialism was elevated from a backburner issue to a matter of constant dispute in the political and electoral realms. At the same time, the major issue cleavages that realignment theory claims emanated from the supposedly pivotal 1896 election and allegedly invested American politics for a generation, were obscured by more compelling international concerns. In fact, contrary to the realignment and APD argument that Republican dominance was inevitable after the 1896 election, the rhetoric and focus of the 1898 midterm and 1900 presidential elections demonstrate that these Republican successes were owed to the emergence of a new, war-spurred set of issues and to the GOP's success in prosecuting the war. The 1898 and 1900 elections are also

---

[5] For instance: David R. Mayhew, "Wars and American Politics," *Perspectives on Politics* 3:3 (Sept. 2005), 473–93; *Shaped by War and Trade*, eds., Ira Katznelson and Martin Shefter (Princeton, NJ: Princeton University Press, 2002).

[6] Puerto Rico and the diminutive island of Guam were also annexed by the United States as a result of the war and – unlike the Philippines – remain unincorporated territories. And while Cuba gained independence, the Americans gained a naval base at Guantanamo Bay. The focus here, though, is on the Philippines because it was a significantly larger and more important acquisition. In addition, it represented a stark break with American expansionism up to that point. Previous territorial advances had been undertaken within the confines of Manifest Destiny and with the understanding that such acquisitions could conceivably become American states at some point in the future. International involvement outside of the North American continent was essentially limited to the Americas, representing only a broad interpretation of the Monroe Doctrine. Puerto Rico, being within the Americas and containing the potential for statehood, fit within that traditional mold. As Raymond Aron writes: "The right to keep watch on the Caribbean was simply an extension of the standard practice of territorial expansion. Regions bordering on the United States were part of its sphere of influence; without undue scruples or repugnance it engaged in the art of recruiting satellites within these zones [and] instigating revolts against uncooperative governments.... Otherwise, the United States had not made any choice between the consciousness of a global role and the predominant interest in protecting trade and investment..." The Philippines represented something new and constituted a decisive break from "the old framework and logic of the original national purpose." Raymond Aron, *The Imperial Republic* (Englewood Cliffs, NJ: Prentice-Hall, 1974), xxxii–xxxiii.

important because they mark the opening of a new dimension in American politics and presidential elections. Foreign affairs and international conflicts had not been a part of American politics since the Mexican War. Presidential elections in the 1870s and 1880s resembled gubernatorial campaigns in that no "higher" dimension of international affairs played a significant role. The Spanish-American War, however, brought foreign affairs to the forefront of U.S. politics.

THE SPANISH-AMERICAN WAR IN BRIEF

The Spanish-American War was fought in and around the Spanish colonial holdings in the Caribbean and the Pacific from April through August of 1898. The Treaty of Paris, signed in December, formally ended the conflict.

Spain's hold on its vast colonial empire had been slipping for centuries when a revolt broke out in 1895 in Cuba. Initially, both major political parties in the United States encouraged a negotiated settlement to the conflict. President Grover Cleveland's sympathies, though, rested with Spain. The 1896 election brought Republican William McKinley to office and the new president – while avoiding a direct alliance with Cuba – staked out a slightly different course from his predecessor by demanding that negotiations between Spain and the Cuban revolutionaries result in an agreement that was acceptable to Cuba. This new position essentially pushed McKinley closer to the Cubans because they would not accept any peace agreement that did not provide for their independence. Nonetheless, the McKinley administration and both political parties continued to press for a negotiated solution into 1898.

The sinking of the *U.S.S. Maine* in Havana, Cuba was the single most important event that drew the United States into the conflict. The battleship had been sent to Havana to protect American citizens living on the island. On February 15, 1898, the ship exploded while docked in the harbor, killing 226. Spain was immediately assumed to have used a mine or a missile to destroy the ship. These assumptions were reinforced in the United States by the "yellow journalists" who had been stoking anti-Spanish sentiment for some time. With the benefit of hindsight, it seems highly unlikely that Spain was responsible for the incident. It is much more probable that the explosion was an accident resulting from the *Maine*'s gunpowder being stored too close to a heating source. A less credible theory suggests that it was actually Cuban revolutionaries who destroyed the ship on the assumption that Spain would be blamed and the United States would enter the war.[7] Nonetheless, American public opinion, Congress, and the media all demanded war. But, as Gould notes, McKinley "delayed as long as he could to find a way out of the crisis.... Contrary to the historic canards

---

[7] Many historical accounts discuss the controversy. See, for instance, David F. Trask, *The War With Spain in 1898* (New York: Macmillan Publishing Co., 1981), 35.

about his performance, McKinley had worked hard for peace until war became inevitable."[8]

War was officially declared on April 20, 1898, shortly after McKinley requested authority to send troops to Cuba.[9] An accompanying congressional resolution deemed Cuba "free and independent," demanded Spain's withdrawal, allowed the president to use military force, and stated that the U.S. had no territorial interests with regard to Cuba.

For the United States, the war itself was short and sweet, leading John Hay, the American ambassador to England (and soon-to-be secretary of state), to famously declare it "a splendid little war." The first significant battle occurred not in the Caribbean but halfway around the world in the Pacific, which proved to be one of the war's three major theaters. McKinley dispatched Commodore George Dewey and his fleet to the Philippines, another Spanish colonial holding. As will be discussed later, most scholars suggest the war was taken to the Pacific as a means to pressure Spain on all fronts and to quickly conclude the war. Dewey arrived in the Philippines and engaged the Spanish fleet on May 1. The Battle of Manila Bay was over within hours and was complemented by Filipino nationalists engaging the Spaniards on the islands' interior. Dewey then blockaded Manila's port and waited for ground troops. Four months later soldiers arrived, the brief Battle of Manila ensued, and the Spanish forces on the islands quickly surrendered.

The second major theater of the war was on and around Cuba. After establishing a naval base at Guantanamo Bay and putting ground forces on the island, Theodore Roosevelt led his Rough Riders to their famous victory in the Battle of San Juan Hill on July 1. Two days later, the American navy quickly defeated the Spanish maritime force near Santiago as it attempted to flee Cuba. The United States had full control of the island within a month. The third theater was Puerto Rico. After shelling San Juan from the sea, soldiers went ashore on July 25 and took control of the island without difficulty.

With the end of fighting in August, a peace commission was sent to Paris to negotiate a settlement with a delegation from Madrid. As Gould writes, the quick victory "enhanced McKinley's prestige and identified the Republicans with another military triumph."[10] The Treaty of Paris was signed in December 1898 and ratified by the Senate the following February. The United States received most of Spain's colonies including the Philippines, Guam, Wake Island, and Puerto Rico. Cuba was declared independent. The altered political climate caused by the war was also instrumental in the annexation of Hawaii.[11]

---

[8] Gould, *Grand Old Party* (New York: Random House, 2003), 129.

[9] The resolution was actually passed on April 25 but was backdated to April 20.

[10] Gould, *Grand Old Party*, 129.

[11] Annexationists attempted to acquire Hawaii in 1893 but failed to gain President Cleveland's support. Concerned about increasing Japanese influence over the islands, McKinley voiced support for acquisition shortly after taking office. Congress, however, had nothing close to

THE SPANISH-AMERICAN WAR AND THE AMERICAN STATE: ARMY REFORM AND IMPERIALISM

Despite rapid victory, the war exposed serious problems in military prepared-ness and the resulting shift to a standing army was a key element of U.S. state building as well as an important signal of America's emergence as a global power. The war is also often seen as the United States's first step on the road to imperialism – that is, the extension of American authority by territorial acquisition or the establishment of political hegemony. In reality, the Spanish-American War was not a result of imperialism. Rather, imperialism was an unintended consequence of the war and its emergence was at least partially an historical accident. Although it is true that the United States was attempting to break into new markets, these efforts did not include serious consideration of territorial expansion until after the Spanish-American War. To the extent the United States was an imperial power, this status was largely a result of the Spanish-American War rather than its cause.[12] After hostilities ceased, Presi-dent McKinley was immediately confronted with a crucial decision about the Philippines. His choice to acquire the islands thrust the United States into a new role in the world – as an imperial power with new land holdings. This unusual and halting episode in American state building highlights the unan-ticipated consequences wars often produce. It resulted in a prolonged, and often overlooked, conflict on the islands with significant human and monetary costs. In addition, and as discussed later in this chapter, imperialism created an important split between Republicans and Democrats. Prior to the war, both supported Cuban independence (the war's instigating issue). But the emergence of imperialism as a key political issue following the war divided the parties and helped the Republicans maintain control of the White House and Capitol Hill.

The Development of a Standing Army

The Spanish-American War was the chief impetus for a crucial step in the devel-opment of the American state: military professionalization and institutional-ization in the form of a standing, centralized army. In Stephen Skowronek's

---

the necessary two-thirds support for acquisition. As a result, McKinley withdrew the treaty and asked for a joint congressional resolution. But Congress was not able to muster even a simple majority. In short, prior to the war there was a consensus that imperial holdings would likely extend, and ultimately undermine, the American republic as they had the Roman republic. In the Spanish-American War's wake, however, Congress' support was strong. By that point, the Hawaiian islands were seen as a valuable strategic position, especially in light of American control over the various former Spanish colonies. In the summer of 1898, with wide Congressional support, Hawaii was annexed to the United States.

[12] The focus here is on global imperialism. Of course, territorial expansion was a major theme of pre-Civil War U.S. policy in North America and resulted in the acquisition of, among other land, Texas and California.

words, a standing army can be characterized as "a mass citizen army that [is] rigorously trained in peacetime, readied for immediate mobilization, and commanded by a highly educated and centrally coordinated cadre of staff and line officers." America's development of a standing army signaled "an institutional standard of the modern state" and was a clear indication that the United States had emerged as a world power in the same category as the traditional European powers.[13]

Prior to the Spanish-American War, the U.S. Army was far from the highly organized, professional institution it is today. Rather, it was characterized by periodic efforts to mobilize a force to deal with specific problems that states and localities were ill-equipped to manage. For instance, following Southern secession, the remaining Union states were unable to coordinate a response among themselves and relied instead on the federal government. Similarly, following the Civil War, federal forces were employed to confront Native Americans in the western territories. In short, the vast majority of soldiers in the U.S. Army were enlisted for brief periods of time in response to isolated problems. Once a crisis passed, soldiers returned home; there were scarcely any Army regulars during peacetime. Thus, although the Union Army employed 1 million men in 1865, it had been drawn down to 30,000 in 1870 – and this while federal troops were still occupying the former Confederacy and the Indian wars were being waged in the West.

In place of a regular, standing army, the country relied on state-run national guard units or local militias – a relic of the founding era republican ideal of the citizen-soldier. These militias were voluntary, organized by status and ethnicity, associated with political parties, and served just as much of a social as a protective role in communities.[14] During crises, they would join together with the small standing Army. Needless to say, these militias were not as reliable or formidable as the standing armies maintained by European states.

In the years between Reconstruction and the Spanish-American War, there were many calls for reform and modernization of the Army. Intellectuals, the War Department, and regular Army officers, few as they were, led this effort. Foremost among those trumpeting reform was West Point professor Emory Upton, who studied the Army and determined the militia system was inefficient. The essence of the problem, he concluded, was its lack of centralized organization. Each militia was trained differently, and levels of preparedness varied widely. Additionally, the communication structure among the militias was poor. In place of this national guard system, Upton suggested reforms to

---

[13] Stephen Skowronek, *Building a New American State* (New York: Cambridge University Press, 1982), 85. For more on the National Guard and the U.S. Army, see: Russell F. Weigley, *Towards an American Army: Military Thought from Washington to Marshall* (New York: Columbia University Press, 1962); Martha Derthick, *The National Guard in Politics* (Cambridge, MA: Harvard University Press, 1965); Weigley, *History of the United States Army* (New York: Macmillan, 1967); Paul J. Hammond, *Organizing for Defense* (Princeton, NJ: Princeton University Press, 1961).

[14] Skowronek, 86–7.

create an educated leadership, a trained body of reserves, and a comprehensive administrative system capable of mobilizing quickly and efficiently.

The existing state-based institutional structure, however, mounted a fierce opposition to reform efforts in an attempt to maintain the prominence of state-run militia. This group consisted of, among others, state governors and political insiders who often reaped patronage benefits in the form of militia positions. Skowronek notes: "The challenge of the professionals' reform program reached into all areas of the integrated structure of political and institutional power that governed late-century America."[15] The opponents of a regular army formed the National Guard Association in 1878 as a means to neutralize the criticisms of Upton and his cohort. In essence, this was an attempt to find a middle ground between the old militia structure and the professional army Upton envisioned. They endorsed maintaining the state-run units but suggested they be organized like those in the regular Army, establishing state run-military academies, eliminating party control of militias in favor of a meritocracy, and instituting militia inspections by Army regulars. These efforts, combined with Upton's lack of political skill, were sufficient to temporarily quell this initial reform movement.

The Spanish-American War, though, highlighted the militia system's continuing problems and propelled the reform and modernization agenda to eventual success. The explosion of the *U.S.S. Maine* brought the issue back to the forefront. In anticipation of war, the reformers tried to get a bill through Congress to revamp the Army by giving it a more centralized and professional structure. But the bill was defeated and McKinley, in his official call for volunteers, gave a prominent role to the National Guard and said the standing Army would only increase in size on a temporary basis. According to Skowronek, these developments, "all too clearly fit the nineteenth-century pattern of military policy that Upton had so bitterly denounced in the name of professionalism, nationalism, and peacetime preparation. The early weeks of the war were a grim vindication of the Uptonian warnings."[16]

Indeed, there were serious shortcomings that would eventually lead to accusations that McKinley and the War Department mismanaged the conflict. The National Guard's limitations became apparent almost immediately. Veteran guardsmen dropped out at the prospect of having to serve abroad for two-year periods as opposed to the brief stints of service, usually in their home states, to which they had grown accustomed. As a result, states were forced to enlist new recruits. Although these volunteers were enthusiastic, they lacked formal training. In addition, this dilemma put the National Guard in competition with the regular Army's recruitment efforts and undermined the militias' claim to be ready for action. Other problems included the lack of a clear command structure. That is, it was not clear whether the National Guard or the Army regulars

---

[15] Ibid., 96.
[16] Ibid., 115.

were in charge. Finally, there were costly and constant challenges in mobilizing material resources for the conflict which were compounded by the fact that this was the nation's first overseas war. There were not enough supplies, and those that were available were unable to reach the troops. As Gould notes:

> Conditions in the camps where the troops assembled offered the most public evidence of the problems that the War Department faced. The army's outmoded and inefficient procedures could not deal with the masses of men to be fed, housed, clothed, and trained in the early weeks of the war. Few officers knew how to manage large numbers of troops, and conflicting responsibilities among quartermaster, ordnance, and medical officers caused frictions that multiplied the disorganization. Some camps had too much of a particular piece of equipment; others were short of everything.[17]

Simply put, the war effort was chaotic. This was largely the result of the main fighting force, the National Guard, being under the control of state governors or local officials rather than one centralized command.

The logistical problems received widespread media coverage that likely spurred the reform effort. In particular, chaos in Tampa, Florida, a major staging ground for the war, garnered considerable attention in the national press,[18] making a big impression in Washington.[19] One crucial ingredient, then, in realizing the long-sought army reforms was the spotlight the media shone on the conduct of the war over a several-month period and, in particular, the alleged fecklessness surrounding the Army's logistical provisioning in Tampa. This episode and the media spotlight it garnered indicate that change often comes about in response to short-term incidents that garner media attention, thus mobilizing and channeling elite and public opinion.

---

[17] Gould, *The Spanish-American War and President McKinley*, 71.

[18] The problems in Tampa received widespread and constant media attention beginning in June 1898. For a sampling from *The New York Times*, see: "The Long Delay at Tampa," *The New York Times*, 15 June 1898, 1; "The Embarkation at Tampa," *The New York Times*, 15 June 1898, 6; "Chaos at Tampa Continues," *The New York Times*, 26 June 1898, 2; "Supplies at the Front: Lack of Mule Trains Due to Scarcity of Transports, Makes Conveyance Difficult," *The New York Times*, 2 July 1898, 2; "Officers Blamed by Alger: He Expresses Regret at the Stranding of Sick Soldiers at Tampa," *The New York Times*, 18 Aug. 1898, 2; "Were Officers to Blame? Trainmaster Harrison of the Plant System Declares They Were Responsible for Muddle at Tampa," *The New York Times*, 1 Sept. 1898, 1; "Our Military Mismanagement and Its Causes," *The New York Times*, 25 Sept. 1898, 21.

[19] Newspaper accounts highlight Washington's knowledge of and dismay over the problems. Again, for a representative sampling from the *Times*, see: "The Army of Invasion: Lack of Method in Moving It from Tampa the Talk of Washington," *The New York Times*, 16 June 1898, 1; "Miles's Alleged Criticisms: Interesting Developments Likely to Follow the General's Return to Washington from Tampa," *The New York Times* 17 Jun. 1898, 2; "Report From Gen. Miles: Commander of the Army Describes the Departure of the First Expedition for Cuba, Delay at Tampa Explained, Many Difficulties Which Had to be Overcome," *The New York Times*, 18 June 1898, 2; "The War Investigation: President's Commission Hears the Testimony of Officers at Camp Cuba Libre," *The New York Times*, 19 Oct. 1898, 4; "The War Investigation: The President's Commission Hears More Stories of Mismanagement in the Army," *The New York Times*, 2 Nov. 1898, 4.

There were additional difficulties after the war, which further epitomized the disasters Upton predicted. As Skowronek notes: "America had become an imperial power but maintained a provincial army. The legislation for army expansion in April 1898 had been a hodgepodge of temporary expedients. The state units began to disband immediately, and the national [regular] troops faced immediate reversion to prewar size."[20] These were serious problems considering the job at hand had not yet been completed and still required troops. Unlike the nation's previous conflicts, there was now a need to provide order and stability in a variety of foreign lands separated by thousands of miles. In addition, new governments had to be established. Most importantly, Americans were faced with an insurrection in the Philippines. In short, the old-style militia structure was fundamentally unprepared to deal with the results of this new type of conflict. Another round of congressional action again tried to institutionalize a larger and better organized regular army but ultimately failed in the face of a filibuster (a temporary bill was passed to ensure enough troops to oversee the postwar issues). Despite this second failed attempt to reform the Army, the tide had shifted. The National Guard was humbled by the problems it faced in the war, and there was a growing consensus that a more professional army was necessary.

Although the entire process of reform would continue until the onset of World War I, the Spanish-American War marked the turning point for the reformers. Before the war, those seeking army professionalization had little political power in the face of the entrenched militia system buoyed by old-style patronage. But after the war and the uncovering of obvious systemic failures, the political mood changed. President Roosevelt, the Elihu Root-led War Department, and Republicans in Congress recognized the need for reform. Over the next three years, Secretary Root quadrupled the size of the standing Army (see Figure 2.1), established the Army War College, gained federal oversight of the National Guard, and established what later became known as the Joint Chiefs of Staff.[21] Needless to say, federal government expenditures for the Army increased dramatically and permanently (see Figure 2.2).

Root also changed the expectations of the National Guard. The militias would now only be used to stop invasions and quell domestic insurrections. No longer would they be expected to carry out long-term operations abroad. However, the National Guard units were allowed to remain under state control and, in return for agreeing to Army inspections, were given more discretionary federal dollars. In addition, efforts were made to utilize National Guard personnel by forming a national voluntary reserve. Root was able to modernize and professionalize the federal, regular Army while, at the same time, respecting the traditional significance of the National Guard. Similar initiatives were continued until the outbreak of World War I.

---

[20] Skowronek, 116.
[21] Ibid., 215–6.

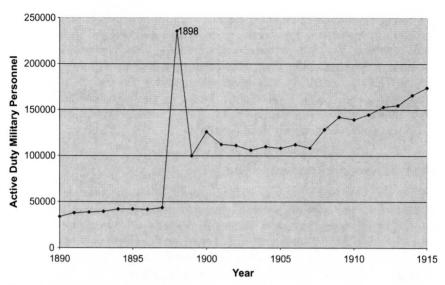

FIGURE 2.1. Military Personnel on Duty.[22]

In sum, the Spanish-American War was a key factor in the development of
the U.S. state. The patronage and devolved command structure that characterized the Army since the founding era proved to be fundamentally incapable

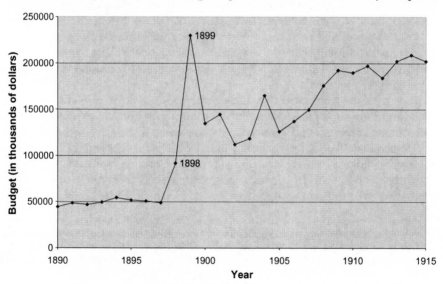

FIGURE 2.2. Annual Federal Army Budget.[23]

[22] U.S. Bureau of the Census, *Historical Statistics of the United States* (Washington: U.S. Government Printing Office, 1975), 1141–2.
[23] U.S. Bureau of the Census, 1114.

of meeting the challenges posed by a foreign war and the peacekeeping efforts needed in its aftermath. Numerous reform efforts had failed in the years preceding the war. The ill-fated attempt to modernize the National Guard for the Spanish-American War then reinforced the problems inherent in the old system. These failures that became apparent during the war created a new and broad consensus for fundamental reform of the militia-style Army. The establishment of a standing Army elevated the United States to a new, more prominent position in international politics.

The Philippines and American Empire

Perhaps the most important and unanticipated result of the Spanish-American War was President McKinley's decision to annex the Philippines. It opened a new chapter in American history and thrust the state into a new role as a colonial power. For the first time, the United States took possession of new territory and attempted to exert control over it.[24] Perhaps because the results were uninspiring, the affair is often overlooked in American history, as well as in the most common APD studies of the state, which focus on massive, domestically based, and largely successful and enduring federal initiatives.[25] This episode of state development did not endure in the usual sense. It was, however, a precursor of future American initiatives abroad that met with similarly ambiguous results, at best. The case is also noteworthy in the annals of American state development because it happened largely by accident. Unlike most of the state building periods on which APD scholars focus, the U.S. acquisition of the Philippines was not a well thought out response to an identifiable problem, but rather an unanticipated consequence of the Spanish-American War. The experience can most clearly be understood through an examination of McKinley's agonizing decision making process.

By way of context, 1890s America witnessed increasing domestic support for establishing imperial holdings abroad. Calls for overseas expansion became increasingly common, and leading politicians came to be identified as pro- or anti-imperialist. In addition to the economic incentives of colonialism, supporters spoke – often in overtly racist and paternalistic fashion – of God's desire for the United States, with its superior way of life, to enlighten the less fortunate around the world. As one imperialist put it: "Let us take this course because

---

[24] Again, the focus here is on global imperialism and attempts to gain territorial holdings disconnected from the United States and with little to no indigenous desire for annexation. There were critical differences between the territories gained in the Mexican War and those resulting from the Spanish-American War.

[25] A recent and welcome exception is: Paul T. McCartney, *Power and Progress: American National Identity, the War of 1898, and the Rise of American Imperialism* (Baton Rouge, LA: Louisiana State University Press, 2006). Deemphasizing economic motives, McCartney argues that Americans' sense of "mission" played a key role in the United States declaring war on Spain and in annexing the Philippines.

it is noble and just and right, and besides because it will pay."[26] The Republicans tended to be more supportive of bold international expansion, whereas Democrats were more reluctant or voiced outright opposition. The split became apparent during the 1896 election between McKinley and Democrat William Jennings Bryan. Though this election focused on domestic issues, the GOP platform clearly articulated the party's pro-expansion majority.[27] Despite this significant uptick in agitation for overseas holdings during the 1890s, no significant expansions actually occurred. Only with the Spanish-American War were imperialists able to implement their agenda.

There has been considerable scholarly debate surrounding McKinley's annexation decision and the extent to which he was an eager or reluctant expansionist.[28] Although there is a relatively small amount of available evidence, scholars have come to starkly different conclusions regarding McKinley's role in the annexation. Early accounts viewed McKinley and his intentions favorably during and after the war.[29] But a group of revisionist historians followed who were heavily critical of McKinley, seeing the war and the annexation as grave mistakes. Some of these critics viewed McKinley as a weak and unengaged president who fell under the sway of either public opinion or various members of his administration and was manipulated into annexing the Philippines.[30] Another revisionist interpretation suggests the President was a

---

[26] This quote comes from Army General James Harrison Wilson, arguing for annexing Cuba. George C. Herring, *From Colony to Superpower: U.S. Foreign Relations since 1776* (New York: Oxford University Press, 2008), 305. See also, 299–309.

[27] "Republican Platform," *History of American Presidential Elections, 1789–1968*, Vol. 2, ed., Arthur M. Schlesinger, Jr. (New York: Chelsea House Publishers, 1971), 1831–5.

[28] One reason for the lack of consensus is that McKinley did not leave a substantial record of his thoughts. He wrote few letters, and his public statements were often ambiguous and open to interpretation. For an overview of relevant scholarship see: Ephraim K. Smith, "William McKinley's Enduring Legacy: The Historiographical Debate on the Taking of the Philippine Islands," ed., James C. Bradford, *Crucible of Empire* (Annapolis, MD: Naval Institute Press, 1993).

[29] These accounts emphasized America's benign intentions. Most scholars argued that McKinley had no real alternative but to take the islands and that part of his calculation involved a concern for the welfare of the Filipinos. Even these early accounts, though, suggested capitalist and missionary motivations were also at work. The period's most prominent McKinley scholar, Charles S. Olcott, portrayed his subject as a strong president but a reluctant imperialist who found himself in a difficult position. Charles S. Olcott, *The Life of William McKinley* (Boston and New York: Houghton Mifflin Co., 1916). See also: Willis Fletcher Johnson, *America's Foreign Relations* (London: E. Nash Co., 1916); Carl Russell Fish, *American Diplomacy* (New York: H. Holt and Co., 1919); John Holladay Latane, *America as a World Power, 1897–1907* (New York: Harper and Brothers, 1907).

[30] The alleged conspirators range from prominent figures such as Theodore Roosevelt and Henry Cabot Lodge to a "small rather self-conscious, politically effective group of expansionists" who "schemed the annexation of colonies in the China Sea" and used the "cover of a war to liberate Cuba and complete the American hegemony of the Caribbean." A. Whitney Griswold, *The Far Eastern Policy of the United States* (New Haven, CT: Yale University Press, 1962, c1938), 34. See also: Harold Underwood Faulkner, *American Economic History* (New York: Harper &

sort of conspiring genius who initiated the war over Cuba but whose secret agenda always called for acquiring an economic and colonial foothold in Asia.[31]

For the most part, the past several decades have seen McKinley's rehabilitation. The general consensus now holds that he was a strong president who attacked the Philippines as a means to draw the war to a close and then, having defeated Spain in the archipelago, discovered that the only reasonable follow-up decision was to annex the islands. Ephraim K. Smith's extensive review of

Brothers, 1924); Julius W. Pratt, *Expansionists of 1898: The Acquisition of Hawaii and the Spanish Islands* (Gloucester, MA: Peter Smith, 1936), 327.

A more moderate strain within this school of thought argues that Social Darwinists set the intellectual climate for expansionism, which, for different reasons, the business community and the religious community supported. After the Battle of Manila Bay these interests and public support were too difficult to combat for the weak-willed McKinley. On this point, see: Richard Hofstadter, "Cuba, the Philippines, and Manifest Destiny," *The Paranoid Style in American Politics and Other Essays* (New York: Knopf, 1965), 145–87; Frederick Merk, *Manifest Destiny and Mission in American History: A Reinterpretation* (New York: Vintage Books, 1963), 231–57; Ernest R. May, *American Imperialism: A Speculative Essay* (New York: Atheneum, 1968).

These criticisms were reinforced by "realist" historians and political scientists during the Cold War years who saw the conflict and the Filipino acquisition as contrary to the national interest and viewed McKinley as incompetent.

[31] According to this camp, McKinley took the Philippines for religious (i.e., missionary) or economic reasons. These scholars tend to argue that the islands should have been given back to Spain or granted their independence. Rejecting the argument that McKinley was a weak president, they see a man who deliberately shaped U.S. policy to create new markets and imperial holdings in Asia. Few go so far as to argue that McKinley went to war over Cuba solely to obtain the Philippines, but some speculate that this could have been a contributing factor. Thus, this school of thought suggests McKinley always had his eye on the Philippines and actively sought their acquisition. John A.S. Grenville and George Berkeley Young add that, to the extent McKinley appeared ambivalent, he was actually just biding his time, knowing that public opinion would eventually turn in his favor. He "made it appear that he had only gradually and reluctantly been driven to the conclusion that his duty to God, national honor, the Filipinos, and the Cubans demanded that the United States assume the burden of governing the Spanish colonies." John A.S. Grenville and George Berkeley Young, *Politics, Strategy, and American Diplomacy* (New Haven, CT: Yale University Press, 1966), 288. See also: James Ford Rhodes, *The McKinley and Roosevelt Administrations, 1897–1909* (New York: The Macmillan Co., 1922), 108; Scott Nearing and Joseph Freeman, *Dollar Diplomacy: A Study in American Imperialism* (New York: B. W. Huebsch and the Viking Press, 1925); Thomas McCormick, Jr., "Insular Imperialism and the Open Door: The China Market and the Spanish-American War," *Pacific Historical Review* 32:2 (1963), 155–69; Walter LaFeber, *The New Empire: An Interpretation of American Expansion, 1860–1898* (Ithaca, NY: Cornell University Press, 1963); William Appleman Williams, *The Tragedy of American Diplomacy* (New York: Dell Pub. Co., 1962); McCormick, *China Market: America's Quest for Informal Empire, 1893–1901* (Chicago: Quadrangle Books, 1967); Williams, *The Roots of the Modern American Empire* (New York: Random House, 1969); Paolo E. Coletta, "McKinley, the Peace Negotiations, and the Acquisition of the Philippines," *Pacific Historical Review* 30 (Nov. 1961), 341–7; H. Wayne Morgan, *America's Road to Empire: The War with Spain and Overseas Expansion* (New York: John Wiley & Sons, 1965); Gould, *The Presidency of William McKinley* (Lawrence, KS: Regents Press of Kansas, 1980), 121, 150.

this literature concludes: "there does seem to be a consensus that McKinley was an able president who, particularly after the Battle of Manila Bay, dominated decisions on the islands." Scholars who continue to contend otherwise, Smith argues,

> have carried revisionism beyond the existing evidence. Weaving a tale of conspiracy and intrigue on McKinley's part, these studies seem to ignore the president's innately conservative and cautious personality. According to this approach, McKinley never had a moment's doubt or miscalculated as he faced one of the most momentous decisions of his career. Such accounts, while stimulating, have as much value as the earlier canard that McKinley had "no more backbone than a chocolate éclair."[32]

Indeed, the evidence suggests that McKinley was not eager for war, had no early plans to take the Philippines, and was a reluctant imperialist. America's conquests resulted from a series of unanticipated events; there were no imperialistic designs that prompted the war or the acquisition. The purpose of confronting the Spanish forces in the Philippines was simply to put pressure on the enemy in a vulnerable outpost. Finally, McKinley hesitated to hold on to the islands until it became clear that public opinion strongly favored annexation.

In his own words and writings, McKinley repeatedly asserted his initial reluctance to acquire the Philippines and stressed the strategic nature of attacking the Spanish fleet in the Pacific. Although McKinley did not leave a detailed paper trail, he did discuss his decision with a number of friends and advisors. His most famous and detailed explanation was given to a visiting Methodist delegation. According to a published account of the meeting, McKinley said that the "truth is I didn't want the Philippines, and when they came to us, as a gift from the gods, I did not know what to do with them." The sole intention of sending Dewey to the Pacific was to exert pressure on Spain and hasten the end of the war. The Philippines "had dropped into our laps."[33] These sentiments are consistent with McKinley's comments to two other confidants.[34]

However, once the islands had been taken from Spain and no viable alternatives presented themselves (from his perspective), McKinley acquiesced and agreed to annexation. He asserted this position in a letter to William Day, his former secretary of state, who was negotiating the peace agreement:

---

[32] Smith, "William McKinley's Enduring Legacy," 236–7. See also, Ivan Musicant, *Empire of Default: The Spanish-American War and the Dawn of the American Century* (New York: Henry Holt and Company, Inc., 1998); Trask, 78.

[33] James F. Rusling, "Interview with President McKinley," *Christian Advocate* (New York) 78 (22 Jan. 1903), 137–8.

[34] McKinley made similar remarks to Jacob Schurman, the president of Cornell University, and confidant Henry S. Pritchett. See: Jacob Gould Schurman, "The Philippine Situation," *The Outlook* 63 (4 Nov. 1899), 534–8; Henry S. Pritchett, "Some Recollections of President McKinley and the Cuban Intervention," *North American Review* 189 (March 1909), 397–403.

There is a very general feeling that the United States, whatever it might prefer as to the Philippines, is in a situation where it cannot let go. The interdependency of the several islands, ... the very grave problem of what will become of the part we do not take are receiving the thoughtful consideration of the people, and it is my judgment that the well-considered opinion of the majority would be that duty requires we should take the archipelago.[35]

McKinley gave a more detailed account of his assessment of the available options to the Methodist delegation. One possibility would have been to return the Philippines to Spain, but this would be "cowardice and dishonorable." Another option was to give the islands to a third country. McKinley, though, thought it would be "bad business and discreditable" to turn the Philippines over to "our commercial rivals." Finally, McKinley might have granted the Filipinos independence, but it was conventional wisdom at the time that the locals "were unfit for self-government." [36] The *Chicago Times-Herald* assessed the decision:

To return these islands to Spain would be to remand the Filipinos to the same condition the Cubans were in before the war. More disastrous yet would be the attempt to establish an independent native government among people who are incapable of self-government and whose present chosen leader is but little more than a barbarian, full of intrigue and dishonesty. To allow them to be sold to any foreign power would be to invite European strife. Any one of these three courses would stultify the United States, for all of them are in conflict with the interests of humanity. The only humane course is to retain the islands and govern them ourselves.[37]

As a result of these considerations, McKinley thought there was no other viable alternative, as he told the Methodists, but "to take them all, and to educate the Filipinos, and uplift and civilize and Christianize them, and by God's grace do the very best we could by them, as our fellow-men for whom Christ also died."[38] Incidentally, this hoped-for Christianization of the Filipinos arose despite the fact that Catholic Spanish missionaries had been hard at work and enjoying great success in the Philippines for approximately 300 years. Perhaps due to then-common anti-Catholic bias, this fact was apparently lost on McKinley and many others who genuinely believed America had a missionary calling in the Philippines.

McKinley's reluctance at this point is consistent with his speeches prior to the Spanish-American War. He did not encourage expansionism, and at times specifically denounced it. McKinley's inaugural address, while noting the

---

[35] Letter printed in: Charles S. Olcott, *William McKinley*, vol. 2 (Boston and New York: Houghton Mifflin Company, 1916), 107–8.

[36] Rusling, 137–8. While this assumption was widespread in 1898, in hindsight it appears quite dubious. Nonetheless, the point here is not to assess the validity of this view or to condemn those who held it. Rather, the more simple aim at present is to ascertain McKinley's state of mind.

[37] *Times-Herald*, in *The Literary Digest*, 29 Nov. 1898, 510.

[38] Rusling, 137–8.

need to fully utilize international trade opportunities, emphasized the peaceful nature of this pursuit and pointedly shunned territorial acquisition. The new president's firm denunciation of aggressive imperialism could not have been more clearly stated:

It has been the policy of the United States, since the foundation of the government, to cultivate relations of peace and amity with all the nations of the world, and this accords with my conception of our duty now. We have cherished the policy of non-interference with the affairs of foreign governments.... Our diplomacy should seek nothing more and accept nothing less than is due us. We want no wars of conquest; we must avoid the temptation of territorial aggression. War should never be entered upon until every agency of peace has failed; peace is preferable to war in almost every contingency.[39]

International business and trade were frequently discussed when McKinley stepped to the lectern (the nation was mired in a recession), but there were no appeals to imperialism. The President's emphasis was always on the exchange of goods and services between businessmen. The proper role for government in this sphere was merely to maintain the peace between the various nations to allow the market to function properly. There were no suggestions of aggressive acquisition of new territories or colonies. As McKinley said in a June 1897 speech in Philadelphia: "A spirit of friendly and mutually advantageous interchange and cooperation has been exemplified, which is in itself an inspiring help not only to trade and commerce, but to international comity and good will. Good will precedes good trade."[40]

Several months later in Cincinnati, McKinley discussed the importance of international trade in greater depth and sought to demonstrate its compatibility with, and reinforcement of, peaceful relations between nations. He started by stating that the material well-being of the United States was an important issue. The President continued:

No subject can better engage our attention than the promotion of trade and commerce at home and abroad. Domestic conditions are sure to be improved by larger exchanges with the nations of the world.... Our manufactured products go to every nation of the world, and I hope the time may be not far distant when our ships... will be on every sea where commerce is carried.... Commerce is a teacher and a pacifier. It gives mankind knowledge of one another. Reciprocity of trade promotes reciprocity of friendship. Good trade ensures good will. The heart as well as the mind contributes directly to the progress of mankind, and wherever we secure just and fair commercial relations with other nations we are sure to have with them friendly political relations.... It should be our settled purpose to open trade wherever we can, making our ships and our commerce messengers of peace and amity.[41]

[39] William McKinley, "Inaugural Address, Delivered From East Front of the Capitol, Washington, March 4, 1897," *Speeches and Addresses of William McKinley* (New York: Doubleday & McClure, Co., 1990), 11–2.

[40] McKinley, "Address at the National Opening of the Philadelphia Museums, Philadelphia, June 2, 1897," 25.

[41] McKinley, "Speech at the Dinner of the Commercial Club of Cincinnati, Saturday, October 30, 1897," 54–5. McKinley makes similar comments in January 1898 at a speech to the Banquet

The primary point here is the absence of imperialistic designs by McKinley. Of course, it is conceivable that the President was being coy and not expressing his true desires. The problem with this possibility is that it simply does not conform to the other available evidence. As previously noted, McKinley's statements after victory in the Philippines suggest that his initial motivations there were of a military rather than expansionist nature.[42]

It was only well after the conclusion of the war – when the benefits of colonial holdings had had time to sink in – that McKinley began to openly engage in imperialistic talk. For instance, during an October 1898 speaking tour in advance of the midterm elections, McKinley hardly beat around the bush about the expansionist benefits of the Spanish-American War. At the time of the trip, McKinley had not announced his intentions regarding the Philippines. In nearly every speech on the tour, though, he alluded to the decision he faced. In Omaha, Nebraska, paraphrasing his remarks at several earlier stops, he stated: "We did not seek war. To avoid it . . . was our constant prayer. The war was no more invited by us than were the questions which are laid at our door by its results."[43]

In addition to this constant refrain, McKinley's rhetoric regarding America's place in the world was markedly different than it had been prior to or during the war. He adopted the language of Manifest Destiny and expansionism, speaking openly about new settlements and territory and alluding to the role of God. "That hostilities have ceased upon terms so satisfactory to the people of the United States," McKinley said in Cedar Rapids, Iowa, " . . . calls forth sentiments of gratitude to divine Providence for those favors which he has manifested unto us."[44] America's inevitable expansion was also alluded to in Clinton, Iowa. McKinley said that the nation had "the courage of destiny." Impressed by the way the country drew together in support of the war, Mc-Kinley went on to encourage his audience to "continue to act together until the fruits of our war shall be embodied in solemn and permanent settlements."[45]

McKinley's statements became even more explicit as the tour wore on. On the third day, he specifically mentioned the new territory that had come to the United States and, for the first time, hinted that America might retain the Philippines. At a stop in Chariton, Iowa, the President said: "Territory sometimes comes to us when we go to war in a holy cause, and whenever it does that banner of liberty will float over it and bring, I trust, blessings and benefits to all the people."[46] Later that same day in Illinois, he again alluded to possible annexation: "The army and the navy from Manila to Santiago have

---

of the National Association of Manufacturers of the United States at the Waldorf-Astoria in New York City. See: McKinley, 61–3.

[42] Musicant, 261–2.
[43] McKinley, "Address at the Trans-Mississippi Exposition at Omaha, Nebraska, October 12, 1898," 105.
[44] McKinley, "Speech at Cedar Rapids, Iowa, October 11, 1898," 87.
[45] McKinley, "Speech at Clinton, Iowa, October 11, 1898," 85.
[46] McKinley, "Speech at Chariton, Iowa, October 13, 1898," 114.

nobly performed their duty. It is left for the citizens of this country to do theirs. May God give us the wisdom to perform our part with fidelity, not only to our own interests, but to the interests of those who, by the fortunes of war, are brought within the radius of our influence."[47] The following passage from his Chicago speech offers perhaps the most comprehensive insight into McKinley's evolution into a postwar imperialist:

The war has put upon the nation grave responsibilities. Their extent was not anticipated, and could not have been well foreseen. We cannot escape the obligations of victory. We cannot avoid the serious questions which have been brought home to us by the achievements of our arms on land and sea.... Accepting war for humanity's sake, we must accept all obligations which the war in duty and honor imposed upon us.... The war with Spain was undertaken, not that the United States should increase its territory, but that oppression at our very doors should be stopped. This noble sentiment must continue to animate us, and we must give to the world the full demonstration of the sincerity of our purpose.... Looking backward, we can see how the hand of destiny builded for us and assigned us tasks whose full meaning was not apprehended even by the wisest statesmen of their times. Our colonial ancestors did not enter upon their war originally for independence. Abraham Lincoln did not start out to free the slaves, but to save the Union. The war with Spain was not of our seeking, and some of its consequences may not be to our liking.... The progress of a nation can alone prevent degeneration. There must be new life and purpose or there will be weakness and decay. There must be broadening of thought as well as broadening of trade. Territorial expansion is not alone and always necessary to national advancement. There must be a constant movement toward a higher and nobler civilization, a civilization that shall make its conquests without resort to war, and achieve its greatest victories pursuing the art of peace. In our present situation, duty and duty alone should prescribe the boundary of our responsibilities and the scope of our undertakings.[48]

McKinley suggested that wars often bring new and unforeseen challenges and opportunities. Like the Revolution and the Civil War, the Spanish-American War brought with it unanticipated consequences. Thus, although McKinley was not focused on territorial expansion before or during the war, he saw reasons to embrace it once the possibility arose and the unappealing alternatives were understood.

It was shortly after the speaking tour that McKinley officially announced his intention to retain the Philippines – a decision that would have serious ramifications for American foreign policy, as well as domestic politics, for years to come. Most prominently, a new war arose. Although the Filipinos fought alongside the United States to oust Spain, they were no more pleased to have America as an imperial overseer. When it became apparent that the United States intended to permanently retain the islands, native insurgents began fighting their new occupiers. The Philippine-American War, or the Philippine Insurrection, began in February 1899 – just months after the Treaty of Paris was signed – and

[47] McKinley, "Speech at Monmouth, Illinois, October 13, 1898," 116.
[48] McKinley, "Speech at the Citizens' Banquet in the Auditorium, Chicago, October 19, 1898," 133–5.

would last for fourteen years. Despite officially concluding in 1902, a smaller number of insurgents continued the fight until 1913.[49] Foreshadowing future American conflicts, the war was marked by guerrilla fighting and included all of the customary attributes of such engagements. Atrocities were common on both sides and civilians paid a high price. Approximately 120,000 U.S. soldiers were engaged during those years, more than 4,000 were killed, and nearly 2,800 were wounded. This casualty rate of 5.5 percent was among the highest for any American war. Although the exact numbers are unknown, deaths likely exceeded 200,000 on the Filipino side, the bulk of which were civilian. Additionally, through 1902 – when the worst of the fighting ended – the Philippine-American War cost the U.S. $600 million to prosecute.[50] The conflict finally ended in 1913 when President Woodrow Wilson announced a policy shift that would eventually lead to the Philippines's independence.

The Philippines also had to be managed during these years. McKinley's initial policy of "benevolent assimilation" in 1898 was intended to convince Filipinos that American intentions were benign. To this end, the Army attempted to establish local government as well as legal, education, and sanitation systems. These initiatives were largely unsuccessful due to a lack of follow-through by the Americans and a plethora of attacks by Filipino insurgents. In 1900, the McKinley administration shifted gears and sent the Taft Commission to set up a civil government in the Philippines. Led by then-federal Judge William Howard Taft, the commission had broad authority to legislate, set up municipal organizations, tax and spend, and establish educational, judicial, electoral, and civil service systems.[51] This commission served as the primary governing authority on the islands until President Wilson shifted American policy under a new program called "Filipinization," in which indigenous leaders gradually assumed greater roles on the commission and within the bureaucracy. This move was accompanied by an unprecedented step for imperial powers: a promise of eventual independence. The Philippines were granted autonomy in 1935 and, eleven years later, their independence.[52]

In sum, the Spanish-American War had the unanticipated consequence of immersing the United States in a protracted and costly conflict thousands of miles away in the Philippines. This example highlights a central theme: Foreign conflicts are usually entered into for specific purposes, yet by the end of a given conflict (even one as short as ten weeks), the set of considerations and available options is often drastically altered. Wars inevitably bring unintended and unexpected consequences that change the set of considerations and available alternatives. In this case, McKinley originally saw the Philippines as a venue

[49] For more on the Philippine-American War, see: Brian McAllister Linn, *The Philippine War, 1899–1902* (Lawrence, KS: University Press of Kansas, 2000); Stanley Karnow, *In Our Image: America's Empire in the Philippines* (New York: Ballantine Books, 1989).

[50] Herring, *From Colony to Superpower*, 329.

[51] Gould, *The Spanish American War and President McKinley*, 123–6. See, also, Herring; Karnow.

[52] Herring, 367.

to pressure Spain in the hopes of quickly ending the war. American success in this initial enterprise, though, left the President with control of vast land holdings and, as a result, several undesirable options. His decision to annex and hold the islands was a fulfillment of the hopes of the expanding cohort of imperialists who for years had been advocating for international territorial holdings. Prior to the war, their calls were ignored, but the conflict with Spain altered the set of considerations. Annexation of the Philippines quickly led to an insurrection, more than a decade of costly guerilla warfare, and fifty years of colonial presence, all of which required considerable sums of money and manpower.

THE SPANISH-AMERICAN WAR AND THE PARTY SYSTEM OF 1896

The Spanish-American War and its unanticipated aftermath had a crucial effect on the 1898 midterm and the 1900 presidential elections. The incumbent Republican Party would have likely suffered significantly had it not been for the war. In addition, without the conflict, one of America's most transformative presidents would never have gained the notoriety that catapulted him into office.

The 1898 Midterm Election

A strong case can be made that, because the Spanish-American War was deemed to be a resounding success, the sitting president's party reaped the benefits. The 1898 results, then, are similar to others (such as 1816 and 2002) in which a governing party gained an advantage because of military events or a national security crisis. Surprisingly, the 1898 election has been underappreciated. Continuous GOP congressional control from 1894 through 1910 – highlighted by realignment theory as the "System of 1896" – likely led to the conclusion that Republican dominance was simply inevitable.[53] But such an assumption, despite creating an appealing narrative for realignment theorists, is wrong – nothing is inevitable. Events matter. In this instance, Republicans likely would have lost badly without the Spanish-American War and its "rally 'round the flag" effect.[54]

Several factors helped Republicans translate success in war to success at the polls. First, McKinley had the public's strong support going into the conflict. Second, the war was a clear victory, was concluded with unprecedented speed, and resulted in relatively low human and monetary costs. Third, the prewar

---

[53] See, for instance: Walter Dean Burnham, "Periodization Schemes and 'Party Systems': The 'System of 1896' as a Case in Point," *Social Science History* 10 (1986), 263–313; Burnham, "The System of 1896: An Analysis," *The Evolution of American Electoral Systems*, ed., Paul Kleppner (Westport, CT: Greenwood Press, 1981), 147–202. Sundquist.

[54] For a full discussion of the "rally 'round the flag" hypothesis, see: John E. Mueller, *War, Presidents, and Public Opinion* (Lanham, MD: University Press of America, 1985).

aim was satisfied with Cuba's independence. This success created a swell of patriotism that naturally benefited the ruling party and shifted the public's attention away from problems that otherwise would have hurt the incumbent Republicans.

McKinley toured the Midwest for the latter half of October and highlighted the successful war. Although McKinley did not explicitly ask his audiences to support Republican candidates – doing so at this time would have been poorly received and nearly unprecedented (the only previous president to do so, Andrew Johnson, was met with a striking rebuke) – undertaking such a trip at all just before an election was highly unusual.[55] The tour's timing was clearly designed to give Republican congressional candidates a boost. The President was met with large and enthusiastic crowds and garnered extensive newspaper coverage throughout the country.

Historians assert that McKinley's Republican Party did much better than expected in 1898 because of the war and the president's extensive speaking tour undertaken just before the election. Lewis Gould and others suggest the war allowed the Republicans to do better than most incumbent parties. He argues: "The Republicans faced the congressional elections in 1898 as the party associated with the victory over Spain, but they still anticipated the losses that the incumbent party usually suffered two years after a successful presidential election. President McKinley capitalized on the opportunity that celebrations of the American triumph provided" by embarking on his Midwest speaking tour.[56] The combination of the successful war and the McKinley victory lap, according to Gould, "helped to hold down" typical losses and the "customary reversal" for the incumbent party in the House.[57]

This argument appears somewhat overstated. Although the Republicans picked up seven Senate seats (Democrats surrendered eight), they lost twenty-one seats in the House whereas the Democrats gained twenty-nine (many of these coming at the expense of the Populists).[58] On the surface, this split decision of sorts hardly suggests an extraordinary election for the Republicans.

---

[55] For more on presidential rhetoric at this time, see Tulis, 25–94.

[56] Gould, *Grand Old Party*, 129–30.

[57] Ibid., 130; Gould, *The Presidency of William McKinley*, 137.

[58] Harold W. Stanley and Richard G. Niemi, *Vital Statistics on American Politics, 2003–2004* (Washington: CQ Press, 2003), 38. At this time U.S. senators were indirectly elected by state legislatures. Nonetheless, the literature concludes that U.S. Senate elections were still representative of public opinion. Just weeks after the first Tuesday in November when state legislative elections were held, the newly elected legislators met to select their U.S. senator. Thus, there was no significant time lag – public opinion was registered in state level elections and the winners of those contests met soon thereafter to choose their U.S. senator. Furthermore, as Rothman notes, "Constituents demanded that a candidate for the legislature declare his allegiances [for a U.S. Senate candidate] well in advance, and state laws often compelled him to respect the pledge. Invariably the Washington contest entered every election district" (160–1). David J. Rothman, *Politics and Power: The United States Senate, 1869–1901* (Cambridge, MA: Harvard University Press, 1966). See also: William H. Riker, "The Senate and American Federalism," *American Political Science Review* 49 (1955), 452–69; Charles H. Stewart III, "Responsiveness in the

TABLE 2.1. *Incumbent Party Performance in Midterm Elections*

For each midterm election, the number of senators/representatives in each chamber is displayed, followed by the number of seats gained or lost in that election, and then the percentage of change represented by those gained or lost seats. The analysis begins in 1870 because prior midterm elections are not comparable. The 1866 midterm election is not included because the presence of the Union Party thwarts a comparison. The Civil War and the establishment of the Republican Party immediately precede that.

Year	# Senators	Sen. ±/−	% Change	# Reps.	Reps ±/−	% Change
1930	96	−8	−8.3%	435	−49	−11.3%
1926	96	−6	−6.3%	435	−10	−2.3%
1922	96	−8	−8.3%	435	−75	−17.2%
1918	96	−6	−6.3%	435	−19	−4.4%
1914	96	+5	+5.2%	435	−59	−13.6%
1910	92	−10	−10.9%	391	−57	−14.6%
1906	92	−3	−3.2%	386	−28	−7.3%
1902	90	+2	+2.2%	386	+9	+2.3%
1898	90	+7	+7.8%	357	−21	−5.9%
1894	88	−5	−5.7%	357	−116	−32.5%
1890	88	0	0.0%	333	−85	−25.5%
1886	76	+3	+3.9%	325	−12	−3.7%
1882	76	+3	+3.9%	325	−33	−10.2%
1878	76	−6	−7.9%	293	−9	−3.1%
1874	76	−8	−10.5%	293	−96	−32.8%
1870	74	−4	−5.4%	243	−31	−12.8%

Ave. Sen. Seats Lost: −2.75   Ave. House Seats Lost: −43.19
Ave. % Change in Senate: −3.11%   Ave. % Change in House: −12.18%

Sources: Harold W. Stanley and Richard G. Niemi, *Vital Statistics on American Politics 2003–2004* (Washington, DC: Congressional Quarterly Press, 2003), 37–8; Norman J. Ornstein, Thomas E. Mann, Michael J. Malbin, and John F. Bibby, *Vital Statistics on Congress, 1982* (Washington, DC: AEI Press, 1982), 28–9.

GOP losses in the House in 1898 were less than normal, but such results did not quite constitute an historical anomaly (see Table 2.1). Additionally, gains in the Senate were not unheard of in the era, occurring in four of the other sixteen midterm elections.

Nonetheless, while some historians may have exaggerated the case, it is undeniable that 1898 was a good election for the Republicans. Their seven seat

Upper Chamber: The Constitution and the Institutional Development of the Senate," *The Constitution and American Political Development*, ed., Peter F. Nardulli (Urbana, IL: University of Illinois Press, 1992). For some partial caveats to this conventional understanding, see: Stewart and Wendy Schiller, "Party Control and Legislator Loyalty in Senate Elections Before Adoption of the 17th Amendment," working paper, accessible online at: http://web.mit.edu/cstewart/www/papers.html, last accessed 4 May 2009.

gain in the Senate ranks as the second highest ever in the current two-party system, dating back to before the Civil War. Only the 1934 Democrats, on the heels of Franklin Roosevelt's popular New Deal, gained more seats in the upper chamber. In addition, Republicans did much better than average. In the period from the establishment of the Republican Party to the beginning of the New Deal, the in-party lost an average of 2.75 Senate seats and 43.19 House seats (see Table 2.1).[59] As such, the 1898 GOP's respective gain of seven and loss of twenty-one appear quite good. Increases in each chamber's membership over these years can be controlled for by determining the percentage of seats gained or lost in each election (see Table 2.1). Here again, the 1898 Republicans do much better than the norm, benefiting from a +7.8 percent shift in the Senate as compared to the era's average of −3.11 percent. The party's losses in the House were only 5.9 percent – well under the average 12.18 percent reduction.

It is highly plausible that much of the explanation for the Republicans' good showing in the 1898 election lies in the Spanish-American War. Indeed, substantial evidence points to the GOP having ridden a patriotic wave generated by the war and making off like bandits in the midterm. The 1898 election gave the in-party majorities in both chambers of Congress. A midterm had only produced such a result once in the five previous off-year elections. In addition, the positive influence of the Spanish-American War becomes increasingly clear when one considers the circumstances surrounding the election. That is, even though the Republicans fared only slightly better numerically than would have been expected, their position going into the election (without the Spanish-American War) was grim, and would almost certainly have led to a much worse midterm result.

First and most obviously, history demonstrates that it is extremely unusual for the president's party to avoid losing seats in midterm elections. Only the 1934, 1998, and 2002 midterms failed to provide any congressional gains for the out-party. But other factors also pointed toward Republican disaster. The influence of patronage, for example, was a problem faced by every incumbent party during midterm elections in this era and, no doubt, contributed to the typical incumbent party losses. As Ohio Senator Marcus Alonzo Hanna explained shortly before the election:

History shows that usually the Congress elected during the middle of an Administration has a majority adverse to the dominant party. There are many reasons for this action by the people, the chief among them being the apathy among the voters and the result of patronage. The offices have been distributed and the men who worked in the Presidential campaign with the hope of reward afterward have either secured places or have been

---

[59] The analysis begins in 1870 because prior midterm elections are not comparable. The 1866 midterm election is not included because the presence of the Union Party thwarts a comparison. The Civil War and the establishment of the Republican Party immediately precede that. The analysis ends in 1930 because the presidential election two years later ushered in a widely accepted pivot point in American political history.

disappointed, and they lose interest in the Congressional election or remain away from the polls because of the disappointment.[60]

This lack of excitement from the party's strongest supporters often created a general sense of lethargy in midterm campaigns for the incumbent party. The effect was pronounced in this particular midterm because of the intensity attached to the 1896 election. In addition, the GOP had no money in its coffers.[61]

Still another bad omen for Republicans came the year before, in the form of the 1897 elections. In this era there were many more of these "off-off year elections," and this one was a significant setback to the GOP. They lost races in Nebraska, New Jersey, New York, and Kansas, and saw a substantial loss of support in Ohio and Pennsylvania.[62] As the *New York Tribune* succinctly observed, "Republican majorities of a year ago have been reduced or extinguished in most of the states voting."[63]

Yet in the face of such influences and indications, the expected Republican defeat in 1898 was avoided, and the existing evidence suggests that the Spanish-American War and McKinley's speaking tour highlighting that military success were critical in this reversal. At this early date, there was no systematic polling to gauge public opinion on the war or the election. Newspaper and periodical accounts, though, strongly suggest McKinley and his Republican Party benefited from the war in the 1898 midterm election.

The war was clearly a pivotal issue in the campaign according to party leaders and newspaper accounts. Both major political parties tried to use the war to their advantage. Democrats attempted to play on what they hoped would turn into widespread discontent over the War Department's alleged blunders with regard to care for the troops.[64] When the issue garnered considerable public attention for a few weeks that fall, Democratic operatives tried to turn the controversy into a full blown scandal, hoping it would reflect poorly on the Republican Party as a whole. As reported by the *New York Times*, Democrats thought this could be a winning issue and tried "to keep the pot boiling while the fight is on."[65] Longtime Democratic leader and Congressman James G. McGuire gave an important speech during the campaign that emphasized this strategy and noted the prominence of the war as a campaign issue. The *San Francisco Chronicle* reported that the congressman "declared that the Republican Party was trying to march to victory on the strength of a successful war having been completed, and [McGuire] held that there had been gross neglect

[60] *The New York Times*, "Hanna Advises Activity," 4 Oct. 1898, 3.
[61] Gould, *The Presidency of William McKinley*, 137.
[62] Ibid., 54–5.
[63] *New York Tribune*, 4 Nov. 1897, 1.
[64] For an account of the problems see: Gould, *The Spanish-American War and President McKinley*, 91–4.
[65] *The New York Times*, "Democratic Campaign Shots," 21 Oct. 1898, 1.

in the care of troops, and if the Republican Party was to claim all the credit for the war, it should also claim the discredit for this."[66]

The Republicans realized the harm these charges could cause to their electoral prospects. Indeed, according to Republican campaign strategist Representative John A.T. Hull of Iowa, the Democrats' strategy might have succeeded under slightly different circumstances.

If the election had been held [in late August or early September] I believe we would have been beaten. A feeling that pretty much everything in connection with the war had been mismanaged swept over the country like a wave. Since then I believe there has been a revulsion in our favor.... The people have seen that the complaints were in many instances exaggerations, and the feeling of pride... has overcome the indignation at what were first thought to be avoidable evils. The people now see the necessity of electing a Congress that will hold up the President's hands throughout the difficult and delicate peace negotiations. They believe Mr. McKinley has managed the war pretty well, and they can see the unwisdom of putting a hostile House at his back while the fruits of the war are being reaped.[67]

This bleak prognosis for the GOP in September 1898 is reminiscent of the party's position entering the 1864 presidential election – another contest that hinged on a war. Abraham Lincoln almost certainly would have lost an election held as late as August of that year. Only the Union's capture of Atlanta and similar last-minute military successes elsewhere allowed Lincoln to win reelection.

In the face of these Democratic charges before the 1898 election, the Republican campaign tried to associate their partisan rivals with the nation's recently defeated international foe. The Republican-affiliated *New York Tribune* ran a front page story suggesting that support for the Democratic Party would be an effective way to aid the nation's Spanish enemies. By rhetorically asking readers whether they would vote to help Spain, the paper said a Democratic victory "may enable Spain not only to obtain more favorable terms in the Philippines, but perhaps to retain them altogether.... [Spain] looks forward with confidence to a Democratic victory on Tuesday, which would... best serve the vital interests" of that country.[68]

The Democrats' attempts to use the war to their political advantage underscore its status as a key issue in the campaign. Secretary James Kerr, of the Democratic Congressional Committee, put war-related issues at the top of the agenda when he announced his party's plan for the fall election at the end of the summer.[69] Reports from Republicans reveal the same focus. Their campaign "handbook" also emphasized the war and, in particular, McKinley's conduct

---

[66] *San Francisco Chronicle*, "Maguire on Campaign," 16 Oct. 1898, 16.

[67] *The New York Times*, "To Secure 56th Congress," 9 Oct. 1898, 1.

[68] *New York Tribune*, "Will You Vote to Aid Spain?" 6 Nov. 1898, 1. Many papers at this time were formally affiliated with a political party.

[69] *The New York Times*, "Democrats Define Issues," 18 Aug. 1898, 3.

of it.[70] Republican Congressional Committee Chairman (RCCC) Joseph W. Babcock, in discussing the upcoming election, said that "people do not want to hear anything about free silver . . . [or] tariff legislation . . . they do not want to hear anything more about that. Practically, the only thing that interests the public now is the war situation and the general policy of the Government in regard to the acquisition of foreign territory."[71]

Election forecasting was a rudimentary art in the nineteenth century, but was nonetheless a source of great interest. At the time, this kind of analysis was often undertaken by party officials. In 1898, Babcock presented his forecast shortly before the election. Foreshadowing the internal campaign polls of the future, Babcock's partisan affiliation likely caused him to slightly overestimate the share of seats his Republican Party would take. After the ballots were counted, the Republicans held 185 House seats, twelve short of Babcock's prediction. But the main point is that, as reported by the *New York Tribune*, the war led him to greatly increase his estimate: "If Chairman Babcock had been required to publish a political forecast three weeks ago . . . it would have been much less favorable than the one he issued today, and a month ago it would have been absolutely disheartening to every supporter of the Administration." In Babcock's own words: "This campaign has been very different from the campaigns of 1894 and 1896, from the fact that so many new conditions have come to the front." The two previous elections, he went on, centered on domestic concerns such as the tariff and monetary issues. In contrast, his statement continues:

During the present campaign, the Administration has prosecuted the most successful war known to modern history. Notwithstanding the brilliant achievements of the Army and Navy, the Democratic party and its allies have endeavored to belittle and criticize, not so much the results of the war as the methods of the War Department. . . . The facts in regard to the conduct of the war have been shown up completely, and the criticism and the attempted opposition to the Administration on this account have fallen flat; and the change in sentiment in the last month . . . has been simply wonderful.[72]

Popular support for the war and its successful outcome was utilized by McKinley shortly before the election in the same Midwest speaking tour discussed earlier in this chapter. Indeed, the successful war became the tour's defining theme and was constantly referenced by McKinley and those who joined him at the podium. The *San Francisco Chronicle* reported on one event in Chicago that captured the spirit of the tour: "Rev. Dr. Thomas P. Hodnett, a Catholic clergyman, caught the fancy and applause of the audience by repeated references to Dewey, [other Spanish-American War luminaries], and the Rough Riders, and when he mentioned President McKinley by name

---

[70] *The New York Times*, "The Republican Handbook," 19 Aug., 1898, 7.
[71] *The New York Times*, "Republicans are Hopeful," 25 Aug. 1898, 4.
[72] *The New York Tribune*, "Forecast of Next House," 28 Oct. 1898, 1.

the people became so demonstrative that the President was compelled to rise in his box and bow his acknowledgments."[73]

For his part, McKinley's initial speeches on the tour included the war as one of several discussion points. Encouraged by the enthusiastic response to mentions of the war at the beginning of the tour, McKinley's comments became increasingly focused on it and the issues that emanated from its conclusion. As one newspaper described it: "As the train moved eastward, the tenor of the President's speeches to the various crowds seemed to center more and more on the question of the foreign policy of the government, and, judging by the applause of his auditors, they were largely in accord with his sentiments."[74]

This initial outpouring of support continued. By all accounts, the trip was a remarkable success and arguably marked the high point of the McKinley presidency. The crowds he encountered were consistently larger than expected and unusually unified in their support of the President and the war. Hundreds of newspaper and periodical articles demonstrate the enthusiasm surrounding the train tour. One report offers a glimpse of the early portion of the trip: "At every station at which the Presidential train stopped on its way to Omaha the crowds were so dense that hundreds could not even gain a glimpse of the President."[75] On arrival in Omaha, the President was greeted by a typical audience:

President McKinley probably never received a more enthusiastic greeting than that which awaited him at the Exposition grounds. By far the greatest crowd in the history of the fair – so large a crowd that its numbers are almost impossible to estimate – thronged about the platform from which the President made his address. Hardly a sentence was spoken by him which did not evoke from the people cheer upon cheer . . . it was fully five minutes before the subsiding of the applause permitted the President to begin speaking.[76]

The rest of the tour was marked by similarly receptive audiences. "In Western Iowa the crowds were large and clamorous at every point, but when the eastern part of the State was reached their magnitude seemed to swell at every stopping place."[77] Even bad weather could not suppress turnout. The *New York Times'* account of McKinley's speech in Columbus, Ohio, notes that, "notwithstanding the heavy downpour of rain an immense crowd had assembled at the depot, and the building resounded with cheers." Further, the President's address was "frequently interrupted by enthusiastic applause."[78] Likewise, in Indianapolis, "all of the city itself turned out to give him welcome."[79]

---

[73] *San Francisco Chronicle*, "Ovation to M'Kinley," 17 Oct. 1898, 1.
[74] *San Francisco Chronicle*, "Iowa Greets M'Kinley," 14 Oct. 1898, 3.
[75] *San Francisco Chronicle*, "Omaha Greets the President," 12 Oct. 1898, 2.
[76] *New York Tribune*, "The President on the War," 13 Oct. 1898, 1.
[77] *San Francisco Chronicle*, "Iowa Greets M'Kinley," 14 Oct. 1898, 1.
[78] *The New York Times*, "President in Columbus," 22 Oct. 1898, 1.
[79] *The New York Times*, "Speech in Indianapolis," 22 Oct. 1898, 1.

McKinley's speaking tour in the Midwest enhanced the advantage Republicans already had on account of the war. Gould contends that "the trip immediately made a favorable impact upon Republican fortunes in the campaign."[80] Though McKinley avoided directly asking his audiences to vote Republican, *The Literary Digest* saw "the president's tour as clever political campaigning."[81] Even this type of semi-campaigning was a bit untoward at the time. But as the *New York Times* articulated, McKinley's efforts were beneficial to his party:

It is a long time since the assistance of a President in a political campaign was so candidly admitted to be necessary as it is now by the Republican Party managers here. They acknowledge that the assistance of President McKinley is essential to the stimulation of the voters of the country. Since the President's trip across Iowa and back was reported to have stirred up the hitherto languid voters of that State, and his appearance in Nebraska was asserted to have had a decidedly favorable effect upon the prospects of the Republicans there, every state that is affected by the common "off year" apathy has been making itself heard in requests that Mr. McKinley pay it a visit, and thus help out the cause.[82]

McKinley's successful tour – characterized by his electioneering and (as previously discussed) imperialist rhetoric – is also important because it suggests he played a larger role in the development of the modern presidency than previously recognized. The leading work in this literature by Jeffrey K. Tulis argues that Theodore Roosevelt and Woodrow Wilson inaugurated a shift from the "old way" to a modern presidency marked by popular rhetoric. In this formulation, McKinley, despite "push[ing] against clearly perceived limits" and "appear[ing] in public quite often" is relegated to the "old way." As Tulis writes:

There is no speech that even alludes to the Spanish-American War, the sinking of the Maine, . . . or United States policy toward the Philippines, all major issues faced by McKinley. Indeed, much of McKinley's rhetoric was characteristic of the century as a whole: expressions of greeting, inculcations of patriotic sentiment, attempts at building "harmony" among the regions of the country, and very general, principled statements of policy, usually expressed in terms of the policy's consistency with that president's understanding of republicanism.[83]

Tulis's account of McKinley is incomplete for two reasons. First, as discussed extensively earlier in this chapter, and contrary to Tulis's contention, the President did talk about the war and the Philippines. In fact, on this Midwest tour these topics were about the only things McKinley discussed. Second, the timing of the tour indicates a shift in presidential speech. As Tulis aptly demonstrates,

---

[80] Gould, *The Spanish-American War and President McKinley*, 105.
[81] *The Literacy Digest*, "President McKinley on National Duty and Destiny," 19 Oct. 1898, 510.
[82] *The New York Times*, "Republicans are Anxious," 20 Oct. 1898, 1.
[83] Tulis, 61, 65, 87. See also: James Ceaser, Glen Thurow, Tulis, and Joseph M. Bessette, "The Rise of the Rhetorical Presidency," *Rethinking the Presidency*, ed., Thomas Cronin (Boston: Little, Brown & Co., 1982).

pre-modern presidents' "policy rhetoric... [was] written, and addressed principally to Congress," thereby avoiding popular appeals to the public that might appear demagogic.[84] Pre-modern presidents also avoided taking partisan positions or doing anything that could be construed as campaigning.[85] McKinley did all of these things. His Midwest speaking tour in the fall of 1898 served as a platform for discussing his imperial plans for the Philippines before an official policy was declared and as "clever political campaigning" designed to have "a decidedly favorable effect upon the prospects of the Republicans."[86] McKinley, at least in the context of this speaking tour, could be considered in the same transformative category Tulis ascribes to his successors Teddy Roosevelt and Wilson.

The actual results of the election were viewed as a Republican success. After the ballots were counted, the GOP held majorities in both chambers. Given the party's prospects ahead of the election, the minor losses in the House and gains in the Senate were excellent results. Press accounts highlighted the uniquely positive midterm results for Republicans. For instance, *The Free Press*, a Democratic paper in Detroit, noted that "For an 'off year' election the Republicans appear to have come through yesterday's ordeal very well indeed.... This result in favor of the party in power at a congressional election immediately following a Presidential campaign is rather unusual, and on this account will be all the more gratifying to the Administration, by whom it will naturally be taken as a splendid indorsement."[87]

Post-election analysis generally centered on the reasons for the relatively strong Republican showing. A handful of accounts, though, argued that the election was a rebuke of McKinley. For instance, the *New York Times* called the election "a distinct and severe blow to the administration."[88] Other accounts said it was a Republican triumph but that it owed more to certain domestic factors (such as monetary policy) than to the war. Most argued, however, that the war loomed large as an explanation for the GOP success. The Republican-affiliated, Chicago-based, *The Inter-Ocean* used the opportunity to compliment itself while emphasizing the importance of the Spanish-American War:

Had it not been for *The Inter-Ocean* and a few other courageous Republican newspapers, this campaign of slander and misrepresentation [Democratic criticism of the War Department] might have been more effective.... Wherever Republicans were united on the war issue the results were very encouraging. We have lost only one State that gave its electoral vote to McKinley, and we have made gains in States like Nebraska and Kansas, carried by Bryan. In Minnesota local issues and rivalries were thrown to the

---

[84] 46. See also, 27–33.
[85] Tulis cites Andrew Johnson as "the great exception" (87) to this rule. Most notable among the reasons cited for this dubious title, was a pre-election tour very similar to McKinley's. Tulis, 87–93.
[86] *The Literacy Digest*, "President McKinley on National Duty and Destiny," 19 Oct. 1898, 510; *The New York Times*, "Republicans are Anxious," 20 Oct. 1898, 1.
[87] *The Free Press*, in *The Literary Digest*, 19 Nov. 1898, 598.
[88] *The New York Times*, "The Country to Mr. M'Kinley," 9 Nov. 1898, A6.

front.... But in most of the States the paramount issue of McKinley's policy was the one that appealed to voters. Had McKinley been a candidate for President this year he would have, on the returns, received a larger electoral vote than in 1896.[89]

While this kind of self-congratulatory analysis might be expected from the Republican press, it was not unique. Independent and Democratic papers came to similar conclusions about the war's influence on the election. For example, W.R. Hearst's Democratic paper in New York, *The Journal*, concurred:

It is both right and reasonable that the Administration which, despite its mistakes, carried this glorious war to a successful conclusion, should receive a vote of confidence.... The Democratic defeat is not due to the Democratic people, or to Democratic principles, but to Democratic leaders. They, having brought on the war, refused to share the honors of the war, or to acquire for the people the lasting benefits of the war. The Democratic leaders do not speak for the Democracy, and the Republicans have everywhere been elected with the aid of Democratic votes.[90]

Finally, Washington's *The Star*, an independent newspaper, made another strong case for the war's role:

The national issues in this year's campaigns were sound money and the Administration's policy in the war with Spain. They were very clearly defined, and there was every reason why both should be heartily indorsed.... The argument as to the war was most cogent. Brilliant victories had been won, under the Administration's direction, on land and sea, and the contention with the enemy brought to a speedy and triumphant close. What was the duty, therefore, of those who ... rejoiced in the country's martial achievements? Clearly to support the candidates who stood distinctly and directly for the two issues involved.[91]

As before, these examples are intended to be illustrative and do not attempt to exhaust all the supporting accounts.

In sum, substantial evidence suggests that the Spanish-American War profoundly influenced the 1898 congressional elections. Realignment theory posits that Republican control of Congress was essentially inevitable, especially following the 1896 election. But without the nation's quick and overwhelming victory over Spain, coupled with McKinley's triumphant speaking tour, the 1898 election could have been disastrous for the GOP. Indeed, few things are inevitable in politics, and events – especially those as profound as wars – exert a tremendous influence. The supposed realignment of 1896 is an insufficient explanation, particularly in light of the issues that dominated this campaign. As John Hay told McKinley after the election, "You have pulled us through with your own strength; this makes the work for 1900 simple and easy."[92]

---

[89] *The Inter-Ocean*, in *The Literary Digest*, 19 Nov. 1898, 598.
[90] W.R. Hearst, *The Journal*, in *The Literary Digest*, 19 Nov. 1898, 598.
[91] *The Star*, in *The Literary Digest*, 19 Nov. 1898, 598.
[92] Gould, *The Spanish-American War and President McKinley*, 105.

The 1900 Presidential Election

Though the Spanish-American War had been over for more than two years, its influence was still being felt in November 1900. One of the major issues in the presidential campaign that once again pitted McKinley against William Jennings Bryan emanated directly from the war. Indeed, issues revolving around the war were far more prominent than those associated with the 1896 election that realignment theory and the APD literature credit with investing American politics for a generation. In addition, the president had a new running mate on his ticket, Theodore Roosevelt, who would never have been in a position to secure this spot had it not been for his popularity after the war.

Foreign affairs were a major issue in the 1900 election, as acknowledged by both candidates and political parties. Several months before the election, McKinley told confidants he thought "the Philippines would be the paramount and dominating issue in the campaign."[93] From his front porch in Canton, Ohio, McKinley accepted the Republican nomination and declared that imperialism was the most important campaign issue. More than half of his address was dedicated to the subject. The only other topics mentioned were the gold standard and tariffs, and both were dealt with in a few sentences. McKinley pointedly addressed the war with Spain and its unexpected consequences in the Far East:

A just war has been waged for humanity and with it have come new problems and responsibilities.... The Philippines are ours and American authority must be supreme throughout the archipelago. There will be amnesty broad and liberal but no abatement of our rights, no abandonment of our duty. There must be no scuttle policy. We will fulfill in the Philippines the obligations imposed by the triumphs of our arms and by the treaty of peace; by international law; by the nation's sense of honor, and more than all by the rights, interests and conditions of the Philippine peoples themselves. No outside interference blocks the way to peace and a stable government. The obstructionists are here, not elsewhere. They may postpone but they cannot defeat the realization of the high purpose of this nation to restore order in the islands and establish a just and generous government, in which the inhabitants shall have the largest participation for which they are capable.... There will be no turning aside, no wavering, no retreat. No blow has been struck except for liberty and humanity and none will be. We will perform without fear every national and international obligation. The Republican party... broke the shackles of 4,000,000 slaves and made them free, and to the party of Lincoln has come another supreme opportunity which it has bravely met in the liberation of 10,000,000 of the human family from the yoke of imperialism.[94]

The Democrats, led by Bryan, also realized the importance of the Philippines, and foreign affairs more generally, and quickly made imperialism their primary

---

[93] Gould, *The Presidency of William McKinley*, 214.
[94] McKinley, "Acceptance Speech by President William McKinley, Canton, Ohio, July 12, 1900," *History of American Presidential Elections*, vol. 3, ed., Schlesinger (New York: Chelsea House Publishers, 1971), 1940–1.

campaign issue. Initially, some Democrats thought a reaffirmation of their 1896 pledge regarding the free coinage of silver should be the prime issue. Ultimately, though, imperialism was selected because, as Democrats highlighted in their platform, "the burning issue of imperialism growing out of the Spanish war involves the very existence of the Republic and the destruction of our free institutions. We regard it as the paramount issue of this campaign."[95] The platform went on to detail the party's position:

We condemn and denounce the Philippines policy of the present administration. It has involved the Republic in an unnecessary war, sacrificed the lives of many of our noblest sons, and placed the United States, previously known and applauded throughout the world as the champion of freedom, in the false and un-American position of crushing with military force the efforts of our former allies to achieve liberty and self-government.... We oppose militarism. It means conquest abroad and intimidation and oppression at home. It means the strong arm which has ever been fatal to free institutions. It is what millions of our citizens have fled from Europe. It will impose upon our peace loving people a large standing army and unnecessary burden of taxation, and will be a constant menace to their liberties.... This republic has no place for a vast military establishment, a sure runner to compulsory military service and conscription.... For the first time in our history, and coeval with the Philippine conquest, has there been a wholesale departure from our time honored and approved system of volunteer organization. We denounce it as un-American, un-Democratic, and un-Republican, and as a subversion of the ancient and fixed principles of a free people. [96]

The platform and Bryan's acceptance speech laid out Democratic plans to end the war in the Philippines immediately, grant the islands independence, and protect them from outside antagonists. Like McKinley's, well over half of Bryan's acceptance speech was dedicated to these and other issues revolving around the outcome of the Spanish-American War.[97]

In short, then, the Democrats made imperialism – an issue that arose directly as a result of the war with Spain – the primary focus of their campaign. They staked out a position in stark contrast to that of the McKinley administration and, in focusing so much attention on the matter, clearly hoped to reap electoral gains. This was a new and significant split between the parties on foreign affairs. Before the war, the parties were unified in their desire to see an independent Cuba. It was only after the war that imperialism became a dominant issue and split the parties. By 1900, the Republicans embraced a limited imperialism in the name of humanity and liberty, while Bryan used the acquisition of the Philippines to make anti-imperialism a key aspect of the Democrats' platform.

Bryan's efforts to capitalize on the imperialism issue failed because Republicans were able to undermine the effort in several ways. First, McKinley easily and effectively linked the Democrats, and Bryan in particular, to the decision to

---

[95] "Democratic Platform," *History of American Presidential Elections*, ed., Schlesinger, 1920.
[96] Ibid.
[97] William Jennings Bryan, "Acceptance Speech of William Jennings Bryan," *History of American Presidential Elections*, ed., Schlesinger, 1943–56.

go to war, and to the ratification of the peace agreement that left the Philippines in American hands. As Walter LaFeber argues, "Bryan helped confuse the imperialism debate himself."[98] Bryan's position on the war and its aftermath was consistent but involved a level of nuance that, to the casual observer, probably appeared more like disorganized hypocrisy. He certainly had been pro-war, declaring: "Humanity demands that we shall act." As historian Michael Kazin explains, "In Bryan's view, the public's enthusiasm for the war did not contradict his deep-seated belief that militarism was an unchristian tool of the upper classes. He opposed the big increases in the standing army that top Republicans were promoting. But the Cubans were suffering to win their freedom, and for Bryan this gave them an unimpeachable moral claim."[99] He apparently took this conviction to heart, because he promptly enlisted in the Third Nebraska National Guard unit, in which he was elected colonel. He and his men got as far as Jacksonville, Florida, before Spain surrendered. When the Philippines issue emerged, Bryan was strongly opposed to annexation. But then he took the surprising – and miscalculated – step of supporting the treaty with Spain that would hand the Philippines to the United States. Bryan reasoned that, because the treaty was going to pass anyway and the issue had the potential to split the Democrats, it was better to support it so American troops could go home, and then grant the islands independence later. When the treaty only passed by two votes, it was suggested that Bryan's support made the difference.[100] Thus, although Bryan never wavered in his support for the war with Spain or in his opposition to occupying the Philippines and to imperialism, his position was complicated. Bryan made tactical mistakes that, at best, made his stance seem unclear and, at worst, insincere and hypocritical.

Second, Republicans achieved a major foreign policy success during the Democratic convention, which served to undermine Bryan's imperialism position. McKinley and Secretary of State John Hay had been concerned that troops sent by various nations to China in response to the Boxer Rebellion might be used to make territorial acquisitions.[101] In his Second Open Door Notes, Hay asked European and Asian countries to preserve Chinese borders and maintain open trade. This request was met with surprisingly satisfactory responses from the involved nations. LaFeber notes the importance of the development:

[98] Walter LaFeber, "Election of 1900," History of American Presidential Elections, ed., Schlesinger, 1893.

[99] Michael Kazin, A Godly Hero: The Life of William Jennings Bryan (New York: Alfred A. Knopf, 2006), 86–7.

[100] Ibid., 86–91.

[101] In addition to the protracted Philippine-American War, there was another regional consequence of the Spanish-American War and the ensuing acquisition of the Philippines–namely, America's entry into Far East politics. China was of particular global interest at the time and the United States wanted to increase its trade with that country. However, the European powers of England, France, Germany, and Russia, along with Japan posed a threat to this interest as they began to divide China into "spheres of influence." This led to the prolonged diplomatic exchange that resulted in the Open Door Policy and saw 2,500 American troops sent to China to help the Europeans suppress the Boxer Rebellion.

This foreign policy success affected domestic American politics directly. Democrats and Republicans alike were determined to keep China whole. Bryan had even suggested as one plank in the Democratic platform: "[W]e believe it is the duty of the government to protect the lives, the property and the commercial interests of its citizens in China, yet we protest against the use of present disturbances in China as a pretext for the seizing of territory or as an excuse for joining with European nations in the dismemberment of that ancient empire." McKinley and Hay had fulfilled Bryan's plank to the letter.[102]

The final and most important reason Bryan's effort failed was that McKinley realized that the imperialism issue could hurt his reelection chances, and therefore steered his foreign policy in a way to minimize the divide between the two candidates. The shift occurred shortly after Bryan's August acceptance speech and was predicted by former Democratic President Grover Cleveland. He told a friend in July that if imperialism was the focal point, the President would have significant flexibility and, thus, could minimize its electoral affect: "Bear in mind," Cleveland said, "that McKinleyism has not so far committed itself concerning the treatment and disposition of our new possessions that it could not be frightened into decency by the organization of an opposition."[103] Indeed, this is exactly what McKinley did. He released a series of papers that focused on the moral reasons that compelled him to retain the islands in 1898 and documented the findings of a commission, containing anti-imperialist Democrats, that the war in the Philippines was the fault of stubborn Filipinos rather than the administration. He also rallied supporters to provide him with cover on this issue. One such effort involved former Republican President Benjamin Harrison, who had been a vocal opponent of imperialism. To gain his support, the White House offered him a government position. Soon after, Harrison came out in opposition to Bryan's candidacy. Additionally, McKinley unleashed allies such as prominent Ohio Senator Marcus Alonzo Hanna and Theodore Roosevelt to link imperialism to legitimate business concerns and the interests of working Americans. Roosevelt went so far as to suggest the Democratic platform was the cause of continued bloodshed in the Philippines because it offered the insurgents hope. This series of events led Bryan to alter his strategy in the middle of September and shift his attention to trusts and, after this failed to take hold, to free silver. In the end, Bryan never found an issue with traction.

In the 1900 election, then, foreign affairs were pivotal but in a rather unusual manner. Both parties immediately identified imperialism as the "paramount issue." Ultimately, though, much of the action went on behind the scenes. McKinley was able to take preventative steps to negate his vulnerability on the issue. LaFeber concludes: "Overall, however, foreign affairs were important... in the sense that McKinley (with Hay's help) neutralized it, removed it from debate, and presented himself as the consistent, conservative protector of America's traditional interests in the Pacific and Latin American areas."[104]

---

[102] LaFeber, "Election of 1900," 1893.
[103] Ibid., 1895.
[104] Ibid., 1915–6.

Interestingly absent from the campaign were the supposedly crucial issue cleavages coming out of the 1896 election that factor so prominently in political science explanations of the era. This disappearance presents a serious problem for the standard realignment and APD accounts.

The 1900 election was also important because it brought Theodore Roosevelt to national office. Without the cult-like following he gained in the Spanish-American War, he never would have become president. It is true that he was not new on the scene when he led the Rough Riders up San Juan Hill. He had been appointed to the Civil Service Commission by presidents Benjamin Harrison and Grover Cleveland, served as president of the New York Board of Police Commissioners, and was assistant secretary of the Navy at the beginning of McKinley's first term. However, his service in the war was clearly what earned him his lasting fame and propelled him first to the governor's mansion in Albany and, from there, to the White House.

Ironically, neither Roosevelt nor McKinley initially wanted the New York governor to be on the ticket. Roosevelt thought the vice presidency was far less important than the "real job" he had in Albany.[105] In letters, he called the position "about the last office that I personally care for"; one in which "there is not much to do"; "an irksome, wearisome place where I could do nothing"; and "about the last thing for which I would care."[106] McKinley and party insiders were equally reluctant. They saw him as unreliable. This reputation was due both to Roosevelt's iconic persona and to his policy stances. He had been slow, for example, to support a protective tariff and had at one point, years before, championed free trade.[107]

Three considerations, though, made Roosevelt the obvious choice. First, he was wildly popular and would undoubtedly give McKinley a boost. He was a passionate and exciting orator on the campaign trail, which was important because it was traditional for incumbent presidents to avoid personally campaigning – a tradition McKinley would uphold. Second, despite his reluctance, there were compelling reasons for Roosevelt to jump at the opportunity. New York governors only served two year terms. If he ran and won again he would only have a job until early in 1903, at which time he would cease to have a political base to make a run for the presidency in 1904. Although Roosevelt would have preferred to be secretary of war or governor-general of the Philippines, McKinley did not offer him these positions. As such, the vice presidency became the best of two imperfect options for Roosevelt. Lastly, Republican leaders in New York were furious with the Governor. Roosevelt was seen as insufficiently pro-business and his prominence irritated the state party's leader,

---

[105] Theodore Roosevelt, "To Henry Clay Payne," *The Letters of Theodore Roosevelt, Volume II: The Years of Preparation, 1898–1900*, ed., Elting E. Morison (Cambridge, MA: Harvard University Press, 1951), 1162.

[106] Roosevelt, "To Lemuel Ely Quigg," 1391; "To Henry Cabot Lodge," 1106; "To Benjamin Barker Odell," 1159; "To George Hinckley Lyman," 1112.

[107] Gould, *Grand Old Party*, 133.

Senator Thomas Collier Platt. To New York Republican insiders, then, the vice presidency was a means to get Roosevelt out of the state. As a combined result of these factors, Roosevelt became McKinley's running mate.

Many Republican leaders, though, remained unimpressed. Senator Hanna, for instance, on news of Roosevelt's position on the ticket, remarked, "don't you know there's only one life between that madman and the Presidency?"[108] Much to Hanna's chagrin, Roosevelt became president a year later. What is most important to note here, though, is the improbability of Roosevelt's rise to the presidency. Without his incredible popularity after the war, he would not have become governor or been in a position to join the national ticket. Indeed, it is surely the case that, without Roosevelt, the convention would have settled on another vice president much more in keeping with the leadership's preferences.

Roosevelt's ascension was no insignificant development. His presidency left a lasting mark on American politics and the Republican Party. It is not at all clear, for example, that McKinley or any other president for that matter would have pursued "trust busting" with Roosevelt's ferocity. Similarly, his conservation efforts were without precedent. Foreign policy was altered and the Panama Canal was constructed. The Progressive Movement would have been without arguably its most prominent leader. And lastly, Roosevelt helped swing the 1912 election to yet another figure who had a pivotal influence on American political history, Woodrow Wilson.

CONCLUSION

President McKinley's "splendid little war" had big ramifications for the American state and the party system. It led directly to two major episodes of state development. Prior to the war, the military amounted to little more than disorganized, often motley, bands of state-run national guard units and local militia groups. During crises, the necessary manpower could usually be mustered, but only in a chaotic manner characterized by great variance in the units' preparation and training. For the modern state America had become by the end of the nineteenth century, this founding era relic was outdated. Initial reform efforts, though, were unsuccessful. Not until the Spanish-American War highlighted the need for a professional, standing army was there a consensus in favor of major reform. In this manner, the Spanish-American War initiated a major overhaul of the nation's armed forces, leading to the establishment of a professional army and the institutional infrastructure to support it.

The second Spanish-American War-induced state building enterprise offers a unique but illustrative glimpse into the unpredictable nature of the ramifications of war. In seeking to end the war as quickly as possible, President McKinley attacked Spain's colonial holdings in the Philippines and, after succeeding,

---

[108] Margaret Leech, *In the Days of McKinley* (New York: Harper, 1959), 537.

faced the unappealing quandary of what to do with the formerly Spanish-controlled islands. Ultimately choosing to take the archipelago as an American possession, McKinley thrust the United States into a new role as a world power with imperial holdings. For several years, imperialists had argued that it was America's destiny to expand overseas in such a manner, but their calls went unheeded until the war. Following more than half a century of costly occupation, this imperialistic episode mercifully ended with Filipino independence in 1946. This unusual and halting state-building initiative, though, foreshadowed similar difficulties the U.S. would encounter in Southeast Asia and the Middle East.

In addition, the Spanish-American War influenced the 1898 and 1900 elections. The 1898 midterms were dominated by the recently concluded war, and the Republicans' success was largely owed to the victory over Spain in what otherwise would have been a difficult electoral climate. The likelihood that the war substantially helped Republicans that year makes this contest similar to other elections, such as 1816 and 2002, in which a governing party gained an advantage through military events or a national security crisis. The 1900 presidential election was similarly influenced by the war and the imperialism issue, which boiled over directly as a result. In addition, these two elections marked the return of foreign affairs as a major feature of American politics. Largely absent from campaigns and elections since the Mexican War, international concerns were back.

3

The War to End All Wars

Looking back, World War I is largely overshadowed by its not-so-innovatively named counterpart some two and a half decades later. But at the time, the conflict was called the "War to End All Wars" and the "Great War" because it was impossible for many, especially in Europe, to envision anything more horrific. At its height, it involved most countries in Europe, Asia, and Africa, several from the Americas, Australia, and numerous other scattered island nations. Lives were lost on an unprecedented scale, and the era witnessed the brutality of trench warfare and the advent of sinister new weapons. Although the United States made a fashionably late appearance and suffered only a fraction of the casualties (and none of the domestic destruction) endured by European states, the conflict was nonetheless grueling. For the first time, hundreds of thousands of Americans went abroad to fight, and many failed to return. This mobilization caused equally disruptive changes in and to the federal government's coffers, the American workplace, the neighborhood bar, and the ballot booth.

Like other chapters, this is not an attempt to document every domestic political effect wrought by war. Rather, this chapter identifies key themes that run consistently across major American wars. With regard to the American state, World War I's influence on the institutionalization of the income tax is highlighted. Tax policies, directly initiated by this war, created new and enduring layers of federal bureaucracy and have continued, to this day, to provide the government with most of its resources. World War I taxation also illustrates the general economic ramifications of wars (other examples of war-induced economic effects include the end of the Great Depression, "guns and butter" trouble for the Great Society, high debt levels during the Cold War, and record deficits during the War on Terror and the Iraq War). Further, with regard to the state's role, World War I was a major influence on the passage of the Eighteenth Amendment, which outlawed alcohol. Like the acquisition of the Philippines following the Spanish-American War, Prohibition eventually came to an end. Yet, these episodes were also similar in that they established important and enduring legacies. Whereas the Philippines was the first major overseas military operation and occupation of foreign territory, Prohibition is notable for the federal government's encroachment into what had previously been a matter reserved to the states.

Additionally, World War I contributed to the extension of important democratic rights to a segment of the population that played a vital role in the conflict. In this instance, a "minority" group constituting slightly more than half of the U.S. population gained the right to vote through the Nineteenth Amendment, largely as an outgrowth of the transition of women into the domestic work force in support of the war effort.

Finally, World War I had a dramatic effect on the party system, as can be seen in the 1918 and 1920 elections. The latter is at least as remarkable as realignment theory's revered 1896 contest because it halted a decade of Democratic success and initiated a long run of complete and total Republican dominance that is more impressive than that inaugurated in 1896.

WORLD WAR I IN BRIEF

World War I began as a European conflict in 1914. Acting on a request from President Woodrow Wilson, Congress, by wide margins in each chamber, declared war on Germany in April 1917. Two primary factors formally drew America into the war (although the United States had previously been supplying and financially aiding the Allies). First, the British intercepted the infamous Zimmermann telegram in which the Germans asked Mexico to join a secret alliance against the United States. Additionally, Germany had just resumed its policy of unrestricted submarine warfare, which had long been a significant source of friction because it occasionally affected American citizens or ships, most notably with the sinking of the *Lusitania* in 1915. (Though the ship was British, it had departed from New York with many Americans aboard.)

Known for its brutal and bloody chemical and trench warfare, the Great War involved twenty-nine countries and 65 million soldiers, 4.3 million of them from the United States. The war exacted a heavy human toll. More than 8.5 million people died, including approximately 126,000 Americans. The fighting came to an end on November 11, 1918, when Germany agreed to an armistice. The Treaty of Versailles, signed on June 28, 1919, officially ended the war. Germany was made to accept full responsibility for the conflict and to pay reparations. Versailles also sought to create the League of Nations, an international body intended to hear disputes and, hopefully, avoid future wars. Despite President Wilson's vigorous campaigning on behalf of both the treaty and especially the League, the Senate and the U.S. public were opposed to the League, and so the Treaty of Versailles – although signed – was never formally adopted in America.

TAXING, BOOZING, AND THE AMERICAN STATE

World War I drove the American state into the areas of taxation and alcohol regulation. The war affected numerous other policy areas related to the state including changes to the protective tariff, the establishment of a national budgeting system, the origins of a domestic intelligence apparatus, and new railroad regulations.[1] But taxation and Prohibition are afforded special attention for two reasons. First, they are important in their own right. The new tax policies proved to be of lasting significance in that they established the enduring backbone of governmental financing. Prohibition led to a constitutional amendment and, although generally mocked as a policy failure, is still constantly referenced by libertarians, if only as a lesson in what to avoid. In addition, Prohibition thrust the federal government into a new zone of influence, authority, and responsibility. Alcohol regulation had previously been under state and local control. Prohibition placed superceding power and authority in federal hands. This episode, then, highlights the broad nationalizing effects wars tend to provoke. These cases are also highlighted because they demonstrate the diverse range of effects that wars can have. While the income tax was the most important instance of state building, Prohibition, though seemingly less relevant today, indicates the extent to which wars can influence domestic policy. In addition, Prohibition offers comparative variation because it was ultimately repealed. It thus serves as a good reminder that, while wars might generally be expected to produce permanent state expansion, the relationship does not play out on a one way street. In the case of Prohibition, a war-induced policy centered on increasing state capacities came to be regretted once the intense war environment subsided and the policy's difficulties became undeniable. However, the larger issues Prohibition speaks to surrounding federalism endure.

A Permanent Income Tax

World War I thrust new institutional and logistical challenges onto the American state that demanded attention. The federal government's response shaped a central feature of a fully developed state; namely, the federal tax system and the bureaucracy overseeing it. While numerous public financing changes occurred during, and as a result of, the war (including the estate tax and taxes on corporate profits), the income tax – because of its prominence as the main source of federal revenue – is particularly important.[2] It was World War I that transformed the income tax into a permanent fixture affecting American paychecks and government revenue.

The influence of World War I will be discussed at length, but it is helpful to briefly examine the origins (also war-borne) of the income tax system to fully appreciate the transformation. The income tax has a long history of

---

[1] David R. Mayhew, "War and American Politics," *Perspectives on Politics* 3:3 (2005), 477–8.

[2] For a specific discussion of the estate tax see: Michael J. Graetz and Ian Shapiro, *Death by a Thousand Cuts: The Fight Over Taxing Inherited Wealth* (Princeton, NJ: Princeton University Press, 2005). For a general account of World War I financing and taxing see: Charles Gilbert, *American Financing of World War I* (Westport, CT: Greenwood Publishing Corporation, 1970); Randolph E. Paul, *Taxation in the United States* (Boston: Little, Brown and Company, 1954) 110–22.

association with wars because of the severe expenditures such conflicts entail. Prior to World War I, the federal government relied primarily on the tariff and excise taxes for its revenue. The income tax was first proposed, though not passed, during the War of 1812 amidst a skyrocketing debt. Nearly fifty years later, an income tax became law during the Civil War's initial phase because the conflict had left the federal government in an economic crisis. The national debt was a staggering (albeit, by contemporary standards, enviable) $505 million. The income tax was instituted only after Thaddeus Stevens (R-PA), chairman of the House Ways and Means Committee, failed to enact a land tax. Stevens's effort was foiled by the poorer and non-industrialized Southern and Western states, which viewed the tax as disproportionately favoring the industrialized North. This regional fissure, as in so many other areas, would be a constant source of strife with regard to tax policy for decades. With this failure, an income tax was introduced and passed in 1862 as a means to bridge the revenue gap. Due to the significance of the budget problems, the tax was made progressive.[3] Incomes exceeding $600 were taxed at a rate of 3 percent, while those earning $10,000 or more paid 5 percent. As economist Sidney Ratner emphasizes, it is important to note that the progressive element of the tax was taken not to ensure equality but as a means to bring in more cash because of the war-induced debt.[4] Two years later, in the face of an even larger debt and a significant deficit, a second income tax was enacted, which raised the top rate bracket to 10 percent. In effect, though, many citizens paid no income tax whatsoever because they earned less than the $600 basement rate. Efforts to repeal the income tax began almost immediately upon the war's conclusion and were ultimately successful in 1872. The North was particularly eager for elimination because its citizens, by earning higher incomes, accounted for the vast majority of the tax's revenue. New Yorkers alone paid one-third of the total.[5]

Despite repeal, two ideological trends kept the idea of an income tax alive. First, the increasingly influential Progressive movement took up the income tax banner and pushed for its reinstatement. The Progressives, a loose coalition including members of both major political parties, encouraged various types of governmental and democratic reforms and sought to curb the influence of big business and "trusts," and the uneven distribution of wealth in society. At the same time as the Progressives' rise, the Democrats' ideology was evolving in a direction that favored an income tax. The party's longstanding opposition to the tariff and its successful efforts to reduce it created a revenue problem. If money was not to be generated by the tariff, it had to come from a different source. The income tax came to be seen as a good substitute for customs

---

[3] John F. Witte, *The Politics and Development of the Federal Income Tax* (Madison, WI: University of Wisconsin Press, 1985), 69.
[4] Sidney Ratner, *Taxation and Democracy in America* (New York: John Wiley & Sons, Inc., 1967), 84.
[5] Witte, 70.

revenue, partly because the Democrats were shifting to a populist, class-based ideology in the 1890s and early 1900s, which engendered a favorable disposition toward the redistribution of wealth.[6]

The early onset of the Democrats' ideological evolution and a severe economic depression in 1893 provided the political momentum to reinstitute the income tax the following year. The Supreme Court, however, quickly struck down the relevant bill because other provisions of the legislation were deemed unconstitutional.[7] In the years and decades following the decision, the Progressive movement fully emerged, and the Democratic Party continued its shift toward embracing wealth redistribution, helping to lead to the tax's resurrection.

The first permanent income tax was implemented at the height of the Progressive Movement but was characterized by its modest effects. By 1909, the Progressives were hitting their stride and there was a renewed effort to institute an income tax via a constitutional amendment. Citizens in the non-industrialized South and West paid a disproportionately high share of consumption-based taxes (relative to their income) compared to those in the industrialized North. As a result, Populists and Progressives based in these areas pushed for an income tax to ease this burden. Four years later, the amendment had garnered the necessary support of three-fourths of the states and took effect on the heels of Woodrow Wilson's election to the presidency. With the constitutional question settled, the Individual Income Tax of 1913, the first permanent income tax, consisting of three brackets, was instituted. An exemption shielded those earning less than $4,000 a year from paying any tax and thereafter varied from 1 percent up to a maximum rate of 7 percent for those few citizens earning more than $500,000 a year. Although the income tax was now permanent, in effect only 2 percent of U.S. households were required to pay anything, "a fact," John F. Witte notes, "that contributed greatly to the political popularity of the tax."[8] The tariff and excise taxes still provided for the overwhelming majority of the federal government's revenue.

The income tax, then, was used several times on a temporary basis and ultimately became permanent because of the Progressive Movement, regional politics, and shifting ideologies within the Democratic Party. These initial incarnations of the income tax, though, generated relatively little revenue, affected few, and were characterized by low rates. Thus, prior to World War I, the income tax was merely a pale and undeveloped image of its contemporary self.

The income tax only became a permanent feature, in the sense of being the primary source of revenue for the federal government, as a result of World

---

[6] John Gerring, *Party Ideologies in America, 1828–1996* (New York: Cambridge University Press, 1998), 169, 193–200.

[7] *Pollock v. Farmers' Loan & Trust Company*, 157 U.S. 429 (1895).

[8] W. Elliot Brownlee, "Tax Regimes, National Crisis, and State-Building in America," *Funding the Modern American State, 1941–1995*, ed., Brownlee (New York: Cambridge University Press, 1997), 60. Witte, 77.

War I. Witte argues that the war was "the single most important influence on the formation and structure of the tax code."[9] Like the War of 1812 and the Civil War, World War I quickly drained readily available resources, and policy makers began seeking other forms of revenue. The initial shift actually occurred before, but in anticipation of, U.S. entry into the war. The Revenue Act of 1916, in the words of economic historian W. Elliot Brownlee, "started out as emergency tax legislation, became potent tax reform, [and] shap[ed] the structure of taxes in a decisive way until World War II."[10] The act served to increase revenue for war preparation and was notable for its progressivity. The lowest tax rate doubled to 2 percent and the highest rate became 15 percent.[11] Wilson was able to secure new military spending – which in and of itself was seen as an affront to Americans' ingrained hostility to concentrated power – by emphasizing the tax's progressive nature. As Brownlee maintains, "[t]he boldness of the progressive shift is without equal in the history of American taxation" and was an effective "solution to the dilemma of financing modern war and, more generally, the modern state in a society fraught with hostilities to concentrations of wealth and power."[12]

The new tax structure was more fully developed under the 1917 War Revenue Act, which addressed the wartime revenue shortfall and radically altered the government's tax system. First, the $4,000 exemption instituted in the Individual Income Tax of 1913 was cut in half. This alteration meant that many people who had previously not been paying income tax were now contributing to the federal government's revenue supply.[13] The rates continued to rise – along with the number of people included in each bracket – all the way up to 67 percent, a stunning increase from the prior top rate of 15 percent.[14] Corporate taxes increased modestly. Needless to say, federal revenue increased dramatically as a result of these changes. In 1917, the federal government took in $800 million and, just a year later, had increased its revenue to $3.7 billion, of which the income tax constituted the largest share.[15]

Apparently pleased with these increased earnings, President Wilson recommended, and Congress approved, further increases in the 1918 War Revenue Act. The minimum rate was increased to 5 percent, earnings over $4,000 were taxed at 12 percent, and the maximum rate reached 77 percent.[16]

---

[9] Witte, 79.

[10] Brownlee, "Woodrow Wilson and Financing the Modern State: The Revenue Act of 1916," *Proceedings of the American Philosophical Society* 129:2 (1985), 173.

[11] "History of the U.S. Tax System," United States Department of the Treasury, http://www.treas .gov/education/fact-sheets/taxes/ustax.shtml, last accessed 15 Oct. 2007.

[12] Brownlee, "Woodrow Wilson and Financing the Modern State," 173, 174.

[13] Witte, 84–5.

[14] "History of the U.S. Tax System."

[15] Corporate taxes, along with minor excise taxes on items such as tobacco and alcohol were also increased. Witte, 84–5.

[16] Witte, 85.

TABLE 3.1. *Individual Income Tax Rates*

	Bottom Rate	Top Rate
Prewar	1%	7%
Revenue Act, 1916	2%	15%
War Rev. Act, 1917	4%	67%
War Rev. Act, 1918	5%	77%

Source: "History of the U.S. Tax System," United States Department of the Treasury, http://www.treas.gov/education/fact-sheets/taxes/ustax.shtml, last accessed 15 Oct. 2007; John F. Witte, *The Politics and Development of the Federal Income Tax* (Madison, WI: University of Wisconsin Press, 1985), 85.

Obviously, these changes were significant (see Table 3.1). More people – though still only 5 percent of the population – were now paying into the system, and the rate structure had increased dramatically with top earners being taxed at a rate more than ten times the prewar maximum. Although ensuing years saw a gradual reduction of this rate, the maximum rate would never again drop below 24 percent (see Figure 3.1). The die was cast and the income tax has remained the major source of governmental revenue ever since.[17]

Finally, new institutions were created to oversee the more complicated World War I tax system. The Budget and Accounting Act of 1921 created a national budget system. It established the president's responsibility for producing a comprehensive budget, and created two new and influential agencies. Housed in the Treasury Department, the Bureau of the Budget was tasked with helping to prepare the budget, while Congress's General Accounting Office was given wide watchdog authority to investigate and conduct audits of the government.[18] Both are still active, though the Bureau of the Budget was reorganized and renamed the Office of Management and Budget in 1970.

In sum, then, World War I was a major turning point in American financial history. No longer would the tariff and excise taxes be the major sources of federal revenue. Besides bringing in more money, the income tax was also easier to enact and enforce. As Witte notes: "Consumption taxes fostered long, fragmented political struggles between specific groups or producers and consumers. This made it difficult to raise large amounts of revenue quickly. In contrast, the income tax had the appearance of universal applicability, and at that time few special interest ties had been formed to restrain its effects. The

---

[17] David Brumbaugh, Gregg A. Esenwein, and Jane G. Gravelle, "Overview of the Federal Tax System," Congressional Research Service, Library of Congress, order code RL32808, 10 Mar 2005.

[18] Brownlee, "Tax Regimes, National Crisis, and State-Building in America," 70. Charles Stewart III, *Budget Reform Politics: The Design of the Appropriations Process in the House of Representatives, 1865–921* (New York: Cambridge University Press, 1989), 172–215.

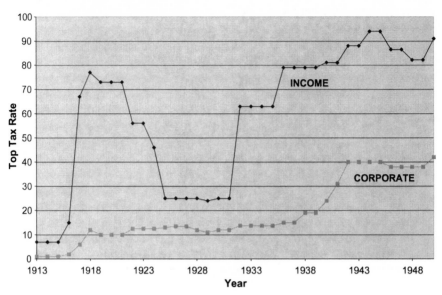

FIGURE 3.1. Top Income and Corporate Tax Rates.[19]

tax's appeal was enhanced by its progressivity."[20] Although the seeds of our present day income tax were sown long before World War I (mostly in other wars), the tax came into its own during this conflict. Prior to the war, the income tax brought in less than 4 percent of the federal government's revenue, applied to only 1 percent of all citizens, and had a maximum rate of 7 percent.[21] Four years later, though, it provided nearly 60 percent of the government's revenue, applied to a still small but significantly increased 5 percent of all citizens, and had a maximum rate of 77 percent. While the ensuing years saw a partially successful effort to dismantle the war-time tax system, the income tax has been the largest source of government revenue ever since.

This progressive income tax system would not have emerged as it did without World War I. W. Elliot Brownlee argues that the "financial demands of World War I . . . accelerated tax reform far beyond the leisurely pace [it was on]. In fact, the wartime crisis produced a brand-new tax regime. This new tax system, the most significant domestic initiative to emerge from the war, probably would not have taken the form it did had the United States not entered the war."[22] A group of Democrats opposed to consolidated wealth, including Claude Kitchin (NC) and Cordell Hull (TN), held powerful positions in Congress (Kitchin was the House Ways and Means Committee chair), and saw taxation as an

[19] National Taxpayers Union Foundation, "History of Federal Individual Income and Top Bracket Rates," www.ntu.org/main/page.php?PageID=19, last accessed 1 Oct. 2007.

[20] Witte, 86.

[21] Ratner, 556 (see Ratner's Table 1).

[22] Brownlee, "Tax Regimes, National Crisis, and State-Building in America," 60.

avenue to achieve social justice and redistribute wealth. They were adamant that any funding of war preparation or conduct be paid for on their terms. President Wilson, who under normal circumstances likely would have taken a more moderate and incremental approach, made the "single most important financial decision of the war" when he agreed to work with these insurgent Democrats in Congress and fund the war on the basis of dramatically increased progressive taxation.[23] As Brownlee concludes:

Without the wartime crisis, the growth of the federal government almost certainly would have been slower and reliant on some combination of tariff revenues, sales taxes, and low-rate taxation of personal and corporate incomes or spending. . . . But the system for financing World War I involved a substantial raising of the stakes of conflict over tax policy. Along with highly progressive taxation came opportunities both for undertaking massive assaults on wealth and corporate power and for carving out lucrative enclaves of special privilege within the tax code. These high stakes helped keep taxation at the center stage of politics through World War II.[24]

Thus, the war-induced need for cash forced Wilson and Congress to acquiesce to the ideological priorities of the Democratic Party's left-wing power brokers.

Not only has the income tax retained its prominent position in American life, its creation also initiated an enduring controversy – one that fueled the Republican Party and helped it gain and maintain power for twelve years following the Wilson presidency and that remains a key link in the party's ideology. In David Mayhew's words, the tax policies resulting from World War I created a new "issue regime," or major controversy, that played a significant role in American politics for numerous years.[25]

Controversy over the income tax's new role became a long-term issue. Brownlee contends that the World War I initiatives made tax policy the primary political issue for the next twenty-five years. Republicans gained control of Congress in 1918 and two years later won the presidency. They would retain both branches for ten years. During this time, they conscientiously set out to dismantle Wilson's tax policies. Top income tax rates plummeted as did those for corporations. For instance, the top tax rate of 77 percent in 1918 was reduced six times before reaching a postwar low of 24 percent in 1929. Despite these reductions, there were still many Republicans who rejected any form of progressive taxation. This faction of the party sought the income tax's complete elimination and argued for a national sales tax in its place. Treasury Secretary Andrew Mellon, though, successfully convinced his fellow Republicans to retain a progressive tax on the grounds of promoting social justice and avoiding political attacks on the administration's policy.[26] Thus, the progressive income tax policy ushered in by World War I became a permanent feature.

---

[23] Ibid., 61.
[24] Ibid., 71–2.
[25] Mayhew, "War and American Politics," 475, 477.
[26] For a more detailed analysis see: Brownlee, 67–72.

If ever there was a time to launch a full-scale assault on progressive taxation, it was in the years following the Republicans' return to power, before the policy became untouchable due to longevity and the silent acquiescence of the opposition party. After the war, Republicans succeeded in greatly reducing the tax burden on individuals, particularly the wealthy. At the same time, however, they came to embrace the fundamental legitimacy of a progressive income tax.

Of course, political debates about the appropriate level of income taxation played a major role in the second half of the twentieth century as well. Income tax reform remains at the top of many politicians' agendas. Examples are plentiful. The issue was among the most important legacies of Ronald Reagan's presidency. Steve Forbes was a one-issue candidate advocating a "flat tax" in his runs for the presidency in 1996 and 2000. Income tax reform was also a major aspect of President George W. Bush's campaign in 2000. Seeking re-election four years later, he campaigned on the need to make his first-term tax cuts permanent. Nonetheless, it was the fiscal demands of World War I that resulted in an untouchable and fully institutionalized income tax. Debates may rage about appropriate rates, but virtually no one contests the basic legitimacy of the income tax as was common prior to World War I. Indeed, even President Bush acknowledged that a 33 percent rate on the highest earners is appropriate.[27]

Prohibition

Typical American political development accounts of the state focus on major and enduring changes in federal policy and institutions. In this sense, of course, Prohibition does not measure up. Prohibiting alcohol production, distribution, and sales under the Eighteenth Amendment began in 1920 but was subsequently deemed a failed policy and was ultimately rebuked thirteen years later by the Twenty-First Amendment. It is typically remembered only in comedy routines or in slippery-slope arguments proffered by libertarians. In another sense, though, Prohibition exemplifies a key facet of early 1900s state development – as spurred on by World War I – because it is an example of a federal regulatory regime replacing a prerogative of states and localities. That is, the national government greatly expanded its reach during, or as a consequence of, World War I, and the Prohibition episode demonstrates how this alteration to the system of federalism occurred.

The Temperance movement began in the 1820s in conjunction with drives for women's rights and the abolition of slavery but likely would never have succeeded, even in its destined-to-fail form, had it not been for World War I. Early Prohibitionists, or Drys, were successful in passing anti-liquor laws in various localities and even bans on production and distribution in eleven states in the 1850s. Over the ensuing decades, the Prohibition Party (modeled after

---

[27] David A. Crockett, "George W. Bush and the Unrhetorical Rhetorical Presidency," *Rhetoric & Public Affairs* 6:3 (2003), 476.

the Republican rise via anti-slavery) as well as the Woman's Christian Temperance Union and the Anti-Saloon League of America were formed to provide an institutional foundation.[28] Although national in scope, these groups operated locally by pressuring politicians to support alcohol bans in towns and counties and, when the political stars aligned, statewide. By 1912, their efforts had brought modest success. Half of all Americans lived in areas with at least some type of alcohol restriction. However, liquor was easily and frequently smuggled into dry localities. In addition, keeping alcohol bans on the books was a constant struggle in some areas, while other, important parts of the country, especially urban centers, were essentially untouched. As historian David E. Kyvig observes, "this situation was unsatisfactory to a reform movement that increasingly viewed the urban saloon as a source of social problems, an encouragement to family neglect, a contributor to worker inefficiency and incompetence, a center of political corruption, and a shelter for immigrant cultures against pressures to assimilate."[29] In short, the localized approach was deemed insufficient and a change in strategy was needed.

A national push for a constitutional amendment became the focus for Dry advocates.[30] Proponents saw an amendment as the only way to permanently prevent liquor from entering dry areas because regional bans were not entirely effective at stomping out the proliferation of contraband. A mere federal law was seen as insufficient because it might be easily reversed with the ebb and flow of election cycles. An amendment, on the other hand, once passed, would be exceedingly difficult to overturn. The first effort to pass an amendment took place in the House of Representatives in 1914 but, in a 197–190 vote, fell far short of the necessary two-thirds approval.[31]

Although the Prohibition movement had clearly been gaining momentum, it is far from clear that these efforts would have ultimately succeeded without the United States's entry into World War I. The House vote in 1914 shows

---

[28] For more on the Prohibition Party see: Jack S. Blocker, Jr., *Retreat from Reform: The Prohibition Movement in the United States, 1890–1913* (Westport, CT: Greenwood, 1976), 39–153. For the WCTU see: Ruth Bordin, *Woman and Temperance: The Quest for Power and Liberty, 1873–1900* (Philadelphia, PA: Temple University Press, 1981). The Anti-Saloon League is detailed in: K. Austin Kerr, *Organized for Prohibition: A New History of the Anti-Saloon League* (New Haven, CT: Yale University Press, 1985). Also see: Peter H. Odegard, *Pressure Politics: The Story of the Anti-Saloon League* (New York: Columbia University Press, 1928).

[29] David E. Kyvig, *Explicit and Authentic Acts: Amending the U.S. Constitution, 1776–1995* (Lawrence, KS: University Press of Kansas, 1996), 219.

[30] In addition to concerns over the localized approach, passage of the Webb-Kenyon Act in 1913 further encouraged the Drys to go national. This act was inspired by two Supreme Court rulings in 1889 (*Leisy v. Hardin*) and 1898 (*Rhodes v. Iowa*) striking down state laws banning shipments of liquor on the grounds that only Congress could regulate interstate commerce. The Anti-Saloon League responded by pressuring Congress to pass a law forbidding the importation of alcohol into a dry state. Congress passed the Webb-Kenyon Act and then overrode President William Howard Taft's veto by a majority in excess of that required for a constitutional amendment. This victory and the extent of Congress' support encouraged anti-alcohol forces to push for an amendment.

[31] For extensive accounts of this process see: Kyvig, 216–26, or Kerr, 115–59.

that Drys might have had the votes to pass a piece of legislation, but they were a long way from the necessary threshold for amending the Constitution. Two factors helped push the Eighteenth Amendment to passage. First, Dry advocates redoubled their efforts and elected more Prohibitionists to Congress. By pressuring congressional candidates into pledging their support for an amendment, Prohibitionists were ensured of these members' votes once sworn into office.

More important, though, was the influence of World War I. The Dry movement was greatly aided by the anti-German sentiment that accompanied the Zimmermann Telegram and American entry into the war. As a result, and as a forerunner to the "Freedom Fries" phenomenon of 2003, citizens shunned products associated with Germany – beer and schnapps headed the list.[32] The Anti-Saloon League also "seized every opportunity to associate beer with the enemy."[33] This anti-German sentiment, and the resulting beer self-denial, had the side effect of swelling the Prohibition movement with new supporters eager to show their bitterness and distaste for Germany. In addition, the outbreak of war shattered the German-American Alliance, a large organization opposing Prohibition.[34]

The Great War also brought about a series of alcohol restrictions that further bolstered the movement. Laws were passed to prevent soldiers from becoming intoxicated by banning alcohol sales near military bases. A halt to the production of distilled spirits also won quick congressional approval as a means to conserve grain for American soldiers and European allies. As a result, the liquor production business was effectively shut down for the war's duration.[35] The ease and speed of this congressional action, argues historian John Milton Cooper, added a sense of momentum to the dry effort and "emboldened Prohibitionists to strike for their ultimate goal, a constitutional amendment."[36] In a related effect, anti-German sentiment, concerns over drunken soldiers, and the grain conservation effort brought converts into the movement, providing even more momentum to the dry cause. Prominent figures including former President Theodore Roosevelt, President Wilson, and future President Herbert Hoover, all of whom had been opposed to Prohibition before the war, joined forces with the Drys to pass the temporary ban on brewing and distilling.[37]

---

[32] Michael A. Lerner, *Dry Manhattan: Prohibition in New York City* (Cambridge, MA: Harvard University Press, 2007), 13, 29–34, 38–9; Kyvig, 224. It should be noted that in this case, people actually ceased or reduced their alcohol consumption rather than merely changing the name of the offending product as in the case of "Freedom Fries."

[33] Jack S. Blocker, Jr., *American Temperance Movements: Cycles of Reform* (Boston: Twayne Publishers, 1989), 118.

[34] Ibid., 118.

[35] Kyvig, 222.

[36] John Milton Cooper, Jr., *Pivotal Decades: The United States 1900–1920* (New York: W.W. Norton & Co., 1990), 307

[37] Robert H. Ferrell, *Woodrow Wilson and World War I* (New York: Harper & Row, 1985), 189.

Finally, the war hastened ratification in the states. Prohibition forces were savvy and took advantage of the patriotism and anti-German sentiment. As discussed previously, the conflict provided another reason to support the Prohibition effort but, equally important, it generated a sense of urgency. Drys were able to insist that Prohibition was in the broad national interest because it would contribute to the conservation effort and the quicker the amendment was passed, the sooner it would help American troops on the front lines.[38] In sum, the Prohibition ranks swelled as a result of U.S. entry into the war, thus providing new momentum and bolstering numerical strength and public opinion.[39]

A further reason to conclude that World War I played a critical role in American Prohibition is because it provoked prohibition in numerous other countries. Russia, for instance, adopted prohibition in 1914 to guarantee that

[38] Not all scholars maintain Prohibition was significantly aided by the war. For instance, historian Jack S. Blocker, Jr. disagrees, asserting: "For the prohibition crusade, however, American involvement in the war came too late and ended too soon to be of great assistance.... The ratification process may have been hastened by the wartime atmosphere, but the process was completed suddenly by the actions of twenty-one state legislatures during the month of January 1919, more than six weeks after the war's end" (118). This position, though, suffers from several flaws. First, the Zimmermann telegraph was sent in January 1917 and the United States entered the war that April while the votes in Congress took place in August, four months later. The states began ratifying the amendment in January 1918 and completed the process, as Blocker notes, six weeks after the war's conclusion. This timeline is certainly sufficient for war-wrought changes to set in. By the time congressional action was taken, new proponents had voiced support for the amendment, public opinion had been moved to oppose beer because of its German connections, the leading anti-Prohibition organization had fractured, and wartime rationing and mobilization had taken effect. Thus, Blocker's argument that the war came too late to influence prohibition is not convincing. Even less credible is his assertion that the war ended too soon. After all, by the time the armistice was reached in November 1918, both chambers of Congress had passed the amendment and fourteen states had already ratified it. Thus, most of the action took place during the war. Blocker implies that the passage of six weeks between the armistice and the final state ratifications demonstrates a lack of war-induced effects. This claim is hard to sustain. Six weeks is not a particularly long period of time in the scope of governmental activity, particularly at the state level. Furthermore, the issue was on the agenda in the other states where newly elected legislatures promptly ratified the amendment, thus providing its necessary margin for adoption, upon being sworn-in that January.

[39] As Kerr argues: "The mobilization for World War I reshaped American politics. Despite the rhetoric of politicians to the effect that a suspension of politics should occur in the interests of national unity, special interest groups of all kinds tried to turn mobilization policies to their particular advantage. The wet and dry forces were no exception, and the 'social and moral' prohibition issue became embroiled in wartime affairs. The Drys initiated efforts to turn the war into a compelling requirement for reform" (199). For further scholarship supporting this conclusion, see: Lerner, 38. See, also: Mayhew, "Wars and American Politics," 447. Mark Lawrence Schrad, *The Political Power of Bad Ideas: Networks, Institutions, and the Global Prohibition Wave* (New York: Oxford University Press, 2009); Schrad, "Constitutional Blemishes: Understanding American Alcohol Prohibition and Repeal as Policy Punctuation," *Policy Studies Journal* 35:3 (2007), 437–64; Schrad, "The First Social Policy: Alcohol Control and Modernity in Policy Studies" *Journal of Policy History* 19:4 (2007), 428–51; Kyvig, 224; Cooper, 307.

its war mobilization would proceed smoothly. In total, the war pushed eleven countries to enact prohibition policies at roughly the same time.[40] Though short lived, America's Prohibition era was part of an international push toward sobriety.

As Robert H. Ferrell argues, "prohibition could have come without war, but war... made easier what many people then believed an invasion of their rights.... After the war there was no stopping the Eighteenth Amendment."[41] Prohibition provides an example of the broad, and oftentimes incongruous and unforeseen possible effects war can engender. In this case, it thrust the federal government into a new role – overseeing the production, distribution, and sale of alcohol – that had once been the province of states and localities. Prohibition may not have endured, but this change to federalism has.

"OUR BOYS NEED SOX, KNIT YOUR BIT": WOMEN AT WORK AND AT THE POLLS

Like most of America's major wars, and amidst some severe but temporary rights retractions, World War I led to an extension of rights for a marginalized minority – albeit one that was actually a numerical majority.[42] The war's importance in the fight for women's suffrage has frequently been overlooked despite clear evidence that World War I had a galvanizing effect on the movement.[43] With many men fighting in Europe, women held a crucial position in the domestic war effort. As in other foreign conflicts, this highly visible role, played by a readily identifiable group, accelerated the expansion of their rights. After their undeniably pivotal part in the war effort, the moral claims emanating from the women's movement could no longer be denied. Their wartime service in a time of crisis solidified and enhanced American women's status as deserving citizens. Similar gains were made by European women in the war's aftermath. These changes eventually would have been achieved without the war, but World War I undoubtedly expedited the process.

The women's movement is widely considered to have begun at the Seneca Falls Convention in 1848.[44] Led by Elizabeth Cady Stanton, Lucretia Mott,

---

[40] Schrad, *The Political Power of Bad Ideas: Networks, Institutions, and the Global Prohibition Wave.*

[41] Ferrell, 189–90.

[42] The U.S. government engaged in various types of suppression during World War I. For an excellent overview of the era's rights retractions, see: Geoffrey R. Stone, *Perilous Times: Free Speech in Wartime* (New York: W.W. Norton, 2004), 135–233.

[43] Neil A. Wynn, *From Progressivism to Prosperity: World War I and American Society* (New York: Holmes & Meier, 1986), 148.

[44] For a more detailed consideration of the early feminist movement see: Kyvig, 226–239; Alexander Keyssar, *The Right to Vote: The Contested History of Democracy in the United States* (New York: Basic Books, 2000), 172–221; Ellen Carol Dubois, *Feminism and Suffrage: The Emergence of an Independent Women's Movement in America, 1848–1869* (Ithaca, NY: Cornell University Press, 1978); Aileen S. Kraditor, *The Ideas of the Woman Suffrage Movement, 1890–1920* (New York: Columbia University Press, 1965).

and Susan B. Anthony, among others, the early feminist movement was initially linked to, and grew out of, the anti-slavery and Prohibition movements. However, Anthony and others ultimately abandoned these causes in favor of concentrating solely on women's enfranchisement after being denied leading, or even prominent speaking, roles in the Dry effort. There were splits within the feminist movement. The National Woman Suffrage Association, led by Stanton and Anthony, pursued a broad, national agenda centered on a constitutional amendment, whereas its rival organization, the American Woman Suffrage Association (AWSA), targeted its efforts toward obtaining the franchise at the state and local levels. The AWSA was successful in organizing state associations and obtaining the franchise in several Western states in the 1890s.[45] In the 1890s and early 1900s, the two groups formed an alliance and began working together as the National American Woman Suffrage Movement (NAWSA). Congressional votes on a constitutional amendment failed in 1914, 1915, and 1916 by wide margins.[46]

With U.S. entry into World War I, however, the political landscape changed. Historian Alexander Keyssar argues that the war "accelerated the progress of suffrage reform.... [T]he most critical impact of the war was the opportunity it gave suffragists to contribute to the mobilization and in so doing, to vanquish the age-old argument that women should not vote because they did not bear arms."[47] Among other activities, the NAWSA organized volunteer efforts, assembled and distributed food, sold bonds, produced clothes, and aided the Red Cross.[48]

Individually, women also made critical economic contributions to the war effort. With men leaving for Europe, women were needed in the workforce. Presaging Rosie the Riveter, World War I posters implored women to join the cause with captions reading: "Our Second Line of Defense," "The Girl Behind the Man Behind the Gun," "For Every Fighter a Woman Worker," and "Our Boys Need Sox, Knit Your Bit."[49] Women heeded the call. During the Great War, 1 million women went to work, many in jobs directly connected to industrial mobilization for the war. The number of women in manufacturing jobs, for instance, doubled while those employed as servants, dressmakers, and laundresses plummeted. The transition was not luxurious. Women worked long

---

[45] These states included Wyoming (1890), Colorado (1893), Idaho (1896), and Utah (1896). However, as Kyvig notes (227), these Western successes were arguably based more on the consolidation of political power than on deference to women's rights. These territories and states allowed women the vote to ensure that long-settled families retained their influence in the face of a largely male influx of fortune-seekers and transients.

[46] A two-thirds majority vote in each congressional chamber is necessary to send an amendment to the states for ratification. A 1914 Senate vote failed 34–35 while 1915 and 1916 House votes were defeated 174–207 and 174–204, respectively.

[47] Keyssar, 215–6.

[48] Ibid.

[49] George Theofiles, *American Posters of World War I* (New York: Dafran House, 1973), 151, 152, 165.

hours and faced discrimination in pay. As Wynn maintains, women, like men, "suffered all the disruptive consequences of the war, . . . but with the additional burdens of lower rates of pay and a working existence in a male world. Even worse, many of their jobs were either temporary in their very nature or viewed as temporary by male counterparts."[50] In short, women left their traditional jobs or their positions in the home to directly contribute to that segment of the economy that fueled and sustained the war, often under difficult circumstances. These efforts, though, demonstrated their importance to the nation's economic vitality in a difficult time.

The war also brought a crucial change in President Wilson's thinking. Wilson, like much of his Democratic Party, had a long history of opposing gender equality. Campaigning for the presidency in 1911, Wilson told his staff that he was "definitely and irreconcilably opposed to woman suffrage," that a "woman's place was in the home, and the type of woman who took an active part in the suffrage agitation was totally abhorrent to him."[51] However, World War I altered his considerations. Women's direct aid to the war effort and their newly pivotal economic position were crucial to his reversal on this matter.[52]

Another possible factor in Wilson's conversion was the strong political support he received from the NAWSA.[53] Not only did the organization support the war effort, it also publicly supported Wilson at a time when many Americans were critical of the conflict. Shortly after the NAWSA's pledge of solidarity and support of the war, Wilson acknowledged women's importance in the war effort and became more accommodating toward their demands for suffrage.[54] He spoke before the NAWSA's national convention and pledged his support for female suffrage.[55] In May 1917, Wilson also directed the House of Representatives to form a women's suffrage committee and vocally supported a

---

[50] Wynn, 145–7.

[51] Frank Parker Stockbridge, "How Woodrow Wilson Won His Nomination," *Current History* 20 (1924), 567.

[52] Beth A. Behn, "Woodrow Wilson's Conversion Experience: The President, Woman Suffrage, and the Extent of Executive Influence," paper presented at the Midwest Political Science Association annual conference, Chicago, 7–10 April 2005.

[53] Ibid. Not all prominent women and women's groups supported the war. For instance, Montana Representative Jeannette Rankin, the first woman elected to Congress, vocally opposed it. Other women protested outside the White House, denouncing as hypocritical an international war fought in the name of democracy when women in the United States were denied the vote. The NAWSA, though, was the most important women's organization and overshadowed dissenters.

[54] See: Christine A. Lunardini and Thomas J. Knock, "Woodrow Wilson and Woman Suffrage: A New Look," *Political Science Quarterly* 95 (1980–1981), 655–63. Wilson's conversion may have begun a few years before the war. Despite his longtime opposition to the feminist agenda, Wilson supported the 1916 Democratic platform that called for women's suffrage, although he maintained his position that, ultimately, it was a state issue (the Republican agenda and Wilson's opponent, Charles Evans Hughes, by contrast, endorsed a constitutional amendment). Nonetheless, Wilson was, at best, a reluctant supporter until World War I.

[55] Woodrow Wilson, "An Address in Atlantic City to the National American Woman Suffrage Association," 8 Sept. 1916, *The Papers of Woodrow Wilson: Volume 38, August 7–November 19, 1916*, ed., Arthur S. Link (Princeton: Princeton University Press, 1984), 161–4.

suffrage referendum in New York state (its success was the first major victory for the movement in the Northeast). The following year President Wilson, long a champion of states' rights on this issue, went even further and endorsed a national solution in the form of a constitutional amendment. In his endorsement, Wilson indicated his full reversal on the subject, calling women's suffrage "an act of right and justice" and "a vitally necessary war measure."[56] Wilson also came to feel that, in addition to women's wartime activity, the nation had a moral imperative to extend suffrage and risked losing international prestige if an amendment was not passed.[57] "Clearly," Kyvig argues, "'the war to make the world safe for democracy' led Wilson to revise his position on woman suffrage."[58] Indeed, he told his brother-in-law that women's service during the war changed his mind. "The women earned it," Wilson confided, and he was "only sorry it had to come through war."[59]

Wilson's change of heart, according to Kyvig, "no doubt helped the measure achieve the necessary two-thirds vote."[60] In January 1918, the amendment passed the House 274–136, a dramatic reversal from its 174–204 defeat just two years before. The Senate vote proved more difficult. Fearing the amendment would fail in that chamber's vote in September 1918, Wilson, without precedent, delivered an impromptu speech on the Senate floor. The war's link to women's suffrage was highlighted:

[The women's suffrage amendment is] vitally essential to the successful prosecution of the great war of humanity in which we are engaged.... We have made partners of the women in this war; shall we admit them only to a partnership of suffering and sacrifice and toil and not to a partnership of privilege and right? This war could not have been fought... if it had not been for the services of women.... The tasks of the women lie at the very heart of the war... [and this amendment] is vital to the winning of the war and to the energies alike of preparation and of battle.[61]

Keyssar argues that Wilson's support indicates an extension, rather than a rejection, of the standard argument that the vote ought to be tied to military service. "[A]s was appropriate, perhaps, in the nation's first modern war (which

[56] Wilson, "A Statement," 9 Jan. 1918, *The Papers of Woodrow Wilson: Volume 45*, 545; Wilson, "An Address to the Senate," 30 Sept. 1918, *The Papers of Woodrow Wilson: Volume 51*, 160. See also: Kyvig, 233.

[57] Wilson said: "If we indeed be democrats and wish to lead the world to democracy, we can ask other peoples to accept in proof of our sincerity and our ability to lead them whither they wish to be led nothing less persuasive and convincing than our actions.... They are looking to the great, powerful, famous Democracy of the West to lead them to the new day for which they have so long waited; and they think, in their logical simplicity, that democracy means that women shall play their part in affairs alongside men and upon an equal footing with them. If we reject measures like this... they will cease to believe in us; they will cease to follow or to trust us...." Wilson, "An Address to the Senate," 158–60.

[58] Kyvig, 234. See also: Sally Hunter Graham, "Woodrow Wilson, Alice Paul, and the Woman Suffrage Movement," *Political Science Quarterly* 98:4 (Winter 1983/4), 674, 678.

[59] Ferrell, 220.

[60] Ibid., 234.

[61] Wilson, "An Address to the Senate," 30 Sept. 1918, 158–60.

demanded a new level of mass mobilization), the president claimed that women should be enfranchised because of their contributions to the war rather than despite their failure to bear arms."[62] Similarly, Kyvig notes that "the war served as the centerpiece of his argument. Having made women partners in the war, he said, the nation needed to enfranchise them to demonstrate its commitment to democracy. Suffrage was 'necessary to the successful prosecution of the war' and 'vital to the right solution of the great problems which we must settle, and settle immediately, when the war is over.'"[63] Despite this impassioned effort, the amendment was still three Senate votes short of the necessary two-thirds threshold.[64] But nine months later, with a new Congress seated, the measure finally passed with a wider margin in the House and, for the first time, by a vote of 56–25 in the Senate (thanks in part to the 1918 midterm defeat of key opposition leaders in both parties). By August 1920, the necessary three-fourths of the states had ratified the Nineteenth Amendment and women had gained the franchise.

As a result, the number of people voting in elections rose dramatically. Prior to passage of the Nineteenth Amendment, the percentage of the total U.S. population casting ballots in presidential elections was always in the teens or lower. In 1920, with women throughout the nation casting votes for the first time, this percentage shot up to more than 25 percent (see Figure 3.2).

This trend was not unique to the United States and reinforces the relationship between World War I and woman's suffrage. Many other countries extended voting rights to females during, or shortly following, World War I based on women's wartime service or other war-induced pro-democracy sentiments. Suffrage rights were extended in Britain, Canada, Germany, Austria, Poland, Czechoslovakia, Sweden, Belgium, and the Netherlands.[65] Though some of these countries were not Great War participants, Mayhew reasons that spillover effects might account for their altered status. It is unlikely that women's suffrage and the war coincide by mere chance because following

---

[62] Keyssar, 216–7.

[63] Kyvig, 234.

[64] The amendment actually failed by a vote of 53–31, although ten supportive senators, knowing the measure would fail, did not attend the formal floor vote.

[65] Mayhew, "Wars and American Politics," 478. On Canada: Harry S. Albinski, *Canadian and Australian Politics in Comparative Perspective* (New York: Oxford University Press, 1973), 103. On Belgium: Thomas T. Mackie and Richard Rose, *The International Almanac of Electoral History* (New York: Free Press, 1974), 39; Norman Ward, *Dawson's the Government of Canada*, 6th ed. (Buffalo, NY: University of Toronto Press, 1987), 100; Kurt Steiner, *Politics in Austria* (Boston: Little, Brown, 1972), 31–4; Eric S. Einhorn and John Logue, *Modern Welfare States: Politics and Policies in Social Democratic Scandinavia* (New York: Praeger, 1989), 32; Neil Elder, Alastair H. Thomas, and David Arter, *The Consensual Democracies?: The Government and Politics of the Scandinavian States* (New York: Blackwell, 1988), 145; Nils Andren, *Government and Politics in the Nordic Countries: Denmark, Finland, Iceland, Norway, and Sweden* (Stockholm: Almqvist & Wiksell, 1964), 36, 66, 120; E.H. Kossmann, *The Low Countries, 1789–1940* (New York: Oxford University Press, 1978), 476, 477, 503, 510, 555, 561; A.J.P. Taylor, *English History, 1914–1945* (New York: Oxford University Press, 1965), 93–4, 115–6, 262.

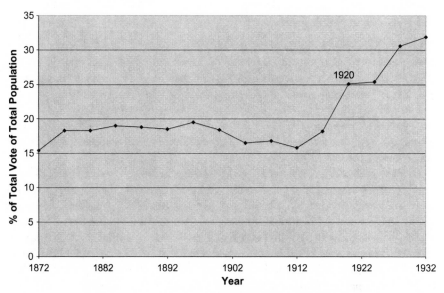

FIGURE 3.2. Relation of Total Vote for President to Total U.S. Population.[66]

World War II there was a similar burst of international gains for women's suffrage. France, Italy, Hungary, and Japan all extended the vote to women in that war's immediate aftermath.[67]

WORLD WAR I AND THE PARTY SYSTEM OF 1896

Occurring in World War I's final days, the 1918 midterm election was dominated by the conflict. The Republican takeover of Congress that year seems to have been influenced by an embittered German-American defection from the Democratic Party in the Midwest. World War I remained a major electoral issue two years later in the 1920 presidential election, a contest in which the major issues emanated directly or indirectly out of the war. Surprisingly, political scientists have not only failed to highlight this relationship in the 1920 contest, but barely even acknowledge that an election was held. Rather, attention has focused on another contest held twenty-four years earlier. To the extent it is mentioned at all, 1920 is considered a mere extension of that all-important vote. However, there is a strong case to be made that 1920 offers at least a comparable – and arguably a more important and dramatic – shift than that accredited to the revered 1896 contest.

[66] Robert E. Lane, *Political Life: Why People Get Involved in Politics* (Glencoe, IL: The Free Press, 1959), 19.

[67] Mayhew, "Wars and American Politics," 478, 487; Mackie and Rose, 223; Dorothy Pickles, *The Government and Politics of France: Vol. 1: Institutions and Parties* (London: Methuen, 1972), 27; Denis Mack Smith, *Modern Italy: A Political History* (Ann Arbor, MI: University of Michigan Press, 1997), 33, 123, 228–30, 423.

The 1918 Midterm Election

Historian Seward W. Livermore asserts that "the war [was] the paramount issue" of the 1918 midterm elections.[68] Going into those contests, President Wilson was in his second term and his Democratic Party held a majority of U.S. Senate seats and controlled the House.[69] World War I's fighting came to a close only days after the election when Germany agreed to an armistice. But, although the campaign and vote both took place while the conflict still raged, Wilson had already announced his Fourteen Points peace plan, and it was clear that America and her allies would prevail.[70]

Democrats tried to leverage the war to their benefit. They charged Republicans with being unpatriotic. A GOP victory, Democrats suggested, "would be a source of comfort to the Kaiser and his cohorts." Another Democrat encouraged voters to "Beat the Huns and the [Republican] Governor."[71] Meanwhile, Wilson purged Bryanite anti-war Democrats from the party, replacing them with candidates embracing his interventionist foreign policy. These activities, though, met with the public's disapproval and, in response, the President declared a truce, proclaiming in May that "politics is adjourned." But in a monumental miscalculation, Wilson pulled down his own white flag shortly before the election in his "October Manifesto" by publicly – and in rather pathetic style – appealing for a Democratic Congress and calling the election a referendum on the party, the war, and his personal leadership:

> If you have approved of my leadership and wish me to continue to be your unembarrassed spokesman in affairs at home and abroad, I earnestly beg that you will express yourselves unmistakably to that effect by returning a Democratic majority to both the Senate and the House.... I am your servant and will accept your judgment without cavil.... [But the] return of a Republican majority to either House of the Congress would ... be interpretative on the other side of the water as a repudiation of my leadership.[72]

The Republican campaign was also structured around World War I. Initially, GOP strategy centered on criticizing Wilson's prosecution of the war. As the campaign progressed and it became increasingly clear the conflict was

---

[68] Seward W. Livermore, "The Sectional Issue in the 1918 Congressional Elections," *The Mississippi Valley Historical Review* 35:1 (1948), 35.

[69] The Democrats lost their House majority in 1916 but still held more seats than the Republicans and continued to effectively control the chamber through an alliance with the Progressives and progressive Republicans. Andrew E. Busch, *Horses in Midstream: U.S. Midterm Elections and Their Consequences, 1894–1998* (Pittsburgh, PA: University of Pittsburgh Press, 1999), 87.

[70] Livermore, *Politics is Adjourned: Woodrow Wilson and the War Congress 1916–1918* (Middletown, CT: Wesleyan University Press, 1966), 210–5.

[71] George H. Mayer, *The Republican Party, 1854–1964* (New York: Oxford University Press, 1964), 352; Livermore, "The Sectional Issue in the 1918 Congressional Elections," 31, 35.

[72] "Text of President Wilson's Appeal," *New York Times* (26 Oct. 1918), 1. See also: Busch, 88; Mayer, 353; Arthur Walworth, *America's Moment: 1918* (New York: W.W. Norton, 1977), 110–3.

drawing to a satisfactory close, however, Republicans shifted course and began criticizing Wilson's "utopian" Fourteen Points. Senator Henry Cabot Lodge and former president Teddy Roosevelt (now reconciled with the GOP after his third party "Bull Moose" candidacy in 1912) led the rhetorical campaign.[73] Demanding an unconditional German surrender, the Republicans positioned themselves as patriots resisting Wilson's "temptation to be easy on the Germans."[74] When Germany offered peace largely in line with Wilson's proposed Fourteen Points in early October, the President was forced to reject the overture, lest he appear weak amidst the tense political climate at home.[75] As a result, the war continued for another month. The Republicans also pounced on Wilson after his public appeal for a Democratic Congress later in October (such presidential public campaign appeals were less common at this time than they are today), contrasting "the partisan behavior of the President with their own self-restraint" and arguing that he wanted to be a dictator.[76] The GOP also effectively refuted allegations of a lack of patriotism by citing their own higher level of congressional support for Wilson's war policies as compared to the President's own party (these votes having taken place prior to his purge of Bryanite anti-war party members).[77]

When the results were tallied, Democrats had lost control of both congressional chambers, dropping nineteen House and six Senate seats. In terms of the raw number of seats changing hands, political scientist Andrew E. Busch asserts that the 1918 results represented only "modest gains for midterm elections."[78] Indeed, it is certainly common enough for the president's party to lose seats in a midterm, and 1918 did not produce exceptional losses.[79] But this 1918 midterm is one of only six instances in which the president's party lost control of both chambers.[80] Republican ascension in Congress also carried critical implications. Progressivism's influence was halted, never to be resurrected. Furthermore, as a result of Wilson's public appeal, Republicans were able to claim

---

[73] Busch, 88; Livermore, "The Sectional Issue in the 1918 Congressional Elections," 31, 59–60.

[74] Mayer, 353.

[75] Busch, 88.

[76] Mayer, 353; Henry Cabot Lodge, Reed Smoot, Frederick H. Gillett, and Simeon D. Fess, "Not Wilson's War, Republicans Say," *New York Times* (26 Oct. 1918), 1. On presidential campaign rhetoric, see: Jeffrey K. Tulis, *The Rhetorical Presidency* (Princeton: Princeton University Press, 1987).

[77] Mayer, 353; Busch, 88; Lodge, Smoot, Gillett, and Fess.

[78] Busch, 88–9.

[79] Ibid., 5; Robert S. Erikson, "The Puzzle of Midterm Loss," *Journal of Politics* 50:4 (1988), 1011–29; Alberto Alesina and Howard Rosenthal, "Partisan Cycles in Congressional Elections and the Macroeconomy," *American Political Science Review* 83:2 (June 1989), 373–98; Samuel Kernell, "Presidential Popularity and Negative Voting: An Alternative Explanation to the Midterm Decline of the President's Party," *American Political Science Review* 71:1 (1977), 44–66; Erikson and Gerald C. Wright, "Voters, Candidates, and Issues in Congressional Elections," *Congress Reconsidered*, eds., Lawrence C. Dodd and Bruce I. Oppenheimer (Washington: CQ Press, 1977), 135.

[80] James W. Ceaser and Daniel DiSalvo, "Midterm Elections, Partisan Context, and Political Leadership: The 2006 Elections and Party Alignment," *The Forum* 4:3, article 11.

a mandate. As such, any remaining hope for Wilson's postwar plan for a League of Nations was dashed, as were his domestic priorities.[81]

The "modest" cumulative results also obscure a distinct sectional dimension of the 1918 election. Nationally, and taking both congressional chambers into account, Republicans captured thirty-five seats from the Democrats whereas Democrats picked up nine from the GOP, for a net twenty-six seat Republican gain (these figures omit five seat transfers involving a third party).[82] Regionally, the results become more remarkable. In the Northeast, the GOP picked up ten seats from the Democrats while losing six, for a net gain of four.[83] In the West, Republicans gained five Democratic seats and lost two to them – a net gain of three.[84] The eleven Southern states of the old Confederacy had no changes. Finally, in the Midwest, the GOP gained a stunning twenty seats from the Democrats while losing only one, for a net gain of nineteen.[85] In the whole country, the states with the biggest net shifts of U.S. House seats – all to the benefit of the GOP – were Indiana (four), Kansas (four), Ohio (four), Missouri (three), and Nebraska (three).[86] Democrats lost Congress in the Midwest.

What explains this? Among other concurrent possibilities, these results were influenced by a German-American backlash against the Democrats. German-Americans – who constituted the most numerous, heterogeneous, and influential non-English speaking ethnicity at the time – were severely repressed in response to their community's widespread support for the homeland from 1914 to 1917. Long simmering tensions exploded, as American society "lashed out" in "anti-German hysteria." As historian Frederick C. Luebke notes, "[c]itizens of German origin were individually harassed and persecuted, German ethnic organizations were attacked, and serious efforts were made to eliminate German language and culture in the United States."[87] Numerous official or pseudo-official government policies targeted – or were unpopular with – the group, including the declaration of war itself, the establishment of the American-Protective League, U.S. Post Office censorship, the Espionage Act, the Trading-with-the-Enemy Act, the Sedition Act, investigations of the German-American Alliance, Prohibition, and the Treaty of Versailles. As the ruling party at the time, Democrats were punished by German-Americans in the ballot booth.[88] All of the high-turnover states in the 1918 election had large

---

[81] Busch, 89.

[82] "House General Election Returns, 1824–2004," *Guide to U.S. Elections, Volume II*, 5th ed. (Washington: CQ Press, 2005), 1056–65; "Senate General Election Returns, 1913–2004," *Guide to U.S. Elections, Volume II*, 5th ed. (Washington: CQ Press, 2005), 1322–59.

[83] For these purposes, the Northeast comprises twelve states including Delaware, Maryland, and West Virginia.

[84] The West is defined here as the eleven Mountain and Pacific states.

[85] Here the Midwest includes Kentucky, Missouri, and Oklahoma.

[86] "House General Election Returns, 1824–2004."

[87] Frederick C. Luebke, *Bonds of Loyalty: German-Americans and World War I* (Dekalb, IL: Northern Illinois University Press, 1974), xiii, 323.

[88] Ibid., 296–8; Samuel Lubell, *The Future of American Politics* (New York: Harper & Brothers, 1952), 139–40; William E. Leuchtenburg, *The Perils of Prosperity: 1914–32* (Chicago:

German-American populations. The other Midwestern states – Michigan, Wisconsin, Minnesota, and Iowa – also had high German-American populations but sent virtually no Democrats to Congress ahead of the 1918 election and, thus, were not in a position to see seats switch parties.[89] In sum, the 1918 midterm elections played out under the specter of World War I. Although Republicans picked up an unremarkable number of congressional seats for an out-party in a midterm election, the Midwest – with its large and disgruntled German-American population – saw a dramatic shift toward the GOP. In this sense, then, the 1918 election indicates how wars can mobilize groups in powerful ways.

The 1920 Presidential Election

Political scientists have generally viewed the Wilson years as an anomaly within the "System of 1896," leading them to minimize the importance of the 1920 Republican victory.[90] They argue that the GOP, dating back to William McKinley's "realigning" 1896 victory, was still dominant and constituted the reigning political order. This connection is important because it suggests the return to Republican rule in 1920 was natural and predictable, if not inevitable, given the dominant 1896-based political system. As Mayhew has suggested, though, this analysis is "questionable" and has left the 1920 election "underanalyzed."[91] Contrary to the standard view, the 1920 results were far from inevitable and were heavily influenced by World War I.

The Failure of the System of 1896 in Explaining the 1920 Election. Realignment theory has guided the political science literature with regard to the 1920 presidential election.[92] It suggests that Ohio Republican Warren G. Harding's

University of Chicago Press, 1958), 43–4. The American Protective League was a government-encouraged amateur spying network (211–2). The Trading-with-the-Enemy Act, passed in 1917, restricted trade with Germany and other countries hostile to the United States (24–42). The German-American Alliance was an organization in that community that professed its loyalty to the U.S. Initially, the group supported Germany in World War I. When the United States entered the conflict, they switched sides, backing their adopted homeland.

[89] Luebke, 3127–38.

[90] Quote from: Walter Dean Burnham, *Critical Elections and the Mainsprings of American Politics* (New York: Norton, 1970); Burnham, "Periodization Schemes and 'Party Systems': The 'System of 1896' as a Case in Point," *Social Science History* 10 (1986), 263–313; Burnham, "The System of 1896: An Analysis," *The Evolution of American Electoral Systems*, ed., Paul Kleppner (Westport, CT: Greenwood Press, 1981), 147–202. For minimizing the importance of 1920 see: James L. Sundquist, *Dynamics of a Party System: Alignment and Realignment of Political Parties in the United States*, revised edition (Washington: Brookings Institution, 1983) 180–1; Jerome M. Clubb, William H. Flanigan, and Nancy H. Zingale, *Partisan Realignment: Voters, Parties, and Government in American History* (Beverly Hills, CA: Sage, 1980), 165; E.E. Schattschneider, *The Semisovereign People: A Realist's View of Democracy in America* (New York: Holt, Rinehart, and Winston, 1960).

[91] Mayhew, "Wars and American Politics," 484.

[92] Burnham, "Periodization Schemes and 'Party Systems': The 'System of 1896' as a Case in Point"; Burnham, "The Changing Shape of the American Political Universe," *American Political Science*

victory over Democrat James M. Cox, also of Ohio, marked a return to the status quo ushered in under the "System of 1896." James L. Sundquist, for example, concludes that "[b]y 1920 the two-party system had essentially returned
to the pattern of 1896, with Republican hegemony throughout the North and
West and a normal Republican majority nationally. So a decade and a half
of great political, social, and institutional change proved, in the end, to be a
period of stability in the party system."[93] Similarly, E.E. Schattschneider, never
mentioning Woodrow Wilson's two-term presidency (or the Democrats' eight
years of majority control in the House and six in the Senate), claims "[t]he 1896
party alignment is important... because it was remarkably stable and because
it was powerful enough to determine the nature of American politics for more
than thirty years."[94] For Schattschneider and the other realignment theorists,
Democratic control for roughly a quarter of this era is either completely ignored
or mentioned only in passing. For instance, Walter Dean Burnham refers to it
as a "special case" while Sundquist calls it an "accident" and, in a footnote, "a
temporary interruption."[95] Succinctly summarizing the thrust of this literature,
Mayhew notes that "the leading interpretation is a questionable teleological
case that the Democrats, that era's natural minority party, *had* to fall from
power somehow once the fluky Wilson presidency, the product of an unusual
four-way election contest in 1912, was out of the way."[96] In other words, the
political science literature's dominant strain views Harding's proclamation of
a "return to normalcy" as more than a mere end to the foreign entanglements,
which inspired the famous speech; it also described a return to the "System of
1896."

Yet, as Mayhew suggests, there are reasons to doubt this analysis. First,
Wilson's victory was not just a bizarre historical fluke – there was much more
to it. Of course, there is certainly some truth to the point that Wilson's election was helped by Theodore Roosevelt's run as a Progressive (or Bull Moose)
after a bitter split in the Republican Party. But it cannot all be attributed to the
strange political circumstances at the top of the ticket. Other Democratic candidates were also faring well in congressional elections and, tellingly, this success

Review 59 (1965), 7–28; Burnham, "Party Systems and the Political Process," *The American
Party Systems: Stages of Political Development*, eds., William N. Chambers and Burnham
(New York: Oxford University Press, 1967), 277–307; Burnham, *Critical Elections and the
Mainsprings of American Politics*; Burnham, "The System of 1896: An Analysis"; V.O. Key,
"A Theory of Critical Elections," *Journal of Politics* 17:1 (Feb. 1995), 11; Schattschneider,
The Semisovereign People; Schattschneider, "United States: The Functional Approach to Party
Government," *Modern Political Parties: Approaches to Comparative Politics*, ed., Sigmund
Neumann (Chicago: University of Chicago Press, 1956) 194–215; Sundquist.
[93] Sundquist, 181.
[94] Schattschneider, *The Semisovereign People*, 78.
[95] Burnham, "Party Systems and the Political Process," 300; Sundquist, 177, 181.
[96] Sundquist, 181; Schattschneider, *The Semisovereign People*, 78; Burnham, "Party Systems and
the Political Process," 300; Sundquist, 177 and 181 (see Footnote 14); Mayhew, "Wars and
American Politics," 484.

TABLE 3.2. *Congressional Seats Held by Party, 1894–1928*

	House		Senate	
	Rep	Dem	Rep	Dem
1894	246	104	44	39
1896	206	134	46	34
1898	185	163	53	26
1900	198	153	56	29
1902	207	178	58	32
1904	250	136	58	32
1906	222	164	61	29
1908	219	172	59	32
1910[a]	162	228	49	42
1912[b]	127	290	44	51
1914[b]	193	231	39	56
1916[b]	210	216	42	53
1918	237	191	48	47
1920	300	132	59	37
1922	225	207	51	43
1924	247	183	54	40
1926	237	195	48	47
1928	267	163	56	39

[a] Indicates Democratic control of the House.
[b] Indicates Democratic control of the House and the Senate.
Source: Harold W. Stanley and Richard G. Niemi, *Vital Statistics on American Politics 2003–2004* (Washington, DC: Congressional Quarterly Press, 2003), 37–8.

unmistakably began two years before Wilson's election. Starting with the 1910 midterm, Democrats made significant gains in both chambers of Congress. (See Table 3.2 for congressional seats held by each party throughout the era.) In the House, the Democrats gained fifty-six seats and became the majority. In the Senate, the Democrats picked up ten seats. Thus, the Democrats did much more than haphazardly enter Washington in 1912 through the backdoor and on the coattails of a president who merely happened to be in the right place at the right time to take advantage of the Republicans' internal strife. Rather, Wilson's election came two years after his Democratic Party had already made remarkable gains in Congress. Indeed, it seems that if Wilson benefited from good timing, it had as much to do with a Democratic surge initiated in 1910 as it did with Republican disarray in 1912. Furthermore, the fact that the GOP was plagued by a bitter internal split that led to a breakaway faction and contributed to their loss of the presidency and congressional majorities for several election cycles, undermines realignment assertions that this was, in Sundquist's words, an "era of Republican dominance."[97]

[97] Sundquist, 181.

TABLE 3.3. *Presidential Elections, 1896–1928*

Year	Candidates	Electoral Vote[a]	Popular Vote[b]
1896	McKinley, R	271 (60.6%)	51.0% (+4.3)
	Bryan, D	176	46.7%
1900	McKinley, R	292 (65.3%)	51.6% (+6.1)
	Bryan, D	155	45.5%
1904	T. Roosevelt, R	336 (70.6%)	56.4% (+18.8)
	Parker, D	140	37.6%
1908	Taft, R	321 (66.5%)	51.6% (+8.6)
	Bryan, D	162	43.0%
1912	Wilson, D	435 (81.9%)	41.8%
	T. Roosevelt, Prog.	88	27.4%
	Taft, R	8	23.2%
1916	Wilson, D	277 (52.2%)	49.2% (−3.1)
	Hughes, R	254	46.1%
1920	Harding, R	404 (76.1%)	60.3% (+26.2)
	Cox, D	127	34.1%
1924	Coolidge, R	382 (71.9%)	54.0%
	David, D	136	28.8%
	LaFollette, Prog.	13	16.6%
1928	Hoover, R	444 (83.6%)	58.2% (+17.4)
	Smith, D	87	40.8%

[a] Each candidate's electoral votes are displayed. The winner's percentage of the total electoral votes is displayed in parentheses.

[b] Each candidate's share of the popular vote is displayed as a percentage. The Republican margin is displayed in parentheses. The Republican margin is not displayed in 1912 and 1924 because prominent third party candidates skew the comparison.

Source: Harold W. Stanley and Richard G. Niemi, *Vital Statistics on American Politics 2007–2008* (Washington, DC: Congressional Quarterly Press, 2008), 28.

Second, and also undermining the "fluky Wilson presidency" thesis, Democrats maintained their advantage for several election cycles (see Table 3.1). Though the presidential election garnered the most attention in 1912, the congressional Democrats made even more dramatic advances in 1912 than they had two years before with gains of sixty-two House seats and nine Senate seats. Like the House, these results gave the Democrats a Senate majority. For the next six years, the party controlled both chambers, often with large majorities. House Democrats reached their peak with an overwhelming 290–127 (70 percent) advantage, while their counterparts in the Senate, following another cycle of impressive gains in 1914, enjoyed a strong 56–39 (59 percent) majority for two of those years. Finally, Wilson, this time in a normal two-way race with a unified Republican Party, was reelected in 1916 (see Table 3.3). Not bad for a party supposedly doomed to minority status in the wake of the "System of 1896." The key point here is that the Democrats controlled the presidency and both houses of Congress for an extended period. This success cannot be casually dismissed as an electoral aberration and a quirky presidential election that deprived Republicans of their natural position atop Capitol Hill and in the White House. Rather, the 1912 presidential election was only one of many contests, in only one of several election cycles, in which the Democratic Party fared quite well and gained or maintained majority status.

Not only were the Democrats winning at the ballot box, but there is also reason to believe their policies were popular with the American people throughout this period. This, again, is a difficulty for advocates of the "System of 1896" because the progressives in the Democratic Party championed a very different set of policy initiatives than the supposedly dominant Republican Party. President Wilson and congressional Democrats pursued a progressive agenda that differed markedly from the Republicans – even the GOP's progressive wing.[98] Specifically, the "New Freedom" agenda, developed by Wilson and liberal attorney Louis Brandeis, went much farther than progressive, not to mention conservative, Republicans in promoting a governmental role in economic regulation. New Freedom initiatives sought to break up industrial trusts and advance the interests of small business owners and farmers. Teddy Roosevelt, with strong progressive credentials of his own, condemned the plan as "rural Toryism."[99] A 1916 progressive-style lawmaking binge included measures such as the Federal Farm Loan Act, workmen's compensation for federal employees, a ban on the interstate sale of goods produced by child labor, the Adamson Act instituting an eight-hour workday for railroad employees, and the Revenue Act of 1916. Brandeis was also elevated to the Supreme Court that year. In sum, there was a significant gulf between the two parties. If the GOP was truly dominant during these years it is unclear why voters continually backed the Democrats and their starkly different policies.

Another difficulty for "System of 1896" proponents is rooted in elections during the 1920s. The results of the 1920 presidential election and those four and eight years later are more dramatic than their counterparts some two decades before. The presidential popular vote margins (Table 3.3) for the three contests in the 1920s (60.3 percent, 54.0 percent, and 58.2 percent; average: 57.5 percent) are more impressive than those for 1896 and its three ensuing elections (51.0 percent, 51.6 percent, 56.4 percent, and 51.6 percent; average: 52.7 percent). Similarly, the 1920s Republicans took larger shares of the available electoral votes (76.1 percent, 71.9 percent, and 83.6 percent; average: 77.2 percent) than did their fellow partisans a generation before (60.6 percent, 65.3 percent, 70.6 percent, and 66.5 percent; average: 65.8 percent). Statistical analyses by Larry Bartels and Jerome M. Clubb, William H. Flanigan,

---

[98] David Sarasohn, *The Party of Reform: Democrats in the Progressive Era* (Oxford, MS: University Press of Mississippi, 1989).

[99] Jules Witcover, *Party of the People: A History of the Democrats* (New York: Random House, 2003), 308–9.

and Nancy H. Zingale bear this out too.[100] Their work shows that the 1920 presidential contest produced an electoral change similar to those trumpeted by realignment theorists. In fact, both studies demonstrate that 1920 produced a more profound change than did the 1896 election.

In short, the Republican Party fared much better in 1920 than it did in 1896 and sustained a higher level of success in ensuing elections. Given that these two periods of GOP control were buffered by ten years in which Democrats controlled at least one congressional chamber or the White House – and six years of holding all three – the argument that the "System of 1896" explains the elections of the 1920s appears to be quite a stretch.

Thus, the conventional political science view seems to overlook three crucial points. First, the Democrats shared or had total power for ten years, something counterintuitive for a supposedly Republican-dominated era. Second, the 1920 election brought this period of Democratic control to a dramatic and decisive close. Third, once the "System of 1896" blinders are removed and the 1920 election is allowed to stand on its own, it appears just as significant as other important elections in American history. In fact, a strong case can be made that this shift was more profound and set a stronger precedent than that of 1896. These realizations do not mean that 1896 was not an important election. Indeed, there is much well-documented evidence to support such a claim. It does mean, however, that 1896 does not explain everything. In particular, it fails to account for the ten years of Democratic control in the 1910s and the following era of Republican dominance in the 1920s.

These difficulties, then, raise serious questions about realignment theory's most hallowed ground – the "System of 1896." In particular, the supposed inevitability of the Republican victory in 1920 seems quite dubious. If the 1896 realignment fails to account for the sudden, dominant, and lasting 1920 Republican resurgence, what does? A strong case can be made for World War I and its immediate effects.

World War I's Influence on the 1920 Election

The 1920 election was held at a time of transition and turmoil. President Woodrow Wilson was bedridden after suffering a debilitating stroke and Teddy Roosevelt had just died unexpectedly. More than 100,000 soldiers had not returned from World War I. The League of Nations – centerpiece of the Treaty of Versailles – was unpopular and obviously not going to be ratified. The economy had drifted into a postwar slump, while race riots and extremist groups dominated newspaper headlines. Amidst these factors, it is not a surprise that the Republicans came to power in one of the biggest landslides in electoral

---

[100] Larry M. Bartels, "Electoral Continuity and Change, 1868–1996," *Electoral Studies* 17(3), 301–26; Clubb, Flanigan, and Zingale, 90–102. See also: Mayhew, "Wars and American Politics," 482–3; Mayhew, *Electoral Realignments: A Critique of an American Genre* (New Haven, CT: Yale University Press, 2002), 44–50.

history. World War I was no longer a primary political issue because the fighting had been over for two years. But the war loomed large in that its direct effects were a major influence on the election.

It had already tallied a significant influence on the American population. Millions of men were sent abroad to fight for the first time in the nation's history. Of those, more than 126,000 were killed in action and many others came home physically or emotionally scarred. World War I also sent many Americans, including women, into cities to work in new, industrial jobs. An African American exodus out of the South and into Northern industrial centers constituted part of this urban migration. John Milton Cooper, Jr., writes: "Economic incentives became particularly important after 1914, when the outbreak of World War I effectively ended European immigration. Northern employers hurried south to recruit blacks for factory work."[101]

Although the war had initially created an economic boom, its conclusion led to a collapse. The World War I-associated economic slump from 1916–1921 was the U.S.'s second worst twentieth century recession (behind only the Great Depression).[102] When the war ended, concern turned toward balancing the budget and paying down debt. As a result, the government stopped borrowing money and raised taxes. These policy shifts occurred during a period of speculative investing based on credit, which drove prices higher. Realizing this, the federal reserve raised interest rates and urged a halt to loan renewals. As historian George Soule maintains, "Merchants and manufacturers who could no longer carry their inventories by means of bank credit were forced to sell at reduced prices. The fall of prices in turn endangered more loans and induced further credit restrictions. The downward spiral of deflation was in process."[103] By 1921, for instance, the index of wholesale prices for commodities fell from a high of 227.9 down to 150.6. Retail prices dropped approximately 13 percent. The economic downturn hit agriculture especially hard, with many farmers losing their land. Industry suffered as well, and bankruptcies and unemployment were common.

These economic and demographic changes linked to the war and its aftermath had a profound influence on American society. New sources of tension and conflict emerged and fed the rise of groups like the Ku Klux Klan on the right, and labor and anarchist groups on the left. Race riots were not unusual.[104] Unions held high profile strikes and became increasingly associated with leftist

---

[101] Cooper, 78–9.

[102] Robert J. Barro and José F. Ursúa, "Stock Market Crashes and Depressions," NBER Working Paper Series. http://papers.nber.org/papers/w14760.pdf?new_window=1, 26 (last accessed 20 Nov. 2009).

[103] George Soule, *The Economic History of the United States: Prosperity Decade: 1917–1929*, vol. 8 (London: The Pilot Press Limited, 1947), 98. See also: 96–106.

[104] Donald R. McCoy, "Election of 1920," *History of American Presidential Elections 1789–1968*, vol. 3, ed., Arthur M. Schlesinger, Jr. (New York: Chelsea House Publishers, 1971), 2349–50. See also: David M. Kennedy, *Over Here: The First World War and American Society* (New York: Oxford University Press, 1982).

groups, which contributed to the Red Scare.[105] Anarchists were chief suspects in a bombing campaign targeting, among others, John Rockefeller, J.P. Morgan, a U.S. senator, the Seattle mayor, and most notoriously, Wall Street, where forty people were murdered on September 16, 1920. The Espionage Act of 1917 and the Sedition Act of 1918 led to the infamous Palmer raids and Eugene V. Debs's imprisonment. Anarchists Nicola Sacco and Bartolomeo Vanzetti were convicted of murder and robbery in 1921 in an extremely controversial case and were later executed.[106]

The ruling Democrats had also stoked ethnic tensions during and after World War I. As discussed earlier, Democratic policies were offensive to German-Americans and caused a backlash in that community, which favored Republican candidates in 1918. That trend continued in 1920.[107] Democrats also alienated other ethnic groups. Scandinavians tended to oppose the war and sympathized with German-Americans. Irish Catholics were displeased about American support for England and thought their newly independent homeland was treated unfairly at Versailles. Similarly, Italian-Americans considered the treaty unfair to Italy.[108] President Wilson, frustrated with what he referred to as the "hyphenated Americans" during his efforts on behalf of the Versailles Treaty, alleged that "[h]yphens are the knives that are being stuck in this document."[109]

In addition to these difficulties, Wilson's campaign for the League of Nations was unsuccessful and unpopular.[110] The League was the heart of the President's "Fourteen Points" speech to Congress on January 8, 1918, and his plan for postwar peace. Wilson said a "general association of nations must be formed under specific covenants for the purpose of affording mutual guarantees of political independence and territorial integrity to great and small states

---

[105] On labor unrest, see: David Brody, *Labor in Crisis: The Steel Strike of 1919* (Champaign-Urbana, IL: University of Illinois Press, 1987).

[106] Stanley Coben, "A Study in Nativism: The American Red Scare of 1919–20," *Political Science Quarterly* 79 (March 1964), 52–75; David R. Colburn, "Governor Alfred E. Smith and the Red Scare, 1919–20," *Political Science Quarterly* 88:3 (Sept. 1973), 423–44; W. Anthony Gengarelly, *Distinguished Dissenters and Opposition to the 1919–1920 Red Scare* (Lewiston, NY: Edwin Mellon Press, 1996); Leuchtenburg, 66–83; Robert K. Murray, *Red Scare: A Study in National Hysteria, 1919–1920* (Minneapolis, MN: University of Minnesota Press, 1955); Roberta Strauss Feuerlicht, *America's Reign of Terror: World War I, the Red Scare, and the Palmer Raids* (New York: Random House, 1971); Neil A. Wynn, *From Progressivism to Prosperity: World War I and American Society* (New York: Holmes and Meier, 1986), 196–225.

[107] Luebke, xiii, 323; Lubell, 135.

[108] Wesley M. Bagby, *The Road to Normalcy: The Presidential Campaign and Election of 1920* (Baltimore, MD: Johns Hopkins University Press, 1962), 21, 23. Leuchtenburg, 43, 58, 89, 206; Lubell, 135.

[109] Leuchtenburg, 206.

[110] Sidney M. Milkis and Michael Nelson, *The American Presidency* (Washington, DC: CQ Press, 2003), 237–8.

alike."[111] Sidney M. Milkis and Michael Nelson maintain that Wilson committed a serious mistake in deciding to bypass Congress in developing his proposal for the international body. Regardless of his "formal constitutional responsibilities and informal obligations as party leader, Wilson believed that the initiative in foreign policy belonged to the executive 'without any restriction'.... No sooner had the Fourteen Points been pronounced and peace negotiations begun than Congress, tiring of Wilson's independent course, began to challenge his conduct of foreign affairs."[112] In the face of congressional skepticism, Wilson chose to take his message to the American people and began a speaking tour in the West in the fall of 1919. The President's health was failing on the trip and the tour was ultimately unsuccessful, serving only to highlight Wilson's sagging influence.[113] The Treaty of Versailles and its provision for the League of Nations never received Senate ratification.

The Republicans made a triumphant return to power amidst these converging forces. Warren Harding defeated James Cox in the 1920 presidential election by a 404 to 127 margin in the Electoral College, while garnering more than 60 percent of the popular vote. The GOP had a strong congressional showing as well. After achieving small majorities in 1918, Republicans gained sixty-three seats in the House and eleven in the Senate for commanding margins of 300–132 and 59–37, respectively.

There were a variety of explanations for the lopsided result. The *Literary Digest* provided an interpretation of the landslide as a response to World War I and its aftermath:

A thundering protest, an overwhelming repudiation, an irresistible demand for a change in the administration of the nation's affairs – these things are recognized by editorial observers of all parties in the unprecedented avalanche of votes that has swept the Republican party into power after eight years of Democratic control. But when it comes to determining exactly what kind of administration is demanded for the future, interpretations begin to diverge and conflict.... They all, however, unite in hailing the result as a crushing condemnation of "Wilsonism" – a point conceded even by many Democratic papers with the comment that if the Republican party had been in power through the soul-shaking ordeal of the world-war and disillusioning period of the armistice, it would have been the victim of a similar revulsion of popular feeling.[114]

Other contemporary sources offered similar explanations for the Republican triumph. Many, such as the Republican, Philadelphia-based *Public Ledger*, argued that it was simply a matter of war and peace. "The nation has emphasized its disapprobation and disgust of the way in which the Wilson oligarchy made war and muddled the making of peace."[115] Other accounts maintained

---

[111] Woodrow Wilson, "Fourteen Points," *Guide to the Presidency* (Vol. 2, 3rd ed.), ed., Michael Nelson (Washington, DC: CQ Press, 2002), 1642–3.
[112] Milkis and Nelson, 245.
[113] For a more detailed account, see: Tulis, 147–61.
[114] *The Literary Digest* "The Republican Avalanche," LXVII:7 (13 Nov. 1920), 11.
[115] Ibid.

that the result was a product of both the war and the war-induced economic downturn. The Republican *Philadelphia Enquirer* suggested "that the Wilson Administration has had the extravagances and wastefulness of the war to carry on its shoulders; it has been without vision as to the needs of the country; it has had no definite policy concerning high prices, heavy taxation, and the restoration of the country to something like a normal condition."[116] Wilson's League of Nations was also singled out. The voters, according to the Republican *Pittsburgh Gazette-Times*, "have saved their country from the threat of exploitation by an alien supergovernment and have preserved American institutions for the benefit of Americans."[117] Finally, the *Milwaukee Journal*, an independent paper, suggested it was a combination of these and other related factors. The election, it argued, was "a reaction to the war, to the tug on every one's heart-strings, to the loss of life and the crippling, to the high prices, to the taxes, to prohibition, to the very exaltation of spirit that carried us through, to the overturning of our whole economic system."[118]

Democratic-affiliated papers and officials had similar accounts. The *Richmond Times-Dispatch*, for instance, maintained that the result:

was a psychological condition that was natural following the termination of a great war, in which, while the nation was triumphant, a burden of taxation was piled up that bore heavily on the shoulders of the people. During the period of reconstruction, with its high prices and vexatious governmental interference with business, the Administration has had to bear the blame for all the unavoidable, yet annoying, incidents growing out of the process of readjustment. Unreasoning and illogical, the people demanded the change, which they now have effected by their votes.[119]

Meanwhile, the *New Orleans Times-Picayune* cited the war-related economic problems. "Excessive living cost, the rampant profiteering, speculation and inflation of the post-armistice period were charged, by the bitterly resentful masses who bore the pressure thereof, to the Democratic party because a Democratic President occupied the White House."[120] Semi-retired party leader and former presidential nominee William Jennings Bryan cited Wilson's League of Nations bungling:

Knowing full well that the majority in the nation was against him, he refused to deal with the Senate as a coordinate branch of Government.... By thus preventing ratification the President assumed responsibility for the nation's failure to enter the League, and thrust the League into the campaign as a partisan issue. The people confronted with a choice between Presidential infallibility and respect for the opinion of the majority in the Senate, naturally chose the latter...[121]

---

[116] *Philadelphia Enquirer*, "Voting for a Change of Administration," 3 Nov. 1920, 12.
[117] *Pittsburgh Gazette-Times*, "The Country is Safe," 3 Nov. 1920, 6.
[118] *Milwaukee-Journal*, "The Election," 3 Nov. 1920, 8.
[119] *Richmond Times-Dispatch*, "Nation Votes for a Change," 3 Nov. 1920, 6.
[120] *New Orleans Times-Picayune*, "A 'Change' is Ordered," 3 Nov. 1920, 8.
[121] "The Republican Avalanche," *The Literary Digest*, LXVII:7 (13 Nov. 1920), 13.

It is not entirely clear which of these claims accounts for the Republican victory in 1920. It seems likely that all these elements played a role. What is much more clear is that all of these suggestions are tied to the war in one way or another. Some effects, such as dissatisfaction over the war itself, the armistice, and the League of Nations are directly tied to World War I. Others, including the economic downturn and Prohibition, are indirectly tied to the war. Either way, though, the war set in motion a series of events that had a profound influence on the 1920 election.

As discussed above, the political science literature tends to either ignore this election entirely or create a haphazard connection to the "System of 1896." On the other hand, historians, like the era's journalistic accounts, not only acknowledge that an election took place in 1920 but place emphasis on the war's electoral influence. Jules Witcover, for instance, characterizes the 1920 election as one with "an electorate eager to leave the war behind."[122] Similarly, Lewis L. Gould, writes that after World War I, the "sense that the United States could and should play a limited role in the world established itself as political dogma in many areas of the nation's heartland where Republicans were strong after 1920."[123] Donald R. McCoy concurs: "In short, the Republicans owed their triumph to Wilson's failure to achieve the better nation and better world of which he had so often talked and to their own ability to conjure up a pleasant picture of the 'normalcy' to which they would return the country."[124]

CONCLUSION

World War I, like other major American wars, has been overlooked as a causal factor in understanding domestic politics. The crisis spurred the United States to develop its revenue system – a vital state capacity – by implementing a permanent income tax along with the regulatory institutions to oversee its administration. In addition, the Eighteenth Amendment's passage and the onset of Prohibition owed much to resource mobilization for – and anti-German sentiment emanating out of – the European conflict. Furthermore, the war gave the women's suffrage movement a boost. Their service on the homefront made women full partners in the war and, as a result, created a consensus that they deserved full citizenship rights. Additionally, these cases highlight war's role as an accelerant in U.S. domestic politics. In each of these cases, forces had been pushing for government action. But these calls for change were only successful once World War I's influence was brought to bear. That is, the war was the crucial factor that finally brought major change to tax policy, alcohol regulation, and women's voting rights. This is the same kind of influence the Spanish-American War had on the professionalization of the army and in the U.S.'s territorial expansion in the Philippines.

---

[122] Witcover, *Party of the People*, 334.
[123] Lewis L. Gould, *Grand Old Party* (New York: Random House, 2003), 219.
[124] McCoy, 2385.

All of these developments were also extensions of the federal government into areas once reserved for the states. The women's suffrage success, in particular, marked a further change in the system of federalism in favor of the national government and at the expense of state power. Among other things, the franchise extension was a move to nationalize a policy area. The states had been making the decisions in this realm; now the federal government would dominate. Taken as a whole, the new federal tax policies, the Eighteenth Amendment instituting Prohibition, and women's suffrage all show the national government greatly expanding its reach during, or as a result of, World War I.

Other war-induced developments not explored here also bolster this claim. The federal government instituted economic controls during the war by centralizing the direction of firms, wages, and prices, and by temporarily nationalizing the railroads. There was also a military draft. In addition, the federal government instituted various surveillance activities, both during the war and in its aftermath, as carried out in the Red Scare. Certain sectors of the population – especially Socialists and German-Americans – experienced repression through direct government action or with its encouragement.[125] Finally, and for the first time, the national government became immersed in immigration policy as never before. Following decades of failed attempts, substantive immigration restrictions were established in 1917 amidst war-induced calls for Americanization, concern over nefarious radicals, and the collapse of key pro-immigration groups like the German-American Alliance.[126] Like women's suffrage and Prohibition, new immigration policies signaled a fresh arena for tough national regulation.[127] A key point here is that World War I ushered in a new role for the federal government that touched U.S. society in general, but it also transformed policy areas that had traditionally been reserved for the states.

Nowhere have World War I's effects been more glaringly overlooked, though, than with regard to the party system. There is a strong case to be made that the 1918 midterm – and the resulting Republican congressional

---

[125] See, for instance: Cooper, *Pivotal Decades*; Luebke, *Bonds of Loyalty*.

[126] Daniel J. Tichenor, *Dividing Lines: The Politics of Immigration Control in America* (Princeton, NJ: Princeton University Press, 2002), Chapter 5; Mayhew, "Wars and American Politics," 478.

[127] There is a transnational element to immigration restriction. As Eric P. Kaufmann argues, America's World War I-era immigration restrictions served as an example to other countries like Britain, France, Canada, Switzerland, and Germany, where immigration "remained essentially uncontrolled until World War I. Therefore, far from being exceptional in its tolerance, the United States was actually a pioneer in the field of immigration restriction!" Following the Great War, according to Hugh Davis Graham, U.S.-like "neo-European" ex-settler nations such as Canada, Argentina, Brazil, and Australia cut back on immigration "to prevent a worldwide flood of refugees from war-torn Europe." Kaufmann, *The Rise and Fall of Anglo-America* (Cambridge, MA: Harvard University Press, 2004), 56; Graham, *Collision Course: The Strange Convergence of Affirmative Action and Immigration Policy in the United States* (New York: Oxford University Press, 2002), 47.

majorities – were heavily influenced by the Democrats' treatment of German-Americans during the war. Furthermore, the 1920 election, at least in terms of setting an electoral precedent, was at least as important as the oft-revered 1896 election. While the GOP had a period of electoral success in the years following 1896, Democrats enjoyed ten years in power starting in 1910. This stretch of Democratic dominance cannot be fully dismissed, as has often been the case in the political science literature, because of Teddy Roosevelt's 1912 third party candidacy. The Democrats began their surge two years before that and, equally troubling for realignment theorists, 1912 was not a one-hit wonder. Democrats maintained their hold on Congress until 1919 and President Wilson won reelection in 1916 despite facing a united Republican Party sporting a respectable nominee. Furthermore, and in contrast to 1896, the GOP's return to power in 1920 was total and complete, including large congressional gains and Warren Harding taking over 60 percent of the popular vote. World War I and its immediate effects played an enormous role in this election and provide the obvious linchpin explaining this dramatic reversal. Indeed, the war makes much more sense as an explanatory variable than does the conventional explanation offered by the political science literature – namely, that the 1920 election was merely the natural reemergence of the "System of 1896." Additionally, this election set a stronger precedent than did 1896 in that the ensuing presidential elections were won by larger margins than those following 1896.

4

The Good War

Taxes, civil rights, and party ideology are not often referenced in accounts of World War II. But if these topics have yet to generate the pages upon pages devoted to Pearl Harbor, D-Day, and the Big Three at Yalta, it's not because they weren't, in their own way, critically important and enduring. This chapter examines three of the most important domestic ramifications as they relate to American political development.

First, World War II led to the further growth of a crucial feature of the American state by providing the impetus for a mass-based, progressive tax system. Shortly after World War I produced important changes in the federal tax structure, its successor dramatically transformed that system yet again. Prior to World War II, and despite the changes wrought by the Great War, governmental revenue was structured very differently – only a relatively small portion of the American public actually paid income taxes. The World War II mass-based tax system has remained the foundation for Washington's revenue gathering ever since.

Second, with regard to democratic rights policy, African American participation drew attention to, and generated policy developments in, the arena of racial politics. Although there have been well-known instances of civil rights' violations in times of war (and perhaps none more infamous than the World War II-era internment of Japanese descendants), marginalized groups that contribute to war efforts – at home or abroad – have made remarkable democratic strides during those wars and in their aftermaths. There is no better case in point than that of African Americans during World War II. Not only did black wartime service prompt the extension of tangible new voting rights; the war years also laid much of the crucial foundation for the Civil Rights Movement. Ironically, these requisite initial gains have been overshadowed by the Civil Rights Movement they helped initiate.[1]

---

[1] World War II, of course, had other domestic policy implications beyond the income tax and African American voting rights. Among other things, it also played a role in curbing labor union

The third effect treated here is war's tendency to recast key elements of the party system. Because major wars are such profound events, they have the ability to directly produce changes in a party's public philosophy. The late 1940s saw such a period of ideological repositioning within the Democratic Party. The need for national solidarity in prosecuting World War II, and a number of indirect effects emanating out of the conflict, caused the party to shift from an ideology rooted in class-based populism to one focused on minority rights as a means of promoting inclusion.

WORLD WAR II IN BRIEF

World War II lived up to its billing, spanning the globe with primary theaters in Europe and the Pacific. The Allies – France, Great Britain, and later, the Soviet Union and the United States – fought against the Axis powers, Germany, Italy, and Japan. The war originated in Europe when Adolf Hitler's Nazi Germany invaded Poland in September 1939 on the heels of territorial gains in Austria and Czechoslovakia. Britain and France then declared war on Germany but were unable to prevent Hitler from overtaking Denmark, Norway, Belgium, the Netherlands, and France in 1940. Hitler's Italian ally, Benito Mussolini, launched an invasion of his own in North Africa that ultimately succeeded in 1941 following German assistance. Joseph Stalin's Soviet Union was next on Hitler's chopping block, and the Nazis invaded in June 1941. Initially, it appeared as though the German troops were going to roll through the USSR, but the vastness of the countryside – combined with a brutal winter and the Soviet Army's resurgence – proved too much for the Germans. After the pivotal and bloody battle of Stalingrad in February 1943, Hitler's army was forced to retreat back to Germany, with the USSR in hot pursuit.

In the midst of Germany's foray into Russia, the United States entered the war following Japan's December 7, 1941, surprise attack on the American naval base at Pearl Harbor on the Hawaiian island of Oahu. Over the next four years, the United States, led by President Franklin D. Roosevelt, fought bitter battles against the Japanese throughout the South Pacific, slowly but steadily advancing toward Japan. At the same time, American and Allied forces began seeing success in Europe. Having already recaptured North Africa from the Italians, the Allies invaded Sicily in the summer of 1943 and eventually deposed Mussolini. The 1944 D-Day invasion of occupied France established a beachhead and resulted in the Allies pushing Germany off the coast and into a retreat. The Nazis, now fighting the Soviets on one side and the British and

---

and executive branch power, and in advancing scientific research, education, atomic energy policy, and a new national security apparatus. See: David R. Mayhew, "Wars and American Politics," *Perspectives on Politics* 3:3 (Sept. 2005), 479. The three issues discussed here were selected because they are important in their own right, have had lasting consequences, highlight key themes cutting across other major wars, and, in one way or another, have largely been overlooked by political scientists.

Americans on the other, surrendered in May 1945. Several months later, the war in the Pacific ended too. Faced with what military experts predicted to be a hard-fought and costly ground invasion, the United States, now under President Harry Truman, dropped two atomic bombs on Japan, leading to that nation's surrender days later on August 15, 1945.

FROM UPPER CLASS TO MIDDLE CLASS: THE LEGACY OF WAR TAXATION

As Benjamin Franklin once poignantly observed, "in this world nothing can be said to be certain, except death and taxes." World War II brought plenty of both.[2] While fighting never touched the continental United States, a large and nearly universal tax system did. As economist John Joseph Wallis maintains, "the country emerged from the war with a completely different revenue structure, one that has remained largely in place until the present."[3] Although World War I made the income tax permanent, it affected only a sliver of the American public. Not until the arrival of World War II and its hefty spending demands did the income tax become a mass-based revenue source.

Federal government expenditures – especially those relating to military spending and attendant war debt – dramatically multiplied during World War II. Prior to 1940, defense spending exceeded 1 percent of the gross national product (GNP) on only two occasions, during the Civil War and World War I. Not surprisingly, World War II saw a substantial increase in such costs. Interestingly, though, defense expenditures remained higher for decades, thereafter accounting for 5 percent to 10 percent of GNP annually through the late 1980s.[4]

---

[2] It also brought a number of important pieces of legislation with implications for the American state that are not explored here, including the GI Bill, the Atomic Energy Act of 1946, and The National Security Act of 1947.

[3] John Joseph Wallis, "American Government Finance in the Long Run: 1790 to 1990," *The Journal of Economic Perspectives* 14:1 (2000), 73. See also: William J. Barber, "Government as a Laboratory for Economic Learning in the Years of the Democratic Roosevelt," *The State and Economic Knowledge: The American and British Experiences*, eds., Mary O. Furner and Barry Supple (New York: Cambridge University Press, 1990), 129–31; John L. Campbell and Michael Patrick Allen, "The Political Economy of Revenue Extraction in the Modern State: A Time-Series Analysis of U.S. Income Taxes, 1916–86," *Social Forces* 72:3 (1994), 643–99; Michael Edelstein, "Wars and the American Economy in the Twentieth Century," *The Cambridge Economic History of the United States, Volume III: The Twentieth Century*, eds., Stanley L. Engerman and Robert E. Gallman (New York: Cambridge University Press, 2000), 357–66; Randolph E. Paul, *Taxation in the United States* (Boston: Little, Brown and Company, 1954); Sidney Ratner, *Taxation and Democracy in America* (New York: John Wiley & Sons, Inc., 1967), 491–521; Herbert Stein, *The Fiscal Revolution in America* (Chicago: University of Chicago Press, 1969), 177–87. Great Britain offers a comparable case of World War II-induced effects: Michael J. Oliver and Hugh Pemberton, "Learning and Change in 20th-Century British Economic Policy," *Governance: An International Journal of Policy, Administration, and Institutions* 17:3 (2004), 415–41.

[4] Wallis, 72.

These increasing federal expenditures required financing and there was a precedent for a war-time income tax. As previously discussed, World War I saw the permanent establishment of the income tax, which had been used occasionally during previous crises but was always rescinded following the period of turmoil. There was no such rescission after World War I. Permanency, therefore, became the hallmark of World War I's income tax influence. But that war also introduced elements of broader applicability, progressivity, and a higher top rate into the income tax. Even so, World War I's tax legacy was limited because, although the tax never disappeared, its impact and applicability was diluted. Prior to World War II, only 4 million Americans, roughly 3 percent, filed tax returns and the top rate had been dramatically slashed from its Great War high of 77 percent. Historian David Kennedy writes that "to all but a plutocratic few Americans the prewar federal tax system was an utter irrelevancy, or at most a decidedly minor nuisance."[5]

With World War II, the income tax became more than a "minor nuisance." There was initial opposition to a mass-based income tax because some in the Roosevelt administration felt taxing lower income earners meant "abandoning advanced New Deal ground with a vengeance."[6] Roosevelt even suggested that "to win the war, no American citizen ought to have [an] income, after he has paid his taxes, of more than $25,000 a year."[7] But Congress worried that a tax plan based purely on taxing the rich and corporations, though popular, could undermine predictability and stability and, thus, the overall economy. This concern was widely held in Congress, and Roosevelt knew his flexibility was limited. In addition, the income tax was a kind of compromise with the business establishment, which preferred a sales tax. These considerations, coupled with the staggering costs of the war, led Roosevelt to reluctantly accept a broad yet progressive income tax, which was established in the Revenue Act of 1942. It was the passage of this law that allowed the government to raise vast sums of money through taxing middle class salaries. The act dropped the couples' exemption to $1,200 ($600 for singles), increased the bottom tax bracket rate by more than 100 percent, and more than doubled the total number of workers paying income tax.[8]

Roosevelt did not, however, give up hope of increasing the progressive nature of the tax and thus increasing the burden on corporations and the wealthy. The Revenue Act of 1943 became a second battle ground over allocation of the tax burden. Roosevelt asked Congress for substantial tax increases on upper-income earners. Congress presented the President with a bill that included

---

[5] David M. Kennedy, *Freedom From Fear: The American People in Depression and War, 1929–1945* (New York: Oxford University Press, 1999), 624.

[6] W. Elliot Brownlee, "Tax Regimes, National Crisis, and State-Building," *Funding the Modern American State, 1941–1995: The Rise and Fall of the Era of Easy Finance*, ed., Brownlee (New York: Cambridge University Press, 1996), 88 and 93.

[7] John F. Witte, *The Politics and Development of the Federal Income Tax* (Madison, WI: University of Wisconsin Press, 1985), 116.

[8] Brownlee, 90–1. Witte, 117–8.

new exemptions for business and only minor tax increases, far short of FDR's request. He vetoed the legislation, calling it "not a tax bill but a tax relief bill," only to see Congress override him.[9]

As economic historian W. Elliot Brownlee asserts, Roosevelt's 1943 failure to adjust the 1942 bill was a turning point in the history of American taxation. "The humiliating defeat convinced Roosevelt that he had to accept the structure of the income taxation without further complaint. [This defeat] essentially ended the conflict, which had begun during World War I between business and progressive advocates, over soak-the-rich income taxation."[10] Thus, the World War II revenue crisis brought an end to the debate over whether the tax burden should be broad-based. A mass-based progressive tax was to become the norm. Progressive and New Deal suggestions of putting the entire burden on corporations and the wealthy subsided. In short, a major tax transformation occurred: Class taxation was replaced with mass taxation.[11]

For government coffers, the altered tax structure rooted in the 1942 Revenue Act was a windfall. Federal tax revenue increased from $2.2 billion before the war to $35.1 billion by 1945. In addition, the federal government was now taking a majority of all tax revenue. Prior to the war, only 16 percent of collected taxes at every level of government went to Washington. But by 1950, more than half went to the federal treasury.[12] Perhaps most dramatically, though, the mass-based income tax also fundamentally altered the sources of federal revenue. Before World War II, corporate and individual income taxes accounted for roughly 40 percent of federal revenue; however, by the war's conclusion, the income tax made up about 75 percent. This sourcing remained essentially the same for decades. Only recently have Social Security taxes rivaled income taxes for primacy.[13]

For American citizens, rates shot up, personal deductions decreased, new taxpayers were tapped, and the now-familiar withholding plan was implemented. The lowest bracket's rate was 24 percent – about the same as the *maximum* prewar rate – and the highest earners were taxed at 93 percent (see Figure 4.1). In addition, the number of people in each bracket shot up.[14] For the first time individuals were now paying more income taxes than corporations. Unlike previous incarnations of the income tax, the new tax structure established by the Revenue Act of 1942 affected most citizens. By the end of the war, 60 percent of the workforce, or 42.6 million people, paid income taxes – more than ten times as many as the 3.9 million before the war. Another 30 percent were submitting tax returns.[15]

Part of the altered tax system was the structural change of withholding wages from employee paychecks. The Current Tax Payment Act of 1943 required

[9] Brownlee, 93.
[10] Ibid.
[11] Ibid.
[12] Ibid.
[13] Witte, 123.
[14] Ibid., 117–8. Kennedy, 624.
[15] Brownlee, 93.

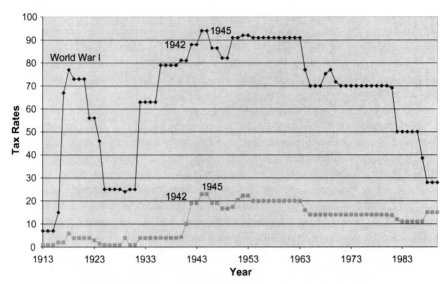

FIGURE 4.1. Top and Bottom Income Tax Rates.[16]

employers to take income taxes directly out of their employees' earnings. The initial reason for the withholding system was a fear of widespread noncompliance on the part of the millions of new taxpayers. The income tax had previously been seen as a tax on the wealthy. Now most people were obligated to pay. The new mass-based income tax, thus, required the entire taxpaying culture to change. The prospect of arresting millions of otherwise law-abiding people living and working in the United States would create obvious logistical challenges.[17] Thus, withholding was, and continues to be, a means to ease lower-income earners into the taxpaying fold. It also had the benefit of ensuring the timely deposit of funds into the Federal Reserve. In these ways, according to law professor Carolyn C. Jones, "the withholding system revolutionized the income tax. Elimination of delay in payments made the income tax more responsive to wartime revenue expansion."[18]

Even with the withholding plan in place, there was widespread concern that many citizens would see the tax as an undue burden. Accordingly, two appeasement strategies were implemented. First, against Roosevelt's wishes, most of the 1942 taxes were forgiven. This step was pragmatic because the new payroll deduction program created a logistical glitch. Under the old system, taxes for the prior year were due shortly after the new year. Therefore, when the withholding system went into effect in 1943, taxpayers were responsible

---

[16] National Taxpayers Union Foundation, "History of Federal Individual Income and Top Bracket Rates," www.ntu.org/main/page.php?PageID=19, last accessed 24 May 2009.

[17] Carolyn C. Jones, "Mass Based Income Taxation: Creating a Taxpayer Culture, 1940–1952," *Funding the Modern American State, 1941–1995: The Rise and Fall of the Era of Easy Finance*, ed., Brownlee (New York: Cambridge University Press, 1996), 107–9.

[18] Ibid., 130.

for paying their 1942 taxes – in keeping with the prior program – but also immediately had income withheld under the new system. To alleviate this burden and the "double taxation" feeling that accompanied it, the 1942 taxes were eliminated for most citizens (only those owing more than $50 remained subject to the tax, and they only had to pay 25 percent of what they otherwise would have owed).[19]

The second and more interesting appeasement strategy designed to quell anger over the new mass tax was an appeal to patriotism.[20] This strategy was particularly important because – with more people paying taxes – the traditional populist, class-based justification for income taxation was no longer sufficient. Previously the Roosevelt administration had justified the income tax as a corrective measure for what it saw as excessive concentrations of wealth and power in the hands of the few. In light of the new mass-based income tax, patriotic propaganda messages were deployed in magazines, pamphlets, street corners, and over the radio. Popular refrains included "Taxes to Beat the Axis" and Roy Rogers informing listeners that "Your income tax money pays for Victory." One subtle radio ad said: "Well, nobody says filling out these forms is fun. But it's more fun than sitting down in a foxhole, and it's more fun than being shot down in a plane. And it's more fun than waiting for a torpedo to hit."[21] The federal government commissioned "God Bless America" and "White Christmas" composer Irving Berlin to write the somewhat less memorable, "I Paid My Income Tax Today." Hundreds of radio stations broadcast the jingle repeatedly. Its attempt to link the tax to the war effort was obvious:

> I said to Uncle Sam
> "Old Man Taxes here I am"
> And he – was glad to see me
> Lower brackets that's my speed
> Mr. Small Fry yes indeed
> But gee – I'm proud as I can be
> I paid my income tax today
> I'm only one of millions more
> Whose income never was taxed before
> A tax I'm very glad to pay
> I'm squared up with the U.S.A.
> You see those bombers in the sky
> Rockefeller helped build them and so did I
> I paid my income tax today.[22]

This was just one of many propaganda efforts aiming to tie taxes to patriotism, war support, and victory itself.

[19] Sidney Ratner, *Taxation and Democracy in America* (New York: John Wiley & Sons, 1967), 517.

[20] Jones, "Class Tax to Mass Tax: The Role of Propaganda in the Expansion of the Income Tax during World War II," *Buffalo Law Review* 37 (1989), 685–737.

[21] Jones, "Mass Based Income Taxation," 114.

[22] Ibid., 122.

Ultimately, the new mass-based tax system succeeded for several reasons. First, the war effort was widely popular. As a result, the public was willing to help finance it. "More so than in World War I," Brownlee writes, "Americans concluded that their nation's security was at stake and that victory required both personal sacrifice through taxation and indulgence toward the corporate profits that helped fuel the war machine."[23] The administration's propaganda campaign on behalf of the tax no doubt reinforced these sentiments. Second, some argued that excessive corporate taxation could lead to another economic depression. These fears understandably created a greater willingness to experiment with new economic arrangements if it meant avoiding a repeat of the 1930s. Third, despite Roosevelt and other New Dealers' initial hesitancy to embrace a mass-based income tax, many of them grew to accept it and defend it as a means to ensure steady revenues and to finance federal social programs.[24]

While the war was the precipitating reason for creating a mass-based income tax, it has remained a central feature of government revenue ever since because of its effectiveness during the conflict. Immediately following the war, there were questions about whether the tax would continue, given that its primary justification was gone. But as path dependency theorists might predict, once the tax structure was in place, it endured.[25] New ways of spending the money were discovered, and policy makers realized that crude on-again, off-again taxation schemes created problems. A Treasury Department paper, "Report on Postwar Taxation," concluded that "The individual income tax . . . must be kept a mass tax, because after the war very large amounts of revenue will still need to be raised for many generations to come." During the war years, the tax had come to be seen as "the most important" governmental revenue source. Although the report suggested altering particular rates, it specifically ruled out more exemptions. Consistency was seen as critical for "tax morale."[26] Thus, the war established a new and far-reaching tax policy with profound effects on

[23] Brownlee, 94.

[24] Ibid.

[25] Margaret Levi has defined path dependency as follows: "Path dependency has to mean, if it is to mean anything, that once a country or region has started down a track, the costs of reversal are very high. There will be other choice points, but the entrenchments of certain institutional arrangements obstruct an easy reversal of the initial choice." Margaret Levi, "A Model, a Method, and a Map: Rational Choice in Comparative and Historical Analysis," *Comparative Politics: Rationality, Culture, and Structure*, eds., Mark I. Lichbach and Alan S. Zuckerman (New York: Cambridge University Press, 1997), 28. See also: Paul Pierson, *Politics in Time: History, Institutions, and Social Analysis* (Princeton, NJ: Princeton University Press, 2003); Pierson, "Increasing Returns, Path Dependence, and the Study of Politics," *American Political Science Review* 94:2 (2000), 251–67; Gerard Alexander, "Institutions, Path Dependence, and Democratic Consolidation," *Journal of Theoretical Politics* 13:3 (2001), 249–69; Herman Schwartz, "Down the Wrong Path: Path Dependence, Increasing Returns, and Historical Institutionalism," unpublished manuscript, http://www.people.virginia.edu/~hms2f/Path.pdf, last accessed 6 May 2009.

[26] Jones, "Mass Based Income Taxation," 146–7.

both government revenue and U.S. citizens. The American state has subsisted on this tax design ever since.

World War II had a decisive influence on the lives of African Americans.[27] As Gunnar Myrdal predicted in his 1944 classic, *An American Dilemma*, their valuable contributions to the war effort, combined with an altered moral and intellectual climate emanating out of the war, created the opportunity for significant precursors to the Civil Rights Movement.[28] Of course, it is somewhat problematic to discuss democracy's expansion during this era because any such advances have been overshadowed by President Roosevelt's executive decision to intern Japanese descendants during the war.[29] Though uncontroversial at the time, internment is now widely regarded as one of the greatest miscarriages of justice and denials of fundamental civil rights in American history.

White Attitudes, Black Organization, and the Intellectual Environment

Speaking in 1922, black leader Marcus Garvey anticipated the effect another world war could have for the cause of black freedom:

I feel sure we are well prepared for the work that is ahead of us. We face the future as never before. We will watch developments in Europe as before. I do hope for war; I am not such a Christian as not to desire war at this time. I am that Christian that believes that except for the shedding of blood there will be no remission of sins, and I believe that the unspeakable is going to be the agent through whom four hundred million Negroes see salvation, and if it comes to-morrow, or the next day or a month from now, I am praying that it will come because only through the coming of another great war in Europe will we get the opportunity to strike the blow for our freedom.[30]

Indeed, Garvey accurately predicted the key role such a conflict might play in advancing African American civil rights.

---

[27] Neil A. Wynn, *The Afro-American and the Second World War* (London: Paul Elek, 1976), 12. See also, Mayhew, "Wars and American Politics," 479.

[28] Gunnar Myrdal, *An American Dilemma: The Negro Problem and Modern Democracy* (New York: Harper & Brothers Publishing, 1944).

[29] For a discussion of various World War II-era curtailments of rights, see: Geoffrey R. Stone, *Perilous Times: Free Speech in Wartime* (New York: W.W. Norton, 2004), 235–310. There is an extensive literature discussing internment and its legacy. See, for example: Robert P. Saldin, "Executive Power and the Constitution in Times of Crisis," *White House Studies* 4:4 (Dec. 2004), 489–504; Greg Robinson, *By Order of the President: FDR and the Internment of Japanese Americans* (Cambridge, MA: Harvard University Press, 2001); Michi Weglyn, *Years of Infamy: The Untold Story of America's Concentration Camps* (New York: William Morrow and Company, Inc., 1976); Audrie Girdner and Anne Loftis, *The Great Betrayal: The Evacuation of the Japanese-Americans During World War II* (London: The Macmillan Company, 1969).

[30] Joseph G. Tucker, "Report by Special Agent Joseph G. Tucker – Oct. 7, 1922," *Marcus Garvey*, http://www.marcusgarvey.com/wmview.php?ArtID=431 (last accessed 5 June 2007).

Three factors elevated the status of African Americans during World War II and provided key arguments for beneficial policy changes. First, their military service led to altered white attitudes. Second, African American leaders leveraged the war domestically and laid the rhetorical, procedural, and organizational foundation of the Civil Rights Movement that would emerge some fifteen years later. And finally, World War II produced a moral and intellectual environment that made racial discrimination appear particularly hypocritical.

Initially, African Americans were not high on the list of desirable soldiers. In striking contrast to the Vietnam War when charges were leveled that blacks ended up on the front lines because they were expendable, World War II-era African American men were deliberately kept away from the front lines because they were thought to be unreliable. In pressure situations, some worried, blacks would flee or be more likely than whites to aid the enemy.[31]

Eventually, though, the World War II manpower shortage left the military desperate to fill holes with any available personnel. Accordingly, 1 million African Americans served in the armed forces and millions more served in the broader defense industry.[32] Black women also served.[33] Although African Americans had participated in all of the nation's previous wars, they were always subject to segregation and discrimination, and were generally used on a temporary basis. Once the crises of previous wars abated, black regiments were disbanded. In the years immediately prior to World War II, the Marines and the Army Air Corps had no blacks, and those few in the Navy were only permitted to serve in dining facilities.

Part of the reason for a shortage of soldiers during World War II was the initial, systematic exclusion of blacks. Although all military branches technically accepted blacks by 1942, Selective Service literacy tests held down African American enrollment. As a result of this and other restrictive measures, 300,000 blacks had been denied admission to the armed forces by 1943, and those admitted were in segregated units relegated to support – rather than combat – roles.

Yet the need to utilize African Americans as Army replacement soldiers could no longer be ignored following the casualties in 1944's Battle of the Bulge. Dozens of black platoons were hastily formed. While they served side-by-side with whites in the same companies, their smaller subunits were still segregated by race. The Navy was facing similar shortages and thus increased

---

[31] Kennedy, 772.

[32] On this topic see: Alexander Keyssar, *The Right to Vote: The Contested History of Democracy in the United States* (New York: Basic Books, 2000), 244–53; Philip A. Klinkner and Rogers M. Smith, *The Unsteady March: The Rise and Decline of Racial Equality in America* (Chicago: University of Chicago Press, 1999), 161–201; *The Invisible Soldier: The Experience of the Black Soldier, World War II*, ed., Mary Penick Motley (Detroit, MI: Wayne State University Press, 1975).

[33] See: Maureen Honey, *Bitter Fruit: African-American Women in World War II* (Columbia, MO: University of Missouri Press, 1999); Martha S. Putney, *When the Nation was in Need: Blacks in the Women's Army Corps During World War II* (Metuchen, NJ: The Scarecrow Press, 1992).

black enrollment, although segregation was still maintained. In addition, the Air Force was eventually forced to train and outfit several black pilots in 1943 – including the famous Tuskegee Airmen – during a shortage in North Africa.[34] All these changes were made reluctantly by the military and the political power structure. But ultimately, winning the war was deemed more important than maintaining social divisions. As General George Patton remarked with typical subtlety and elegance: "I don't care what color you are, so long as you go up there and kill those Kraut sonsabitches."[35] This pragmatic mentality, rather than any idealistic moral imperative, was the key factor in the introduction of African Americans into combat roles.

Regardless of motives or rationales, this black wartime service was important in that it altered white attitudes. Many whites – at least those who served with blacks – emerged from the war with different racial opinions. A survey of white officers and noncommissioned officers demonstrates this transformation in stark terms. Initially, 64 percent of respondents had unfavorable feelings toward serving with black units, but after serving together, 77 percent had "more favorable" feelings while 0 percent had "less favorable" feelings. Similarly, white opinion ratings of black combat performance were high, with more than 80 percent of the white respondents giving black soldiers the highest possible grade.[36] One South Carolinian echoed the survey results, saying: "When I heard about it I said I'd be damned if I'd wear the same patch they did. After that first day when we saw how they fought I changed my mind. They're just like any of the other boys."[37] At home, the war was also a unifying force and weakened traditional ethnic cleavages. Public and private associations began educational initiatives to ensure these divisions did not hinder the war effort.[38] From Hollywood to the Office of War Information, pluralistic conceptions of citizenship were the order of the day.[39] According to historian David Bennett, "By war's end nativism was all but finished."[40]

The war also galvanized African American organizing efforts in pursuit of increased civil rights. World War II laid some of the rhetorical, procedural,

---

[34] Kennedy, 773.

[35] Ulysses Lee, *United States Army in World War II Special Studies: The Employment of Negro Troops* (Washington, DC: Department of the Army, 1963), 661.

[36] Klinkner and Smith, 190.

[37] Jean Byers, "A Study of the Negro in Military Services," Department of Defense Monograph, June 1947, 172–3. For other anecdotal accounts see Klinkner and Smith, 189–90.

[38] Robert L. Fleegler, "Theodore G. Bilbo and the Decline of Public Racism, 1938–1947," *Journal of Mississippi History* 68:1 (2006), 2–3; Richard W. Steele, "The War on Intolerance: The Reformulation of American Nationalism," *Journal of American Ethnic History* 9 (Fall 1989), 9–35; Richard Polenberg, *One Nation Divisible* (New York: Viking, 1980), 46–9; John Blum, *V Was for Victory* (New York: Harcourt Brace Jovanovich, 1976), 147–72.

[39] Philip Gleason, *Speaking of Diversity: Language and Ethnicity in Twentieth Century America* (Baltimore, MD: Johns Hopkins University Press, 1992), 153–87; Eric Foner, *The Story of American Freedom* (New York: W.W. Norton, 1998), 237–9.

[40] David H. Bennett, *Party of Fear: The American Far Right From Nativism to the Militia Movement* (Chapel Hill, NC: University of North Carolina Press, 1995), 285.

and institutional groundwork for the Civil Rights Movement. Black leaders such as A. Philip Randolph recognized the opportunity the war provided to advance racial equality. If the nation was in need of African American support for the war effort, it should come at a price. Randolph made this point several months before the Pearl Harbor attack but in the midst of European turmoil and growing speculation that the United States would increase its support for the Allies:

Negro America must bring its power and pressure to bear upon the agencies and representatives of the Federal Government to exact their rights in National Defense employment and the armed forces of the country. I suggest that ten thousand Negroes march on Washington, D.C. with the slogan: "We loyal Negro American citizens demand the right to work and fight for our country." No propaganda could be whipped up and spread to the effect that Negroes seek to hamper defense. No charge could be made that Negroes are attempting to mar national unity. They want to do none of these things. On the contrary, we seek the right to play our part in advancing the cause of national defense and national unity. But certainly there can be no national unity where one tenth of the population are denied their basic rights as American citizens.[41]

Foreshadowing Martin Luther King, Jr., Randolph couched his appeal in definitively American terms by invoking rights, citizenship, and national unity. Shortly after America's official entry into World War II, the same sentiment was expressed in the *Pittsburgh Courier*, the nation's most widely circulated black newspaper: "What an opportunity this crisis has been and still is for one to persuade, embarrass, compel and shame our government and our nation . . . into a more enlightened attitude toward a tenth of its people!"[42]

Blacks took strategic action during World War II to organize civil rights groups. Underlying these steps, argue political scientists Philip A. Klinkner and Rogers Smith, "was the belief that although the war would entail profound sacrifices, it also presented black Americans with an unprecedented opportunity to leverage the government and society for greater rights. . . . Waiting until the war was over to press for equal rights would be foolish and futile."[43] First, the Congress of Racial Equality (CORE), a new civil rights group, was formed in 1942.[44] Recognizing the opening the war provided, the group staged protests and sit-ins in an effort to integrate public facilities and also expanded its organizational capacity throughout the North and Midwest. Meanwhile the well-established National Association for the Advancement of Colored People

---

[41] A. Philip Randolph, "Statement Made on the Proposed March on Washington," 15 Jan. 1941, http://www.spartacus.schoolnet.co.uk/USArandolph.htm, last accessed on 11 May 2009.

[42] "Voiceless in Congress," *Pittsburgh Courier* (10 Jan. 1942), 6. See also: Richard M. Dalfiume, "The 'Forgotten Years' of the Negro Revolution," *Journal of American History* 55 (June 1968), 96–7.

[43] Klinkner and Smith, 164. See also: Harvard Sitkoff, *The Struggle for Black Equality, 1954–1980* (New York: Hill and Wang, 1981), 11; John Dittmer, *Local People: The Struggle for Civil Rights in Mississippi* (Urbana, IL: University of Illinois Press, 1994), 1–18.

[44] For more on CORE, see: August Meier and Elliot Rudwick, *CORE: A Study in the Civil Rights Movement, 1942–1968* (Urbana, IL: University of Illinois Press, 1975).

(NAACP) grew its membership list to 500,000 by 1945, ten times the numbers it had in 1939.[45] Although its success was limited, CORE's work during the war provided a procedural example, rooted in nonviolence, that would become a cornerstone of the Civil Rights Movement.[46] In addition, both CORE and the NAACP realized the advantages of organizing large numbers of citizens to bring pressure on the government.

The third and final factor that raised the status of blacks during World War II, and in the process spurred fundamental policy changes, was the new moral and intellectual environment. Comparisons between the Allies and the Nazi regime were inevitable. Adolph Hitler felt Germany was strong compared to the United States. For the Fuhrer, as historian David M. Kennedy states, Americans were an unintelligent, "mongrel race, doomed to the trash heap of history when...the national bloodstream [was opened] to indiscriminate immigrant inflows and, worse, black contamination. Even Aryan peoples could be corrupted by infection with the bacillus of American mediocrity."[47] Shortly after Pearl Harbor, Hitler reiterated this view: "I don't see much future for the Americans.... It's a decayed country. And they have their racial problem, and the problem of social inequalities.... American society [is] half Judaized, and the other half Negrified. How can one expect a State like that to hold together?"[48] On the other side of the Atlantic, the United States took solace in what it considered to be its moral superiority. But, as the Germans and Japanese constantly noted, the widespread existence of systematized discrimination in America undermined U.S. claims to be the model for democracy.[49]

Some black opinion leaders and intellectuals agreed. Scholar and journalist Horace Clayton, for instance, argued that "the only difference between Hitler's plans for non-Aryans (were he to win the war) and the treatment of African-americans in the South was that Hitler was talking in future terms, while in the South the treatment was current practice."[50] Similarly, an NAACP newspaper advertisement asked, "Is This the Way of Life That Congress Has Voted 24 Billion Dollars to Defend? Could Hitler Be Worse?"[51] Though obviously hyperbolic, the general charge of hypocrisy clearly had merit and was an embarrassment to U.S. assertions of moral superiority.

In this manner, the war against the Nazi regime undermined any ideology of racial supremacy in the United States because the intellectual fight against Germany exposed unavoidable contradictions at home. For example, several

---

[45] For more on the NAACP, see: Gilbert Jonas, *Freedom's Sword: The NAACP and the Struggle Against Racism, 1909–1969* (New York: Routledge, 2007).

[46] Klinkner and Smith, 165. See also: Meier and Rudwick.

[47] Kennedy, 392.

[48] William L. Shirer, *The Rise and Fall of the Third Reich* (New York: Simon and Schuster, 1960), 895n.

[49] Keyssar, 245.

[50] Azza Salama Layton, *International Politics and Civil Rights Policies in the United States, 1941–1960* (New York: Cambridge University Press, 2000), 40. See also pages 39–41.

[51] Ibid., 39.

months before the United States even entered the war, President Roosevelt and British Prime Minister Winston Churchill met in Newfoundland to issue the Atlantic Charter, a brief statement laying out the eight "common principles in the national policies" of the United States and Great Britain "on which they base[d] their hopes for a better future for the world." One of these principles was respect for "the right of all peoples to choose the form of government under which they will live; and [the United States and Britain] wish to see sovereign rights and self government restored to those who have been forcibly deprived of them."[52] *The New Republic* summed up the difficulty, arguing that racial discrimination at home made a "mockery of the theory that we are fighting for democracy, and we are giving aid and comfort to the enemy thereby."[53] The editors also worried that whites engaged in stoking racial tension in cities such as Detroit "were assuredly doing Hitler's work. We don't doubt that the story of that riot was told all over Asia, with Nazi trimmings."[54] Similarly, in 1943, *The Nation* argued: "It is time for us to clear our minds and hearts of the contradictions that are rotting our moral position and undermining our purpose. We cannot fight fascism abroad while turning a blind eye to fascism at home. We cannot inscribe on our banners: 'For democracy and a caste system.' We cannot liberate oppressed peoples while maintaining the right to oppress our own minorities."[55]

This difficulty was most famously analyzed by Swedish scholar Gunnar Myrdal in his book *An American Dilemma*.[56] He argued that the American creed – rooted in the ideals of liberal democracy – did not measure up to the realities of the African American experience. Race was a particularly vexing problem because the United States was the obvious nation to lead the then ongoing global fight against fascism and dictatorship. Yet the oppressed black population at home weakened America militarily and, more importantly, ideologically. Myrdal's project was tightly connected to World War II. Biographer Walter Jackson writes that Myrdal and others viewed *An American Dilemma* "as if it were part of the war effort – a large, collaborative enterprise to produce a report for the general public on a sensitive issue bound up with the morale of American troops, the productivity of the war industries, and the ideology of the war against fascism."[57] The Swede thought the good in America far outweighed the bad, was optimistic that U.S. democracy could overcome the

---

52 "The Atlantic Charter," ed., Samuel Rosenman, *Public Papers and Addresses of Franklin D. Roosevelt*, vol. 10 (New York: Random House: 1938–1950), 314.

53 "Back to Jim Crow," *The New Republic* (16 Feb. 1942), 221.

54 Peter J. Kellogg, "Civil Rights Consciousness in the 1940s," *Historian* 42 (November 1979), 31. Klinkner and Smith, 167–8.

55 "Defeat at Detroit," *The Nation* (3 July 1943), 4.

56 Myrdal, *An American Dilemma: The Negro Problem and Modern Democracy* (New York: Harper & Brothers, 1944).

57 Walter A. Jackson, *Gunnar Myrdal and America's Conscious: Social Engineering and Racial Liberalism, 1938–1987* (Chapel Hill, NC: University of North Carolina Press, 1990), 262. See also, Klinkner and Smith, 183–6. Kennedy, 762–3.

race problem, and hoped that his book, published in the middle of the war, would play a role in the process. Kennedy writes: "The book's release in [1944] reflected [Myrdal's] confidence that even in the midst of a global war, perhaps precisely *because* of the war, the American people were prepared to hear a probing report about their country's most enduringly painful social issue: race."[58]

The book became a bestseller and was widely praised. Following the attention it gathered upon publication, *Life* magazine declared race "America's No. 1 social problem."[59] *Time* magazine compared Myrdal to Alexis de Tocqueville.[60] Klinkner and Smith attribute the book's popularity and acclaim to the war. "If the book had appeared only a decade earlier, reactions would likely have been sharply different; but the catalyst of war had fundamentally altered racial attitudes.... Tellingly, *Time* reviewed *An American Dilemma* under the heading, 'U.S. at War.'"[61]

While Myrdal's work arguably had the greatest influence, Klinkner and Smith demonstrate that it was merely one example of an undeniable growth of racial liberalism linked to World War II. Liberal intellectuals, historian Alan Brinkley notes, started moving "from a preoccupation with 'reform' (with a set of essentially class-based issues centering around confronting the problem of monopoly and economic disorder) and toward a preoccupation with 'rights' (a commitment to the liberation of oppressed peoples and groups)."[62] In addition, Klinkner and Smith argue, changes occurring in popular culture suggested that "civil rights was emerging as an important national issue."[63] Popular literature, nonfiction writing, and movies portrayed race in a new light.[64] For example, the films *Bataan* and *Sahara* not only brought increased attention to racial issues, but also portrayed heroic African American soldiers (even though few blacks were actually allowed in combat situations when the movies were released).[65] A vast political science literature has demonstrated the importance of elite opinion and the media in shaping mass public opinion.[66] While the evidence

[58] Kennedy, 762. Italics are Kennedy's.
[59] Klinkner and Smith, 184.
[60] "U.S. at War: Races," *Time* (7 Feb. 1944), 16.
[61] Klinkner and Smith, 184.
[62] Alan Brinkley, *The End of Reform: New Deal Liberalism in Recession and War* (New York: Knopf, 1995), 170; Klinkner and Smith, 186. See, also: Fleegler. Steve Lawson, *Running for Freedom: Civil Rights and Black Politics in America since 1941* (New York: McGraw-Hill, 1997), 10.
[63] Klinkner and Smith, 183–6.
[64] See, for instance: Lillian Smith, *Strange Fruit* (San Diego, CA: Harcourt, Brace, Jovanovich, 1992); Richard Wright, *Black Boy* (New York: Harper, 1945). Movies: *Bataan* (1943); *Casablanca* (1943); *The Ox-Bow Incident* (1943); *Sahara* (1943).
[65] Klinkner and Smith, 184–5.
[66] See, for instance: John Zaller, *The Nature and Origins of Mass Opinion* (New York: Cambridge University Press, 1992); Edward G. Carmines and James A. Stimson, *Issue Evolution: Race and the Transformation of American Politics* (Princeton, NJ: Princeton University Press, 1989); Philip Converse, "The Nature of Belief Systems in Mass Publics," *Ideology and Discontent*,

presented here suggests World War II influenced both mass opinion (at least that of the soldiers) and elite opinion, this literature would suggest that the transformation at the elite level was the most critical.

In sum, World War II's ideological environment highlighted racial inequality in 1940s America, shifted the manner in which race was discussed, and set the stage for the Civil Rights Movement. The war itself contributed directly to this altered environment because race relations were an embarrassment to America's claim to the moral high ground. Once a manpower shortage developed, and blacks were allowed to enlist in the armed forces, the problem became even more difficult to ignore. It seemed particularly perverse and hypocritical to ask blacks to risk their lives fighting for a country in which they were denied full political participation.

This new war-engendered environment also, of course, led to new policy debates. Specifically, it raised the question of how blacks' service during the war would alter their status in America. As historian Neil Wynn asserts: "The mass of writings dealing with [African Americans] during the war years in books, learned journals and popular magazines, equals that of the 1960s, and reflected the new awareness of America's social problem. Implicitly or otherwise, it too demanded that Negro participation in the defense of democracy be given its just rewards."[67] Klinkner and Smith concur that these societal trends rooted in World War II forced the federal government to make policy changes on behalf of blacks. "In this climate of shifting attitudes and domestic political pressures, the problems of racial violence, and especially the severe needs of the war, federal officials found it increasingly difficult to delay addressing racial inequalities."[68] It has frequently been the case that groups that contribute to a war effort receive benefits in return; this was certainly true with regard to World War II.

Policy Changes

As a result of the war-induced factors described above – altered white attitudes, African American organization, and the changed intellectual climate – tangible policy benefits were achieved. African American participation in the war effort, at home and abroad, created a compelling reason to reward their contributions. Like other groups which sacrificed in support of a war effort, blacks were recognized for their contributions. Although these wartime advances have been overshadowed by achievements made during the Civil Rights Movement of the 1950s and 1960s, the policy victories were remarkable and only a few years before would have been unthinkable. The previously discussed reforms in the

ed., David Apter (New York: Free Press, 1964); Walter Lippman, *Public Opinion* (New York: Penguin, 1946). See also, Fleegler, 2, 4, 13–27.

[67] Wynn, "The Impact of the Second World War on the American Negro," *Journal of Contemporary History* 6:2 (1971), 50.

[68] Klinkner and Smith, 186.

armed forces (such as altered enrollment policies and blacks serving in combat units) were of obvious importance. Of even greater significance, though, was the war's influence on labor and, especially, voting rights.

Several labor policies related to African Americans were initiated as a result of World War II. The number of blacks working in defense industries sky-rocketed during the war, and much of this employment came in higher paying, skilled jobs. While this transition resulted primarily from wartime labor short-ages, it was due in part to several federal government initiatives designed to increase African American employment. The War Labor Board, for instance, barred wage differences based on race in 1943.[69] In addition, labor unions restricting black membership were no longer offered the necessary certifica-tions by the National Labor Relations Board. Finally, the U.S. Employment Service banned job listings by race.[70] Combined, these policies amounted to what economist William J. Collins calls "the federal government's first effort to enforce a wide-ranging anti-discrimination policy."[71]

While these employment advances were significant, the most profound World War II era policy changes for African Americans occurred in the realm of voting rights. As women gained suffrage – at least in part – due to their efforts during World War I, and as 18 to 20 year olds – based on their eligibil-ity for military service – would gain the vote during Vietnam, black soldiers in World War II gained increased voting rights as an outgrowth of their wartime service.

The Soldier Voting Act of 1942 was the first of two major World War II-era advances in African American suffrage. This law federalized the right of soldiers to register and to vote absentee. Even more importantly, the Soldier Voting Act abolished the poll tax. Eliminating the tax, which was designed to – and had the effect of – decreasing black access to the ballot in Southern states, was obviously crucial to providing full political participation to all citizens. Liberals in Congress had been attempting to eliminate the poll tax for several years but had made little headway because bills were blocked in the Democratic-controlled House Judiciary Committee. But with the war under way, eliminating the poll tax for soldiers was difficult to oppose and proponents of the measure emphasized its new relevance. As Florida Senator Claude Pepper said, eliminating the poll tax for soldiers "would ring around the world that America was carrying out its professions of democracy."[72] Historian Steven Lawson maintains that it was this new war-related argument that carried the day. Opponents had no cover to "filibuster [the bill] because they found it difficult to justify the deprivation of the right to vote to men fighting for

---

[69] Ibid., 191–2.
[70] Richard Polenberg, *War and Society: The United States, 1941–1945* (Westport, CT: Greenwood Press, 1972), 116–7; Klinkner and Smith, 191.
[71] William J. Collins, "The Political Economy of State-Level Fair Employment Laws, 1940–1964," *Explorations in Economic History* 40:1 (2002), 28.
[72] Klinkner and Smith, 174.

their country."[73] While states would still retain administrative control over absentee voting, the Soldier Voting Act was a turning point in the campaign for African American voting rights. As Alexander Keyssar argues, the "federal government's disapproval of poll taxes had become a matter of law, and the wartime climate of opinion contributed to the repeal of the poll tax in Georgia in 1945 as well as to the postwar passage of state laws exempting veterans from poll taxes."[74] Tellingly, the Soldier Voting Act marked the first expansion of African American voting rights since Reconstruction.

Smith v. Allwright, a 1944 U.S. Supreme Court case, carried even more significance for black voting rights.[75] In an 8–1 decision, the Court reversed 1935's *Grovey v. Townsend*, which had held that political parties were private associations and thus not subject to the Fifteenth Amendment's protections against racial discrimination.[76] *Smith*, conversely, declared the so-called "white primary" unconstitutional. The crux of the case centered on a black citizen, Lonnie Smith, who was not allowed to vote in the Texas Democratic primary because he was not white. Of course, hearkening back to the Civil War and Reconstruction, the Republican Party was so weak in Texas, and the rest of the South, that winning the Democratic primary meant, in effect, winning the general election as well. Smith argued that the white primary disenfranchised him because he was excluded from the only election that mattered. The Supreme Court agreed despite the fact that, as the majority opinion acknowledged, no facts had changed since the *Grovey* decision nine years earlier. One thing that had changed, though, was the Court's composition. Only two justices from the *Grovey* decision remained on the bench. Franklin Roosevelt's appointees in the interim tended to be more willing to assert federal authority over states and, as political scientist Kevin J. McMahon argues, extend civil rights.[77]

But in the years since *Grovey*, the country had also become engaged in World War II. Indeed, "of perhaps equal importance" as the Court's membership, Keyssar posits, "the justices were not immune to events transpiring in the world around them.... They were well aware of the links between the ideological dimensions of World War II and the exclusion of blacks from voting in the South."[78] Historian Darlene Clark Hine notes, the "white primary was one of the first casualties of World War II."[79] Contemporaneous accounts also made

---

[73] Steven F. Lawson, *Black Ballots: Voting Rights in the South, 1944–1969* (New York: Columbia University Press, 1976), 66.

[74] Keyssar, 247.

[75] *Smith v. Allwright*, 321 U.S. 649 (1944).

[76] *Grovey v. Townsend*, 295 U.S. 45 No. 563 (1935).

[77] Kevin J. McMahon, "Constitutional Vision and Supreme Court Decisions: Reconsidering Roosevelt and Race," *Studies in American Political Development* 14 (Spring 2000), 20–50; McMahon, *Reconsidering Roosevelt on Race: How the Presidency Paved the Road to Brown* (Chicago: University of Chicago Press, 2004).

[78] Keyssar, 248.

[79] Darlene Clark Hine, *Black Victory: The Rise and Fall of the White Primary in Texas* (Millwood, NY: KTO Press, 1979), 236–7.

TABLE 4.1. *Black Voter Registration in the South**

Year	Estimated Number	Percentage of Eligible Blacks
1940	250,000	5
1947	595,000	12
1952	1,008,614	20

* South includes: Alabama, Arkansas, Florida, Georgia, Louisiana, Mississippi, North Carolina, South Carolina, Tennessee, Texas, and Virginia.

Source: Philip A. Klinkner and Rogers M. Smith, *The Unsteady March: The Rise and Decline of Racial Equality in America* (Chicago: University of Chicago Press, 1999), 196.

the connection. *The New York Times* Washington bureau chief Arthur Krock pinned the decision directly on the altered intellectual environment emanating from the war. "The real reason for the overturn," Krock wrote, was "that the common sacrifices of wartime have turned public opinion and the court against previously sustained devices to exclude minorities from any privilege of citizenship the majority enjoys."[80]

Smith's results were dramatic. By 1952, more than a million Southern blacks were registered to vote – four times as many as in 1940 (see Table 4.1). In addition, these voters were allowed to cast ballots in the crucial Democratic primary, not just the frequently irrelevant general election.[81] In addition to shutting down the white primary, *Smith* set the stage for *Brown v. Board of Education* ten years later. Thurgood Marshall, the lead attorney in both cases and later the first African American Supreme Court Justice, said *Smith* was his greatest victory.[82] There was obviously more work to be done before African Americans enjoyed full voting rights – hence the need for the Voting Rights Act of 1965, which dealt with many of these same issues. Nonetheless, the seeds of later, more dramatic, developments were planted and nourished during World War II, and the most effective means of preventing blacks from accessing the ballot booth had been eliminated.

Further, as Mayhew has noted, these changes to the racial status quo emanating out of World War II provided one of the foundational elements of Harry Truman's Fair Deal.[83] Civil rights was not a New Deal issue. Rather, it

[80] Arthur Krock, "In the Nation: Self Reexamination Continues in the Supreme Court," *New York Times*, 4 April 1944, 20. See also, Keyssar, 248; Harvard Sitkoff, *A New Deal for Blacks* (New York: Oxford University Press, 1981), 229–37; Ward E.Y. Elliott, *The Rise of Guardian Democracy: The Supreme Court's Role in Voting Rights Disputes, 1845–1969* (Cambridge, MA: Harvard University Press, 1974), 78–80.

[81] Klinkner and Smith, 195. Incidentally, it was about this time that general elections became competitive in the South – at least at the presidential level.

[82] Keyssar, 248.

[83] Mayhew, "Wars and American Politics," 480.

emerged during World War II and was embraced by Truman. Thus, the 1964 and 1965 policy achievements constituting the high-water mark of the Civil Rights Movement, had little or nothing to do with the New Deal. They should more properly be considered products of the World War II-inspired Fair Deal.

This sanguine view of World War II's influence on the status of African Americans is not universally shared. Political scientist Daniel Kryder offers the most persuasive counterargument.[84] He contends that any policy advancements during these years were at best peripheral to the larger goals of winning the war and maintaining the Democratic Party's electoral coalition based on conservative Southerners, liberal Northerners, and urban blacks. "The Roosevelt administration implemented policies that may have appeared progressive, but other purposes – the full mobilization of industrial production and the maintenance of the party coalition – outweighed in importance the principle and the goal of egalitarian social reform."[85] He concludes that the war did not bring the improvements Myrdal predicted and that are presented here. These criticisms of the Roosevelt administration and federal bureaucrats clearly have some merit – particularly with regard to the landmark executive order creating the Fair Employment Practices Committee.[86]

Although Kryder's careful study echoes the scholarly consensus on Roosevelt, it has recently been countered by McMahon who argues that FDR consciously pursued civil rights advances indirectly by appointing liberals to the Supreme Court.[87] Instead of Kryder's cynical and calculating Roosevelt, McMahon portrays a president implementing a long-term strategy to address civil rights – a strategy that bore fruit more than a decade later in *Brown v. Board*. McMahon, for instance, argues that FDR's "court-packing" plan was a key part of this process. This typology that elevates Roosevelt to the status of a civil rights crusader seems forced next to Kryder's elaboration on the standard view. Ultimately, though, with regard to the matter at hand, Roosevelt's "true" intentions and racial views are of little importance.

What counts is whether or not World War II produced significant and lasting civil rights achievements. On this score, Kryder wants to throw the baby out with the bathwater. Just because FDR's administration and the military bureaucracy failed to rally to the African American cause with moral indignation does not mean that significant progress was not made. And even if one

[84] Daniel Kryder, *Divided Arsenal: Race and the American State During World War II* (New York: Cambridge University Press, 2000). See also: Russell L. Riley, *The Presidency and the Politics of Racial Inequality: Nation-Keeping from 1831 to 1965* (New York: Columbia University Press, 1999); Edward Carmines and James Stimson, *Issue Evolution: Race and the Transformation of American Politics* (Princeton, NJ: Princeton University Press, 1989), 31–4; Nancy J. Weiss, *Farewell to the Party of Lincoln: Black Politics in the Age of FDR* (Princeton, NJ: Princeton University Press, 1983); Frank Freidel, *F.D.R. and the South* (Baton Rouge, LA: Louisiana State University Press, 1965).

[85] Kryder, 4.

[86] Ibid., 52–66.

[87] McMahon, *Reconsidering Roosevelt on Race*.

were to concede that the progress came in spite of Roosevelt, the fact remains that major advances were achieved during the World War II years. Further, much of the World War II story occurred within the black community at the grassroots level and had nothing to do with FDR or any other political elites. In other words, crucial aspects of the World War II-induced change came not from elites handing down new policies, as Kryder and McMahon emphasize, but from groups pushing up from below.

For Kryder, the real success came during the Civil Rights Movement of the 1950s and '60s. He argues that to the extent World War II played a role in black advances at all, it likely slowed down the march to equality.[88] Of course, it is impossible to argue that progress during World War II overshadows milestones such as the Civil Rights Act of 1964 or the Voting Rights Act of 1965. But this is not the point. Gains for African Americans were made slowly over the course of many decades and, at least to some extent, built on each other. Just because events of the 1940s appear modest compared to those twenty years later does not mean that they were unimportant in the overall process. Indeed, the racial initiatives of the 1940s only look minor when compared to the following decades. If one examines the Soldier Voting Act and *Smith v. Allwright* with reference to the 1920s and '30s, the progress is undeniable. During those decades, the federal government did nothing to address racial issues (except, perhaps, to reinforce and institutionalize inequalities). By contrast, during World War II, concrete steps were taken to address the blatant repression under which blacks lived. It matters less what motivated the changes than that the changes were made. In addition, it was during and because of the war that crucial organizational steps were taken within the black community. This process was important because these forces would later shape the Civil Rights Movement.

In principle, the United States could have turned back from civil rights progress in the 1950s or '60s, as it did in the 1870s. In fact, to some extent, the momentum from World War II was lost. Racism enjoyed a postwar resurgence.[89] In addition, despite Truman taking some important actions in his first years in office, his second term is often characterized as a time of promises unfulfilled.[90] As such, Kryder is undoubtedly correct that World War II did not determine everything. Yet civil rights never left the national agenda after World War II as it did following the Civil War and Reconstruction. Certainly the increased organization within the black community played a role in keeping the issue alive. But, whatever the reasons, it is not the purpose here

---

[88] Ibid., 250–4.
[89] Riley, 158; Dalfiume, *Desegregation of the U.S. Armed Forces* (Columbia, MO: University of Missouri Press, 1969), 132–4; Robert J. Donovan, *Conflict and Crisis: The Presidency of Harry S. Truman, 1945–1948* (New York: Norton, 1977), 243–5.
[90] McMahon, *Reconsidering Roosevelt on Race*, 177–96; Sidney M. Milkis, *The President and the Parties: The Transformation of the American Party System Since the New Deal* (New York: Oxford University Press, 1993), 157–9. See also, William C. Berman, *The Politics of Civil Rights in the Truman Administration* (Columbus, OH: Ohio State University Press, 1970).

to explain why there was no turning back like there was after Reconstruction. Rather, the aim is simply to show what happened during and immediately after World War II. And in this respect, the advances were quite dramatic given the preceding decades and helped elevate civil rights to the status of a frontburner issue, thus setting the stage for the extraordinary progress to follow.

DEMOCRATS' POSTWAR IDEOLOGICAL TRANSFORMATION

World War II has the distinction of being America's only uncontroversial major war. Unlike the other conflicts in this study, the public and the three federal branches of government were virtually unanimous in their unwavering support for the war effort. What few critics there were often had ulterior motives. For instance, Montana Representative Jeanette Rankin's vote against a declaration of war had more to do with feminism and pacifism than a true belief that Japan's attack on Pearl Harbor and Germany's declaration of war should be ignored. As a result of this virtual unanimity, the era's elections were not forums for debate about the war in any fundamental sense. Republican candidates pledged to carry on the conflict in much the same manner as President Roosevelt. Indeed, the GOP slogan in 1944 – "end the war quicker with Dewey and Bricker" – was a testament to the marginal differences between the candidates.[91] Those disagreements that did exist tended to focus on mundane matters regarding postwar planning.[92] The one area in which the war was important was in convincing Roosevelt to run for a third and fourth term, and in the public's support for him. Minus the war, FDR probably would not have run again in 1940 and, prior to the fall of France and the recognition of the international crisis, opinion polls indicate that he probably would have been defeated if he had.[93] Four years later, observers pinned Roosevelt's victory on public unwillingness to change leadership at the height of a crisis.[94] In short, while

[91] Robert A. Divine, *Foreign Policy and U.S. Presidential Elections, 1940–1948* (New York: New Viewpoints, 1974), 162.

[92] For instance, 1944 Republican presidential candidate Thomas E. Dewey proposed bringing servicemen home more quickly following Axis surrender than Roosevelt was planning. Thomas E. Dewey, "Campaign Speech, Philadelphia, September 7, 1944," *History of U.S. Political Parties: 1910–1945, From Square Deal to New Deal*, vol. 3, ed., Arthur M. Schlesinger, Jr. (Philadelphia, PA: Chelsea House Publishers, 2002), 2361.

[93] Mayhew, "Incumbency Advantage in U.S. Presidential Elections: The Historical Record," *Political Science Quarterly* 123:2 (2008), 227–8. On Roosevelt not running for a third term, see: Kenneth S. Davis, *FDR: Into the Storm, 1937–1940* (New York: Random House, 1993), 532–5, 584–6; Frank Freidel, *Franklin D. Roosevelt: Rendezvous with Destiny* (Boston: Little, Brown, 1990), 327–8, 341, 346; Robert E. Sherman, *Roosevelt and Hopkins* (New York: Harper and Brothers, 1948), 169–73. On public opinion, see: Paul Lazarsfeld, Bernard Berelson, and Hazel Gaudet, *The People's Choice*, 3rd ed. (New York: Columbia University Press, 1968), 71; Mathew A. Baum and Samuel Kernell, "Economic Class and Popular Support for Franklin Roosevelt in War and Peace," *Public Opinion Quarterly* 65 (Summer 2001), 198–229; James MacGregor Burns, *Roosevelt: The Lion and the Fox* (New York: Harcourt, Brace and World, 1956), 422.

[94] Divine, 162.

World War II loomed large in these elections, their outcomes did not turn on conflict over issues associated with the war because there was little difference of opinion on the matter. In this sense, then, World War II was an anomaly. Whereas all of America's other major wars have produced contentious partisan disputes, World War II spawned cohesiveness and unity.

World War II had a more interesting and lasting influence on the Democratic Party's public philosophy.[95] John Gerring's leading account of American party ideologies contends that prior to the war, Democrats' were characterized by class-based populism; and that after the war, Democrats transitioned to an ideology based around solidarity and universality.[96] Gerring accurately assesses the important differences in the party's prewar and postwar public philosophies, and he is right in identifying the late 1940s as the key point in Democratic ideology. Yet his analysis omits a key causal variable in that transition: World War II. Mobilizing for and fighting the war required a unified country. The class-based rhetoric Democrats employed prior to the outbreak of hostilities was divisive, pitting different segments of the country against one another. The war – if only by necessity – required a new approach that brought people together in solidarity for a national cause. This need encouraged the party to adopt a more unifying, inclusive ideology that became evident in the war's aftermath. Other factors indirectly tied to the war also bolstered this ideological transformation.

Prewar Democrats

Until recently, there was a general consensus that 1932 marked a critical hinge point for the Democratic Party. Prior to Franklin Roosevelt's election in that pivotal year, the party was plagued by constant disputes between its disparate, and often fundamentally opposed, elements. The party, for instance, contained natural combatants: Northerners and Southerners; urban workers and rural farmers; nativists and immigrants; progressives and conservatives. In essence, the Democrats were a motley array of opposing forces unable to unify around a coherent ideology.[97]

---

[95] As discussed extensively in Chapter 1, my analysis of party ideology follows John Gerring in focusing primarily on what he calls "presidential parties" (6). For more on this approach, see the "Party Ideology" section in Chapter 1 and Gerring, *Party Ideologies in America, 1828–1996* (New York: Cambridge University Press, 1998), 6, 22–7.

[96] Gerring, 187–253.

[97] See, for instance: Walter Dean Burnham, "The System of 1896: An Analysis," *The Evolution of American Electoral Systems*, eds., Paul Kleppner, et al. (Westport: Greenwood Press, 1981), 158; Jerome M. Clubb, "Party Coalitions in the Early Twentieth Century," *Party Coalitions in the 1980s*, ed., Seymour Martin Lipset (San Francisco, CA: Institute for Contemporary Studies, 1981), 120–2; Richard Hofstadter, *The Age of Reform: From Bryan to FDR* (New York: Alfred A. Knopf, 1955); Everett Carll Ladd, *American Political Parties: Social Change and Political Response* (New York: W.W. Norton, 1970), 161; Milkis, *The President and the Parties: The Transformation of the American Party System Since the New Deal*, 21; James L. Sundquist,

All this changed, the standard view maintains, in 1932. Roosevelt not only saved the nation from the throes of the Great Depression, but also rescued his party from irrelevance. For the first time in decades, the party had an identifiable ideology centered around the public philosophy of the welfare state. That is, the majority of Democrats were united in their support for redistributive social and economic policies, statism, and science.[98] As political scientist Sidney Milkis has argued, Roosevelt's reinterpretation of America's "liberal" ideals marked a profound break with the nation's limited government tradition. Prior to the 1930s, liberalism had always been linked to "Jeffersonian principles and the natural rights tradition of limited government drawn from Locke's Second Treatise and the Declaration of Independence. Roosevelt pronounced a new liberalism in which constitutional government and the natural rights tradition were not abandoned but linked to programmatic expansion and an activist national government."[99]

This account of Democratic ideological history complements realignment theory's emphasis on 1932. That year's "critical election" and the federal government's ensuing activist policies created a massive partisan realignment in favor of the Democrats. James Sundquist writes: "The millions of voters who switched from the Republican to the Democratic Party or were mobilized into the electorate as Democrats for the first time, attracted by the Democratic

---

Dynamics of the Party System: Alignment and Realignment of Political Parties in the United States (Washington, DC: Brookings Institution Press, 1983), Chapter 3.

[98] This is not to say that the party's ideology was synonymous with the liberal Democrats' position. The Democratic Party was, in Milkis' words, a "bifactional party with durable ideological and policy divisions" (75–6). Conservative Southern Democrats were powerful and influential in many respects. Nonetheless, Roosevelt's policies did represent the dominant strain of the party and was clearly in control of the party's national rhetoric (the "presidential party," as Gerring calls it). Milkis, *The President and the Parties*, 75–6; Gerring, 6. For more on the Southern Democrats, see: Nicol Rae, *Southern Democrats* (New York: Oxford University Press, 1994).

[99] Milkis, "Programmatic Liberalism and Party Politics: The New Deal Legacy and the Doctrine of Responsible Party Government," *Challenges to Party Government*, eds., John Kenneth White and Jerome M. Mileur (Carbondale and Edwardsville, IL: Southern Illinois University Press, 1992), 109. For most scholars, then, this was the decisive break in Democratic ideology. Today's party is still the same as the one forged by Roosevelt in the 1930s. See, for instance: Samuel Beer, "Liberalism and the National Idea," *Left, Right and Center: Essays on Liberalism and Conservatism in the U.S.*, ed., Robert A. Goldwin (Chicago: Rand McNally, 1965), 145–6; Steve Fraser and Gary Gerstle, *The Rise and Fall of the New Deal Order, 1930–1980* (Princeton, NJ: Princeton University Press, 1989); Ladd and Charles D. Hadley, *Political Parties and Political Issues: Patterns in Differentiation since the New Deal* (Beverly Hills, CA: Sage, 1973); Ladd and Hadley, *Transformation of the American Party System* (New York: Norton, 1975); William E. Leuchtenburg, *In the Shadow of FDR: From Harry Truman to Ronald Reagan* (Ithaca, NY: Cornell University Press, 1983); Herbert S. Parmet, *The Democrats: The Years after FDR* (New York: Oxford University Press, 1976); David R.B. Ross, "The Democratic Party, 1945–60," *History of U.S. Political Parties*, vol. 4, ed., Schlesinger (New York: Chelsea House, 1973); Theda Skocpol, "The Legacies of New Deal Liberalism," *Liberalism Reconsidered*, eds., Douglas MacLean and Claudia Mills (Totowa, NJ: Rowman & Allanheld, 1983); Richard C. Wade, "The Democratic Party, 1960–1972," *History of U.S. Political Parties*, vol. 4, ed., Schlesinger (New York: Chelsea House, 1973).

program and the Rooseveltian personality and leadership . . . made the latter the country's clear majority party for the first time in eighty years."[100] Even critics of realignment theory recognize the 1932 election as a turning point in American political history. Indeed, for realignment skeptics, 1932 is perhaps the only election in the canon that actually meets the theory's requirements.[101] In addition, a key statistical study demonstrates the significance of 1932. Jerome Clubb, William Flanigan, and Nancy Zingale measure the amount of enduring electoral change each presidential election produced from 1836 to 1964. They show that Roosevelt's first contest for the White House produced the largest and most significant lasting change of any election in their study.[102] Thus, not only did 1932 purportedly bring about a sea change in the dominant strain of Democratic ideology, but it also brought the party to power for the better part of the next several decades.

Yet it is important to note that these two outcomes (ideological change and electoral dominance) represent two separate and not necessarily connected claims. The first identifies an intraparty ideological hinge point. Theoretically, a shift in Democratic ideology could make the party less popular, more popular, or result in no popularity change and could occur independently of any specific election. By contrast, realignment's emphasis on 1932 is more broadly concerned with the relationship between the two major parties and their relative levels of electoral success. In theory, the two developments are not codependent. Practically, however, it is not a coincidence that these two literatures both emphasize 1932 because there is obvious overlap between them. And this convergence makes for a neat, logical, causal narrative. It is comforting, in a sense, to have everything coalesce around 1932. Under this appealing and accessible plotline, the Democratic Party, led by Roosevelt, reacted to the Depression's economic horrors and the do-nothing policies of Herbert Hoover with a new ideology geared toward the nation's challenges. As a result, the electorate rallied to the Democratic banner, thereby crushing Republican dominance rooted in the "System of 1896" and ushering in a new political era.

---

[100] Sundquist, 214. See also, V.O. Key, Jr., "A Theory of Critical Elections," *Journal of Politics* 17 (Feb. 1955), 3–18; Key, "Secular Realignment and the Party System," *Journal of Politics* 21 (May 1959), 198–210; Walter Dean Burnham, *Critical Elections and the Mainsprings of American Politics* (New York: W.W. Norton & Co., 1970).

[101] Ladd, "Like Waiting for Godot," *The End of Realignment*, ed., Shafer (Madison, WI: University of Wisconsin Press, 1991), 27; Samuel T. McSeveney, "No More 'Waiting for Godot': Comments on the Putative 'End of Realignment,'" *The End of Realignment*, ed., Shafer (Madison, WI: University of Wisconsin Press, 1991), 90–1; Joel H. Silbey, "Beyond Realignment and Realignment Theory: American Political Eras, 1789–1989," *The End of Realignment*, ed., Shafer (Madison, WI: University of Wisconsin Press, 1991), 4–5, 14; Mayhew, *Electoral Realignments: A Critique of an American Genre* (New Haven, CT: Yale University Press, 2002), 141.

[102] Clubb, William H. Flanigan, and Nancy H. Zingale, *Partisan Realignment: Voters, Parties, and Government in American History* (Beverly Hills, CA: Sage, 1980), Chapter 3. See especially Table 3.1a, pages 92–3. This analysis covers elections from 1836–1964 and, thus, does not actually cover every election in American history. Yet one can infer that no election since 1964 has had such a dramatic, lasting effect.

However, political scientists James Morone and John Gerring argue that the transition was not quite so seamless. Morone notes that although the administrative state was greatly expanded under FDR, this was merely a natural response to the Depression: "The New Deal administrative inventions did not break sharply with the past. Roosevelt left behind a far greater government, but not one fundamentally different from . . . that he found."[103] Gerring builds on Morone's analysis by demonstrating that the New Deal is the outgrowth of Bryanism and Wilsonianism, and that the party's ideology fundamentally changed not with Roosevelt and the New Deal, but following World War II. Gerring reframes the period by identifying the Democratic Party's ideological hinge point in the late 1940s.[104] Contrary to the traditional view, Gerring maintains the party was unified from the Bryan-era on. "There was more cohesion and continuity within Democratic ideology between 1896 and 1948 than is generally recognized. This ideology was not oriented on Jefferson, nor was it oriented on the technocratic management of the welfare state; rather it was *Populist* in tone and policy."[105]

Prewar Democrats were tied together by a belief in market regulation and wealth redistribution based on the public interest model of evangelical Christianity. "Democrats' political philosophy could be encapsulated in the ideal of majority rule and in the populist narrative in which the people fought for their rights against an economic and political elite. . . . From 1896 to 1948, Democratic candidates sounded the bell of political and economic freedom and advocated for the rights of the common man."[106] Policy proposals, invoking the language of reform, were tailored to benefit and appeal to the "people." Monopolies and big business were targeted because they purportedly operated in opposition to the people's interests.[107]

All this, of course, is not to suggest that the 1932 election and the New Deal were unimportant for the Democratic Party. Indeed, the standard view is certainly correct that key aspects of the party looked very different after 1932. As Milkis argues, the presidency and its relationship to the party system were profoundly affected, and New Deal policies created a federal government that was a much more prominent and vital feature of Americans' daily lives.[108]

---

[103] James A. Morone, *The Democratic Wish: Popular Participation and the Limits of American Government*, revised ed. (New Haven, CT: Yale University Press, 1990), 129.

[104] Gerring says the transition happened between 1948 and 1952. Gerring, *Party Ideologies in America, 1828–1996*.

[105] Ibid., 188. Italics are in original. I follow Gerring in using "*Populism* to refer to the ideology of the Democratic party in the 1896–1948 period and *populism* to invoke the general (nonspecific) concept" (188). For the purposes of this discussion, I also follow Gerring in understanding class warfare to be one possible form of populism. See also: Terri Bimes and Quinn Mulroy, "The Rise and Decline of Presidential Populism," *Studies in American Political Development* 18:2 (2004), 136–159.

[106] Gerring, 189.

[107] Gerring, 193–200.

[108] Milkis, *The President and the Parties*. Milkis argues that political parties had always been primarily ensconced in state and local politics; governing at the national level was often only an afterthought. Roosevelt and his New Deal allies recognized that this feature of American

Yet the vast expansion of government during the 1930s was characterized by experimentation in a direct response to the Great Depression – not a coherent, planned set of policy initiatives long envisioned by Roosevelt. Federal government intervention was initially conceived of as a temporary solution to a crisis and, even then, only after Roosevelt realized that traditional solutions such as balancing the budget would be insufficient.[109] Governing around a welfare state did not fully emerge within the Democratic Party until the 1960s. In sum, as Gerring argues, pre-World War II Democrats were, from a purely ideological standpoint, rooted in a public philosophy of class-based rhetorical appeals pitting the "people" against the "interests."

Postwar Democrats

How, then, was Democratic ideology different after World War II? Most simply, a new strain of universality and solidarity emerged that was not present in the party's public philosophy before the war, and which proved to be an important and enduring feature of its popular appeals. This is not to say that everything changed. Postwar Democrats, for instance, had a similar understanding of social justice, welfare, and wealth redistribution. Yet crucial elements did change. Equality came to be associated with inclusion and formed the basis for postwar Democratic ideology. Gerring writes:

[In] the wake of World War II, the party's egalitarian agenda was broadened to include a host of social groups and political issues that did not fit neatly into the socioeconomic perspective and the masses-versus-elites dichotomy of the Populist period. Equality in the 1890s or the 1930s did not mean the same thing as equality in the 1950s and 1960s. Forsaking the shrill polemics of Bryan, the party now adopted a soothing tone and reassuring demeanor. The rhetoric of reconciliation replaced that of resentment. The all-inclusive American People subsumed the figure of the Common Man ... The organizing theme of Democratic ideology changed from an attack against special privilege to an appeal for inclusion. Party leaders rewrote the Democratic hymn-book; Populism was out, and Universalism was in.[110]

Tolerance, understanding, and inclusion became key components of the Democratic platform, which stood in stark contrast to the divisive "people versus the powerful" rhetoric that preceded it.

> politics limited the ability of a president to initiate the kind of progressive action needed in the early 1930s. As a result, Roosevelt engineered a reshuffling of American government in which the executive was at the center of the action and in a better position to direct a coherent policy agenda.

[109] Roosevelt famously asserted as much in his commencement address at Oglethorpe University in 1932: "The country needs ... persistent experimentation. It is common sense to take a method and try it: If it fails, admit it frankly and try another. But above all, try something. The millions who are in want will not stand by silently forever while the things to satisfy their needs are within easy reach." Franklin D. Roosevelt, "Oglethorpe University Address," 22 May 1932. See also: Gerring, 228.

[110] Gerring, 233.

Two specific changes in Democratic ideology – one rooted in economic policy, particularly with regard to labor issues, and one rooted in minority rights – are evident in the postwar epoch and differentiate the party's prewar and postwar eras. During the first half of the century, Democrats embraced organized labor and the working man, and rhetorically pitted them against business interests. But postwar Democrats worried less about capitalism's excesses because John Maynard Keynes and John Kenneth Galbraith persuaded them that regulatory measures were sufficient to avoid serious economic depressions.[111] Historian Alan Brinkley articulates the scope of the transformation. By the end of the war, he argues, "the concept of New Deal liberalism had assumed a new form.... [Its adherents] largely ignored the New Deal's abortive experiments in economic planning, its failed efforts to create harmonious associational arrangements, its vigorous . . . antimonopoly and regulatory crusades, its open skepticism toward capitalism and its captains, its overt celebration of the state."[112] In sum, liberal Democrats came to embrace capitalism. The lessons learned during the war, combined with previous New Deal policies, led to a dramatic softening of their prior economic views.

Also in the economic realm, organized labor became something of an electoral liability beginning in the 1950s to the extent that candidates went to great lengths to demonstrate that they were not beholden to the American Federation of Labor or the Congress of Industrial Organizations. Additionally, the party became increasingly amenable to business. As Gerring explains:

In the Populist era, Democrats had sought to portray themselves as the friends of the businessman and the upholder of capitalism; however, this position was attenuated by the party's shrill cries against the depredations of "monopoly," "big business," and "usurious" business practices. In the postwar era, the party dropped its litany of economic protest themes, and Populist-leaning candidates generally fared poorly in the candidate selection process.... Democrats' embrace of "the American capitalistic system" was, for the first time in party history, unalloyed by Jeffersonian suspicions.[113]

The party gradually reduced labor's influence, culminating in an altered method of selecting presidential candidates. By 1972, the Democratic nominee was determined by primary elections. As such, union leaders were no longer able to position themselves as powerful forces in the "smoke-filled rooms" where

---

[111] John Kenneth Galbraith, *American Capitalism* (New York: Houghton-Mifflin, 1952).

[112] Alan Brinkley, "The New Deal and the Idea of the State," *The Rise and Fall of the New Deal Order, 1930–1980*, eds., Steve Fraser and Gary Gerstle (Princeton, NJ: Princeton University Press, 1989), 109–10.

[113] Gerring, 235 and 236. Gerring argues that "only McGovern, Carter (in 1976), and Mondale integrated Populist themes into their rhetoric on a regular basis, and these occasional notes of protest were not nearly as vehement or shrill as those registered by their predecessors in the 1896–1948 period. It might also be pointed out that only one of these candidates made it to the White House," with the other two suffering overwhelming defeats. Gerring continues: "Thus, although Populists were the most successful candidates during the 1896–1948 period they were, by and large, the *least* successful candidates in the postwar period."

candidates were previously chosen.[114] Thus, the Democrats had moved from divisive pro-worker, anti-business rhetoric to a public stance of less support for organized labor coupled with less criticism of business interests. Though they certainly did not transform into pure laissez-faire free marketers, the party's postwar acceptance of business was a remarkable development.

The Democrats' ideological pivot can also clearly be seen in their shift from focusing on majority rule to emphasizing pluralism and minority rights.[115] As many have pointed out, blacks especially became a consistent feature in the party's rhetoric.[116] Of course, it should be noted that the staunchest supporters of segregation – including Harry F. Byrd, Sr., James Eastland, Sam Ervin, John Little McClellan, Richard Russell, John C. Stennis, Strom Thurmond, and even eventual convert Lyndon Johnson – all hailed from the Democratic Party. Yet, among those elements of the party supporting racial liberalism (and this became the dominant strain by at least the 1940s), Gerring's extensive content analysis yields interesting findings. Initially, Democrats, especially President Harry Truman, made an attempt to frame racial issues through the party's prewar Populist lens by painting minorities, like laborers, as oppressed common people dominated by a cabal of powerful economic elites. But by 1948, as seen in that year's convention platform, the party had adopted the new and now familiar frame of "civil rights" and "minority rights":

The Democratic Party commits itself to continuing its efforts to eradicate all racial, religious and economic discrimination. We again state our belief that racial and religious minorities must have the right to live, the right to work, the right to vote, the full and equal protection of the laws, on a basis of equality with all citizens as guaranteed by the Constitution.... We call upon Congress to support our President in guaranteeing these basic and fundamental American principles: (1) the right of full and equal political participation; (2) the right to equal opportunity of employment; (3) the right of security of person; (4) and the right of equal treatment in the service and defense of our nation.[117]

This rhetorical shift was significant. It demonstrated that these issues were group-based, rather than afflictions pertaining to the great mass of common

---

[114] James W. Ceaser, *Presidential Selection: Theory and Development* (Princeton, NJ: Princeton University Press, 1979), Chapter 5. James I. Lengle, *Representation and Presidential Primaries: The Democratic Party in the Post-Reform Era* (Westport, CT: Greenwood Press, 1981); Shafer, *Quiet Revolution: The Struggle for the Democratic Party and the Shaping of Post-Reform Politics* (New York: Russell Sage Foundation, 1983), 55–7, 78, 86–7, 92–7, 361; Graham K. Wilson, *Unions in American National Politics* (New York: St. Martin's Press, 1979), 44.

[115] Gerring, 238–45.

[116] Merle Black and George B. Rabinowitz, "American Electoral Change: 1952–1972," *The Party Symbol*, ed., William Crotty (San Francisco: W.H. Freeman, 1980); Carmines and Stimson, 115–37; Ladd, *Where Have All the Voters Gone?* (New York: W.W. Norton, 1978); Gerald M. Pomper, "From Confusion to Clarity: Issues and American Voters, 1956–1968," *American Political Science Review* 66 (1972), 28–45; Pomper, "Toward a More Responsible Two-Party System: What, Again?" *Journal of Politics* 33 (1971), 916–40; Sundquist, 382–93; Jules Witcover, *Party of the People: A History of the Democrats* (New York: Random House, 2003).

[117] "1948 Democratic Platform," *History of American Presidential Elections: 1789–1968*, vol. 4, ed., Schlesinger (New York: Chelsea House Publishers, 1971), 3154.

people. A similar group-based emphasis permeated the Democratic approach to poverty. The class-based rhetoric of Populist-era Democrats was replaced by framing poverty as an abstract "social issue" with complex causes. As Gerring puts it, "there were still victims – the poor – but no longer any victimizers" like trusts or big business.[118]

Democrats no longer saw a nation polarized between two classes: a small economic elite and the masses. The prewar notion of the common people now appeared romantic and ill-informed.[119] Rather, there existed a vast middle into which numerous minority groups did not fit, and remedies were thus required to bring them into the fold. So, while prewar Populist Democrats were focused on bringing down the small economic elite and lifting the masses, postwar Democrats focused on helping relatively small, targeted minority groups and were suspicious of the masses who held them down. Ironically, mass society – once the intended beneficiary of Democratic efforts – had come to replace the conniving economic elite as the party's target.

Gerring provides numerous examples of this new focus throughout the party's postwar epoch.[120] In addition, this change is clearly reflected in Democratic Party platforms. They frequently began to list a series of particular minority groups along with tangible actions the party or candidate pledged to take on their behalf. For instance, the 1952 platform contained specific promises to veterans, children in general, children of migrant workers in particular, American Indians, as well as racial, religious, and ethnic minorities.[121] Reaffirming most of these, the 1956 platform added farmers, the handicapped, poor children, and the elderly to the list, while the 1960 Democrats extended their reach to the mentally handicapped, the temporarily disabled, and women.[122] The party's platforms from its prewar Populist era did not reflect the laundry list approach that the Democrats adopted in the postwar era.

Gerring aptly assesses the eventual results of this group-based focus: "The multifocused Democratic agenda kept spreading outward as the decades progressed, incorporating the demands of an ever wider set of ethnic, racial, sexual, and issue-based groups. Eventually, all sorts of groups were endowed with inalienable rights."[123] The extension appeared to have reached its postmodern zenith when Democrats codified "the right to be different" and "the rights of people who lack rights" in 1972.[124] Yet the extension has continued. "The pinnacle of this help-everybody rhetoric," Gerring writes, "was reached in the party's recent embrace of multiculturalism." The 1992 platform included the

[118] Gerring, 241–5.
[119] Christopher Lasch, *The Agony of the American Left* (New York: Knopf, 1969).
[120] Gerring, 238–45.
[121] "1952 Democratic Platform," *History of American Presidential Elections: 1789–1968*, vol. 4, ed., Schlesinger, 3267–81.
[122] "1956 Democratic Platform" and "1960 Democratic Platform," *History of American Presidential Elections: 1789–1968*, vol. 4, ed., Schlesinger, 3355–85 and 3471–510.
[123] Gerring, 244.
[124] "Democratic Party Platform of 1972," *National Party Platforms, Volume II 1960–1976*, ed., Donald Bruce Johnson (Urbana, IL: University of Illinois Press, 1978), 790–1.

following provision: "As the party of inclusion, we take special pride in our country's emergence as the world's largest and most successful multiethnic, multiracial republic. We condemn anti-Semitism, racism, homophobia, bigotry and negative stereotyping of all kinds. We must help all Americans understand the diversity of our cultural heritage."[125]

These two broad factors – economic moderation and group-based minority rights – engendered a Democratic Party centered around solidarity and inclusion. While the prewar Democrats focused on class divisions within society, the postwar party focused on national unity constructed around a series of disparate groups. Gerring concludes: "Consensus, tolerance, compromise, pragmatism, and mutual understanding . . . were the ideals to which the Democratic leaders aspired, ideals that were central to the party's [postwar] weltanschauung, in which all peoples, all faiths, and all lifestyles were embraced (at least in principle)."[126] As Gerring hints, some have questioned the extent to which this new breed of Democrat has, in practice, embraced, tolerated, and understood conservative peoples, evangelical Christians, and those pursuing traditional lifestyles, but it is the party's ideological foundation that is most important here.

There is a substantial literature demonstrating that similar intraparty changes occurred following World War II throughout the democratic Western world. Otto Kirchheimer has shown that Western political parties transformed from hardened ideological entities into "postwar catch-all" organizations. In addition, like the American Democrats, these parties dropped their emphasis on class and sought to attract members throughout the entire population.[127] These results were reinforced by John Clayton Thomas's study of fifty-four political parties in twelve countries, which found "a dramatic narrowing in the scope of domestic political conflict."[128] In this comparative context, identifying the Democrats' ideological hinge point in the late 1940s makes even more sense.

The Influence of World War II on the Democratic Party's Ideological Shift

The primary question left to be addressed is how the ideology of the Democratic Party was transformed from its prewar class-based populism into postwar solidarity and inclusion. In other words, what accounts for Democrats altering

---

[125] Gerring, 245.

[126] Gerring, 250.

[127] Otto Kirchheimer, "The Transformation of the Western European Party Systems," *Political Parties and Political Development*, eds., Joseph LaPalombara and Myron Weiner (Princeton, NJ: Princeton University Press, 1966), 177–200.

[128] John Clayton Thomas, "The Decline of Ideology in Western Political Parties: A Study of Changing Policy Orientations," *Sage Professional Papers in Contemporary Political Sociology*, 06–012 (Beverly Hills, CA: Sage Publications, 1975), 46. See also: Thomas, "Ideological Trends in Western Political Parties," *Western European Party Systems: Trends and Prospects*, ed., Peter H. Merkl (New York: Free Press, 1980), 348–66.

their economic populism in favor of economic moderation and dropping their "people versus the powerful" rhetoric in favor of a group-based, minority rights approach? World War II played a major role. Most prominently, the war required national unity. Solidarity and cohesiveness were critical in facing what was arguably the nation's gravest threat. Class-based divisions were secondary in this age of all-out war and had to be transcended if the country was to be victorious. This need for national unity caused the old-style Democratic rhetoric to seem out of place and retrograde. In addition, World War II was tied in with other factors that Gerring emphasizes. Several revolved around economics, such as the long postwar period of economic growth, the rise of the middle class, the ascendancy of Keynesianism, and the declining influence of labor unions. The Democratic Party's ideological shift was also influenced by the emergence of racial politics, the lack of a challenge from the left (such as the Communist Party, Huey Long, or the Progressive Party), and the Cold War.[129] In sum, multiple factors pushed the Democratic Party toward this major ideological shift. But a critical point to be noted for present purposes is that the crisis of World War II contributed directly to the shift by compelling the party to focus on national unity. In principle, once the war ended, the Democrats could have reverted back to their Populist era ideological position. However, the complex and mutually reinforcing relationship between the war and the factors Gerring emphasizes helped solidify the change.

Wartime Solidarity. World War II's most important direct effect on the Democratic Party's ideological shift away from class-based appeals and toward solidarity and universality, arose from the necessity of unifying the country behind the war effort. The divisive appeals pitting the "common people" against the "interests" or the economic elite quickly fell out of style after Japanese bombers attacked the United States.

This rhetorical shift is reflected in the party's 1936, 1940, and 1944 platforms, and in President Roosevelt's major speeches. These electoral years offer a good base for a prewar-postwar comparison. Roosevelt ran as a sitting president in all three. The first two occurred before the United States entered World War II, though by 1940 Roosevelt thought it was very possible that the country would ultimately become involved. The 1944 contest, of course, occurred several years after the Pearl Harbor attack brought America into the war.

The 1936 Democratic platform was filled with the party's then-commonplace class warfare appeals. The document is full of pledges on behalf of "the people" and denunciations of the economic elite:

We hold this truth to be self-evident – that 12 years of Republican surrender to the dictatorship of a privileged few have been supplanted by a Democratic leadership which has returned the people themselves to the places of authority.... We shall continue to use the powers of government to end the activities of the malefactors of great wealth

---

[129] Gerring discusses these indirect factors. Gerring, 274.

who defraud and exploit the people.... We have safeguarded the thrift of our citizens by restraining those who would gamble with other peoples savings [sic].... Monopolies and the concentration of economic power... continue to be the master of the producer, the exploiter of the consumer, and the enemy of the independent operator.... The issue in this election is plain. The American people are called upon to choose between a Republican administration that has and would again regiment them in the service of privileged groups and a Democratic administration dedicated to the establishment of equal economic opportunity for all our people.[130]

Similarly, as Arthur Schlesinger, Jr., notes, President Roosevelt's 1936 campaign emphasized class-based appeals, focusing on "the economic gains his Administration had secured [and] appeals to class differences."[131] Roosevelt emphasized these themes throughout his campaign, often alternating between the two touchstones from speech to speech.[132] An address in New York City on October 31, 1936, exemplified the class-based theme:

We had to struggle with the old enemies of peace – business and financial monopoly, speculation, reckless banking, class antagonism, sectionalism, war profiteering. They had begun to consider the Government of the United States as a mere appendage to their own affairs. We know now that Government by organized money is just as dangerous as Government by organized mob... They are unanimous in their hate for me – and I welcome their hatred. I should like to have it said of my first Administration that in it the forces of selfishness and of lust for power met their match. I should like to have it said of my second Administration that in it these forces met their master.[133]

Roosevelt went on to refer to the financial elites as "tyrants" who "attack the integrity and honor of American Government itself" and "campaign against America's working people."[134] The key point here is that in the 1936 presidential campaign, the Democratic Party was emphasizing class-based differences. On one side stood the hardworking common people, and on the other, the elites seeking to exploit the less well off and greedily line their own pockets with the fruits of the working person's labor.

The 1940 Democratic platform is similar in tone and style to that of 1936. Again there is a lengthy discourse on how the Administration had worked to protect average Americans from the selfish elites. A few illustrative lines convey the theme:

We have attacked and will continue to attack unbridled concentration of economic power and the exploitation of the consumer and the investor. We have attacked the

---

[130] "Democratic Platform, 1936," *History of American Presidential Elections, 1789–1968,* vol. 3, ed., Schlesinger, 2851–6.
[131] Schlesinger, *History of American Presidential Elections, 1789–1968,* vol. 3, ed., Schlesinger, 2888.
[132] Ibid.
[133] Franklin D. Roosevelt, "Speech by President Franklin D. Roosevelt, New York, October 31, 1936," *History of American Presidential Elections, 1789–1968,* vol. 3, ed., Schlesinger, 2900–2.
[134] Ibid., 2902.

kind of banking which treated America as a colonial empire to exploit; the kind of securities business which regarded the Stock Exchange as a private gambling club for wagering other people's money; the kind of public utility holding companies which used consumers' and investors' money to suborn a free press, bludgeon legislatures and political conventions, and control elections against the interest of their customers and their security holders.[135]

In keeping with the party's standard prewar rhetoric, references to "the people" and "the average man and woman" are juxtaposed against "the selfish interest of a few" or "a privileged few" bent on "exploitation" as a means to amass "vast political empires."[136]

Roosevelt's acceptance speech to that national convention, by contrast, strikes a very different note and signals a crucial shift in the party's rhetoric. The President spends nearly the entire address discussing the war in Europe, noting that it "is not an ordinary war," that it "threatens all men everywhere," and "would of necessity deeply affect the future of this nation."[137] Given this reality, Roosevelt said he would reluctantly serve a third term. He only briefly touched on domestic politics and the party's standard class warfare theme, and did so in a remarkably less bellicose manner than had been typical:

... we have had to develop ... the answers to aspirations which had come from every State and every family in the land. ... Some of us have labeled it a wider and more equitable distribution of wealth in our land. It has included among its aims, to liberalize and broaden the control of vast industries – lodged today in the hands of a relatively small group of individuals of very great financial power. But all these definitions and labels are essentially the expression of one consistent thought. They represent a constantly growing sense of human decency, human decency throughout our nation. This sense of human decency is happily confined to no group or class. ... You find it, to a growing degree, even among those who are listed in that top group which has so much control over the industrial and financial structure of the nation.[138]

Also notable in Roosevelt's 1940 speech were his appeals for national unity. The President said, for instance: "National unity in the United States became a crying essential in the face of" Europe's turmoil. He went on to honor the sacrifice and national service of private citizens "who have placed patriotism above all else" by leaving their jobs and homes to protect the country in recent years.[139] In closing, Roosevelt referred to selfishness but not with its usual association with the rich. Rather, he used it to implore all Americans to join together in opposing the European forces fighting against freedom:

---

[135] "Democratic Platform, 1940," *History of American Presidential Elections, 1789–1968,* vol. 3, ed., Schlesinger, 2952.

[136] Ibid., 2948, 2953–4.

[137] Roosevelt, "Acceptance Speech by President Franklin D. Roosevelt, Washington, July 19, 1940," *History of American Presidential Elections, 1789–1968,* vol. 4, ed., Schlesinger, 2967–9.

[138] Ibid., 2971.

[139] Ibid., 2968.

It is the continuance of civilization as we know it versus the ultimate destruction of all that we have held dear – religion against godlessness; the ideal of justice against the practice of force; moral decency versus the firing squad; courage to speak out, and to act, versus the false lullaby of appeasement. But it has been well said that a selfish and greedy people cannot be free. The American people must decide whether these things are worth making sacrifices of money, of energy, and of self.[140]

Thus, although the 1940 Democratic platform echoed the party's standard class-based Populist themes, Roosevelt's acceptance speech focused on the war in Europe, scarcely mentioned class divisions, reached out to the economic elite, and called for national unity.

Following the December 7, 1941, Japanese attack on Pearl Harbor, national unity became central to Roosevelt's strategy for winning the war. Any lingering attachment to divisive class-based rhetoric Roosevelt might have had was quickly discarded. As Roosevelt biographer Kenneth S. Davis has demonstrated, FDR's chief worry was that the war "would be forced upon an America that remained deeply divided ideologically." As a result, his job as President "had similarities to that of Abraham Lincoln during the Civil War – the task of uniting the American people.... He must strive to make of himself the very personification of the kind of active American union that was vitally necessary, stressing the positive (all that made for union) while shunning, to the maximum possible degree, divisive words and deeds."[141] In addition, the country was swept up in patriotism, which had a unifying force, rendering class distinctions, at least temporarily, less important.[142]

Roosevelt's new focus on solidarity was evident in his annual State of the Union addresses during World War II, when he made more impassioned appeals for national unity and sought to quell domestic divisions. His 1942 State of the Union Address, for example, warned that "we must guard against divisions among ourselves."[143] Similarly, appearing before Congress one year later, Roosevelt said: "Fortunately, there are only a few Americans who place appetite above patriotism.... We Americans intend to do this great job together. In our common labors we must build and fortify the very foundation of national unity – confidence in one another."[144] FDR's 1944 State of the Union Address contained similar themes and omitted class-based denunciations – even when he detailed his new domestic economic plan, which he hoped would ultimately

---

[140] Ibid., 2973.

[141] Davis, *FDR: The War President, 1940–1943* (New York: Random House, 2000), 72, 361, 746, 756. See also: George McJimsey, *The Presidency of Franklin Delano Roosevelt* (Lawrence, KS: University of Kansas Press, 2000), 215; John E. Mueller, *War, Presidents and Public Opinion* (New York: John Wiley & Sons, Inc., 1973), 63–5, 170–1.

[142] Davis, 348–9, 361.

[143] Roosevelt, "Address to the Congress on the State of the Union, January 6, 1942," *The Public Papers and Addresses of Franklin D. Roosevelt, 1942 Volume* (New York: Harper & Row, 1950), 39.

[144] Roosevelt, "Address to the Congress on the State of the Union, January 7, 1943," *The Public Papers and Addresses of Franklin D. Roosevelt, 1943 Volume*, 28–29.

amount to a "second Bill of Rights."[145] Before the war, such a proposal would almost certainly have been accompanied by stark class-based rhetoric.

All of these speeches were devoid of anything even approaching an appeal to class differences or denunciations of an economic or political elite. In short, as far as Roosevelt was concerned, Americans were in this fight together. Winning World War II required a unified effort, and there was no room for internal divisions. This should not be a surprise. World War II was such a cataclysmic event that it completely reshuffled the American political landscape. The bitter class differences that characterized the prewar era appeared petty and unimportant when the country was faced with war against Nazism and fascism.

By 1944, the Democrats' platform was in line with Roosevelt's nomination speech four years earlier and his subsequent State of the Union addresses. There were appeals to unity and conscious efforts to display solidarity. For instance, the platform stated: "Our gallant sons are dying on land, on sea, and in the air. They do not die as Republicans. They do not die as Democrats. They die as Americans."[146] Notably, the prewar theme of helping "the people" remained, but the once constant references to a greedy oppositional elite were completely absent. The harshest class-based line stated: "We reassert our faith in competitive private enterprise, free from control by monopolies, cartels, or any arbitrary private or public authority."[147]

Similarly, Roosevelt's short 1944 acceptance speech lacked any reference to the class-based appeals seen before World War II. Rather, the President emphasized solidarity even in his brief discussion of domestic economics: "the people of the United States have transcended party affiliation, not only Democrats but also forward-looking Republicans, and millions of independent voters have turned to progressive leadership, a leadership which has sought consistently and with fair success to advance the average American citizen who had been so forgotten during the period after the last war."[148] Remarkably, that sentence about the domestic economy was the closest Roosevelt came to anything that could be construed as a class-based appeal.

Thus, Democratic platforms and President Roosevelt's key speeches from 1936 to 1944 demonstrate a profound transition in the party's rhetoric. The class-based references that marked the prewar Democratic Party had been abandoned. Of course, appeals were still made to average and working Americans

[145] Roosevelt, "Message to the Congress on the State of the Union, January 11, 1944," *The Public Papers and Addresses of Franklin D. Roosevelt, 1944 Volume*, 41. There was mention of "a noisy minority [that] maintains an uproar of demands for special favors for special groups" in 1944. Yet, as the President went on to explain, this was largely geared toward those who had grown complacent and did not think further sacrifice was necessary. This "minority" cut across class divides. In short, Roosevelt was not making a class-based distinction here.

[146] "Democratic Platform, 1944," *History of American Presidential Elections, 1789–1968*, vol. 4, ed., Schlesinger, 3040.

[147] Ibid., 3041.

[148] Roosevelt, "Acceptance Speech by President Franklin D. Roosevelt, San Diego, July 20, 1944," *History of American Presidential Elections, 1789–1968*, vol. 4, ed., Schlesinger, 3062.

but, crucially, the harsh denunciations of the "interests" and the "powerful" were dropped entirely. In their place were statements emphasizing solidarity and national unity. Gerring suggests that the prewar "people versus the powerful" rhetoric characterized the Democratic Party until at least 1948. But interestingly, the only Roosevelt speech Gerring cites after the United States entered the war does not support this assertion. In response to Republican accusations that communist sympathizers held posts in his Administration, Roosevelt said: "This form of fear propaganda is not new among rabble rousers and fomenters of class hatred."[149] Gerring's reliance on this quote to bridge the gap between 1941 and 1948, then, is curious because it is starkly different from the kind of class-based appeals prewar Democrats made. Rather than speaking to the majority of average Americans by attacking a selfish and powerful elite, Roosevelt here seems to have been accusing Republicans of engaging in divisive class warfare.

In sum, World War II marked the crucial hinge point in Democratic ideology with regard to class antagonisms. The war changed the domestic political landscape and the Democrats responded, altering their rhetoric in crucial ways. Appeals to class tensions were out. National unity and solidarity were in. In the aftermath of Pearl Harbor and in the subsequent years of military conflict, class warfare simply did not resonate. In a similar vein, others have noted that overt efforts were undertaken to increase unity across ethnic lines and reduce divisive nativism.[150] Nationalism and patriotism were the order of the day. Although class distinctions remained during these years, the country "rallied around the flag."[151] Class-based appeals have never fully melted away from the Democrats' public philosophy (think of Truman in 1948, Gore in 2000, or Edwards in 2008), but they have not returned to claim the central, dominant role they played in the party's prewar ideology.

Economic Factors. Overlooking World War II-related solidarity, Gerring identifies several economic factors (in addition to other influences discussed in the next section) in explaining the Democratic party's ideological shift. Specifically, he asserts that economic growth, the rise of the middle class, the triumph of Keynesianism, and the sagging influence of labor unions induced the

---

[149] Gerring, 198.

[150] Fleegler, "Theodore G. Bilbo and the Decline of Public Racism, 1938–1947," 1–28.

[151] Mueller, "Presidential Popularity from Truman to Johnson," *American Political Science Review* 64 (1970), 18–34; Mueller, *War, Presidents and Public Opinion*; Richard W. Steele, "The War on Intolerance: The Reformulation of American Nationalism," *Journal of American Ethnic History* 9 (Fall 1989), 9–35; Richard Polenberg, *One Nation Divisible* (New York: Viking, 1980), 46–9; John Blum, *V Was for Victory* (New York: Harcourt Brace Jovanovich, 1976), 147–72; Philip Gleason, *Speaking of Diversity: Language and Ethnicity in Twentieth Century America* (Baltimore, MD: Johns Hopkins University Press, 1992), 153–87; Eric Foner, *The Story of American Freedom* (New York: W.W. Norton, 1998), 237–9; David H. Bennett, *Party of Fear: The American Far Right From Nativism to the Militia Movement* (Chapel Hill, NC: University of North Carolina Press, 1995), 285.

transformation. These factors were undeniably important in the Democrats' shift, but it is worth noting that the war itself was a contributing and reinforcing factor in these very economic changes. The war served, along with the economic considerations Gerring emphasizes, to ensure that the party's ideological shift endured when, in principle, it might have reverted to its earlier Populist style.

The prewar Democratic focus on a "people versus the powerful" rhetorical style is much more likely to be successful in an era of vast economic inequality or a period of economic hardship. Before the war, such appeals had obvious constituencies: first, poor laborers who worked hard under difficult conditions and then, after 1929, victims of the country's worst-ever economic depression. After the war, the burgeoning and dominant middle class of the late 1940s – fueled by the GI Bill – combined with the period's humming economy, gave class-based rhetoric less salience.[152] To have broad-based appeal, such rhetoric would have required the endorsement of the freshly constituted middle class, yet this demographic had new concerns of its own. As a result, the fierce class-based speech of the prewar Democrats fell on deaf ears. The natural audience for this message had dissipated.

These developments were reinforced by the Democrats' adoption of Keynesianism, the economic theory of maintaining a market-based economy augmented by governmental policies geared toward promoting consumption, increasing employment, and stimulating business. Although this embrace signaled the collapse of the hotly contested doctrine of pure laissez-faire economics, it also put the party in a position of defending the market economy. As David Kennedy writes, "if earlier liberals conceived of the economy as a mechanism that needed fixing, the Keynesians thought of the economy as an organism that needed feeding but that otherwise should be left to its own devices."[153] The adoption of Keynesianism, then, shifted the Democratic Party's view of economics in general and of the government's role in the economy in particular. Obviously, the full adoption of Keynes's theories was related to the strong economic growth and the growing middle class it helped produce. It was also tied to the beginning of the end for organized labor.[154]

Labor unions continued a long, slow decline in influence in the postwar era. Organized labor had suffered during World War II because of, among other factors, limits on strikes and internal divisions within the labor movement. Then, following the war, passage of the Taft-Hartley Act in 1947, along with

---

[152] On the GI Bill, see, for instance: Suzanne Mettler, "Bringing the State Back in to Civic Engagement: Policy Feedback Effects of the G.I. Bill for World War II Veterans," *American Political Science Review* 96:2 (2002), 351–65; Mettler, *Soldiers to Citizens: The G.I. Bill and the Making of the Greatest Generation* (New York: Oxford University Press, 2005); Edward Humes, *Over Here: How the G.I. Bill Transformed America* (New York: Harcourt, 2006); Glenn Altschuler and Stuart Blumin, *The G.I. Bill: The New Deal for Veterans* (New York: Oxford University Press, 2009).

[153] Kennedy, 359–60.

[154] Gerring, 233–8.

the growing economy and emergence of a strong middle class (which made the bill viable), all contributed to labor's dwindling power. Historian Nelson Lichtenstein places the turning point between 1946 and 1948, when the union movement's attempts to shape the postwar economy were stopped by business interests, that by then had become at ease with Democrats. "Labor's ambitions were thereafter sharply curbed, and its economic program was reduced to a sort of militant interest group politics, in which a Keynesian emphasis on sustained growth and productivity gain-sharing replaced labor's earlier commitment to economic planning and social solidarity."[155] The salient point that emerges is that the above-referenced economic factors were all intimately tied together. The growing economy and resulting middle class moderated Democrats' suspicion of capitalism and led them to buy into America's market economy – albeit with their New Deal modifications. In addition, the economy's vitality proved the feasibility of, and validated the Democrats' adoption of, Keynesianism. And the party's newly adopted Keynesian policies limited its commonalities with organized labor. These developments, in turn, led to labor's slip.

These related economic factors clearly played a role in the Democratic Party's new ideological makeup. Notably, though, World War II contributed to and reinforced these economic developments. Most economists and historians maintain that the war played an important role in ending the Great Depression and creating the ensuing strong economy.[156] They argue that the

---

[155] Nelson Lichtenstein, "From Corporatism to Collective Bargaining: Organized Labor and the Eclipse of Social Democracy in the Postwar Era," *The Rise and Fall of the New Deal Order, 1930–1980*, eds., Fraser and Gerstle, 122–3. See also, Gerring, 233–8. For more on American labor in the 1940s, see, for instance: Irving Bernstein, *Turbulent Years: A History of the American Worker, 1933–1941* (Boston: Houghton-Mifflin, 1970); Melvyn Dubofsky, *American Labor Since the New Deal* (Chicago: Quadrangle, 1971); Walter Galenson, *The American Labor Movement, 1955–1995* (Westport, CT: Greenwood Press, 1996); Michael Goldfield, *The Decline of Organized Labor in the United States* (Chicago: University of Chicago Press, 1989); Robert Zieger, *American Workers, American Unions* (Baltimore, MD: Johns Hopkins University Press, 1986).

[156] See, for example, Michael A. Bernstein, *The Great Depression* (New York: Cambridge University Press, 1971), 207; John Morton Blum, *V was for Victory: Politics and American Culture During World War II* (New York: Harcourt, Brace, Jovanovich, 1976), 90–1; Tyler Cowen, "Why Keynesianism Triumphed or, Could So Many Keynesians Have Been Wrong?," *Critical Review* 3 (1989), 525–6; Stanley Lebergott, *The Americans: An Economic Record* (New York: W.W. Norton, 1984), 472 and 477; Seymour Melman, *The Permanent War Economy: American Capitalism in Decline* (New York: Simon & Schuster, 1985), 15–6 and 19; Albert W. Niemi, Jr., *U.S. Economic History* (Chicago: Rand McNally, 1980), 390; Richard Polenberg, *War and Society: The United States, 1941–45* (Westport, CT: Greenwood Press, 1980), 36; Robert C. Puth, *American Economic History* (Chicago: Dryden Press, 1988), 521 and 531–2; Stein, *The Fiscal Revolution in America* 169–70; Harold G. Vatter, *The U.S. Economy in World War II* (New York: Columbia University Press, 1985), 14; J.R. Vernon, "World War II Fiscal Policies and the End of the Great Depression," *Journal of Economic History* 54:4 (1994), 850–68; Gary M. Walton and Hugh Rockoff, *History of the American Economy*, 6th ed. (San Diego: Harcourt, Brace, Jovanovich, 1990), 520, 523–4, and 535; Allan M. Winkler, *Home*

Keynesian-inspired massive federal spending galvanized the economy with multiplied effects on the civilian sector. As a result, they contend, the nation reached
full employment and increased GNP and personal consumption, and out of all
this a strong middle class emerged. Economist Herbert Stein is representative
of this camp. He notes that prior to the war, the nation was perpetually mired
in stagnation and permanent deficits with no easy solutions. In addition, there
were still 10 million people unemployed and there was no prospect that private
investment could significantly mitigate the problem. But "the war changed all
of that dramatically." Full employment became a reality; the issue of secular
stagnation was put to rest; businessmen became involved in federal economic
policy; the federal debt, enormous budgets, and the pay-as-you-go tax system
were erased; and opposing economic factions were able to unite behind the
war effort. "All of this," Stein writes, "came about primarily as a result of
conditions created coincidentally and accidentally by the war."[157]

A smaller group of scholars contend World War II's influence on the economic recovery was less profound than is generally thought. None contend that
it played no role, only that it was not the sole cause. Kennedy, for instance, says
the war worked in tandem with the New Deal. "[T]he New Deal petered out in
1938.... [Full economic] recovery awaited not the release of more New Deal
energies but the unleashing of the dogs of war.... When the war brought... a
recovery that inaugurated the most prosperous quarter century America has
ever known, it brought it to an economy and a country that the New Deal had
fundamentally altered."[158] Economists J. Bradford de Long and Lawrence H.
Summers offer a stronger prewar argument. Utilizing pre- and postwar output data, they maintain that 80 percent of the economic recovery had already
taken place by 1942. To the extent this is true, "it is hard to attribute any of
the pre-1942 catch-up of the economy to the war" – although, as De Long
and Summers acknowledge, one could argue that Roosevelt began wartime
mobilization well before the Pearl Harbor attack formally drew the United
States into the war.[159] Still another view is offered by economist Robert Higgs,
who argues that the major shift occurred not prior to (or as a result of) World
War II, but in its immediate aftermath. While the war did push the economy
out of the Depression, it did so indirectly. "Certain events of the war years –
the buildup of financial wealth and especially the transformation of expectations – justify an interpretation that views the war as an event that recreated

Front U.S.A.: America During World War II (Arlington Heights, IL: H. Davidson, 1986), 14
and 20.

[157] Stein, *The Fiscal Revolution in America*, 169–70.

[158] Kennedy, 363.

[159] J. Bradford de Long and Lawrence H. Summers, "How Does Macroeconomic Policy Affect
Output?," *Brookings Papers on the Economic Activity* 19:2 (1988), 433–94, quote on 467.
For similar accounts see: Christina D. Romer, "What Ended the Great Depression?," *The
Journal of Economic History* 52:4 (1992), 757–84, see especially pg. 782; Peter Temin, "The
Great Depression," *The Cambridge Economic History of the United States*, eds., Stanley L.
Engerman and Robert E. Gallman (New York: Cambridge University Press, 2000), 328.

the possibility of genuine economic recovery. As the war ended, real prosperity returned."[160] Thus, Higgs argues that the war ended the Great Depression but in a roundabout way. Rather than the war bringing the economic downturn to an end as most scholars contend, the conflict induced a postwar boom from 1946 to 1949.[161] Clearly, then, there is disagreement over the role World War II played in ending the Great Depression and initiating a strong economy. The timing of these effects is also contested. But the important point to note here is that the war and the economy were, in one way or another, related and mutually reinforcing with regard to the influence they had on the Democratic Party's ideology.

In addition, the war was entangled with the Keynesian triumph and its embrace by Democrats. Economist Tyler Cowen writes: "The onset of the war brought significant increases in demand and government spending, and eventually, government control over investment – precisely what Keynes had recommended."[162] As a consequence, instead of merely pointing out the inequalities and downfalls associated with a pure market economy, Democrats were now in a position of supporting the economic system. As Alan Brinkley puts it, "Keynes's economic doctrines ... suggested ways to introduce in peacetime the kinds of stimuli that had created the impressive wartime expansion. They offered, in fact, an escape from one of liberalism's most troubling dilemmas and a mechanism for which reformers had long been groping. They provided a way to manage the economy without directly challenging the prerogatives of capitalists."[163] That is, the war experience demonstrated that governmental intervention in the private sector was extremely complicated and at some point became unnecessary. In addition, it showed that vast new regulatory functions were not required either. Rather, indirect economic oversight through monetary and fiscal "levers" combined with a moderate welfare state was sufficient. These initiatives were no longer viewed as temporary solutions to stem the flow until a more fundamental solution was settled on. Instead, these measures had become the solution. The renewed wartime faith in economic growth, Brinkley continues, led to "several ideological conclusions of considerable importance to the future of liberalism. It helped relegitimize American capitalism [amongst those] who had developed serious doubts about its viability.... It robbed the 'regulatory' reform ideas ... of their urgency and gave credence instead to Keynesian ideas."[164]

These factors contributed directly to labor's initial decline. While the war did not directly induce labor's less prominent position in the Democratic Party, it did directly contribute to these main factors for labor's diminished position.

[160] Robert Higgs, "Wartime Prosperity? A Reassessment of the U.S. Economy in the 1940s," *The Journal of Economic History* 52:1 (1992), 58.

[161] Ibid., 41.

[162] Cowen, 525.

[163] Brinkley, "The New Deal and the Idea of the State," 108–9.

[164] Ibid., 109.

The party's adoption of Keynesianism, the strong economy, and a burgeoning middle class – all of which the war played a role in creating and cultivating – gave labor's appeals to the American working class less credibility.

In sum, while the economic changes that Gerring identified clearly played key causal roles in the Democratic party's ideological shift at the end of the 1940s, World War II just as clearly contributed to and reinforced those developments.

Other Factors. At least three other factors – the emergence of racial politics, the lack of a leftist challenge, and Cold War anticommunism – also played an indirect role in the Democratic Party's postwar ideological shift.[165] Yet, like the economic considerations, these factors were also intertwined with the war in important ways. And the fact that race played an important role in altering the Democrats' ideological position was all the more notable for a party that had traditionally been rooted in white supremacy. Civil rights did not fit comfortably into the Democrats' old majoritarian ideology. Rather, it was a new issue requiring the extension of new rights to a targeted minority group. The party's adoption of the issue spurred it to identify other groups in need of rights extensions.[166] Like the economic factors, though, civil rights did not emerge out of thin air. Although the new attention to civil rights on the national agenda and in the Democratic Party's ideology clearly had multiple propellants, African American involvement in the war reinforced its emergence. As discussed earlier, the black community's contribution to the war effort spurred a new intellectual environment that was more sympathetic to race issues. In addition, the war galvanized the black community to organize itself by developing some of the key groups that would lead the Civil Rights Movement in coming decades.

Along the same lines, the lack of a significant challenge from the left was at least partially a consequence of the economic factors addressed above. Before the war, there was no shortage of left-wing challengers, including the Union Party, Huey Long, the American Labor Party, and the Communist Party. The strong postwar economy and developing middle class limited the constituency to which such leftists could easily appeal.

Another factor in the Democrats' ideological shift was Cold War anticommunism. It, too, was partially linked to the war. As Kennedy asserts, "World War II led directly to the Cold War and ended a century and a half of American isolationism."[167] Indeed, the war initiated an ongoing era of involvement in international relations. Much of the U.S. desire to stay engaged in world affairs emanated out of the war. Because the war affected the United States

---

[165] Gerring notes each of these: 251–3, 274. He also suggests television played a role. The postwar (but apparently pre-Bill O'Reilly) "shift from 'hot' stump speaking to the 'cool' medium of television – mandating a softer, more personal, more conciliatory brand of rhetoric" – was also behind the Democrats' ideological shift according to Gerring. This factor was not related to the war.

[166] Gerring, 253.

[167] Kennedy, 855.

so profoundly and in so many ways, the country sought to do everything in its power to minimize the chances of a similar future war. It laid plans for a world deliberative body similar to Wilson's rejected League of Nations. In addition, the United States sought not only to rebuild benign versions of Germany and Japan, but also to export the ideology of democracy and capitalism. In short, the war changed America's position in, and view of, the world. A widespread consensus developed that authoritarianism had to be confronted lest a Hitler-like figure be allowed to emerge again.[168]

World War II also changed the Soviet Union. For starters, the war was felt much more deeply in the USSR than in the United States. The Soviet Union was left in ruins with roughly 27 million fatalities – 90 times the number of American dead. Joseph Stalin emerged from the war, like his U.S. counterparts, determined to avoid another conflict on that scale. He also felt the USSR was entitled to compensation for its wartime losses but, because of its devastation, the country was in no position to unilaterally take what it wanted. There was, however, a silver lining from Stalin's perspective. Steeped in Marxist-Leninist ideology, he believed capitalism was bound to destroy itself. Stalin thought that once the war ended, Britain and the United States would have no further reason to cooperate, and capitalism's inherent flaws would emerge and plunge its practitioners into another depression. At that point, Stalin theorized, the Soviets could take over Europe as Hitler had amidst squabbling capitalists in the aftermath of World War I.[169]

Thus, the postwar world sported the newly, but fully, engaged United States, on the one hand, as the planet's leading champion of freedom, and, on the other, a devastated, but entitled, Soviet Union as the most authoritarian nation on Earth biding its time for its rightful ascension over all of Europe. In this sense, World War II was very much at the root of the Cold War world that developed in its aftermath. It is difficult to know if this ideological confrontation would have eventually emerged without World War II because those years shaped both countries in ways that made the Cold War so much more likely, if not unavoidable. Admittedly, this tie is indirect. And admittedly, the Cold War itself influenced Democratic ideology. Nonetheless, World War II played a role in setting the stage for this superpower confrontation.

This new international climate – which reinforced domestic anticommunism in the United States – had reverberations on the Democrats' ideological repositioning. Gerring succinctly writes: "it is difficult to overestimate the effects of the Cold War, which helped marginalize the left and legitimate the right; which seemed to vindicate the (Republican) perspective that statism, not individualism, was the primary enemy of the American public; and which granted foreign

---

[168] See, for instance: John Lewis Gaddis, *The Cold War: A New History* (New York: The Penguin Press, 2005), 5–47.

[169] Ibid., 10–4.

policy an ascendance over domestic policy that it had rarely enjoyed."[170] This consideration – along with the economic factors – may also help explain why Republicans enjoyed relative ideological stability in this period of Democratic flux.

It was this powerful anticommunist sentiment in the wake of World War II that created such a difficult environment for labor (and leftists in general) and provided yet another reason for its marginalization. Anticommunist rhetoric became an animating point for Democrats following the war. Preventing communism from taking hold on the homefront was of particular concern.[171] Typical of this new mindset was Democratic presidential nominee Adlai Stevenson's 1952 acceptance speech:

I suggest that we would err, certainly, if we regarded communism as merely an external threat. Communism is a great international conspiracy and the United States has been for years a major target.... Communist agents have sought to steal our scientific and military secrets, to mislead and corrupt our young men and women, to infiltrate positions of power in our schools and colleges, in business firms and in labor unions and in the Government itself. At every turn they have sought to serve the purposes of the Soviet Union.... Along the way they have gained the help, witting or unwitting, of many Americans.... I fear there are still people in our country under illusions about the nature of this conspiracy abroad and at home.... Communism is committed to the destruction of every value which the genuine American liberal holds most dear. So I would say to any Americans who cling to illusions about communism and its fake utopia: Wake up to the fact that you are in an alliance with the devil.[172]

The key point here is that communism and socialism had become public enemy number one for the Democrats. And organized labor – perhaps unfairly, but nonetheless – paid a price. In stark contrast to their prewar stance, the private sector became a point of pride for Democrats, and they distanced themselves from labor. As Stevenson said later in his campaign: "We are for private, and profitable, business. The Democratic Party is against socialism in our life in any form – creeping, crawling or even the imaginary kind which shows up so often in the Republican oratory. I am opposed to socialized medicine, socialized farming, socialized banking, or socialized industry."[173] Although he did not single out labor, the implication was unavoidable: The Democratic Party was not going to support much of the action that labor sought. This development was a striking departure from the party's prewar position. Thus, this new anticommunist focus played a role in labor's demise along with Keynesianism, the strong economy, and the burgeoning middle class.

---

[170] Gerring, 274.

[171] Ibid., 251–53.

[172] "Speech by Governor Adlai E. Stevenson, Albuquerque, September 12, 1952," *History of American Presidential Elections, 1789–1968*, vol. 4, ed., Schlesinger, 3308–9.

[173] Gerring, 252.

CONCLUSION

World War II was a transformative event for the world. Yet the political science literature largely overlooks several of the war's key domestic ramifications in the United States. The state's financing system added on to its World War I development with the establishment of a mass-based, progressive income tax to meet the funding needs of this new global conflict. As in many other major wars, this element of state building was initiated to address a specific crisis, but the new regulatory and institutional structure endured. In addition, World War II brought major advances for African Americans, whose wartime service and sacrifice bolstered claims for full citizenship. Voting rights were extended in the Soldier Voting Act of 1942 and in the U.S. Supreme Court's *Smith v. Allwright* decision in 1944.

African American civil rights advances are often mistakenly remembered as part of the New Deal. But voting rights and the gradual integration of the armed forces appeared on the national agenda after the New Deal, were sparked by the war, and actually came to comprise Harry Truman's Fair Deal program. It was the contributions that blacks made to the war effort that provided a compelling reason to start the several decades-long project of addressing systemic and systematic discrimination.

Finally, the war had a profound effect on the Democratic Party's ideology. Like other major wars, this conflict upended politics in the United States. As a result, Democrats were forced to reposition themselves to maintain their majority status. The party's prewar class-based populism was discarded in favor of a new message based around solidarity and inclusion, with appeals to targeted demographic groups. These postwar Democrats were more economically conservative. In addition, they focused on minority rights as a means of inclusion and abandoned their old rhetoric trumpeting class warfare. World War II was a key influence in this shift. It directly created an environment requiring national unity, which discredited divisive class-based appeals. The war also influenced and reinforced other factors explaining the Democrats' ideological shift including economic growth, a developing middle class, Keynesianism, the decline of organized labor, the emergence of racial politics, the absence of a leftist challenge, and the Cold War.

5

The Forgotten War

Korea is known as "the forgotten war" for several reasons. First, and most obviously, it followed closely on the heels of World War II and seemed less important by comparison. Far fewer Americans served in Korea than in Europe or the South Pacific, and the stakes were lower. In addition, there were, relatively speaking, few American deaths. Another contributing factor is probably the war's conclusion – a frustrating stalemate that essentially reestablished the prewar status quo. And finally, Korea has been overshadowed by Vietnam, the other "hot" conflict of the Cold War era. The United States simply did not go through the domestic, societal, and political upheaval during the Korean years that it did during Vietnam.

Nonetheless, there are at least three important domestic developments that were clear outgrowths of the Korean War. First, like other wars, Korea had ramifications for the American state. Specifically, the federal government instituted – and paid for – a vast national security state. This expansion ranged from the establishment of new bureaucracies, to the initiation of federal aid for higher education. In addition, the military draft offered the state an easy source of personnel and regimented American life for years after the war ended. The office of the presidency also gained new powers to control the state's broad military-related capacities at Congress's expense. Second, and also like other major U.S. wars, Korea brought about an extension of new democratic rights to a marginalized group that contributed to the war effort. In this instance, African American wartime service prompted the military's full desegregation. And third, domestic electoral and party politics hinged on the war, as is evident in the 1952 presidential campaign.

Of course, the conflict in Korea took place within the context of the Cold War. Attributing certain effects to the hostilities in Korea and other effects to the larger Cold War is sometimes difficult; nonetheless, the aim here is to do just that. Every effort is made to tease out the independent effects of the "hot war" in Korea. In other words, this chapter highlights effects that are directly attributable to Korea – not simply those domestic effects wrought by the larger, decades-long ideological conflict.

Beyond the domestic ramifications, the Korean War merits close examination today because it is increasingly compared to the conflict in Iraq. Former Bush Administration officials hopefully point to Korea, and President Harry S. Truman's resurrection in the eyes of historians over the past few decades as compelling analogies. Critics of George W. Bush and his war prefer to cite Vietnam, the next chapter's subject. Many of the claims on both sides are rooted in little more than cherry-picked conjecture. A more serious and thorough examination of the domestic ramifications of the Korean War (and Vietnam) is warranted.

THE KOREAN WAR IN BRIEF

At the end of World War II, the Russians were planning to invade the Japanese-controlled Korean peninsula from the North, and the Americans were poised to strike from the South. With Japanese Emperor Hirohito's surrender, both armies moved in with ease. Moscow and Washington agreed to split the peninsula into temporarily occupied territories at the 38th parallel until a unified Korean government was created, after which all foreign troops would leave. Although the American and Soviet armies did withdraw by 1949, no unification occurred. The democratic Republic of Korea, backed by the United Nations and the United States, was established in the South and the USSR-supported Democratic People's Republic of Korea took control of the North, both claiming to be the Korean people's rightful government.

With Joseph Stalin's blessing, North Korea invaded the Republic on June 25, 1950.[1] Cold War historian John Lewis Gaddis aptly assesses the invasion's profound influence on the American psyche. The surprise attack, he writes, "was almost as great a shock as the one on Pearl Harbor . . . and its consequences for Washington's strategy were at least as profound. South Korea in and of itself was of little importance . . . but the fact that it had been invaded so blatantly – across . . . a boundary sanctioned by the United Nations – appeared to challenge

---

[1] There is an extensive literature on the Korean War and the encompassing Cold War. Historians John Lewis Gaddis, Melvyn P. Leffler, and Walter LaFeber offer a representative sampling: John Lewis Gaddis, *The Cold War: A New History* (New York: Penguin Press, 2005); Gaddis, *We Now Know: Rethinking Cold War History* (New York: Oxford University Press, 1997); Gaddis, *The Long Peace* (New York: Oxford University Press, 1987); Gaddis, *Strategies of Containment: A Critical Appraisal of American National Security Policy During the Cold War* (New York: Oxford University Press, 1982); Melvyn P. Leffler, *The Specter of Communism: The United States and the Origins of the Cold War, 1917–1953* (New York: Hill and Wang, 1994); Leffler, *A Preponderance of Power: National Security, the Truman Administration, and the Cold War* (Stanford, CA: Stanford University Press, 1991); Walter LaFeber, *America, Russia, and the Cold War, 1945–2006*, 9th ed. (New York: McGraw-Hill, 2002).

the entire structure of postwar collective security."[2] President Truman ordered U.S. troops, in coordination with U.N. forces, to support the Republic's army. The U.S.-U.N. contingent narrowly staved off defeat in the South in September, and then proceeded to nearly beat the North Koreans in October while pushing their forces to the brink of the Chinese border at the Yalu River. In another dramatic twist, the U.S.-U.N. contingent was then attacked by China's army at the end of November and, by January of 1951, had been driven back well below the 38th parallel. China's entry was precipitated by concerns in Beijing that U.S.-U.N. forces would continue their advance into the People's Republic of China. After two more years of fighting to a standoff, all sides agreed to an armistice in July of 1953 that established a boundary between North and South Korea at a nearly identical location as three years before. More than 36,000 Americans died, as did 600,000 Chinese and 2 million Korean troops and civilians.

BUILDING A NATIONAL SECURITY STATE

The Korean War prompted another round of state building in America. Like World War I and World War II, money was needed to support the military action. Yet in addition to these typical war-induced costs, the Korean conflict saw the development of a vast national security state. Much of this development had been proposed and discussed in the early Cold War years, prior to fighting on the Korean peninsula. But it was only the outbreak of another hot war that actually brought about significant action.

Cold War National Security before Korea: Cautious Concern

Following World War II, many wanted to demilitarize and revert back to the prewar isolationist status quo. Scholars such as Alfred de Grazia argued that the increasingly executive-centered government led to an expansion of state capacities, and that the United States needed a return to congressional authority to preserve liberty.[3] This widespread sentiment for reducing government made the establishment of a permanent national security state – and its widespread acceptance – much more remarkable.

At the same time, widespread perceptions of a Soviet-centered communist threat provoked new national security concerns in Washington. As early as July of 1946, Truman was concerned enough to instruct White House Counsel Clark Clifford and his assistant George Elsey to study the situation and report back. Their product, entitled "American Relations with the Soviet Union," was

---

[2] Gaddis, *The Cold War: A New History*, 42–3.
[3] Alfred de Grazia, *Republic in Crisis: Congress Against the Executive Force* (New York: Federal Legal Publications, Inc., 1965). See also: James Burnham, *Congress and the American Tradition* (New York: Gateway Editions, 1959).

ahead of the rest of the political establishment in concluding that the Soviet Union was the greatest threat facing the U.S. The report determined Soviet leaders were engaged in "aggressive militaristic imperialism" and were:

increasing their military power and the sphere of Soviet influence in preparation for the "inevitable" conflict [with the capitalist West], and they are trying to weaken and subvert their potential opponents by every means at their disposal. So long as these men adhere to these beliefs, it is highly dangerous to conclude that hope of international peace lies only in "accord," "mutual understanding," or "solidarity" with the Soviet Union.[4]

The report's recommendations for dealing with the USSR included military preparedness, a confinement strategy, and assistance to any democratic countries under Soviet threat. Although Clifford and Elsey's position would come to represent mainstream Washington thought several years later, in this period prior to the Korean War, Truman thought the report was too "hot" and ordered that no copies be distributed outside the Oval Office.[5]

Ensuing years saw numerous Cold War crises, culminating in 1950 with several key incidents. In 1947, the Truman Doctrine was proclaimed and the Marshall Plan was announced, both of which established an active and confrontational stance toward communism. Later that year, the National Security Act of 1947 centralized the armed services and the intelligence community by creating the Department of Defense and the Central Intelligence Agency, respectively. One year later, the USSR established a blockade on goods entering West Berlin and, in response, the Berlin airlift began. In further response to the Soviet threat, the North Atlantic Treaty Organization was created in 1949. By 1950, concerns about the Soviet Union were widespread within the U.S. federal government as well as in the general public. Four major events induced this heightened unease: In September of 1949, Truman announced the Soviets had developed an atomic bomb, thus shattering the security Americans felt as the lone nuclear power; Communist Party leader Mao Zedong formed the People's Republic of China in October of 1949 after defeating the nationalist government led by Chiang Kai-shek; in January of 1950, former State Department official Alger Hiss was convicted of perjury after denying under oath that he had spied for the USSR; and, in that same month, it was revealed that British scientist Klaus Fuchs had leaked the secret of the atomic bomb to the Soviets.[6] Taken together, these events generated a perception of communism on the move and western democracy on the defensive. The result was increased

---

[4] Clark Clifford and George Elsey, "American Relations with the Soviet Union: A Report to the President by the Special Council to the President" (24 Sept. 1946), *Containment: Documents on American Policy and Strategy, 1945–1950*, eds., Thomas H. Etzold and Gaddis (New York: Columbia University Press, 1978), 64–5.

[5] McCullough, 543–5.

[6] There is some debate over how helpful Fuchs's information actually was to the Soviets. See: Robert Chadwell Williams, *Klaus Fuchs: Atom Spy* (Cambridge, MA: Harvard University Press, 1987).

concern over, and discussion of, national security. There was, however, no military buildup. So, while these developments caused increased alarm, they did little else. Expenditures remained stable and no national security buildup was undertaken.[7]

This new environment provided a launching pad for Senator Joseph McCarthy and his well-known efforts to expose "card-carrying" communists.[8] Though McCarthy is remembered as the era's icon, political scientist Nelson W. Polsby demonstrated that McCarthy's rhetorical bark far exceeded his electoral bite. The Wisconsin Republican never had extensive grassroots support and, with the exception of certain circles within the GOP, was not held in high regard.[9] In this sense, then, McCarthy offers an exaggerated characterization of the era. His heightened concern over national security and communism was reflective of the country's growing unease, but his crusading paranoia was far outside the mainstream.

Less remembered yet more indicative of the nation's mood, was a *Life* magazine issue exploring the apparent Soviet military supremacy. Entitled, "War can come. Will we be ready?," this series of stories demonstrated how the United States came up short on nearly every measure of military comparison. One piece asked "How badly off are our Army, Navy and Air Force?" The answers were not encouraging: "We have some good planes but not enough of them;" the U.S. is "vastly outnumbered," has "moth-ball ships," and a "skimpy" defense system. All of this led to the conclusion that "The Reds, Whose War Production Far Outstrips Ours, Might Base Strategy on a Quick Knockout."[10]

Some government officials were also concerned, as reflected in a report known as NSC-68. In April of 1950 Paul Nitze, aide to Secretary of State Dean Acheson, wrote what Cold War historian Melvyn Leffler calls "one of the most significant studies of the entire Cold War era."[11] National Security Council Paper No. 68 resembled Clifford and Elsey's 1946 report but went further. Nitze's document asserted that:

the Soviet Union, unlike previous aspirants to hegemony, is animated by a new fanatic faith, antithetical to our own, and seeks to impose its absolute authority over the rest of the world.... The issues that face us are momentous, involving the fulfillment or

---

[7] Michael Edelstein, "War and the American Economy in the Twentieth Century," *The Cambridge Economic History of the United States, Volume III: The Twentieth Century*, eds. Stanley L. Engerman and Robert E. Gallman (New York: Cambridge University Press, 2000), 371–2.

[8] Much has been written about McCarthy. See, for instance: Richard H. Rovere, *Senator Joe McCarthy* (Berkeley: University of California Press, 2005(reprint)); Fred J. Cook, *The Nightmare Decade: The Life and Times of Senator Joe McCarthy* (New York: Random House, 1971); Arthur Herman, *Joseph McCarthy: Reexamining the Life and Legacy of America's Most Hated Senator* (New York: Free Press, 1999).

[9] Nelson W. Polsby, "Towards an Explanation of McCarthyism," *Political Studies* 8 (Oct. 1962), 250–71.

[10] "War Can Come; Will We be Ready?" *Life* 28:9 (27 Feb. 1950), 19–31.

[11] Leffler, *A Preponderance of Power*, 313.

destruction not only of this Republic but of civilization itself.... [T]his government and the people it represents must now take new and fateful decisions.[12]

Specific recommendations called for developing hydrogen bombs, expanding the military establishment, building an alliance system throughout the free world, undercutting the Soviet Union at home, and increasing taxes to fund these initiatives.[13]

Truman biographer David McCullough contends its "apocalyptic theme" was "intended to shock."[14] Acheson's memoir bolsters that assessment. He recalled that rather than present "a clinic in political science's latest, most fashionable, and most boring study . . . the purpose of NSC-68 was to . . . bludgeon" the government into adopting the measures the report advocated.[15]

Indeed, NSC-68, like the Clifford-Elsey report four years before, still represented only the hardliners in the administration as epitomized by Acheson. Those outside his circle, including the State Department's foremost Russian expert and "the father of containment," George Kennan, found the report ultimately unconvincing. In his view, the USSR at the time did not appear to be the aggressive behemoth Nitze outlined. Many thought the United States, rather than the Soviet Union, would more closely fit the belligerent actor mold if it adopted NSC-68's recommendations. Others agreed in principle but worried about the economic ramifications of Acheson and Nitze's plan. Secretary of Defense Louis Johnson, for instance, thought implementing such policies could bankrupt the nation. On Capitol Hill, nearly all Republicans and many Democrats preferred tax cuts to massive military spending. And – in those earnest days before Lyndon Johnson's "guns and butter" twofer and George W. Bush's Iraq War financing – they actually operated under the assumption that they would have to choose between the two.[16] President Truman was also hesitant and, as historian Michael J. Hogan asserts, "missed no opportunity . . . to postpone action on NSC-68."[17] He worried the Fair Deal would suffer, the costs involved in tripling the military's size might outweigh the benefits gained, and that American militarization might spur a Soviet garrison state and, ultimately, something very similar in the United States.

In sum, the Cold War was well under way by June of 1950. Yet despite widespread concern and several destabilizing events, the United States had not

---

[12] "NSC-68: United States Objectives and Programs for National Security," *Containment: Documents on American Policy and Strategy, 1945–1950*, eds., Thomas H. Etzold and Gaddis (New York: Columbia University Press, 1978), 385–6. For more, see: Ernest R. May, ed., *American Cold War Strategy: Interpreting NSC 68* (Boston: Bedford Books of St. Martin's Press, 1993).

[13] Ibid., 385–442. See especially 438–42.

[14] David McCullough, *Truman* (New York: Simon & Schuster, 1992), 772.

[15] Dean Acheson, *Present at the Creation: My Years in the State Department* (New York: W.W. Norton, 1969), 374.

[16] LaFeber, 103. See also, Arnold A. Offner, *Another Such Victory: President Truman and the Cold War: 1945–1953* (Stanford, CA: Stanford University Press, 2002), 366.

[17] Michael J. Hogan, *A Cross of Iron: Harry S. Truman and the Origins of the National Security State, 1945–1954* (New York: Cambridge University Press, 1998), 303.

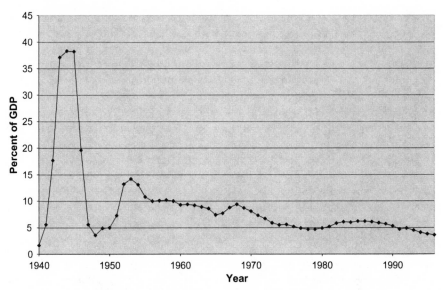

FIGURE 5.1. National Defense Outlays as Percentage of GDP, 1940–1996.[18]

embarked on a defensive buildup – as can be seen in defense spending (see Figure 5.1 above). Following World War II, defense expenditures plummeted from war-time highs of between 30 percent and 40 percent of the national GDP to around 5 percent of GDP for several years. It took the Korean invasion to pave the way toward a big and lasting military expansion, and to drive defense expenditures back into double digits. While there is a decay over time (see Figure 5.1), it takes quite awhile to set in. Defense expenditures do eventually fall back to pre-Korea levels, but only after forty years.

Cold War National Security after the Korean Invasion: Great Urgency

Truman's reluctance to embrace the spirit of, and the specifics within, NSC-68 changed with the Korean invasion and the three year conflict that followed. In effect, the war shifted Washington and the country toward the position of the once marginalized Acheson and his fellow hardliners. And although NSC-68 was once on the fast-track to obscurity, the shock of the Korean invasion and the ensuing war transformed the report into what Cold War historians Thomas H. Etzold and Gaddis call "the definitive statement of American national security policy."[19] As Acheson said three years after the outbreak of hostilities,

---

[18] Source: Office of Management and Budget, *Budget of the U.S. Government, Fiscal Year 1998* (Washington, DC: U.S. Government Printing Office, 1997), Table 3.1: "Outlays by Function and Superfunction: 1940–2002," 42–50.

[19] Etzold and Gaddis, "NSC 68: The Strategic Reassessment of 1950," *Containment: Documents on American Policy and Strategy, 1945–50* (New York: Columbia University Press, 1978).

"Korea came along and saved us."[20] Writing in 1969, he again emphasized the war's crucial role in granting legitimacy to the policies presented in NSC-68: "It is doubtful whether anything like what happened in the next few years could have been done had not the Russians been stupid enough to have instigated the attack against South Korea."[21] Nitze's memoir similarly contends that it was not until well after the Korean War was under way that Truman "had become persuaded that the conclusions and recommendations in NSC-68 were in essence correct and that they should be fully acted upon without further delay."[22]

The President's assessment of the new conflict's larger context shifted.[23] Truman said the communist invasion demonstrated broad new realities and meant that America needed to increase its military strength beyond the requirements of the current, and presumably short-term, conflict in Korea. Truman was clear that it was the conflict in Korea, which had drastically increased the stakes and added urgency to the pre-existing national security concerns:

Under all the circumstances, it is apparent that the United States is required to increase its military strength and preparedness not only to deal with the aggression in Korea but also to increase our common defense, with other free nations, against further aggression.... The defenses of the North Atlantic Treaty area were considered a matter of great urgency by the North Atlantic Council in London this spring. Recent events make it even more urgent than it was at that time to build and maintain these defenses.... the world situation requires that we increase substantially the size and materiel support of our armed forces, over and above the increases which are needed in Korea.[24]

So while this conflict would, like all wars, require manpower and resources, Truman was clear that the country's needs in these areas exceeded those required to effectively deal with this limited conflict. In other words, Korea was only a symptom of what was now obviously a larger problem. The new and dangerous realities, highlighted by – but not limited to – the Korean conflict, required an expanded national security state above and beyond that needed to restore South Korea's territorial integrity.

There is some scholarly debate over whether the President would have adopted NSC-68's recommendations had it not been for the outbreak of Korean hostilities. Most accounts suggest that he would not have.[25] McCullough's

---

[20] Acheson, Princeton Seminar, July 8–9, 1953, Acheson Papers, Truman Library.

[21] Acheson, 374.

[22] Paul H. Nitze, *From Hiroshima to Glasnost: At the Center of Decision* (New York: Grove Weidenfeld, 1989), 106.

[23] Truman never actually used the word "war" in reference to Korea. This was a conscious decision to circumvent Congress' constitutional power to declare war. While such a motion would have had no trouble passing, Truman thought disputes over authority between the U.N., the U.S., and other involved countries were already complicated enough.

[24] Truman, "Special Message to the Congress Reporting on the Situation in Korea."

[25] Gaddis, *We Now Know*, 76; Leffler, *A Preponderance of Power*, 358; Leffler, *The Specter of Communism*, 94–6; Offner, 367; Hogan, 303. One ambiguous exception is LaFeber, 103. LaFeber seems to suggest Acheson and Truman agreed on the necessity of implementing the

analysis is representative. He argues that prior to the war Truman, in typical fashion, "refused to rush to a decision.... Whether he would have attempted anything like the buildup called for in NSC-68 had events not taken the calamitous turn they did in late June, will never be known. But it seems unlikely."[26] It was Korea that erased his doubts about building a vast national security state. The key point here is that while national security was on the agenda long before June of 1950, the conflict on the Korean peninsula put these concerns front and center, providing the decisive push toward implementation.

On July 19, 1950, President Truman addressed the nation and sent a message to Congress to lay out a plan for meeting the country's immediate challenge in Korea and its long-term challenge in light of the new "world situation."[27] He identified three needs: an immediate increase in military assistance for General Douglas MacArthur's U.N. force; a "build up [in] our own Army, Navy, and Air Force over and above what is needed in Korea"; and a strengthened alliance system. To achieve these goals, the President proposed new laws to meet the military requirements, economic controls to preserve the nation's "sound financial condition," and increased production of those goods vital to the national defense. Truman was straightforward about the costs involved, saying it would "be necessary to make substantial increases in taxes. This is a contribution to our national security that every one of us should stand ready to make."[28] Truman proposed doubling the size of the military to 3 million men, reactivating the draft, and dispensing emergency funds totaling $11.6 billion (in addition to that year's previously projected $13 billion military budget). Economist Michael Edelstein documents the lack of opposition to these spending requests and notes, "once a military attack occurred, Senator Robert Taft, the leading Republican conservative, was almost as eager as Truman's planners to fund the war and rearmament, and to fund it with permanent revenues."[29] When all was said and done, Congress appropriated much more than the White House requested – $48.2 billion for fiscal year 1950–51 and $60 billion for fiscal year 1951–52.[30] Tellingly, the Korean conflict completely changed the

NSC-68 recommendations prior to Korea: "Only [Acheson], the President, and a few others seemed to have a clear idea of what had to be done. NSC-68 was a policy in search of an opportunity. That opportunity arrived [with the Korean War]." Another apparent exception: Daniel Yergin, *Shattered Peace: The Origins of the Cold War and the National Security State* (Boston: Houghton Mifflin Co., 1977), 407.

[26] McCullough, 772–3.

[27] Harry S. Truman, "Address on Hostilities in Korea," 19 July 1951, *The Truman Administration: Its Principles and Practice*, ed., Louis W. Koenig (New York: New York University Press, 1964), 345.

[28] Ibid., 346.

[29] Michael Edelstein, "War and the American Economy in the Twentieth Century," *The Cambridge Economic History of the United States, Volume III: The Twentieth Century*, eds., Stanley L. Engerman and Robert E. Gallman, (New York: Cambridge University Press, 2000), 372. See also, Sidney Ratner, *Taxation and Democracy in America* (New York: Octagon Books, 1980), 524–7.

[30] McCullough, 791–2.

terms of debate surrounding Cold War national security. The outbreak of hostilities across the 38th parallel engendered the kind of military buildup called for in NSC-68, a document that only months before appeared reactionary and extreme.

As Truman acknowledged in his address, these expenditures required a significant shift in the tax system. Fortunately, there was no need to reinvent the wheel because the World War I and World War II-era system of government financing via the income tax and the supporting institutional structures were still in place. Following World War II, tax rates were reduced substantially in the Revenue Acts of 1945 and 1948, but the broad range of people subject to the income tax and automatic withholding from paychecks remained. With this structure intact, only an adjustment in rates was required.[31]

Korean War financing was primarily achieved in three revenue acts. On September 22, 1950, Congress passed the first wartime revenue act, which had the effect of increasing personal and corporate marginal income tax rates back to their World War II levels (the range on personal rates went from 21 percent to 90 percent, while corporate rates bounced from 38 percent to 45 percent). The second revenue act was passed on January 3, 1951, boosting the maximum corporate rate up to 47 percent and instituting a 30 percent excess profits tax. Finally, a third revenue act cleared Congress in October of that year to raise an additional $5.4 billion – down from an initial White House request of $16.5 billion – through further increases on individual and corporate rates as well as excess profits and capital-gains incomes.[32]

Again, although a tax hike to fund military and national security expenditures had been suggested prior to the war – most notably in NSC-68 – the proposal was dead on arrival until the hostilities on the Korean peninsula resuscitated it, after which it enjoyed robust political support. The ease with which income taxes were raised at this time indicated the extent to which the federal tax apparatus had become institutionalized. The state's economic development during the world wars had not drifted away but remained in place and proved to be a flexible mechanism in the face of this new crisis. Specifically, the basic structure of the mass-based income tax and its withholding system that had developed because of the world wars could now be manipulated as needed in response to crises.

Korea and Conscription

Shortly after World War II ended, the military draft did too. That particular incarnation of the draft had become law when President Franklin Roosevelt signed the Burke-Wadsworth Act in 1940, prior to Pearl Harbor but after Hitler began his tear across Europe. Conscription, of course, picked up

---

[31] Edelstein, 366–73.
[32] Ibid., 367–8.

dramatically once the United States formally entered the war.[33] However, when Japan surrendered and postwar activities were more or less wrapped up, Truman bowed to Congress's wishes and agreed to end the draft. The country had never had a peacetime draft, and both the public and Capitol Hill were eager to see it scuttled once again. For his part, Truman thought the U.S. needed to focus on recruiting scientists rather than soldiers, although he still favored a kind of draft-light program of compulsory "Universal Military Training" that would be less strenuous and lengthy than typical conscription but would still produce an emergency reserve force.[34] The draft formally ended in 1947. The Korean War not only brought the draft back, but in precedent defying style, conscription then remained in place for nearly a quarter century, including some twenty years after the 1953 armistice.

A weak form of the draft actually returned prior to Korea in 1948, only six months after it was shut down. Economically, the draft was a money saver for two reasons. First, draftees could be paid less. Second, the threat of being drafted had the effect of generating more volunteers because they were compensated better than draftees and were offered greater flexibility in assignments. And with a larger pool of volunteers, less money was needed to induce recruits through higher pay and bonuses.[35] This economically driven renewal of the

---

[33] On the World War II era draft, see: George Q. Flynn, *The Draft, 1940–1973* (Lawrence, KS: University of Kansas Press, 1993), 9–52. Flynn offers the best and most comprehensive account of the draft from World War II through Vietnam. Another account of this period can be found in: James M. Gerhardt, *The Draft and Public Policy: Issues in Military Manpower Procurement, 1945–1970* (Columbus, OH: Ohio State University Press, 1971). See also: Aaron L. Friedberg, *In the Shadow of the Garrison State: America's Anti-Statism and Its Cold War Grand Strategy* (Princeton, NJ: Princeton University Press, 2000), 149–98. For a collection of essays on many topics related to the draft, see: *The Military Draft: Selected Readings on Conscription*, ed., Martin Anderson, (Stanford, CA: Hoover Institution Press, 1982). For more on the ancient military draft and its origins and development in the U.S., see: John Remington Graham, *A Constitutional History of the Military Draft* (Minneapolis, MN: Ross & Haines, 1971). A collection of primary source documents on the U.S. draft is offered in: *The Draft and Its Enemies: A Documentary History*, eds., John O'Sullivan and Alan M. Meckler (Urbana, IL: University of Illinois Press, 1974). For two comparative accounts, see: George Q. Flynn, *Conscription and Democracy: The Draft in France, Great Britain, and the United States* (Westport, CT: Greenwood Press, 2002); Margaret Levi, *Consent, Dissent, and Patriotism* (New York: Cambridge University Press, 1997). Case studies on various societal issues are presented in: *Selective Service and American Society*, ed., Roger W. Little (New York: Russell Sage Foundation, 1969). On the role of local draft boards, see: James W. Davis, Jr. and Kenneth W. Dolbeare, *Little Groups of Neighbors: The Selective Service System* (Chicago: Markham Publishing Co., 1968). For a biography of Lewis Hershey, the director of the Selective Service System, see: George Q. Flynn, *Lewis B. Hershey: Mr. Selective Service* (Chapel Hill, NC: University of North Carolina Press, 1985).

[34] Flynn, *The Draft*, 88–109, 122. See also: Gerhardt, 3–187.

[35] Flynn, *The Draft*, 105–11. See also: Richard Gillam, "The Peacetime Draft: Voluntarism to Coercion," in *The Military Draft: Selected Readings on Conscription*, ed., Martin Anderson (Stanford, CA: Hoover Institution Press, 1982), 97–116; Gary L. Wamsley, *Selective Service and a Changing America: A Study of Organizational Environmental Relationships* (Columbus,

draft had little effect beyond modestly boosting volunteer numbers. Historian George Q. Flynn writes, "the new draft was more a threat than a reality." In its first two years (prior to Korea), only 30,000 men were actually drafted under its terms while 368,000 had volunteered. As a mobilization system, Flynn concludes, this reincarnation of the draft "seemed redundant, a relic of an old-style war."[36]

It seemed much less of a relic when it returned in a serious way after the North Koreans crossed the 38th parallel on June 25, 1950.[37] The 1948 law resurrecting the draft was extended in 1950 and again in 1951 under the Universal Military Training and Service Act. Ironically, the 1951 law was named after Truman's alternative to the draft, but its effect was to extend conscription and table the President's proposal.[38] The war's influence on the number of draftees was remarkable. In 1949, only 7.5 percent of non-commissioned personnel had been drafted. But once the war broke out and the next two extensions took effect, that figure increased to 32.1 percent in 1951, 38.2 percent in 1952, and 58.7 percent in 1953 (see Figure 5.2). At the same time, the raw number of servicemen also shot up.[39] In 1949 after the initial, low-impact draft revival, there were only 398,000 servicemen, of which 30,000 had been drafted. Just two years later there were 1,826,000 servicemen – 587,000 of whom were drafted.[40]

Most notably, the Korea-era draft remained prominently in place after the war, thus becoming the first and only substantial peacetime draft in U.S. history. Draft renewals were passed in 1955, 1959, 1967, and 1971.[41] Between 1951 and 1966, an average of 220,000 men were drafted each year (see Figure 5.3). During the three war years, the figure was much higher at an average of 510,000 annual draftees. But even after the war was over – and before draft numbers shot up again because of Vietnam – an average of 154,000 men were conscripted each year in the peacetime draft. The number dipped as low as 60,000 in 1961; however, it was back up to 158,000 the following year. Similarly, draftees composed a higher portion of total servicemen during the Korean War years, at 42.5 percent, than after, at 26.1 percent. But the point is that Korea induced a major and lasting change in the United States by bringing back the

OH: C.E. Merrill Publishing Co., 1969), 199; United States Selective Service System, *Selective Service Under the 1948 Act* (Washington, DC: U.S. G.P.O., 1951).

36 Flynn, *The Draft*, 109.

37 On the draft during Korea, see: Flynn, *The Draft*, 110–33; Gerhardt, 143–88.

38 Flynn, *The Draft*, 123–6; Gerhardt, 168–9.

39 The term "servicemen" refers to members of the armed forces below the rank of commissioned officers. It includes both "enlistees," or volunteers, and "draftees," who entered the military after being conscripted.

40 Thomas D. Morris, "Report on Studies of the Draft," *The Military Draft*, ed., Anderson (Stanford, CA: Hoover Institution Press, 1982), 550.

41 There was "little debate" over the Reserve Forces Act of 1955 which extended the draft (Flynn, *The Draft*, 158). Another renewal "passed with hardly a second glance" in 1959 (164). The 1967 renewal was "lopsided" and a final 18 month renewal passed in 1971 despite "opposition from both liberal and conservative factions in Congress" (204, 256).

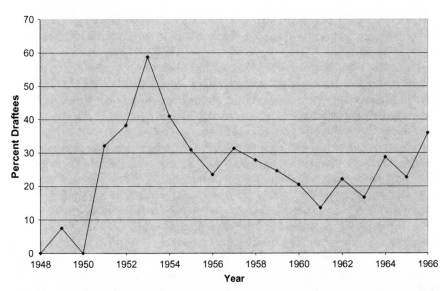

FIGURE 5.2. Draftees as a Percentage of Total Armed Services Personnel, 1948–1966.[42]

military draft, which, once implemented, remained in place as a serious measure, even after its initial reason for revival was taken off the table. The draft lived on until 1973. For most of this time – until the Vietnam War began in

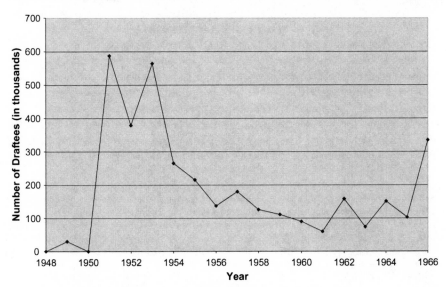

FIGURE 5.3. Number of Draftees in Armed Services, 1948–1966.[43]

[42] Source: Ibid., 550.
[43] Source: Morris, 550.

earnest – it was a peacetime procedure, conscripting hundreds of thousands of young men, famously including Willie Mays in 1952 and Elvis Presley in 1957.

The draft's importance went beyond the obvious influence it had on the armed forces and the lives of many everyday Americans. Indeed, its force was felt throughout society because the draft regimented the economy and provided incentives for people to pursue certain activities over others. Deferments were bound to be controversial because they offered a way out of the draft for what amounted to the educated elite.[44] The rules on deferments varied over the course of the post-1950 draft but, in general, education was prized. As Flynn notes, the "channeling and protection of elites" through the student deferment program "was a reaffirmation of America's commitment to education."[45] Undergraduate students were deferred, as were graduate students for much of the period.[46] Dropouts became eligible for the draft, which encouraged students to stay in school and, especially toward the end of this period, led to universities' reluctance to fail students. Needless to say, taking a "gap year" after high school or college to save sea turtles in Costa Rica, backpack the "Hippie Trail," or indulge in the ski bum lifestyle was not the option for young men that it has been since the draft ended.

In offering a way out of compulsory military service, deferments encouraged young men to attend college. And in providing an incentive to pursue higher education, the draft had the effect of promoting white collar careers over blue collar work. This channeling was, at least to some extent, undertaken purposefully. For many, the atomic bombings of Hiroshima and Nagasaki demonstrated the importance of science and the necessity of continued advancement in this area for purposes of national defense.[47] As such, it was in the national interest to encourage the pursuit of knowledge. In this sense, the draft regimented the American economy and society as a whole. There were strong incentives to immediately enroll in college upon graduating from high school, enter graduate school after that, and then pursue a career in science, medicine, education, or the defense industry. Because married men and fathers were also offered deferments, there was a similar incentive to start a family earlier than one might otherwise.[48] In sum, the military draft altered American life

---

[44] President Eisenhower, for instance, complained that "We've got people who have gone scot free and will soon be out of the age bracket" (Flynn, *The Draft*, 161). Accusations of socio-economic bias were common. For more on the deferment controversy, see: Flynn, *The Draft*, 194, 224, 270. For more on Vietnam-era deferments, see: Lawrence M. Baskir and William A. Strauss, *Chance and Circumstance: The Draft, the War, and the Vietnam Generation* (New York: Alfred A. Knopf, 1978).

[45] Flynn, *The Draft*, 160 and 143.

[46] Scientists, engineers, medical doctors, teachers, married men, fathers, and defense workers among others were also, at times, offered deferments.

[47] Flynn, *The Draft*, 105–7.

[48] Ibid., 137.

in the 1950s and 1960s by channeling young men into education, toward certain types of careers, and away from the kind of pre- and post-college breaks many educated young people engage in today prior to starting a career or family.

Executive Power in War

The Korean War also had a related effect on the question of who controls the American state during wartime, (increasingly) broadly construed.[49] By relying on the Constitution's commander-in-chief clause, Truman effectively fought a war despite the lack of a formal declaration from Congress. He pioneered this feature of presidential power, which, surprisingly, provoked little contemporaneous controversy. In short order, however, the issue became contentious in the scholarly debate between those, such as Alfred de Grazia and James Burnham, who favored congressional supremacy, and others, such as Richard E. Neustadt and Arthur Schlesinger, Jr., who (at least initially) preferred executive leadership.[50] In subsequent years, debates over Truman's actions have come to constitute a sub-literature within a much larger body of work addressing executive power during war.[51] Many constitutional scholars argue that Truman's

[49] There is a related literature addressing the famous steel seizure case. In addition to sources cited in the next several notes, see: *Youngstown Sheet and Tube Company v. Sawyer*, 343 U.S. 579 (1952); Maeva Marcus, *Truman and the Steel Seizure Case: The Limits of Presidential Power* (New York: Columbia University Press, 1977).

[50] Alfred de Grazia, *Republic in Crisis: Congress Against the Executive Force* (New York: Federal Legal Publications, Inc., 1965); James Burnham, *Congress and the American Tradition* (New York: Gateway Editions, 1959); Richard E. Neustadt, *Presidential Power: The Politics of Leadership* (New York: John Wiley & Sons, 1960); Arthur Schlesinger, Jr., "Presidential Powers: Taft Statement on Troops Opposed, Actions of Past Presidents Cited," *New York Times* (9 Jan. 1951), 25. Schlesinger later recanted on his initial defense of Truman on this matter as well as his largely unqualified enthusiasm for the presidency as an institution.

[51] There is an extensive literature on executive power during war. This overview is, by no means, exhaustive. Most of this work has been done by constitutional law specialists. For more mainstream political science-related literature, see, for example: Louis Fisher, *Military Tribunals and Presidential Power: American Revolution to the War on Terrorism* (Lawrence, KS: University Press of Kansas, 2005); Gordon Silverstein, *Imbalance of Powers: Constitutional Interpretation and the Making of American Foreign Policy* (New York: Oxford University Press, 1997), see especially pgs. 65–74; Donald L. Westerfield, *War Powers: The President, the Congress and the Question of War* (Westport, CT: Praeger Press, 1996); Daniel P. Franklin, *Extraordinary Powers: The Exercise of Prerogative Powers in the United States* (Pittsburg, PA: University of Pittsburg Press, 1991); David Gray Adler, "The Constitution and Presidential Warmaking: The Enduring Debate," *Political Science Quarterly* 103:1 (1988), 1–36; Edward S. Corwin, *The President: Office and Powers, 1787–1984* (New York: New York University Press, 1984); Rossiter, *The Supreme Court and the Commander in Chief* (Ithaca, NY: Cornell University Press, 1976); Joseph E. Kallenbach, *The American Chief Executive: The Presidency and the Governorship* (New York: Harper and Row, 1966); Clinton Rossiter, *Constitutional Dictatorship* (Princeton, NJ: Princeton University Press, 1948); Corwin, *Total War and the Constitution* (New York: Knopf, 1947).

actions were unconstitutional "illegalities" or, at best, irresponsible.[52] Others defend Truman based on presidential prerogative.[53] The debate is polarized between scholars such as Louis Fisher who suggest Truman "ignored" Congress, and another camp, led by Robert F. Turner, which maintains that Congress gave its assent. Exaggerations of evidence are plentiful.[54] From Fisher, one gets the false impression that the episode was contentious, and from Turner

Even more has been written by constitutional law scholars, much of it in law review journals. See, for instance: Richard A. Posner, *Not a Suicide Pact: The Constitution in a Time of National Emergency* (New York: Oxford University Press, 2006); Michael D. Ramsey, "War Powers Textualism and War Powers," *The University of Chicago Law Review*, 69:4 (Autumn 2002), 1543–638; John C. Yoo, "War and Constitutional Texts," *University of Chicago Law Review* 69:4 (2002), 1639–84; Michael D. Ramsey, "Text and History in the War Powers Debate: A Reply to Professor Yoo," *The University of Chicago Law Review* 69:4 (Autumn 2002), 1685–720; Yoo, "The Continuation of Politics by Other Means: The Original Understanding of War Powers," *California Law Review* 84:2 (Mar. 1996), 167–305; Bennett C. Rushkoff, "A Defense of the War Powers Resolution," *The Yale Law Journal* 93:7 (June 1984), 1330–54; Raoul Berger, *Executive Privilege: A Constitutional Myth* (Cambridge, MA: Harvard University Press, 1974); Charles A. Lofgren, "War-Making under the Constitution: The Original Understanding," *The Yale Law Journal* 81:4. (Mar. 1972), 672–702; William P. Rogers, "Congress, the President, and the War Powers," *California Law Review* 59:5 (Sep. 1971), 1194–214.

[52] Quote from: Fisher, *Congressional Abdication on War and Spending* (College Station, TX: Texas A&M University Press, 2000), 49 (also relevant are pgs. 40–51). For concurring assessments, see: Corwin, "The President's Power," *The New Republic* (29 Jan. 1951), 15; John H. Ely, *War and Responsibility* (Princeton, NJ: Princeton University Press, 1995), 10–1 and 151–2; Fisher, "The Korean War: On What Legal Basis Did Truman Act?," *The American Journal of International Law* 89:1 (Jan. 1995), 21–39; Fisher, *Presidential War Power*, 2nd ed. (Lawrence, KS: University Press of Kansas, 2004), 97–104; Harold Koh, *The National Security Constitution* (New Haven, CT: Yale University Press, 1990), 106. See also: Arthur M. Schlesinger, Jr., *The Imperial Presidency* (New York: Houghton Mifflin, 1973). Schlesinger's assessment here differs from his initial defense of Truman in 1951: Schlesinger, "Presidential Powers: Taft Statement on Troops Opposed, Actions of Past Presidents Cited," *The New York Times* (9 Jan. 1951), 25.

[53] Robert F. Turner, "Truman, Korea, and the Constitution: Debunking the 'Imperial Presidency' Myth," *Harvard Journal of Law & Public Policy* 19 (1996), 533–85. Schlesinger defended Truman at the time: "From the day that President Jefferson ordered Commodore Dale and two-thirds of the American Navy into the Mediterranean to repel the Barbary pirates American Presidents have repeatedly committed American armed forces abroad without prior Congressional consultation or approval. . . . In the century after 1812 there were at least forty-eight separate occasions of the use of our armed forces abroad without a formal declaration of war." Quote taken from: Schlesinger, "Presidential Powers." Schlesinger reversed his opinion during the Vietnam War. For a blistering account of Schlesinger's "waffling," see: Fisher, *Congressional Abdication*, 50–1. For a much more cautious defense, see: Lofgren, "Mr. Truman's War: A Debate and Its Aftermath," *The Review of Politics* 31:2 (Apr. 1969), 223–41. See also: Yoo, *The Powers of War and Peace: The Constitution and Foreign Affairs After 9/11* (Chicago: University of Chicago Press, 2005), 143.

[54] For example, see Turner's apt discussion of Fisher's selective use of evidence (565–7). Immediately after this convincing case against Fisher, Turner quotes an account of a conversation between Truman and congressional leaders. Turner says this exchange "clearly refutes the conventional wisdom that Truman 'ignored Congress' or merely 'informed' Congress of a *fait*

one comes away dubiously concluding that Truman and Congress worked as a team. The more obvious conclusion, as Fisher himself acknowledges at points, is that Truman took this new and aggressive action with Congress's blessing, encouragement, and cheerful abdication.[55]

Despite Turner's protestations, it is true that the President's decision to take the country to war was not a matter for discussion. Deeming a formal declaration of war from Congress to be overkill and too time consuming, Truman issued his orders after which he informed congressional leaders and, only minutes later, the press.[56] To skirt the thorny issue of constitutionally mandated powers, Truman took the then-novel approach of consciously and carefully avoiding any reference to "war" in his statements and writings. Additionally, he argued that the United Nations charter was a treaty that had been incorporated into American constitutional law and, thus, obligated the United States to act in Korea. When pointedly asked about the situation's status in a news conference, he said "we are not at war."[57] Rather, the situation in Korea was referred to as a "police action" or a "conflict." The White House and its defenders denied it was breaking new ground by citing Jefferson's handling of the Barbary pirates and other limited engagements (most of which were short term). However, as Fisher argues, none of these earlier examples "comes even close to the magnitude of the Korean War."[58] An executive branch statement concluded "that the use of congressional power to declare war has fallen into abeyance because wars are no longer declared in advance."[59]

By and large, Truman's decision to go to war without a congressional declaration was not controversial. This was as true within Congress – the institution with arguably the most to lose – as it was amongst the general public.[60] Congressional Democrats were supportive as were the vast majority of

---

accompli" (567). Turner's stark conclusion falls well short of "clearly refut[ing]" those arguing from Fisher's perspective. For Fisher's response, see: *Congressional Abdication*, 43–4.

[55] See, for instance: Fisher, *Presidential War Power*, 100; Fisher, *Congressional Abdication*, 42.

[56] There are many accounts of this decision. Some include: Glenn D. Paige, *The Korean Decision: June 24–30, 1950* (New York: Free Press, 1968); McCullough, 777–83; James L. Sundquist, *The Decline and Resurgence of Congress* (Washington, DC: Brookings Institution, 1981), 107–10.

[57] Truman, "The President's News Conference of June 29, 1950," *Public Papers of the President*, Truman Presidential Museum and Library online database.

[58] Fisher, *Presidential War Power*, 101. See also: Fisher, *Congressional Abdication on War and Spending*, 50 and 166–7. For another view, see: Turner, 579–80. Tellingly, Turner does not argue that Jefferson's action against the pirates provided a precedent for Truman in Korea. Instead, Turner argues that Jefferson misled Congress when he said that he did not have the constitutional authority to attack the pirates without Congress' consent. Fisher takes Jefferson at his word, but Turner argues the President actually believed he did have the power to act without Congress.

[59] Truman, "The President's News Conference of March 1, 1951," *Public Papers of the President*, Truman Presidential Museum and Library online database.

[60] Sundquist, 108–10.

Republicans. There was little congressional debate.[61] Illinois Democratic Senator Paul H. Douglas, typical of the President's supporters (and echoing Alexander Hamilton's *Federalist* stance), argued that "the speed of modern war requires quick executive action" because "even the slightest delay may prove fatal," and Congress too frequently works slowly and is subject to the Senate filibuster, which can completely halt popular legislation. Sounding like a stand-in for Truman's press secretary, Senator Douglas continued by saying fears that a president might abuse this broad power were ill-founded because of "the sobering and terrible responsibilities of the office" and the "deterring influence" of Congress's impeachment power.[62] Only a few Republicans opposed Truman. Ohio Senator Robert A. Taft was the most vocal critic: "The President is usurping his powers as Commander in Chief.... There is no legal authority for what he has done.... If the President can intervene in Korea without congressional approval, he can go to war [anywhere]."[63] Yet, any serious debate was academic, as an exchange between Senators Arthur V. Watkins (R-UT) and Scott W. Lucas (D-IL) nicely captured. Watkins articulated the core issue: "A question that has never been finally determined is whether that can be done without the consent of the Congress." "Well," replied Lucas, "it has been done."[64] And, aside from a few marginalized critics, the move was popular, even on Capitol Hill where "cheers broke out in the House and Senate when the statement [announcing Truman's decision] was read aloud."[65]

In sum, Truman's approach carved out a new power for the presidency that included greater control of the American state's military capacities during times of war, as defined by the president. This new power came at the expense, and with the enthusiasm, of the legislative branch. It also paved the way for a future major military engagement in Vietnam.[66] This shift in power over the wartime American state owed as much to Congress's acquiescence as it did to Truman's assertiveness.

INTEGRATING THE U.S. ARMY

Political scientists and historians have written extensively about the Cold War's influence on African American civil rights advances.[67] They argue that systematized racial discrimination in the United States undermined American efforts to

---

[61] Truman also relied on executive prerogative in three other areas: sending troops to Europe in accordance with the NATO treaty, addressing railroad and coal strikes, and seizing the nation's steel mills. Drafting coal strikers into the Army and sending troops to Europe did generate a lot of debate on the constitutional issues. For more, see: Silverstein, 65–74.

[62] Paul H. Douglas, *Congressional Record* (July 5, 1950), 9648–9.

[63] Robert A. Taft, *Congressional Record* (June 28, 1950), 9320, 9322–3.

[64] Arthur V. Watkins and Scott W. Lucas, *Congressional Record* (27 June 1950), 9233.

[65] McCullough, 781.

[66] Fisher, *Presidential War Power*, 103–4.

[67] Philip A. Klinkner and Rogers M. Smith, *The Unsteady March: The Rise and Decline of Racial Equality in America* (Chicago: University of Chicago Press, 1999), see Chapters 7–8; Azza Salama Layton, *International Politics and Civil Rights Policies in the United States, 1941–1960*

promote the ideals of freedom and equality in the ideological struggle between democracy and communism. This apparent hypocrisy provided a pressing reason to institute civil rights reforms.

The hot war in Korea is often relegated to the sidelines in this analysis of the decades-long Cold War, if it is mentioned at all. Much of this marginalization is likely due to the relatively short duration of the Korean War, and the fact that the most prominent civil rights developments occurred over a decade later with the Civil Rights Act of 1964 and the Voting Rights Act of 1965. In addition, it is difficult to identify Korea's influence independent of the broader and all-encompassing Cold War. That is, it is hard to untangle and isolate Korea's effects because it is only a small – albeit important – part of the larger Cold War. Thus, when looking at civil rights during the Korean War years, most scholars have focused on connections to the Cold War broadly construed. For their purposes, such an approach makes sense. Indeed, teasing out Korea's specific influence does not substantially bolster or detract from their arguments because their concern is about the Cold War as a whole. Yet for this project's purposes – that is, to assess the domestic effects of hot wars – this is exactly the distinction that needs to be made. In examining the Korean War as distinct from the Cold War, the U.S. Army's integration stands out as a uniquely Korea-induced effect. Perhaps this achievement would have eventually been realized without the military conflict, but it is uncertain when this might have occurred, under what circumstances, and how its later incarnation might have affected the more famous civil rights achievements that followed. What is abundantly clear, though, is that Korea, like other major wars, had a galvanizing influence on the extension of new rights for a marginalized minority group that served honorably in an armed conflict during a time of need.

Two years prior to the Korean conflict, President Truman built on the limited military integration that occurred in World War II.[68] Executive Order 9981 was issued on July 26, 1948, and brought a formal end to segregation in the armed forces. The order read: "It is hereby declared to be the policy of the President that there shall be equality of treatment and opportunity for all persons in the armed services without regard to race, color, religion or national origin. This

---

(New York: Cambridge University Press, 2000), see especially Chapter 2 and pg. 150. See also: Mary L. Dudziak, *Cold War Civil Rights: Race and the Image of American Democracy* (Princeton, NJ: Princeton University Press, 2000); Thomas Borstelmann, *The Cold War and the Color Line: American Race Relations in the Global Arena* (Cambridge, MA: Harvard University Press, 2001); *Window on Freedom: Race, Civil Rights, and Foreign Affairs, 1945–1988*, ed., Brenda Gayle Plummer (Chapel Hill, NC: University of North Carolina Press, 2003).

[68] Michael R. Gardner, *Harry Truman and Civil Rights: Moral Courage and Political Risk* (Carbondale, IL: Southern Illinois University Press, 2002), 105–21. See also: Charles C. Moskos, Jr., "Racial Integration in the Armed Forces," *The Making of Black America: Essays in Negro Life and History, Volume I: The Origins of Black Americans*, eds., August Meier and Elliott Rudwick (New York: Atheneum, 1969), 425–47; Moskos and Joel Sibley Butler, *All That We Can Be: Black Leadership and Racial Integration the Army Way* (New York: Basic Books, 1996).

policy shall be put into effect as rapidly as possible . . . "[69] Integration proceeded smoothly in the Navy and the Air Force. The Navy had begun integrating during World War II and with that head start, promptly brought their policies up to the Executive Order's standards. Following the Navy's lead, Secretary of the Air Force William Stuart Symington initiated integration efforts of his own volition shortly before Truman's announcement.[70] Not surprisingly, then, Symington was particularly receptive to the Executive Order and gathered his senior staff to say, "We're going to integrate the air force now – okay, let's go do it."[71] The Air Force immediately took steps to open its schools to African American service members, disband all-black units and redistribute those personnel to white units, and impose quotas on units' racial balance. Within six months, more than half of its African American personnel had already been reassigned.[72]

Army integration, however, met fierce resistance. Four-star General Omar Bradley, a World War II hero and Truman's Army Chief of Staff, articulated the Army's lack of enthusiasm when he publicly denounced the Executive Order less than 24 hours after it was released, saying "[t]he Army is not out to make any social reforms. The Army will put men of different races in different companies. It will change that policy when the Nation as a whole changes it."[73] Army officers, noting that the Executive Order did not specifically say segregation had to end, reaffirmed the continued status of separating units by race. *The New York Times*' military expert Hanson W. Baldwin said this resistance was widely supported by both whites and blacks within the Army and that there was a consensus that integration would damage morale and efficiency.[74] In sum, the Army was "firmly wedded to its segregation policy," and its bureaucracy effectively prevented the branch's integration. As historian Robert M. Dalfiume observed, the Army's "determination to maintain segregation would not be easy to break."[75]

All this changed in short order, however, once the realities of the Korean War set in. As sociologist Charles C. Moskos says, "The Korean War was

---

[69] Truman, "Executive Order 9981," *Public Papers of the President*, Truman Presidential Museum and Library Online archive.

[70] Richard M. Dalfiume, *Desegregation of the U.S. Armed Forces: Fighting on Two Fronts, 1939–1953* (Columbia, MO: University of Missouri Press, 1969), 178–80.

[71] Gardner, 116.

[72] Dalfiume, 178, 180, and 202. For a full account see Dalfiume, 175–200.

[73] Dalfiume reports that Bradley "had not read the order at the time and had not been aware that reporters were in his audience. He assured the President that the press was in error when it implied that his statement meant the Army would stubbornly resist integration: 'I assure you that nothing is further from our intent'. . . . Unfortunately, Bradley underestimated the will to resist integration within the Army" (pg. 172). By all accounts, Truman accepted Bradley's apology and subsequently awarded the general a fifth star and promoted him to Chairman of the Joint Chiefs of Staff.

[74] Hanson W. Baldwin, "Segregation in the Army: Gen. Bradley's View is Held to Put Morale Above Compulsory Chance," *The New York Times* (8 Aug. 1948), 51.

[75] Klinkner and Smith, 232; Dalfiume, 175, 178, and 182.

the coup de grace for segregation in the Army."[76] More than anything else, segregation was recognized as inefficient, a fact that quickly became evident at Army training camps. The basic training camp at South Carolina's Fort Jackson was faced with a huge influx of new recruits and, in the words of one post commander, it was "totally impractical to sort them out" by race. Integration followed by necessity and was so successful that Department of the Army staffers visited Fort Jackson to see how it was done. On March 18, 1951, all basic training camps were officially integrated.[77]

A similar process played out on the Korean peninsula. Reminiscent of the Navy's experience during World War II, the Army did an about face when it was confronted with heavy casualties and a resultant manpower shortage. Casualties disproportionately affected white units because they were widely considered to be better and more reliable in combat and, thus, were on the front lines. As a result, white units suffered manpower shortages while black units – largely assigned to service and other non-combat roles – were frequently overfilled. Pragmatically, commanders began an informal initiative of reinforcing white units with African Americans. As one officer articulated, "forces of circumstance" demanded a policy shift: "We had no replacements.... We would have been doing ourselves a disservice to permit [black] soldiers to lie around in rear areas at the expense of still further weakening of our [white] rifle companies."[78] Although there was significant miscommunication between officers in the field, commanding General MacArthur (whose office took a "completely negative view" of integration), and the Pentagon over these matters, it was ultimately recognized that the unofficially integrated units worked well together in combat situations. Given the shortage of combat personnel, there was little choice but to continue allowing informal integration. As Assistant Secretary of the Army Earl D. Johnson concluded, "[i]f non-segregation works as well as it has in certain units, I can see no good reason why it should not work for other units."[79]

Although pragmatism and efficiency initially offered the most compelling reasons to integrate, an additional argument eventually emerged: Black soldiers were entitled to equal treatment because of the sacrifices their service to the country entailed. After all, they were in Korea risking their lives just like the white soldiers. And though this sentiment of rewarding sacrifices made by a minority group during wartime was apparently less prevalent in Korea than in other major American wars, it offered an additional rationale for desegregation. Arthur Krock, *The New York Times*' Washington bureau chief, emphasized this point: "recognizing racial prejudice and establishing racial inferiority among Americans who have assumed the risk of dying for their country, freely or

---

[76] Moskos, "Racial Integration in the Armed Forces."

[77] Dalfiume, 203 and 209.

[78] Lee Nicholas, *Breakthrough on the Color Front* (New York: Random House, 1954), 112.

[79] Dalfiume, 209.

by draft, is a system as repugnant to decency as to democracy."[80] President Truman echoed this sentiment, saying segregation in the armed forces was "morally wrong."[81]

This informal integration of the Army was a success as judged by Project Clear, a Pentagon-sponsored group of Johns Hopkins University social scientists that was formed early in 1951 to study the issue.[82] Among other positive findings, Project Clear found that commanders in the field overwhelmingly reported that their integrated units fought well together. White servicemen felt the same and quickly gained respect for the black soldiers serving beside them. There was little racial antagonism and no drop in morale amongst white soldiers. What dissent existed generally came from officers and non-commissioned men who were opposed to desegregation in principle but had no actual experience with integrated units. Dalfiume sums up this aspect of Project Clear's findings: The African American soldier "was generally accepted when he was seen as part of the team, but he aroused criticism when viewed as part of a separate group. The expected violent conflict and opposition to integration by white soldiers did not materialize."[83] Finally, Project Clear determined that black soldiers performed better in integrated units. No doubt, part of this boost in performance was due to the increased morale that integration sparked in black soldiers. In its final report issued late in 1951, Project Clear concluded that "the continued existence of racial segregation limits the effectiveness of the Army" and "integration enhances the effectiveness of the Army.... [As such,] the Army should commit itself to a policy of full and complete integration to be carried out as rapidly as operational efficiency permits."[84] This report silenced most of the remaining critics. By early 1952, the U.S. Army was officially under orders to integrate – a process that was "practically complete" by October 1953 when 95 percent of African American soldiers were serving in integrated units.[85]

The Army's integration was important both for America's image abroad and at home. As Truman proudly asserted at a Howard University address in 1952: "Some of the greatest progress [in civil rights] has been made in the armed services.... From Tokyo to Heidelberg these orders have gone out that will make our fighting forces a more perfect instrument of democratic defense."[86] The

[80] Arthur Krock, "In the Nation: The Senate Vote on the Russell Amendment," *The New York Times* (23 June 1950), 24.

[81] Truman, "Address in Harlem, New York, Upon Receiving the Franklin Roosevelt Award," *Public Papers of the President* (11 Oct. 1952), Truman Presidential Museum and Library Online Archive.

[82] Operations Research Office, *Project Clear: The Utilization of Negro Manpower in the Army* (Chevy Chase, MD: Operations Research Office, Johns Hopkins University, 1955).

[83] Dalfiume, 213.

[84] As quoted in Dalfiume, 215. Project Clear's actual report, *The Utilization of Negro Manpower*, is, according to Dalfiume, "still not readily available" (n. 210).

[85] Dalfiume, 218–9.

[86] Truman, "Commencement Address at Howard University," *Public Papers of the President* (13 June 1952), Truman Presidential Museum and Library Online archive.

country's international image was important because of U.S. claims to moral superiority over the Soviet Union. NSC-68, for instance, argued that "there is a basic conflict between the idea of freedom under a government of laws, and the idea of slavery under the grim oligarchy of the Kremlin."[87] This kind of American boasting about freedom and opportunity in the face of communist oppression was smugly denounced by the Soviets who missed no opportunity to reference racial discrimination as a prime example of U.S. hypocrisy. Indeed, approximately half of the Soviets' anti-American propaganda centered on race.[88] Regardless of whether this was a fair comparison for the Soviets to make, it was clearly a weakness in America's claim to the moral high ground. *The New York Times Magazine* and *The Nation* ran prominent stories on the matter arguing, respectively, that "[s]ome of the flung mud sticks" and that "Jim Crow at home seems to have bankrupted our diplomatic resources."[89] Following the military's desegregation, America could more convincingly lay claim to its ideals of freedom and equality. As Mary Dudziak maintains, "Equality in service meant equality in death... These integrated troops fulfilled the promise of U.S. propaganda. Their bodies held the line in the battle for the hearts and minds of the people of the world."[90]

Military integration also boosted morale among black servicemen, decreased animosity from whites, and laid crucial groundwork for later civil rights progress. To a much greater extent than in World War II, the Korean conflict brought black and white soldiers together in a more or less equal setting. For many, this was a new experience. A *Saturday Evening Post* article quoted one white Georgian who articulated the significance: "I'll tell you rightly. I didn't much like it when they told us boys they's bringing a lot of blacks into the comp'ny. But then they come in and I got kindly used to the idea." A white officer said: "I'll be the first to admit I had my doubts about this whole project when they first unloaded it on me. But it's working and I'd be very much surprised if that fact didn't percolate back to the States and have an effect on us there too."[91]

Polling data back up these anecdotal accounts and further highlight the transformative effects Army integration played in rapidly shifting racial opinions. For instance, 37 percent of white soldiers supported integration in 1943 as compared to 90 percent in 1951. Black soldiers became similarly supportive of integration over this period.[92] These figures run counter to the conventional

---

[87] "NSC-68: United States Objectives and Programs for National Security," 387.

[88] Dalfiume, 139.

[89] Robert E. Cushman, "Our Civil Rights Became a World Issue," *The New York Times Magazine* (11 Jan. 1948), 12 and 22–4; William A. Rutherford, "Jim Crow: A Problem in Diplomacy," *The Nation* 175 (8 Nov. 1952), 428–9.

[90] Dudziak, 88.

[91] Ernest Leister, "For Negroes, It's a New Army Now," *Saturday Evening Post* (13 Dec. 1952), 27.

[92] Samuel A. Stouffer, et al., *The American Soldier: Adjustments During Army Life*, vol. I (New York: John Wiley & Sons, 1965), 568.

wisdom that social attitudes within large populations only change at a slow pace.[93] Additionally, as Moskos argues, the change in black opinion indicates that integration signaled the group's shift away from the "traditional acquiescence to Jim Crow to the ground swell that laid the basis for the subsequent civil rights movement.... The desegregated military, moreover, offers itself as a graphic example of the abilities of both whites and Negroes to adjust to egalitarian racial relations with surprisingly little strain."[94] Additionally, blacks became proportionally more likely to join, reenlist, and forge a career in the armed forces.[95] The authors of *The American Soldier* – an extensive opinion study of non-commissioned personnel – conclude that these and similar findings indicate that the more contact servicemen had with soldiers of a different race, the more supportive they were of integration.[96] According to political scientists Philip A. Klinkner and Rogers M. Smith, these new racial sentiments returned with the soldiers to the United States when the war was over. The experience, they argue, "undoubtedly percolated back home. During the Cold War, millions of Americans served in the military, and it was here that many whites had their first experiences of living, working, and often fighting and dying on an equal footing with blacks."[97] As a further indication of the influence this change had on the homefront, the years following Korea saw the military's integration prominently reflected in popular culture – especially in novels, including John Oliver Killens's *And Then We Heard the Thunder*, Gene L. Coon's *The Short End*, and Hari Rhodes's *A Chosen Few*.[98]

Finally, the military's successful integration was also important because it offered an example of how the country as a whole might deal with the highly charged issue of race and civil rights. Truman seemed to sense this at the time, noting at Howard University that desegregation had been carried out smoothly and left the country better off: "You have seen the results [of integration] in the wonderful performance of our troops in Korea.... All these matters have been taken care of in a quiet and orderly way. The prophets of doom have been proved wrong. The civil rights program has not weakened our country – it has made our country stronger. It has not made us less united – it has made us more united."[99] Because of the more dramatic civil rights achievements that came in the next fifteen years, the military's integration tends to be a forgotten chapter

[93] Stouffer, 168. Moskos, "Racial Integration in the Armed Forces," 436.
[94] Moskos, 436, 426.
[95] Ibid., 425–47.
[96] Stouffer, 594. See also: Operations Research Office, *Project Clear*, 322, 433; Moskos, "Racial Integration in the Armed Forces," 436–7.
[97] Klinkner and Smith, 234.
[98] John Oliver Killens, *And Then We Heard the Thunder* (New York: Knopf, 1963); Gene L. Coon, *The Short End* (New York: Dell Publishing, 1964); Hari Rhodes, *A Chosen Few* (New York: Bantam Books, 1965).
[99] Truman, "Commencement Address at Howard University."

in American political history. Yet, desegregation in this arena demonstrated that major social change was possible without bitter divisiveness or violence. In this sense, the Korea-induced Army integration created momentum toward what would become known as the Civil Rights Movement.

THE PARTY SYSTEM IN THE ERA OF "KOREA, COMMUNISM, AND CORRUPTION"

The American political science literature does not emphasize foreign affairs in its account of elections. The American voter, these studies contend, has little information, holds few opinions, and is largely indifferent to international events.[100] There are several strains within this literature. Some scholars argue that domestic economic issues swing elections.[101] Others say issues of any sort (domestic or international) are unimportant compared to long-term forces

[100] Paul F. Lazarsfeld, Bernard Berelson, and Hazel Gaudet, *The People's Choice: How the Voter Makes Up His Mind in a Presidential Campaign* (New York: Columbia University Press, 1944); Berelson, Lazarsfeld, and William N. McPhee, *Voting: A Study of Opinion Formation in a Presidential Campaign* (Chicago: University of Chicago Press, 1954); Angus Campbell, Philip E. Converse, Warren E. Miller, Donald E. Stokes, *The American Voter* (New York: John Wiley & Sons, Inc., 1960); Converse, "The Nature of Belief Systems in Mass Publics," in *Ideology and Discontent*, ed., David E. Apter (New York: Free Press, 1964), 206–61; Stokes, "Some Dynamic Elements of Contests for the Presidency," *American Political Science Review* 60 (March 1966), 19–28.

    For dissenting views on the general thrust of this literature, see: V.O. Key, *The Responsible Electorate* (Cambridge, MA: Harvard University Press, 1966); Key, *Public Opinion and American Democracy* (New York: Knopf, 1961); John H. Aldrich and Richard D. McKelvey, "A Method of Scaling with Applications to the 1968 and 1972 Presidential Elections," *American Political Science Review* 71 (1999), 111–30; Sowmya Anand and Jon A. Krosnick, "The Impact of Attitudes towards Foreign Policy Goals on Public Preferences among Presidential Candidates: A Study of Issue Publics and the Attentive Public in the 2000 U.S. Presidential Election," *Presidential Studies Quarterly* 33:1 (March 2003), 31–71.

[101] For those emphasizing long-term factors like party ID, the "Michigan School," see: Campbell, Converse, Miller, and Stokes; Larry M. Bartels, "Partisanship and Voting Behavior, 1952–1996," *American Journal of Political Science* (2000) 44: 35–50; Donald Green, Bradley Palmquist, and Eric Schickler, *Partisan Hearts and Minds: Political Parties and the Social Identities of Voters* (New Haven, CT: Yale University Press, 2002).

    For the "Columbia School" and an emphasis on social characteristics, see: Berelson, et al., *Voting*; Katherine Tate, *From Protest to Politics: The New Black Voters in American Elections* (Cambridge, MA: Harvard University Press, 1994); Jeff Manza and Clem Brooks, "The Gender Gap in U.S. Presidential Elections: When? Why? Implications?" *American Journal of Sociology* (1998) 103: 1235–66; Barbara Norrander, "The Evolution of the Gender Gap," *Public Opinion Quarterly* (1990) 54: 566–76; Miller and J. Merrill Shanks, *The New American Voter* (Cambridge, MA: Harvard University Press, 1996); Geoffrey C. Layman, "Religion and Political Behavior in the United States: The Impact of Beliefs, Affiliations, and Commitment from 1980 to 1994," *Public Opinion Quarterly* (1997) 61: 288–316.

    For those emphasizing the economy, see: Robert S. Erikson, "Economic Conditions and the Presidential Vote," *American Political Science Review* 83:2 (June 1989), 567–73; Edward R. Tufte, *Political Control of the Economy* (Princeton, NJ: Princeton University Press, 1978); Douglas A. Hibbs, Jr., *The American Political Economy: Macroeconomics and Electoral Politics in the United States* (Cambridge, MA: Harvard University Press, 1987); Morris Fiorina,

such as partisan identification (the "Michigan School") or social characteristics such as race (the "Columbia School"). Adherents of "components analysis" – an offshoot of the Michigan School – suggest that candidate selection is critical because voter assessments of this component fluctuate the most.[102] In any event, foreign affairs are generally held to be unimportant in elections.[103]

Retrospective Voting in American National Elections (New Haven, CT: Yale University Press, 1981); Gary C. Jacobson and Samuel Kernell, *Strategy and Choice in Congressional Elections* (New Haven, CT: Yale University Press, 1981); Gregory B. Markus, "The Impact of Personal and National Economic Conditions on the Presidential Vote: A Pooled Cross-sectional Analysis," *American Journal of Political Science* (1988) 32: 137–54; Helmut Norpoth, "Presidents and the Prospective Voter," *Journal of Politics* (1996) 58: 776–92; Richard Nadeau and Michael Lewis-Beck, "National Economic Voting in U.S. Presidential Elections," *Journal of Politics* (2001) 63: 159–81; Michael B. MacKuen, Erikson, and James A. Stimson, "Question Wording and Macropartisanship," *American Political Science Review* (1992) 86: 475–86; Lewis-Beck, *Economics and Elections: The Major Western Democracies* (Ann Arbor, MI: University of Michigan Press, 1988). For an opposing view, see: Miroslav Nincic and Barbara Hinckley, "Foreign Policy and the Evaluation of Presidential Candidates," *Journal of Conflict Resolution* 35:2 (June 1991), 333–55.

　　　Campaigns are often said to have "minimal effects": Joseph T. Klapper, *The Effects of Mass Communication* (Glencoe, IL: Free Press, 1960); Markus, "The Impact of Personal and National Economic Conditions on the Presidential Vote: A Pooled Cross-Sectional Analysis," *American Journal of Political Science* 32: 137–54; Steven E. Finkel, "Reexamining the 'Minimal Effects' Model in Recent Presidential Elections," *Journal of Politics* 55 (1993) 1–21.

[102] Ideological proximity is important here, as is party identification. In addition to attitudes toward the Republican candidate and the Democratic candidate, other components are: group-related attitudes, domestic policy attitudes, foreign policy attitudes, and party management attitudes. Stokes, "Some Dynamic Elements of Contests for the Presidency," *American Political Science Review* 60 (1966), 19–28; Stokes, Campbell, and Miller, "Components of Electoral Decision," *American Political Science Association* 52:2 (1958), 367–87. The six-component analysis has been updated since. See: Samuel Popkin, John W. Gorman, Charles Phillips, Jeffrey A. Smith, "Comment: What Have You Done for Me Lately? Toward an Investment Theory of Voting," *American Political Science Review* 70:3 (1976), 779–805; Erikson, "National Election Studies and Macro Analysis," *Electoral Studies* 21 (2000), 269–81.

[103] See, for instance: Gabriel Almond, *The American People and Foreign Policy* (New York: Praeger Press, 1950); Converse, "The Nature of Belief Systems in Mass Publics"; Barry Hughes, *The Domestic Content of American Foreign Policy* (San Francisco: Freeman, 1978); James N. Rosenau, *Public Opinion and Foreign Policy* (New York: Random House, 1961).

　　　There are, to be sure, dissidents within the election studies literature. Perhaps the strongest refutation of the standard view comes from John Aldrich, John L. Sullivan, and Eugene Borgida. Using National Election Studies and Gallup survey data, they demonstrate that politicians are not fools for spending so much time addressing foreign policy issues in presidential campaigns. On the contrary, Aldrich, et al., argue that voters do have attitudes on foreign policy, can perceive differences between candidates on these issues, and that such considerations affect individuals' vote choice. This view, though, is a distinct minority in the elections literature. Aldrich, John L. Sullivan, and Eugene Borgida, "Foreign Affairs and Issue Voting: Do Presidential Candidates 'Waltz Before a Blind Audience?'" *American Political Science Review* 83:1 (Mar. 1989), 123–41. For limited and partial refutations, see: Benjamin I. Page and Richard A. Brody, "Policy Voting and the Electoral Process: The Vietnam War Issue," *American Political Science Review* 66:3 (Sept. 1972), 979–95; David Karol and Edward Miguel, "The Electoral Cost of War: Iraq Casualties and the 2004 U.S. Presidential Election," *Journal of Politics* 69:3 (Aug. 2007), 633–48.

For instance, in keeping with their overall argument, the authors of *The American Voter*, the classic political science election study, downplay Korea while emphasizing partisan identification and Eisenhower's likeability.[104] They do note that the war and charges of corruption against the Truman administration were important issues in the 1952 election.[105] Yet, in their "six components" analysis, "Attitude on Foreign Issues" ranks only fourth, far behind "Attitude towards Eisenhower," "Group-related Attitude," and "Attitude toward Parties as Managers of Government" – although it does eclipse "Attitude on Domestic Issues" (barely) and "Attitude towards Stevenson."[106] Similarly, Larry Bartels and John Zaller suggest Korea was a "politically costly" war for the Democratic Party but that the "impact [was] too small to have swung the 1952 election to Eisenhower."[107] Additionally, in accordance with his econometric model, Robert Erikson emphasizes economic conditions and, to a lesser extent, candidate evaluations in explaining the 1952 election. Compared to the other nine post-World War II elections up to 1984, Erikson demonstrates that 1952 is notable for Democrat Adlai Stevenson's comparative disadvantage in popularity (the worst year for an incumbent party) and for the third worst economy as measured by change in per capita income.[108] The larger point is that as this Michigan School literature was being developed, Korea – and foreign affairs – hardly got mentioned. It seems likely that part of the reason for this omission is because of the manner in which these studies structure their argument. The models they use simply make it difficult for foreign affairs to be important. In other words, it seems possible that the deck

Also in the dissident camp, John Kenneth White is perhaps the only political scientist to specifically emphasize Korea's role as a critical 1952 electoral issue, though his work is narrative in structure and does not engage the discipline's elections literature. John Kenneth White, *Still Seeing Red: How the Cold War Shapes the New American Politics* (Boulder: Westview Press, 1997), Chapter 3. See also: Stephen Hess and Michael Nelson, "Foreign Policy: Dominance and Decisiveness in Presidential Elections," *The Election of 1984*, ed., Nelson (Washington: Congressional Quarterly Press, 1985), 143–4.

[104] Campbell, et al., *The American Voter*, 135. See also: 49–50, 75, and 546. Writing a collected series of essays six years later, the same authors similarly deemphasize Korea in favor of long-term factors in: Converse, "The Concept of a Normal Vote," 30–1; Campbell, "A Classification of the Presidential Elections," *Elections and the Political Order*, 72–3; Stokes, "Spatial Models of Party Competition," 171–2. All these essays are in: *Elections and the Political Order*, eds., Campbell, Converse, Miller, Stokes (New York: John Wiley & Sons, Inc., 1966).

[105] Ibid., 49, 135, and 527.

[106] Stokes, et al., "Components of Electoral Decision," 383.

[107] Bartels and Zaller, "Presidential Vote Models: A Recount," *PS: Political Science and Politics* 34:1 (Mar. 2001), 16. Using Korea in 1952 and Vietnam in 1968, the authors find a (weighted) average parameter estimate of 3.94 percentage points. As they note, this is "an impact too small to have swung the 1952 election to Eisenhower, but certainly big enough to have been decisive in 1968" (16). Bartels and Zaller find that the Democrats' five consecutive terms as the incumbent party cost them about two percentage points in 1952 (17). They also suggest that the opposition party will be more likely to nominate a moderate candidate, as the Republicans did in choosing Eisenhower over Taft in 1952. This paper and its 3.94 percent war effect is addressed again in the section after next, "Assessing the 1952 Presidential Election."

[108] Erikson, "Economic Conditions and the Presidential Vote," 572.

is stacked in favor of other factors. It is quite possible, for example, that the vague notion of likeability is, at least to some extent and in some cases, a proxy for evaluations of a candidate's ability to handle foreign affairs. In elections featuring candidates who largely agree on the major issues of the day (in 1952's case, the Korean War), likeability might be as much of an indication of whom the voters would rather have sitting across the negotiating table from the Soviets as anything else. At the very least, it seems likely that such considerations would play a role in assessments of likeability.

In sum, as John H. Aldrich, John L. Sullivan, and Eugene Borgida conclude: "The prevailing consensus [in the political science elections literature]... is that the public possesses little information and only few, ill-informed attitudes about foreign affairs and is concerned deeply about these issues only when their daily lives are directly affected. As a result, such concerns are not terribly consequential in the voting booth."[109] The traditional treatment of the 1952 election largely conforms to this broader perception of foreign affairs' lack of electoral importance. Yet, a strong case can be made that the Korean War and the 1952 presidential election illustrate how foreign affairs can overtake and ultimately dominate an American election.

The 1952 Presidential Campaign

Dwight D. Eisenhower and his Republican Party brilliantly controlled the 1952 election, as evidenced by their success in fighting the contest on the three issues identified in their campaign's mantra: "Korea, Communism and Corruption." Of these, Korea proved to be the most important.

Public opinion polling clearly demonstrated two things in the months leading up to the 1952 campaign: The Korean War was thoroughly unpopular, and so was the president associated with it. Roughly a year before the election, a Gallup Poll found that 56 percent of the population agreed with a U.S. senator who said "the Korean war is an utterly 'useless war,'" while only 33 percent disagreed.[110] Similarly, in April of 1952 another Gallup Poll showed that a majority thought "the United States made a mistake in going into the war in Korea," whereas only 35 percent did not. Additionally, a plurality in that same poll thought the "enemy" was winning.[111] Tellingly, President Truman was even less popular than the war. By the end of 1951, he only had a 23 percent approval rating in the Gallup Poll and never got above 28 percent prior to the election.[112] In addition to the war, Truman suffered from corruption charges

---

[109] Aldrich, et al., 125.
[110] George H. Gallup, *The Gallup Poll: Public Opinion 1935–1971, Volume Two: 1949–1958* (New York: Random House, 1972), 1019.
[111] Ibid., 1052.
[112] Ibid., 1032, 1040, 1062. Only two other Gallup Polls assessing Truman's performance were taken prior to the election. On February 8, 1952, Truman's approval rating stood at 25 percent and on May 12 it was 28 percent. General MacArthur had been fired a year earlier in April of 1951. This termination was unpopular as illustrated by a May poll showing 25

dating back to 1949. The initial accusations related to a gifts-for-access scheme, and led to embarrassing congressional investigations and Republican assertions of a "mess in Washington." The problem was compounded in 1952 when Attorney General J. Howard McGrath was forced to resign over scandals in the Justice Department and the Bureau of Internal Revenue.[113]

Eventual Democratic nominee Adlai E. Stevenson attempted to distance himself from Truman, but this proved difficult. The President personally asked Stevenson to run on several occasions only to be turned down by the Illinois Governor who told a confidant: "If I do have to run, I must run on my own, with no one telling me what to do or say."[114] He decided to enter the contest only after the convention had begun and it was clear he could win the nomination. Truman, though irritated that Stevenson jumped into the race after denying months of personal White House requests, put on a good show for the convention by emerging all smiles and deeming Stevenson "a winner." Then, either ignoring Stevenson's desire for distance from the White House or oblivious to it, Truman exclaimed: "I am going to take my coat off and do everything I can to help him win."[115] And he did. Despite Stevenson's desire to run as his own man, Truman played an active role in the 1952 campaign. For their part, Republicans consciously sought to solidify this connection. Stevenson's name was not to be uttered. Rather, the Democratic nominee was referred to as "Truman's candidate."[116]

The campaign's three central issues – "Korea, Communism and Corruption" – all played to Eisenhower's advantage. The only overtly domestic issue was corruption and the "mess in Washington." The Eisenhower campaign exploited the administration's scandals and sought to link Stevenson to them. The Republicans' 1952 platform, for instance, contended that, "the present Administration's sordid record of corruption had shocked and sickened the American people.... Immorality and unethical behavior have been found to exist among some who were entrusted with high policy-making positions, and there have been disclosures of close alliances between the present Government and underworld characters."[117]

---

percent approval and 66 percent disapproval, and another poll the next month showing similar findings of 29 percent approval and 56 percent disapproval. But MacArthur's firing did not have a dramatically negative affect on Truman's popularity, probably because it was already so low. Prior to the firing the President's 1951 approval was measured at: Jan. 10, 1951: 36 percent; March 14: 26 percent; April 14: 28 percent. The April 14 poll was released after the firing but the survey had been conducted previously. Following the firing, Truman's approval was measured at: July 11: 25 percent; July 30: 29 percent; Sept. 10: 31 percent; Nov. 9: 29 percent (957–1032).

[113] Jules Witcover, *Party of the People: A History of the Democrats* (New York: Random House, 2003), 443 and 447.

[114] Robert A. Divine, *Foreign Policy and U.S. Presidential Elections: 1952–1960* (New York: New Viewpoints, 1974), 18.

[115] Ibid., 39–40

[116] Ibid., 43.

[117] "Republican Platform," *History of American Presidential Election: 1789–1968*, ed., Schlesinger (New York: Chelsea House Publishers, 1971), 3291.

The Democrats' corruption problem was partially neutralized when a Republican scandal emerged. *The New York Post* reported in mid-September that Eisenhower's vice presidential running mate, California Senator Richard Nixon, had received numerous gifts and had an $18,000 "slush fund" created by Golden State businessmen. The money had primarily been used to finance travel and other political expenses. Nothing was technically illegal (or, as Nixon noted, particularly unusual for a member of Congress); however, it gave the impression of a money-for-influence scheme that contrasted starkly with Eisenhower's anti-corruption pledge. Although modest by today's standards, the low five-figure transgression turned into a media feeding frenzy. The Eisenhower-supporting *Washington Post*, for example, called on Nixon to withdraw in an editorial: "General Eisenhower's principal domestic issue – and one with which we completely agree – is that new leadership is needed to return high moral standards to government. Obviously, this issue would be seriously compromised by Senator Nixon's remaining on the ticket."[118] To clear his name and regain Eisenhower's trust, the Senator delivered a melodramatic, nationally televised address. Nixon said the fund was legal, had only been used for political (as opposed to personal) business, and that no favors had been traded. Additionally, Nixon emphasized his family's middle class credentials, mentioning, for instance, that "[his wife] Pat doesn't have a mink coat." The speech's most memorable moment, though, dealt with the family dog:

We did get something – a gift – after the [1950] election. A man down in Texas heard Pat on the radio mention the fact that our two youngsters would like to have a dog. And, believe it or not...we got a message...saying they had a package for us. We went down to get it. You know what it was? It was a little cocker spaniel dog.... And our little girl Trisha – the 6-year old – named it Checkers. And you know, the kids, like all kids, love the dog, and I just want to say this, right now, that regardless of what they say about it, we're gonna keep it.[119]

Nixon's speech proved a success. Eisenhower embraced his running mate after the address and announced, "You're my boy." As historian Robert A. Divine notes, the speech "transformed Nixon into a political celebrity in his own right, adding strength to the ticket and reassuring party regulars."[120] Yet the episode also distracted from the Republican charge of corruption in the Democratic Administration. So, although corruption had always played second fiddle to foreign policy in the Republican's campaign, this issue – the primary domestic issue in the 1952 election – was a virtual non-factor in the campaign's final six weeks.

The more central campaign issues dealt with foreign affairs. Communism and Korea were front and center throughout the campaign, and the latter became increasingly dominant as the election drew near. In July (which at that time was considered an early stage of a presidential campaign), Nixon identified

[118] "Nixon Should Withdraw," *Washington Post* (20 Sept. 1952), 8.
[119] Richard Nixon, "Checkers Speech" (23 Sept. 1952), *History of American Presidential Election*, 3321.
[120] Divine, 63.

foreign policy as "the big issue of the campaign" because "that is where the Administration has made its greatest failure.... General Eisenhower can offer new leadership in foreign affairs but Governor Stevenson must accept the [Truman] Administration's foreign policy."[121] The Republican Party platform placed a similar emphasis on "Foreign Policy" by addressing it first and with much more print than any other issue.[122] Additionally, Eisenhower's chief political advisor John Foster Dulles told the press that Ike, Nixon, and he agreed that foreign policy would be the campaign's "major issue."[123] The General later confirmed Dulles's assessment that "the great question of peace ... would be the overshadowing issue of the campaign."[124] Finally, of course, the very nomination of a World War II hero-general is an indication of how important foreign policy was in 1952.

While Republicans sought to emphasize foreign policy, others attempted to assert that differences between the candidates in this arena were minimal. McGeorge Bundy, for instance, writing in *Foreign Affairs*, argued that, "[t]he two nominees ... are known as supporters of the basic outlines of the American foreign policy developed since 1947, and both have had a part in this policy" [i.e., containment].[125] Such overt efforts to downplay the issue, though, did as much to elevate the importance of foreign affairs as to minimize or neutralize its significance.

Communism, as it related to the administration's containment policy, was the first of the two major foreign policy issues. Most closely associated with the State Department's George Kennan and his boss, Secretary Dean Acheson, containment was an anti-communist strategy that called for limiting communism to those areas where it already existed and preventing the ideology from spreading to new areas. It was tied to the Domino Theory (which suggested that if one nation or region fell to communism, surrounding areas would become vulnerable and might also fall). Containment became the theoretical foundation for the Truman Doctrine, and was contrasted with a more muscular foreign policy, prominently advocated by Republican Senator Robert Taft, that sought to defeat communism rather than merely prevent its spread.[126]

---

[121] Russell Porter, "Eisenhower Attacks Record and Platform of Democrats," *The New York Times* (27 July 1952), 1.

[122] "Republican Platform," 3281–92.

[123] W.H. Lawrence, "Dulles Questions Stevenson Ability," *The New York Times* (9 Aug. 1952), 1.

[124] Lawrence, "Eisenhower Binds Party to Program that Faces Facts," *The New York Times* (12 Aug. 1952), 1.

[125] McGeorge Bundy, "November 1952: Imperatives of Foreign Policy," *Foreign Affairs* 31 (Oct. 1952), 6.

[126] George Kennan, "Moscow Embassy Telegram #511: 'The Long Telegram,'" (22 Feb. 1946), *Containment: Documents on American Policy and Strategy, 1945–1950*, 50–63; Kennan ("X"), "The Sources of Soviet Conduct," *Foreign Affairs* 25 (July 1947), 566–83. The preceding article was published anonymously under the name "X" and is often referred to as the "X Article." See also, Kennan, *American Diplomacy* (Chicago: University of Chicago Press, 1985).

The essence of Eisenhower's message on this score was that Truman and his administration – and, by association, Stevenson – were weak on communism because of their endorsement of the allegedly flawed containment policy. In August, Dulles spoke of a more aggressive anti-communist policy: "We will abandon the policy of mere containment, and will actively develop hope and a resistance spirit within the captive peoples which, in my opinion, is the only alternative to a general war."[127]

The Dulles-Taft hard-line approach to communism reached its peak when the Eisenhower campaign briefly adopted "liberation" as a policy replacement for containment. As outlined by Dulles, liberation would mean actively trying to destroy the Soviet Union and communism by fomenting internal resistance through the Voice of America and aiding anti-communist forces. This shift away from containment was met with near universal disdain. European allies were aghast, accusing Eisenhower of being a "warmonger" and "out-MacArthuring MacArthur."[128] Meanwhile, Democrats and much of the U.S. press attacked the General for recklessness. Eisenhower attempted damage control in a Philadelphia speech on September 4 by emphasizing the use of peaceful approaches but, as Divine argues: "Liberation had clearly backfired on the Republicans ... [and] thus did not play the major role Dulles had conceived for it in the presidential election.... it disappeared from the national contest by early September."[129] Similarly, Dulles disappeared from Eisenhower's inner circle for the campaign's final two months. Only Nixon continued to attack Truman and Stevenson on communism generally (outside the Korean context), and these attacks did not mention "liberation." Nixon mostly rested on an array of platitudes. For instance, the Democrats "lost the secret of the atomic bomb," "lost 600,000,000 people to the Communists," and permitted them to "honeycomb our secret agencies with treachery."[130] "Nothing would please the Kremlin more" than another "second-rate president." Nixon took to calling Stevenson "Adlai the Appeaser" and a "Ph.D. [in] Dean Acheson's Cowardly College of Containment."[131]

In sum, what started out as a prominent and promising campaign issue – Truman's alleged weakness on communism – fell flat and was largely discarded. Only Nixon, playing the attack dog role that is typical of vice presidential candidates, maintained the harsh anti-communist language, and even that was toned down. Eisenhower needed another foreign policy issue to kindle memories of his wartime accomplishments.

Korea, the final and most prominent issue in the 1952 campaign, helped fill the foreign policy void after Dulles's liberation policy floundered. To this end,

---

[127] Lawrence, "Dulles Questions Stevenson Ability."

[128] Divine, 52.

[129] Ibid., 53–5.

[130] William M. Blair, "Nixon Campaigns Across Missouri," *The New York Times* (22 Oct. 1952), 19; Elie Abel, "Nixon Says Reds Want Stevenson," *The New York Times* (9 Oct. 1952), 25.

[131] Abel, "Nixon Says Reds Want Stevenson"; Abel, "Stevenson Called Appeaser by Nixon," *The New York Times* (17 Oct. 1952), 19.

Eisenhower revisited a central issue from his nomination fight against Taft. To get the Republican nomination, Eisenhower had to defeat the Ohio Senator who was the darling of conservatives.[132] Unlike the General, Taft offered a true contrast to the administration on Korea. The Ohioan continuously charged Truman with weakness in his failure to adopt General MacArthur's aggressive plan to attack China. Charging the administration with having "invited" the war and then failing to adopt sufficiently strong tactics, the war was Taft's central issue in the months preceding the Republican National Convention.[133] Eisenhower never mimicked Taft's fierce condemnation of "Truman's war" at this stage of the campaign. Instead, he relied on his own heroic public image, a strong anti-communist message, and a long standing (albeit distorted and media-induced) charge that Taft was an isolationist. This approach was sufficient to gain the Republican Party's nomination.

Although Eisenhower would begin exploiting the unpopular war at Stevenson's expense in September, the General's position scarcely differed from that of his general election opponent or Truman. All three felt that confronting the blatant communist aggression that provoked the Korean conflict was critical and, thus, supported the war. Yet all three would not go so far as MacArthur, who advocated expanding the war to China and suggested using nuclear weapons. Truman's limited war, they agreed, was necessary, but any larger conflict risked provoking World War III.

After securing the nomination, there was significant internal disagreement over how to handle Korea within the Republican campaign. Not everyone was content to limit Ike's foreign policy appeal to merely a generic anti-communism message. Indeed, if Korea caused a split amongst the American people, it was equally divisive within Eisenhower's campaign. That summer the General's camp was separated between a majority that felt Korea should be politically exploited and placed at the forefront of the campaign, and a minority that urged deemphasizing the conflict at hand and favored a broader anti-communist appeal. As discussed above, Dulles led the informal coalition seeking to focus more broadly on anti-communism and downplay Korea. This cohort's strategy was based on the fact that the war had been Taft's major nomination issue and out of concern that politicizing the war could jeopardize armistice negotiations. But others in Eisenhower's campaign wanted to make Korea the primary issue and urged their candidate to endorse MacArthur's proposal to expand the war into China. As one advisor argued, "[t]his is a military matter. In the eyes of many, Ike will rise or fall on his position on Korea."[134] Dulles was eventually persuaded to relent slightly and advised Eisenhower to publicly propose dropping propaganda leaflets over North Korea. Ike initially agreed

---

[132] For full accounts of the struggle for the Republican nomination see: Divine, 3–41; Barton J. Bernstein, "Election of 1952," *History of American Presidential Elections*, ed., Schlesinger (New York: Chelsea House Publishers, 1971), 3215–40.

[133] Divine, 10.

[134] Ibid., 45.

with Dulles's proposals, saying that taking the fight to China would mean "starting another war far more difficult to stop than the one we are in now." While Eisenhower said he thought Truman had committed some "really terrible blunders," he also thought that the President's overall approach had been correct and in the nation's best interest.[135] Throughout the summer of 1952, then, Eisenhower was reluctant to fully exploit Korea. Although he reveled in his reputation as a military man and took a hard-line on communism, Ike's minor quibbles with Truman's Korea policy limited his desire to exploit the Democrats' political weakness on the issue.

After the national conventions, the Korean War became the main focus of attention, with Eisenhower staking out a clear, if somewhat disingenuous, position of his own. Much of this renewed focus on Korea sprung from Stevenson and Truman emphasizing it. Stevenson maintained his support for Truman's approach. His broadcast comments to soldiers stationed abroad in August were typical:

Had we not resisted aggression in Korea, then we would not only have lost Korea but we would have invited the Soviet Union to pursue aggression elsewhere. The line had to be drawn somewhere and, the earlier it was drawn, the better the chance and the greater the hope of averting general war.... [B]y persevering in this difficult and sometimes exasperating path we can win our way to a peaceful world. It is a goal worth the price, heavy as it is.[136]

Truman jumped in as well, mounting a nation-wide whistle-stop tour in the campaign's final weeks. At each rally he defended his Korea policy, frequently paraphrasing these remarks from an October 4 event in Oakland: "We are fighting in Korea so we won't have to fight in Wichita, or in Chicago, or in New Orleans, or on San Francisco Bay."[137] The President also pointed out Eisenhower's vacillating positions on the issue. Recalling Ike's 1945 statement that the Soviets sought friendship with the United States, Truman argued that the General's new-found stance on Korea demonstrated that he had been co-opted by Republican hardliners. In the same Oakland address, Truman said: "So now he is going around the country, campaigning against his own record, and his own principles. My friends, he is a very sad and pathetic spectacle."[138] Public opinion polls indicated the Democratic approach was working. What once was a double digit lead for Eisenhower had shrunk to a four point margin. At the same time, other polling data indicated Eisenhower had a 67 percent to 9 percent advantage over Stevenson in the public's confidence for handling the Korean conflict.[139]

[135] Ibid., 46. Eisenhower made these comments at a meeting with regional leaders in Kansas City.
[136] Adlai E. Stevenson, "War and Peace" (30 Aug. 1952), *Major Campaign Speeches of Adlai E. Stevenson*, ed., Stevenson (New York: Random House, 1953), 36 and 38.
[137] Truman, "Address in the Oakland Auditorium," (4 Oct. 1952), *Public Papers of the President*, Truman Presidential Museum and Library online database.
[138] Ibid.
[139] Divine, 69–70.

In response to these Democratic attacks on the communist and Korean fronts, Ike dropped Dulles's liberation theory and began hammering the Democratic administration over Korea. Eisenhower's criticism focused on Truman's failure to anticipate and prevent the war in Korea, his inability to win it, and his apparent powerlessness at the negotiating table. The contrast between the old and new strategies can be seen in a few illustrative speeches. In an early September address in Philadelphia, Eisenhower blamed the Democrats for the war, claimed they failed to supply South Korea, and charged them with having "abandoned China to the Communists."[140] On September 22, after the campaign had analyzed the polling data, a Cincinnati audience heard Eisenhower increase the pressure on Truman and Stevenson, charging the administration with "incompetence."[141] First, Ike suggested that a Dean Acheson speech, in which the Secretary of State said Korea was outside of America's defense perimeter, had led to the communist attack on the South. And second, while endorsing the decision to fight, the General accused Truman of fumbling the war's prosecution, declaring: "Our servicemen were summoned to snatch military victory from political defeat. Democracies cannot afford the luxury of assigning armies of soldiers to go around 'picking up' after their statesmen."[142] Eisenhower went even further on October 3 when he offered a new solution for the Korean stalemate. Closely resembling the Vietnamization policy his running mate would implement some twenty years later, Ike suggested that Koreans should gradually take over the fighting from American soldiers. "That is a job for the Koreans.... If there must be a war there, let it be Asians against Asians, with our support on the side of freedom."[143] This suggestion – to increasingly move American soldiers out of harm's way – played well to a public upset over U.S. casualties and became a mainstay of Eisenhower's campaign rhetoric.

Stevenson and Truman, realizing their party's vulnerability on Korea, went to great lengths to control the damage. Responding to Eisenhower's Cincinnati address several days later, Stevenson defended Acheson, charged Eisenhower with hypocrisy, and accused him of exploiting American deaths in Korea for his own political gain.[144] A more expansive defense of the war and the administration came on October 16 in a nationally televised fireside address. The Korean conflict, Stevenson argued, was about much more than a relatively small peninsula thousands of miles away. Rather, it was about confronting an ideology

---

[140] Dwight D. Eisenhower, "Peace Can Be Won," *Vital Speeches of the Day*, Volume XVIII (New York: The City News Publishing, Co.), 709. See also, Divine, 70.

[141] Divine, 70.

[142] "Text of Eisenhower's Address in Cincinnati on Foreign Policy," *The New York Times* (23 Sept. 1952), 16.

[143] Divine, 71. Eisenhower received much criticism for these remarks because he sounded unconcerned about Asians killing Asians, and also because the South Koreans already contributed almost half the front line forces.

[144] "Text of Stevenson's Louisville Speech Attacking Eisenhower on Foreign Policy" *New York Times* (28 Sept. 1952), 63.

bent on aggressively exporting its repressive ideas. Eisenhower's position that only Asians should be fighting "completely misses the significance of the Korean War for America.... The Korean War is not a war that concerns just Koreans. It is our war, too, because – and there should be no mistake about this – world domination is the ultimate target of the communist rulers, and world dominion includes us."[145] Truman similarly kept hammering away at Eisenhower by continuing to justify the war as a way to fight the enemy abroad rather than at home.[146] Beginning on October 16 in Hartford, Connecticut, the President also began calling on Ike to offer up his own war remedy:

Now I want to say to you that he has... stated that he knows a panacea that will cure the Korean situation. He and one of his snollygoster foreign state advisers has said that he knows how to do that job. Now he has been my military adviser ever since I appointed him Chief of Staff of the Army, and I will say to you right here, if he knows a remedy and a method for that situation, it is his duty to come and tell me what it is and save lives – right now.[147]

Eisenhower's response to Truman's challenge sealed his election in the eyes of many observers.

In Detroit on October 24, Eisenhower vowed: "I shall go to Korea." In a sense, the General's stoic pledge was little more than rhetorical grandstanding. There was little that his presence would, or could, change. The Republican nominee admitted as much, saying: "Only in that way could I learn how best to serve the American people in the cause of peace."[148] In essence, Eisenhower said that he would go to Korea and hope something occurred to him while he was there.

Politically, though, the speech was a resounding success. In the words of the Associated Press's Jack Bell, "[f]or all practical purposes, the contest ended that night." Most other contemporary political observers agreed, as have historians in the years since.[149] Stevenson and Truman continued to defend the war and accuse Eisenhower of isolationism, naiveté, and opportunism, but the charges

---

[145] Stevenson, "Second Fireside Speech," *Major Campaign Speeches*, 254.

[146] Divine, 74.

[147] Truman, "Address in Hartford, Connecticut," 16 Oct. 1952, *Public Papers of the President*.

[148] "Text of General Eisenhower's Speech in Detroit on Ending the War in Korea," *The New York Times* (25 Oct. 1952), 8.

[149] Divine, 75; White, *Still Seeing Red*, 97. Campbell, et al., disagree. In analyzing why Eisenhower performed better in the election than in their polling, they argue measurement error and false reports have more to do with the discrepancy than Eisenhower's pledge to visit Korea. Though they acknowledge that "attitude change can occur between the interview and election day," they suggest Ike's last minute pledge to visit Korea could not have boosted his numbers to cover the full discrepancy presented in their data. "Our data suggest strongly that eleventh-hour events such as... the offer of Eisenhower to go to Korea in 1952 could not possibly have had the great impact in the whole electorate with which they are often credited. But there is little doubt that some errors of prediction are due to attitude change induced by events after our pre-election interview" (75).

fell on deaf ears. Humbled by the infamous "Dewey Defeats Truman" headline four years earlier, some pollsters and pundits continued to predict a close election in the campaign's final days.[150] When the results were in, though, the General took 39 states for 442 electoral votes with 55 percent of the popular vote, while Stevenson tallied nine states for 89 electoral votes and 44 percent of the popular vote.

Assessing the 1952 Presidential Election

The era's leading non-academic analyst of elections and public opinion cited Korea as the key issue of the 1952 campaign. Samuel Lubell was an early pioneer of election forecasting. Though not from the academy, he carried considerable influence because of his methodological sophistication.[151] Lubell worked in the field, conducting hundreds of interviews in selected and representative cities and counties. In 1952, his findings all pointed toward the importance of Korea:

> During the whole campaign I traveled through the country, covering thirty cities and seventeen rural counties, asking persons of every description whom they were going to vote for and why.... In 1952 the public's thinking was dominated by the bloody stalemate in Korea. On that issue the popular mood was to demand a decision – to get the war over with one way or another.... I kept a careful record of the main reasons why one-time Democrats were swinging Republican. Eisenhower's popularity stood about fourth in importance, far behind the angers stirred by the Korean War.... The "Communist" issue I found of considerable importance, although its effects tended to merge with angers over Korea.... [T]he frustrations over Korea were the most important single propellent behind Eisenhower's sweep.[152]

A strong case can be made that Lubell – in stark contrast to the consensus position that foreign affairs in general are not electorally important – was accurate in emphasizing Korea's importance. First, one of the prominent pieces in the mainstream literature curiously minimizes Korea's importance in spite of its own statistical data pointing to the contrary. Bartels and Zaller assert that the 3.94 percent estimated influence of the "war dummy variable" was "an impact too small to have swung the 1952 election to Eisenhower."[153] In one sense, of course, this is true. Ike won by more than ten percentage points in the popular vote – more than twice the estimated effect for the war. Nonetheless, 3.94 percent is a large estimate and anything that can make that

[150] Divine, 76–81.
[151] For more on Lubell, see: Ronald Smothers, "Samuel Lubell is Dead at 76; Predicted Election Outcomes," *The New York Times* (21 Aug. 1987), B7. Among others, Warren Miller is quoted in this obituary. See also: Samuel Lubell, *The Future of American Politics* (New York: Harper, 1952); Lubell, *The Hidden Crisis of American Politics* (New York: Norton, 1970).
[152] Lubell, *Revolt of the Moderates* (New York: Harper & Brothers, 1956), 38, 118, 265.
[153] Bartels and Zaller, 16.

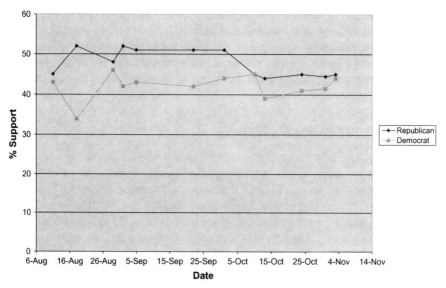

FIGURE 5.4. 1952 Gallup Presidential Election Polls.[154]

much difference in an election is critically important. Despite the minimal difference between the candidates' actual positions on this matter, Korea was still the most important issue in their study. If anything, this fact does more to highlight the war's importance. Had the candidates offered starkly different views, Korea likely would have been even more important.

The war's effect as measured by Bartels and Zaller looms even larger when polling data is considered. Polls consistently showed Eisenhower leading in the campaign's final months, but his edge varied considerably (see Figure 5.4 above). Without the bump of the war effect, Ike would have won by very little, if the Bartels and Zaller counterfactual is accepted. Furthermore, based on the Gallup polling, if the election had been held a week or two earlier, he might have lost without the Korea boost.

Second, the academic underpinnings of the general consensus that foreign affairs (and issues *per se*) are electorally unimportant emerged several decades ago and are now dated. This scholarship represented some of the best work political scientists have produced, but since that time new methods of analysis have been developed that cast doubt on certain aspects of these earlier studies. The best example of a new and dynamic means of analyzing elections comes

[154] Source: Gallup, *The Gallup Poll: Public Opinion, 1935–1971* (New York: Random House, 1972). These polls omitted candidate names, asking "which political party you would like to see win." I chose to use these figures because only eight polls specifically asked about Eisenhower and Stevenson. These eight polls tracked onto the polling date displayed here but because the party and candidate questions were often asked in the same poll, the visual display is awkward.

from Richard Johnston, Michael G. Hagen, and Kathleen Hall Jamieson.[155] This work relies on the 2000 National Annenberg Election Survey (NAES) in which three hundred randomly selected people were interviewed every day. The authors explain the benefit this "rolling cross section" provides: "All that distinguishes one day's sample from another day's, aside from sampling error, is something that has happened in the interval."[156] In other words, the authors were able to chart the ebbs and flows of the Bush-Gore presidential election on a daily basis and assess the influence of campaign events. In essence, Johnston, et al., divide the post-convention campaign into three phases according to basic polling data: Gore ahead, Bush ahead, Gore catches up.[157] They find that the "fundamental factors" traditionally used to explain voting do indeed account for some variation in vote choice. However, they also find that social characteristics are "summarily weak" explanatory variables, and any meaningful account of partisan identification leaves out the large middle swath of the electorate that is not partisan or particularly ideological. Similarly, economic forecasts only fully accounted for the initial phase of the campaign in which Gore was leading. In addition, and most importantly, these factors fail to account for the dynamics and changes in vote choice over the course of the contest.[158]

To get at these underlying dynamics and the campaign's effects, the authors conduct a "natural experiment" with the NAES data, which produces remarkable findings. First, the study demonstrates increased campaign effects in battleground states where candidates concentrated their resources and advertising as compared to states one nominee conceded to the other. And second, their findings register and highlight short-term responses to campaign strategies and events.[159] In other words, Johnston, Hagen, and Jamieson conclude that campaign dynamics and strategy had a marked effect on the 2000 election.

More than anything else, this study demonstrates that while party identification, social characteristics, and the state of the economy are clearly important, the overwhelming and exclusive emphasis traditionally ascribed to them by the mainstream political science literature went overboard. Campaigns are not rigid and fixed affairs. Rather, they are responsive, and contain ebbs and flows that the traditional election studies cannot explain. Issues, events, strategy, and timing are often critical. Comparatively, then, the old studies minimizing the importance of these factors appear static because they are unable to take events and their timing into account. These traditional studies, important as they were, lacked context and were not data-rich enough to fully explore the intricate dynamics of a campaign in the way Johnston, Hagen, and Jamieson

---

[155] Richard Johnston, Michael G. Hagen, and Kathleen Hall Jamieson, *The 2000 Presidential Election and the Foundations of Party Politics* (New York: Cambridge University Press, 2004).
[156] Ibid., 16.
[157] Ibid., Chapter 2.
[158] Ibid., Chapter 3. Quote on pg. 61.
[159] Ibid., Chapter 8.

do. Building on the work of the Michigan and Columbia Schools and proponents of economic voting, Johnston, et al., are able to cast light on the effects of various events, politicians' moves, and their timing – aspects that are obscured in the stagnant cataloging of party identification, social characteristics, and domestic economic measurements.

The NAES data employed by Johnston, et al., did not exist in 1952. Yet its use in analyzing the 2000 election is certainly instructive and suggestive. There is good reason to think that a Johnston-style analysis back in 1952 would have demonstrated Korea's importance and been consistent with the narrative campaign timeline presented above. It likely would demonstrate the significance of the strategies and timing that went into the candidates' positioning on Korea, and the effects of that positioning – think, for instance, of Eisenhower's last minute pledge to go to Korea. Such findings would conform to the non-political science consensus that already suggests as much.[160] So while one cannot be sure that a time-warped Johnston-style analysis would match up exactly along these lines, it seems a good bet that it would come very close.

Also of note is the high turnout in 1952. A remarkable 63.5 percent of the voting age public cast ballots – an increase of 10.4 percent over the 1948 election (see Figure 5.5).[161] This was the highest turnout in a presidential election since 1908 and has only been eclipsed once since then – in 1960 when 65.2 percent of the voting age population cast ballots. The 1952 election also initiated a stretch of high turnout elections that was, and remains, unprecedented in modern election history. From 1868 to 1900 turnout ranged from 71.8 percent to 82.9 percent. But the turn of the century brought, as Walter Dean Burnham argues, "the collapse of [this] earlier political universe," which "was marked by a more complete and intensely party-oriented voting participation among the American electorate."[162] In 1904 and 1908 percentile turnout fell into the 60s. This downward trend continued. In the next ten elections prior to 1952, turnout was in the 40s or 50s with only three exceptions: 1916, 1936, and 1940. The 1936–1940 upswing, though, failed to sustain itself, as turnout

---

[160] Such assessments are common outside of the political science literature. In addition to Lubell, *Revolt of the Moderates*, see, for instance: Robert David Johnson, *Congress and the Cold War* (New York: Cambridge University Press, 2006), 55. Johnson, an historian, asserts: "Korea's most immediate impact came in domestic politics: Truman's inability to end the war doomed Democratic chances in the 1952 elections."

[161] Obtaining reliable voter turnout figures is difficult because respected publications contain different data. Just among *Congressional Quarterly Press* publications, figures vary from book to book – often by wide margins. The figures reported here were used because Rusk's book offers data for all presidential elections through 1996 while most other references only list those from 1960 to the present or some other arbitrary date in the mid-1900s. Thus, the numbers here are consistent relative to one another. Additionally, Rusk's figures fall in the middle and tend not to be outliers in comparison to other reports. There is an extensive literature addressing measurement of voting turnout and the differing figures that get reported. For a good overview of the problems involved, see: Barry C. Burden, "Voter Turnout and the National Election Studies," *Political Analysis* 8:4 (2000), 389–98.

[162] Walter Dean Burnham, "The Changing Shape of the American Political Universe," *American Political Science Review* 59:1 (Mar. 1965), 22.

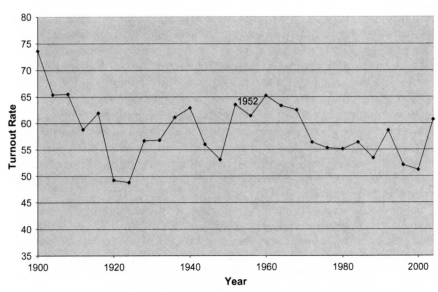

FIGURE 5.5. Voter Turnout Rates in Presidential Elections, 1900–2004[163]

once again dropped off in 1944 and 1948. Only in 1952 did turnout pick up and remain at a high level for several elections. Indeed, the next five presidential elections all had turnout rates in the 60s. This kind of turnout was not seen again until 2004 and 2008.

Many election studies fail to note the 1952–1968 upswing and instead emphasize the decline in turnout following the 1952 and 1960 elections.[164] A likely reason for this blind spot is because many studies do not consider

---

[163] All figures are the presidential vote as a percent of the voting-age population. Sources: Jerrold G. Rusk, *A Statistical History of the American Electorate* (Washington, DC: Congressional Quarterly Press, 2001), 52. For 2000 and 2004 figures: Richard M. Scammon, Alice V. McGillivray, Rhodes Cook, *America Votes 26* (Washington, DC: Congressional Quarterly Press, 2002), 1 and 15.

[164] See, for instance: Miller and Shanks, *The New American Voter*, 21–69. The authors assert that to explore the questions surrounding turnout decline, "we will begin with a generation-by-generation inspection of all the correlates of turnout contained in the NES studies from 1952 to 1988" (70). See also: Steven J. Rosenstone and John Mark Hansen, *Mobilization, Participation, and Democracy in America* (New York: Macmillan, 1993), 211–9; Carol A. Cassell and Robert Luskin, "Simple Explanations of Turnout Decline," *American Political Science Review* 82 (1988), 1321–30; Ruy A. Teixeira, *Why Americans Don't Vote: Turnout Decline in the United States, 1960–1984* (Westport, CT: Greenwood Press, 1987); Paul R. Abramson and Aldrich, "The Decline of Electoral Participation in America," *American Political Science Review* 76 (1982), 502–21; Paul Kleppner, *Who Voted: The Dynamics of Electoral Turnout, 1870–1980* (New York: Praeger, 1982); Stephen D. Shaffer, "A Multivariate Explanation of Decreasing Turnout in Presidential Elections," *American Journal of Political Science* 25 (1981), 68–95; Richard A. Brody, "The Puzzle of Political Participation in America," *The New American Political System*, ed., Anthony King (Washington, DC: American Enterprise Press, 1978), 287–324.

elections prior to 1952. The University of Michigan's National Election Study began that year and has provided analysts with a goldmine of data ever since.[165] As a result, many scholars use 1952 as a starting point and look forward. For most purposes, this approach is reasonable. However, it obscures the larger context surrounding 1952. Turnout had been down for most of the twentieth century and, in particular, in 1948. Then 1952 saw a turnout surge that lasted for five elections, at which point it began declining back to pre-1952 levels. Thus, in looking at the twentieth century as a whole, the period from 1952 to 1968 stands out as a stretch of particularly high turnout and appears to be more of an anomaly than a standard from which we ought to take our bearings. As such, the emphasis on declining turnout in the elections between 1952 and 2004 may be misplaced.

A final observation about the 1952 contest is that, although it has never been regarded as a member of the prestigious class of "critical" or "realigning" elections, Lubell's contemporaneous analysis and two recent studies suggest that it could be considered in this elite company – if only as a bit of an oddball or an aberration.[166] Lubell's interviewing data indicated that:

Republican gains of recent years have come through a shifting of individuals, not groups. At every income level and among all social classes one finds some families who have turned Republican, but there has not yet been any dramatic conversion of whole blocs of voters. This slow tempo of realignment can be attributed largely to the curious paradox that both the voters and the country have changed so much more than have the symbols attached to the parties. To sum up, the usual agitation for a "real two-party politics" has come from those who wanted to draw a sharp line of cleavage which would force all "conservatives" into one party and all "liberals" into the other. But the reappearance of a two-party politics at this perilous point in our history has virtually nothing in common with any such motive. Instead of seeking to sharpen the party cleavage, it is aimed at moderating both parties and using them to preserve the gains of the last two decades. What has happened, in short, is that the moderate elements, by refusing to cast their lot

---

[165] For a discussion of how the NES has contributed to election analysis, see: Erikson, "National Election Studies and Macro Analysis," *Electoral Studies* 21 (2002), 269–81.

[166] The traditional canon of realigning elections includes those in 1800, 1828, 1860, 1896, and 1932. Key, "A Theory of Critical Elections," *Journal of Politics* 17 (1955), 3–18; Key, "Secular Realignment and the Party System," *Journal of Politics* 21 (1959), 198–210; E.E. Schattschneider, "United States: The Functional Approach to Party Government," *Modern Political Parties: Approaches to Comparative Politics*, ed., Sigmund Neumann (Chicago: University of Chicago Press, 1956), 194–215; Schattschneider, *The Semisovereign People: A Realist's View of Democracy in America* (New York: Holt, Rinehart, and Winston, 1960); James L. Sundquist, *The Dynamics of the Party System: Alignment and Realignment of Political Parties in the United States* (Washington, D.C.: Brookings Institution, 1973); Walter Dean Burnham, "The Changing Shape of the American Political Universe," *American Political Science Review* 59 (1965), 7–28; Burnham, "Party Systems and the Political Process," *The American Party System: Stages of Political Development*, eds., William N. Chambers and Burnham (New York: Oxford University Press, 1967); Burnham, *Critical Elections and the Mainsprings of American Politics* (New York: Norton, 1970). For a critique of realignment theory, see: David Mayhew, *Electoral Realignment: A Critique of an American Genre* (New Haven, CT: Yale University Press, 2004).

with either party, have forced both the Democrats and Republicans to turn their backs on the extremists in their ranks and to fight for the middle ground where the balance of victory lies.[167]

So, Lubell argues, although 1952 did not produce a realignment in the traditional sense, it signaled the end of the New Deal coalition and the emergence of a centrist majority.

With the benefit of hindsight and more sophisticated quantitative methods, two political science studies have reached similar conclusions. Jerome M. Clubb, William H. Flanigan, and Nancy H. Zingale contend 1952 signaled the deterioration of the party system inaugurated in 1932 and "created an electorate capable of realignment."[168] Clubb, et al., devised a methodology by which they can gauge an election's lasting influence for each party from 1836 to 1976. Their findings indicate that 1952 is one of only two elections that had a positive "realigning surge" for the Republicans (the other being 1920; 1932 and 1964 brought negative "realigning surges" for the GOP).[169] They find that the 1952 Republican victory was the culmination of the "post New Deal decline in Democratic strength" and a high point in Democrats's ideological divisions.[170] Also demonstrating 1952's importance is Larry Bartels's statistical analysis, which uses election returns and a regression model measuring partisan, national, and sub-national factors for elections from 1868 to 1996.[171] Applying this methodology, only 1920 and 1972 rank as larger Republican "swings" than Eisenhower's first victory.[172] In addition, Bartels demonstrates 1952's lasting long-term coalitional change, its effect on the end of the "New Deal Party system," and the South's realignment toward the Republican Party.[173]

Above all, the 1952 election demonstrates how foreign affairs – especially if a war is involved – can dominate an American election. 1952 is particularly instructive because the Korean War was not merely *an* issue or even *an important* issue, but rather it was, far and away, the campaign's *dominant* issue. The election's ebbs and flows can be mapped onto the contours of that single issue. Early in the campaign, Eisenhower had a large lead. Then, Democratic attacks started to eat away at it. At the same time, the Republicans discovered they had a big advantage on the Korea issue. They exploited it in an increasingly aggressive manner and won (for the first time in twenty years) in a landslide with unusually high turnout. Moreover, they purposefully manipulated the Korea issue. In reality, Ike's position scarcely differed from Stevenson or President

---

[167] Lubell, *Revolt of the Moderates*, 120.
[168] Jerome M. Clubb, William H. Flanigan, and Nancy H. Zingale, *Partisan Realignment: Voters, Parties, and Government in American History* (Boulder, CO: Westview Press, 1990), 134–5.
[169] Clubb, 92–3.
[170] Ibid., 105.
[171] Bartels, "Electoral Continuity and Change, 1868–1996," *Electoral Studies* 17:3 (1998), 301–26. Bartels and Zaller, "Presidential Vote Models: A Recount."
[172] Bartels, 1998, 304–5. See Table 5.1.
[173] Ibid., 307 and 309.

Truman. Yet public disgust with the war was so deep that the Republican campaign could exploit it for political gain. In sum, Korea was a foreign policy issue the American voter had information about, formed an opinion about, and cared about.

Of course, not every election has its own Korea, and this is not to say that foreign affairs always or even frequently dominate a campaign in this manner. But 1952 is a prime case study in how an international crisis can do just that. In addition, when combined with the elections examined in the midst of and following conflicts such as the Spanish-American War, World War I, Vietnam, and the Iraq War, it is clear that 1952 is more than a one-off anomaly. Many elections have been influenced by and, indeed, turned on foreign affairs. Although these elections may not amount to a majority, they certainly constitute a sufficient minority to warrant careful attention and analysis by mainstream American political science election studies.

CONCLUSION

Korea is an often forgotten conflict. Sandwiched between the United States's greatest victory and, as of this writing, her only major defeat, Korea's inconclusive resolution seems to pale by comparison and defies easy categorization. But like other wars, it left a lasting mark on American politics and society. In terms of the American state, the war had profound and lasting effects. A new military draft was initiated and, unlike past incarnations, proved to be an enduring and regimenting feature of American life for many years following the war's conclusion. In addition, the presidency gained a new prerogative power over the American state during crises that came at Congress's expense. But more than anything else, the Korean War was primarily responsible for the creation of the national security state. Many government officials had been pushing for sharp increases in military spending for years. But prior to the war, these forces were viewed as marginal and were largely ignored. Once the guns started firing, though, major resistance to the creation of a national security state evaporated. As with other major wars, these developments of the American national state came marginally and incidentally at the expense of the states. As the national government asserted its power and influence in certain areas, the states were inevitably left with less authority in the overall picture of American life.[174]

With regard to democratic rights policy, Korea was the impetus for the Army's desegregation – a crucial development for America's image at home and abroad and, like World War II-era events, an important precursor to the

---

[174] For more on this relationship, see: Aaron L. Friedberg, *In the Shadow of the Garrison State: America's Anti-Statism and its Cold War Grand Strategy* (Princeton, NJ: Princeton University Press, 2000). Friedberg argues that America's anti-statist ideology shaped the nation's approach to the Cold War, prevented it from becoming overly centralized, and ultimately helped it win. The key point for Friedberg is that, contrary to what might have been expected, the U.S. did not become a garrison state like the Soviet Union. This claim, however, does not mean that there wasn't a dramatic expansion of government activity.

Civil Rights Movement to follow. Talk of desegregating the Army was certainly not new, but full integration never occurred until Korea compelled it. Finally, Korea was the most important issue in the 1952 presidential campaign and provides an important case study in how foreign affairs can play a critical role in elections – a fact generally overlooked in the political science literature.

6

The Lost War

The Vietnam War stands out as an anomaly in United States history. It is hard to say when it began or when it ended – and not just because there was no official declaration of war or a concluding treaty that cemented a new peace. It also stands, as of this writing, as America's only defeat. Like World War II, Vietnam has lingered over American politics for a generation, but unlike the conflict that produced the "Greatest Generation," the Vietnam War has left a legacy of bitterness and division that the shared horror of the September 11, 2001, terrorist attacks failed to fully quell and the Iraq War seemed to reignite.

As in other chapters, there is no effort to address *every* domestic change wrought by the Vietnam War. Significant domestic changes that constitute thematic connections between wars are highlighted here. Like the discussion of Korea, a distinction is made between the larger Cold War and Vietnam. Obviously, the hostilities in Southeast Asia were, at least for Americans, tied up with the larger ideological struggle against communism. Yet the focus here is on those effects that can be linked directly to the hot war in Vietnam. It had a profound influence on one crucial aspect of the American state. The conflict's unpopularity brought the military draft to a halt and, to this day, it shows no sign of coming back. Thus, in contrast to other wars in which state capacities were enhanced, Vietnam saw no significant state expansion.[1] With regard to democratic rights policy, Vietnam led directly to the Twenty-Sixth Amendment and the extension of voting privileges to 18–20 year olds based on the argument that those eligible to be drafted should also enjoy the franchise. Finally, as to the party system, the war's influence on the 1968 and 1972 elections is addressed. In addition, the rise of a large anti-war faction within the Democratic Party and their perception of a rigged system led to an important procedural change in the presidential nomination system. The chapter concludes by examining Vietnam's role in altering crucial aspects of the Democratic Party's ideology.

---

[1] This lack of transformative state growth is considered in the concluding chapter.

THE VIETNAM WAR IN BRIEF

Unlike the other conflicts explored here, there was no clear starting date for the Vietnam War. Rather, it was marked by gradual increases in American involvement. The seeds of major U.S. engagement can be traced to the 1954 battle at Dien Bien Phu when the Viet Minh, a communist and nationalist force, defeated the French army and effectively ended a war between the two parties. As a result, France was ousted as a colonial power in Indochina, and the Geneva Peace Accords created a temporary partition line at the seventeenth parallel separating North and South Vietnam. The North was governed by communist leader Ho Chi Minh with support from China and the Soviet Union, while the South was led by Ngo Dinh Diem and backed initially by the French and later, following their departure, by the United States. Free elections in 1956 – expected to favor Ho Chi Minh – were supposed to erase the temporary partition line and unify the country. However, Diem refused to participate, noting that his regime was not a party to the Geneva Accords, and elections were never held. Diem's communist opponents in the South then formed the Vietcong, a guerilla army allied with the Northern regime, and began carrying out attacks on South Vietnam's army and government.

The first stage of American involvement began during French rule when President Harry Truman offered financial assistance for the war against the Viet Minh. Under President Dwight Eisenhower, America's financial aid increased, ultimately to the point of paying 80 percent of France's war costs. Following the Geneva Accords, the United States funded Diem's regime and sent military advisors to help train the South's Army of the Republic of Vietnam to counter the communist North.

President John F. Kennedy expanded the U.S. commitment in 1961 by sending in new military equipment and more military advisors. At this stage, the United States still hoped to avoid any direct fighting with the communist forces in the North or with the Vietcong. By 1963, the Kennedy administration, frustrated with Diem's failure to quell the Vietcong insurgency and his corruption-plagued regime, supported a successful coup to install new leadership in South Vietnam. A series of military governments followed.

After Kennedy's assassination, President Lyndon Johnson ordered a retaliatory bombing strike against North Vietnam following the 1964 Gulf of Tonkin incident in which North Vietnamese torpedo boats allegedly attacked a U.S. destroyer. Congress passed the Gulf of Tonkin Resolution with only two dissenting votes, giving Johnson the power to take whatever action he deemed necessary in the region. This resolution was the basis for Johnson's massive increase in American involvement, including the introduction of American combat forces. The number of draftees serving in Vietnam increased dramatically starting in 1965. The next several years saw a protracted guerilla-style war and an extensive U.S. bombing campaign of North Vietnam.

The Johnson administration's claims of success over this period were irretrievably undermined by the enemy's well-coordinated Tet Offensive in 1968.

Although the North Vietnamese Army and Vietcong attacks on major Southern cities were ultimately repulsed and technically constituted a military failure, they highlighted the strength of the communist forces and demonstrated that the war would not end anytime soon. These realizations had a dramatic influence on American public opinion and shifted the American focus away from winning the war and toward ending direct military action without abandoning South Vietnam.

In response to the American public's increasing disenchantment with the war, President Richard Nixon ended the draft and began gradual troop withdrawals in accordance with his Vietnamization plan, which called for more and more responsibility to be shifted from U.S. forces to those of South Vietnam. Yet even as Americans began coming home, Nixon expanded the war into neighboring Cambodia and Laos because of the presence of communist forces near the Vietnam border. These actions led to mass demonstrations in the United States and further strengthened anti-war sentiment. American involvement in Vietnam finally came to an end in January of 1973 when the United States and North Vietnam signed the Paris Peace Agreement. Virtually all American personnel were gone by early 1973. Following the U.S. withdrawal, fighting continued in Vietnam, but by 1975 the North prevailed and established a united, communist Vietnam.

THE AMERICAN STATE IN THE ERA OF GUNS, BUTTER, AND PROTESTS

Vietnam is unique among major American wars in that it did not produce a noteworthy expansion of the state. In prior wars, state capacities were increased to address specific emergencies and largely remained in place as lasting changes even after the instigating crises abated. During the Vietnam War, major state building initiatives were being designed and implemented in pursuance of President Lyndon Johnson's Great Society initiative, addressing issues such as health care, poverty, and education. These programs, however, were not related to the war. In fact, the costs associated with the Great Society's state building efforts created tension with the need to pay for military activities in Vietnam, and Johnson's hope to fund both "guns and butter" proved increasingly difficult. The longer LBJ was in the White House, the more these dueling initiatives became a drain on the state's financial resources. There was, however, an interesting and important war-related state development (albeit a retrenchment, as opposed to the more typical expansion) that is examined here. Vietnam ended the latest, Korea-inspired, incarnation of the military draft.[2] This incarnation,

---

[2] Other changes occurred that were also related to the war. For instance, in conjunction with the Watergate scandal, Vietnam contributed to a long period of distrust and loss of faith in government and its institutions (for a review of this literature, see: John H. Aldrich, *Why Parties? The Origin and Transformation of Party Politics in America* (Chicago: University of Chicago Press, 1995), 241–2). Though it is one of Vietnam's enduring legacies, it is not

in contrast to previous drafts, had remained in place as a peacetime measure for two decades and had played a significant role in shaping society before Vietnam brought it to an end.

Vietnam and Conscription

The military draft had been used in the United States during the Civil War, World War I, World War II, and the Korean War. Notably, though, conscription remained in place after Korea, becoming the first peacetime draft in American history. During the quiet years between Korea's conclusion in 1953 and the beginning of serious troop deployments to Vietnam in 1965, the draft was a serious presence in American life and regimented society in important ways. A complicated system of draft deferments provided new incentives to pursue undergraduate and graduate degrees. This emphasis on education, in turn, channeled young men into white collar professions and, especially, toward jobs in areas that also offered draft deferments such as science, medicine, academia, and engineering. At times, deferments were also available to married men and fathers, thus nudging young people toward family life.[3] At the most basic level, hundreds of thousands of young men without deferments or other disqualifying attributes (such as physical infirmities) were conscripted into the armed forces and served two years on active duty. Between 1954 and 1966, an average of 154,000 men were drafted annually and accounted for 26.1 percent of all non-commissioned military personnel.

The number of draftees shot up beginning in 1965. In July, President Johnson more than doubled the number of draft calls to 40,000 per month. From 1966 to 1969, roughly 300,000 men were drafted each year – with most of those being inducted into the Army. At its peak, draftees accounted for 49 percent of non-commissioned personnel. But even that relatively high figure understates

addressed here because it is not explicitly related to the state. In addition, because Congress concluded that it had given away too much authority to the executive branch, attempts were made to reign in presidential power by the Church Committee, the War Powers Resolution, and a general attack on the national security state. While Vietnam clearly influenced this series of changes, other factors, such as the Central Intelligence Agency's foreign escapades, were also major contributors. These initiatives arguably produced only the appearance of change. On these matters, see: Robert David Johnson, *Congress and the Cold War* (New York: Cambridge University Press, 2005); Julian Zelizer, *On Capitol Hill* (New York: Cambridge University Press, 2004); Robert A. Pastor, "Disagreeing on Latin America," *The President, the Congress, and the Making of Foreign Policy*, ed., Paul E. Peterson (Norman, OK: University of Oklahoma Press, 1994).

3 See also, Chapter 5. See also: Aaron L. Friedberg, *In the Shadow of the Garrison State: America's Anti-Statism and its Cold War Grand Strategy* (Princeton, NJ: Princeton University Press, 2000), 149–98; George Q. Flynn, *The Draft, 1940–1973* (Lawrence, KS: University of Kansas Press, 1993), 105–7, 137, 143, 160–1, 194, 224, 270; John Whiteclay Chambers II, *To Raise an Army: The Draft Comes to Modern America* (New York: The Free Press, 1987); Lawrence M. Baskir and William A. Strauss, *Chance and Circumstance: The Draft, the War, and the Vietnam Generation* (New York: Alfred A. Knopf, 1978).

their impact because of the sobering fact that draftees were far more likely to see combat and be killed. In 1969, for instance, only 16 percent of the total armed forces were draftees, but they accounted for 88 percent of the infantry and more than half of all combat fatalities. Draftees tended to be assigned to the infantry and sent from there to the front lines, whereas volunteers and career military personnel were generally placed in safer support areas.[4]

Deferments continued to be offered but became increasingly restricted as the war dragged on. Conscientious objectors – a difficult status to obtain – and fathers were granted deferments throughout the conflict, but deferments for graduate and undergraduate students and married men were eliminated. The elimination of deferment opportunities incented many draft avoiders to join the National Guard or the Reserves or, in more extreme cases, to move to Canada or to attempt to obtain physical rejections in various ways – for example, by gaining debilitating amounts of weight.[5]

The Vietnam era draft sparked widespread popular protests. This movement's primary goal was ending America's military activities in Southeast Asia, but because conscription was seen as an important part of the war effort, the draft became a target, too.[6] Draft resistance was not new, of course, but it was more fierce and widespread than at any time before.[7] Protests began as early as May of 1964 and two years later major protest organizations began forming. Among other activities, public demonstrations were held; draft cards were burned or returned to the Justice Department; and draft officials and their offices were harassed. Participants in this resistance included traditional pacifists, civil rights groups, religious organizations, and the counterculture movement centered on college campuses that came to be known as the New Left. Not all draft resisters were solely preoccupied with Vietnam, but surveys indicated that this was the primary focus for 88 percent of them.[8] As one attorney who defended draft resisters said, "I have never yet found one that did not have, at the very nub of his feelings, his opposition to the war."[9]

Ultimately, the protest movement played a major role in ending the draft. It first succeeded in swaying elite opinion to the conclusion that the draft was unfair. Men who were poor or less educated were much more likely to be drafted than those from the middle or upper classes holding college degrees.

---

[4] Flynn, 170–1.

[5] Ibid., 179–80.

[6] Ibid., 220. Todd Gitlin, *The Sixties: Years of Hope, Days of Rage* (New York: Bantam Books, 1987), 247–55.

[7] There were significant draft riots in New York City during the Civil War. See: Barnet Scheter, *Devil's Own Work: The Civil War Draft Riots and the Fight to Reconstruct America* (New York: Walker & Co., 2005); Iver Bernstein, *The New York City Draft Riots: Their Significance for American Society and Politics in the Age of the Civil War* (New York: Oxford University Press, 1991).

[8] Flynn, 173–7. Others were concerned with various causes, many related to Vietnam, including imperialism, colleges' contracts with defense contractors, and Third World exploitation.

[9] Ibid., 179.

Racial minorities – especially blacks – were also overrepresented (perhaps because they were more likely to be poor and less educated). In short, there was a largely accurate perception that the privileged elite was able to avoid the draft, thus leaving the fighting and dying to the less fortunate and influential elements of American society. This sentiment became especially widespread amongst opinion leaders in Congress and academia.[10] Numerous bills appeared in Congress calling for an end to conscription and, although they failed, they gained increasing support from both liberals and conservatives.

By 1970, public opinion had turned decisively against the draft, and President Richard Nixon had been pushing for an all-volunteer force and other reforms for two years. The draft lottery, intended to make the process random and, thus, more fair, was instituted in 1969.[11] The only question was when, not if, the draft would end. There were complications regarding manpower and money but these issues became less troublesome as the American military presence in Southeast Asia was reduced. During the 1972 campaign, Nixon announced that no more draftees would serve in Vietnam and that the draft would end the following summer. The last combat troops left Vietnam in August of 1972, thereby opening the way for the draft's retirement. The following June, Nixon simply proclaimed that the scheduled lottery was cancelled, effectively ending the military draft. It has not returned.[12]

In sum, Vietnam brought conscription to an end. The controversy surrounding the war made the draft – an established institution in both wartime and peacetime for over twenty years – simply untenable. With the draft's demise, the societal ordering it had engendered was also gone. There were no longer incentives to pursue higher education or to start a family as a means of avoiding military service. In addition, given Vietnam's infamous legacy, there has been no serious effort to bring the draft back, even following the 9/11 attacks, the initiation of the War on Terror, and the launching of a major war in Iraq. In this sense, Vietnam provoked a rare wartime rebuke to state building in the United States. The end of the draft certainly constitutes an enduring war-induced effect on the state, but in contrast to other major wars, this conflict saw an element of the federal government deconstructed.

Yet, in another sense, the draft's termination may have bolstered the state in a roundabout way. The large, well-educated, well-financed, professional, all-volunteer military that emerged after Vietnam may be a stronger and better force than its predecessor, which was populated with short-term, unmotivated, and complaining draftees counting the days until their return to civilian life.

---

[10] Friedberg, 187–96. Flynn, 181. This disparity was also central to Dr. Martin Luther King, Jr.'s, opposition to the war. See: King, "Beyond Vietnam," 4 April 1967, *A Call to Conscience: The Landmark Speeches of Dr. Martin Luther King, Jr.*, http://www.stanford.edu/group/King/publications/speeches/Beyond_Vietnam.pdf (last accessed 31 May 2007), 2–3.

[11] Flynn, 243–9.

[12] Ibid., 259–71. Friedberg, 194–6.

This second perspective coincides with Samuel Huntington's conclusion in his classic 1957 examination of the relationship between the military and the state.[13] He argued that soldiering by professionals is more effective at maintaining national security than is soldiering by a democratic – or drafted – army.[14] Traditionally, professionalization has been difficult and halting in the United States because of an ingrained suspicion of the military establishment. That is, the military was often seen as a threat to America's liberal democratic legacy, leading to repeated efforts to "civilianize" the military.[15] Indeed, Huntington was even critical of World War II-era civil-military relations.[16] In his estimation, these civilianizing initiatives only rendered the military less effective at defending the country.

From this perspective, then, the demise of the draft and its democratic army may well have been a blessing in disguise for the state's power and effectiveness. Though the draft's termination halted the state's ability to forcibly conscript its citizens into service and ended the societal ordering it produced, the change arguably brought about an unintended – if quite different – benefit for the state. While most major U.S. wars through Vietnam entailed conscription, Huntington's analysis suggests this non-professional aspect of the military may have done more harm than good in certain respects. The Vietnam War ended the draft, made its reinstatement politically untenable, and brushed away any lingering romantic notions of a citizen army. The result, it seems, is a system whereby presidents can start and conduct wars without having to worry about the inevitably divisive politics surrounding a draft. Tellingly, a handful of anti-war politicians such as U.S. Representative Charles Rangel (D-NY) have noted this and proposed reinstituting the draft as a means to make presidents and Congress less likely to initiate wars.[17] In this post-draft era, George H.W. Bush fought the Gulf War in 1991, Bill Clinton dispatched troops to Bosnia in 1999, and George W. Bush initiated the ongoing conflicts in Afghanistan and Iraq. All of these wars, with the initial exception of Afghanistan, were controversial and had difficulty gaining congressional approval. Had these debates also been predicated on draftees, rather than professional soldiers, doing the fighting, they almost certainly would have been even more controversial. The absence

---

[13] Samuel P. Huntington, *The Soldier and the State: The Theory and Politics of Civil-Military Relations* (Cambridge, MA: Harvard University Press, 1957).

[14] Ibid., 456–66.

[15] Ibid., 143–62. See also, Chapters 8–16.

[16] Ibid., 315–44. Obviously, there have been times – World War II, for instance – when more personnel was necessary than a volunteer, professional army might have been able to produce.

[17] In 2003, for instance, Rangel introduced a bill to reinstitute the draft, saying: "I truly believe that those who make the decision and those who support the United States going into war would feel more readily the pain that's involved, the sacrifice that's involved, if they thought that the fighting force would include the affluent and those who historically have avoided this great responsibility.... Those who love this country have a patriotic obligation to defend this country.... For those who say the poor fight better, I say give the rich a chance." CNN.com, "Rangel Introduces Bill to Reinstate the Draft," 8 Jan. 2003, http://www.cnn.com/2003/ALLPOLITICS/01/07/rangel.draft/ (last accessed 11 May 2009).

of a draft similarly reduces the pressure on presidents during the prosecution of these conflicts. In this regard, the end of the draft has provided presidents and Congress more latitude in using the military. It has, in effect, lowered the bar for sending troops into harm's way.

As a final note on this point, the end of the draft extended a new *de facto* right to young people: the privilege of being left alone by the Pentagon. In all earlier eras, young men were subject to, if not a formal draft, at least the possibility of one in the event a war broke out. But following Vietnam, a full generation has grown up free from the prospect of being drafted. This new entitlement has gained such strength and popular favor that it did not so much as develop a chink in its armor even after the September 11, 2001 terrorist attack and the initiation of two personnel-sapping foreign wars in its aftermath.

"OLD ENOUGH TO FIGHT, OLD ENOUGH TO VOTE"

The Twenty-Sixth Amendment lowering the voting age to eighteen was passed during, and because of, the Vietnam War.[18] Not all war-related rights extensions have come in the form of amendments. New rights for African Americans, for example, were extended through legislation, litigation, and institutional necessity during World War II and Korea. Yet amendments have been popular vehicles for war-time rights extensions. The Civil War produced three constitutional amendments addressing former slaves, and women gained suffrage rights through the World War I-associated Nineteenth Amendment. Lowering the voting age during Vietnam also required the amendment process, though not for lack of trying other approaches first.

Initial Efforts to Lower the Voting Age

Reducing the voting age was not a new issue on the national agenda. Indeed, it popped up fairly consistently during or shortly after major wars in which numerous young men without the franchise were called on to serve and, in many cases, die for their country. Two years after the Civil War, delegates to New York's constitutional convention offered a series of unsuccessful amendments seeking to provide suffrage rights to males eighteen and over.[19] One delegate argued: "We hold men at 18 liable to the draft and require them to peril their lives on the battlefield."[20]

---

[18] As with most wars, there were significant instances of rights retractions during Vietnam, particularly with regard to freedoms of speech, the press, and association. For an extensive discussion of these issues, see, for example: Geoffrey R. Stone, *Perilous Times: Free Speech in Wartime* (New York: W.W. Norton, 2004), 427–526.

[19] Wendell W. Cultice, *Youth's Battle for the Ballot: A History of Voting Age in America* (New York: Greenwood Press, 1992), 13–4.

[20] Close Up Foundation, "The 26th Amendment: Pathway to Participation," *First Vote* (Alexandria, VA: Close Up Foundation, 2001), 1.

In 1942, during World War II, Senator Arthur Vandenberg (R-MI) sponsored a constitutional amendment to lower the voting age to eighteen. "If
young men are to be drafted at 18 years of age to fight for their government,"
Vandenberg argued, "they ought to be entitled to vote at 18 years of age for
the kind of government for which they are best satisfied to fight."[21] In the
House, Representative Jennings Randolph (D-WV) sponsored the amendment,
and the Judiciary Committee held hearings in October 1943. At those hearings,
Randolph said: "I strongly feel one of the very cogent reasons why we should
consider this proposal today is that the impact of war on our society has lifted,
through the processes of the draft, from our home front millions of young men
and women in the age bracket of 18 to 20."[22] No further congressional action
came out of the Judiciary Committee hearings, though Georgia independently
lowered its voting age to eighteen that year.[23]

The issue emerged again in the midst of the Korean War when President
Eisenhower proposed lowering the voting age in his 1954 State of the Union
Address: "For years our citizens between the ages of 18 and 21 have, in time
of peril, been summoned to fight for America. They should participate in the
political process that produces this fateful summons. I urge Congress to propose
to the States a constitutional amendment permitting citizens to vote when they
reach the age of 18."[24] Now working on the other side of the Capitol in the
Senate, Randolph again sponsored a constitutional amendment. Though the
chamber gave it more attention than it had in 1943, the measure was unable to
eclipse the required two-thirds majority. But once again a lone state, this time
Kentucky, unilaterally lowered its voting age to 18 in 1955.[25]

In the ensuing fifteen years, prior to passage of the Twenty-Sixth Amendment, numerous other states – mostly by voter referenda – considered following
in Georgia and Kentucky's footsteps and independently lowering the voting
age for their citizens. With a handful of exceptions, most of these efforts failed
(see Table 6.1). And in those ten states that did unilaterally lower the voting age by 1970, three of them had only reduced the requisite age to twenty.
Eighteen states had tried and failed to reduce the voting age in those years,
though in 1970 Nebraska succeeded after an initial failure in 1968. Assessing
these numerous state-based initiatives, historian David E. Kyvig concludes that
"voting age reduction appeared to lack majority support, much less a broad

---

[21] Cultice, 20–1.

[22] Ibid., 22.

[23] David E. Kyvig, *Explicit and Authentic Acts: Amending the U.S. Constitution, 1776–1995*
(Lawrence, KS: University Press of Kansas, 1996), 364. See also, Cultice, 24–7.

[24] Dwight D. Eisenhower, "Annual Message to the Congress on the State of the Union, January 7, 1954," *Public Papers of the Presidents of the United States: Dwight D. Eisenhower, 1954* (Washington: Office of the Federal Register National Archives and Records Service, 1960), 22. http://www.eisenhowermemorial.org/speeches/19540107%20State%20of%
20the%20Union.htm.

[25] In 1952, also during Korea, Oklahoma and South Dakota rejected efforts to lower their states'
voting age.

TABLE 6.1. *State Action on Voting Age Prior to Ratification of Twenty-Sixth Amendment*

Lowered Voting Age:			Rejected Lowering Age:	
State	Age	Year	State	Year
GA	18	1943	OK	1952
KY	18	1955	SD	1952
AK[a]	19	1959	SD	1958
HI	20	1959	ID	1960
AK[a]	18	1970	MI	1966
MA	19	1970	NY	1967
ME	20	1970	HI[c]	1968
MN	19	1970	MD	1968
MT	19	1970	NE[c]	1968
NE	20	1970	ND	1968
KS[b]	18	1971	TN	1968
NV[b]	18	1971	NJ	1969
			CO	1970
			CT	1970
			FL	1970
			HI[c]	1970
			IL	1970
			MI	1970
			NJ	1970
			OR	1970
			SD	1970
			WA	1970
			WY	1970

[a] Note that Alaska appears on this chart twice. The voting age was reduced to 19 in 1956 and then to 18 in 1970.

[b] Kansas and Nevada lowered the voting age prior to the Twenty-Sixth Amendment but after *Oregon v. Mitchell* and, thus, were under the same threat of electoral upheaval that spurred quick passage of the amendment.

[c] Later lowered age prior to Twenty-Sixth Amendment.

Source: Wendell W. Cultice, *Youth's Battle for the Ballot* (Westport, CT: Greenwood Press, 1992), 206.

consensus.... [R]esentment against several years of campus demonstrations, sporadic urban rioting, and antiwar protest undoubtedly did more to persuade older citizens not to lower the voting age than it did to convince them that younger people possessed the requisite political maturity."[26]

[26] Kyvig, 365 and 364. For another view, see Carl M. Cannon, "Generation 'We'–The Awakened Giant," *National Journal* (10 Mar. 2007). See also, Cultice. Cultice argues that public opinion supported a lower voting age and refers to "public opinion running at a 61 percent figure in favor of a lower voting age" (33). However, Cultice provides no citation for this figure (or for anything

Although Kyvig is certainly right to note that the overwhelming and widespread support many previous amendment-bound issues enjoyed was absent in this case, he fails to emphasize that the state initiatives appeared to be gaining traction over time. After an eleven year drought, six states lowered their voting ages in 1970, and another two followed in 1971. Other state-based efforts barely failed. Additionally, the mere fact that such efforts were springing up in so many states in the late '60s and early '70s indicated a heightened level of interest in lowering the voting age.

The Twenty-Sixth Amendment

The issue emerged for a final time during the Vietnam War. In the midst of an increasingly difficult and unpopular conflict serviced by the military draft, lowering the voting age became more central in American political discourse than it had ever been. "Old enough to fight, old enough to vote" was a common refrain. The arguments for dropping the age had not changed. The only difference was that more people and organizations were vocally supporting it. Lyndon Johnson became the second president to call for a constitutional amendment shortly after withdrawing from the 1968 election.[27]

Unlike Eisenhower's lonely appeal in 1954, Johnson was not alone. That summer, both the Democratic and Republican parties voiced support for the cause in their 1968 platforms, though they advocated different means. The Democrats called for a constitutional amendment while Republicans said: "We believe that states which have not yet acted should reevaluate their positions with respect to 18-year-old voting, and that each such state should decide this matter for itself. We urge the states to act *now*."[28] Each party's presidential nominee (Democrat Hubert Humphrey and Republican Richard Nixon) vocally supported the change, as had candidate Robert Kennedy in the months before his assassination.[29]

As noted above, increased action at the state level – while often in the form of rejection – was also indicative of newfound, Vietnam-induced momentum. Six of the nine states that took it upon themselves to lower the voting age did so in 1970, in the midst of the war. And even amongst those states that formally rejected an age reduction, such rejections all came during the war: one in 1966, one in 1967, five in 1968, two in 1969, and nine in 1970.

---

else in his book, for that matter), and I was unable to find any such public opinion figures. Kyvig starkly notes these difficulties in Cultice's work, calling it the "only comprehensive study of voting age reform" but one that is "flawed in style, analysis, documentation, and, occasionally, statements of fact." (n532).

[27] Cultice, 93.

[28] Italics in original. "Democratic Platform" and "Republican Platform," *History of American Presidential Elections, 1789–1968*, vol. 4, ed., Arthur M. Schlesinger, Jr. (New York: Chelsea House Publishers, 1971), 3776 and 3786.

[29] Cannon, 22.

The formal process of reducing the voting age to eighteen at the federal level began in February 1970. Senator Birch Bayh (D-IN) held hearings in his Subcommittee on Constitutional Amendments. Among those testifying was Theodore Sorensen, a former aide to President John F. Kennedy, who argued that allowing 18–20 year olds the vote was a "moral issue."[30] "Those between the ages of 18 and 21," Sorensen said, "have no voice whatsoever in the process which determines whether they live or die. If taxation without representation was tyranny, then conscription without representation is slavery."[31]

Dr. Walter Menninger, a member of the National Commission on the Causes and Prevention of Violence, which had been created several years before by President Johnson, told Bayh's subcommittee that lowering the voting age would decrease the frustration youths felt, thereby offsetting their violent tendencies. Based on data the commission collected, Menninger argued that suffrage would provide "a direct, constructive, and democratic channel for making their views felt and for giving them a responsible stake in the future of the nation." Yet not all of his testimony relied on hard scientific evidence; Menninger also cited the Beatles song "Revolution" and its lyrics: "You say you'll change the constitution . . . Don't you know it's gonna be alright, alright, alright."[32]

Despite the growing support on Capitol Hill, there were still plenty of skeptics. Opponents offered a number of arguments over the years as the issue gained traction. House Judiciary Chairman Emanuel Celler (D-NY), a longtime opponent of teen voting, noted that soldiering and voting were starkly different activities and offered the strongest articulation of the potential dangers:

The draft age and the voting age are as different as chalk is from cheese. The thing called for in a soldier is uncritical obedience, and that is not what you want in a voter. To say that he who is old enough to fight is old enough to vote is to draw an utterly fallacious parallel. . . . Eighteen to twenty-one are mainly formative years . . . [offering] fertile ground to demagogues. . . . These are rightfully the years of rebellion rather than reflection. We will be doing a grave injustice to democracy if we grant the vote to those under 21. Leaders of radical movements understand that patience is not a particular virtue of the young. . . . [R]adicalism has had the greatest appeal to the youth . . . Hitler and Mussolini understood this; they advocated and accomplished the granting of the vote to eighteen-year-olds.[33]

The New York Times echoed Celler's point on the differences between fighting and voting. "The requirements for a good soldier and for a good voter are not the same. For the soldier, youthful enthusiasm and physical endurance

---

[30] U.S. Senate, Committee on the Judiciary, Subcommittee on Constitutional Amendments, *Lowering the Voting Age to 18: A Fifty-State Survey of the Costs and Other Problems of Dual-Age Voting*, 92nd Congress, 1st Session, 1971, 8.

[31] Cannon, 22.

[32] Kyvig, 365–6.

[33] Cultice, 46.

are of primary importance; for the voter, maturity of judgment far outweighs other qualifications."[34] Similarly, a former U.S. District Judge testified before Congress that, based on the results of quizzes and polling, teens possessed "a woeful ignorance of even our own country's history, to say nothing of the history of the world. Anybody really qualified to exercise the right of suffrage ought to have a fair knowledge of the course of history."[35]

Others pointed out what they saw as fallacies with the "old enough to fight, old enough to vote" mantra. *Collier's Weekly* editorialized that this pro-youth vote argument "doesn't justify giving young ladies of eighteen the right of franchise. And it brings to mind a remark by one of our colleagues: 'If a man is old enough to vote when he's old enough to fight, then logically the man who is too old to fight ought to lose the right to vote.'"[36] A final argument against federal action rested on states' rights. The *Washington Star* editorialized that the issue was not an urgent matter for the country and, thus, should be left to the states.[37]

Despite these criticisms, the issue continued to progress through the halls of Congress. In March of 1970, Senators Mike Mansfield (D-MT) and Edward Kennedy (D-MA) proposed tacking a lower voting age onto that year's Voting Rights Act renewal. The senators held that the 1966 case *Katzenbach v. Morgan* allowed for such a rider. That decision provided Congress with the authority to pass laws in support of the Fourteenth Amendment. The Senate passed the renewal of the seminal 1965 civil rights law, along with the provision for the voting age adjustment, by a 64–17 vote. The House followed suit in a 272–132 vote, with Celler's blessing. The longtime opponent ultimately voted for the bill because he thought extending the Voting Rights Act was of greater import and because he was confident the Supreme Court would strike down the voting age rider on states' rights grounds. Nixon – a proponent of lowering the voting age – also thought it was unconstitutional as a federal infringement on the states. Nonetheless, he signed the bill on June 22, 1970, throwing the issue to the judiciary.[38]

The U.S. Supreme Court's response that December in *Oregon v. Mitchell* defied all expectations.[39] Four justices sided with Mansfield and Kennedy, arguing that lowering the voting age was within Congress' constitutional

---

[34] "The Right to Vote," *The New York Times* (25 Mar. 1967), 22. See also: "The Right Voting Age," *New York Times* (7 July 1967), 32. In 1970 the paper switched its position and editorialized in favor of a lower voting age: "Enlarging the Electorate," *New York Times* (21 Jun 1970), 160; "The 18-Year Old Vote," *New York Times* (22 Dec. 1970), 32; "Uniform Voting Age," *New York Times* (7 Mar. 1971), E12.

[35] Cultice, 47.

[36] "What's Your Idea About It?," *Collier's Weekly* (11 July 1953), 70.

[37] Cultice, 49.

[38] Keyssar, 280; Cultice, 137; Kyvig, 366.

[39] *Oregon v. Mitchell*, 400 U.S. 112 (1970). For more on this decision, see: Richard S. Greene, "Congressional Power over the Elective Franchise: The Unconstitutional Phases of *Oregon v. Mitchell*," *Boston University Law Review* 52 (1972), 509–69.

authority. Four other justices agreed with Celler and Nixon that the rider was an infringement on states' rights. Justice Hugo Black split the difference, arguing that Congress had the right to take such action for national elections but not for those at the state level. In effect, the ruling created the daunting prospect of eighteen- to twenty-year olds being eligible to vote for president and their representatives in Congress but, in most states, not being allowed to vote for anything farther down the ticket.[40] The only way to create a uniform voting age was through a constitutional amendment. If this was to be done before the fast approaching 1972 elections, speed and efficiency would be necessary in a process designed to be slow and deliberative. Indeed, before moving to the states – three-fourths of which would be needed for approval – the proposal again had to move through Congress, an institution not known for its cat-like reflexes.

Contrary to stereotype, Congress acted "with decisiveness [and] what passed in the Capitol for lightning speed."[41] Randolph again introduced a proposal, this time in the form of an amendment resolution, on January 25, 1971. Bayh's subcommittee passed the resolution on to the full Judiciary Committee on March 2, and it was sent to the Senate floor two days later. That chamber unanimously passed the resolution 94–0. Less than two weeks later, and with Celler's acquiescence in deference to the prospect of an electoral mess, the resolution passed the House in lopsided fashion, 401–19. The whole process on Capitol Hill took less than two months.[42]

Like Congress, the states feared the *Oregon* decision would produce an election day nightmare if the amendment was not ratified. As such, they acted quickly, too. Remarkably, five states – including Connecticut and Washington, whose voters had rejected a voting age reduction only a few months before – acted later in the same day as the U.S. House of Representatives' vote. By July 1, the necessary thirty-eight states had completed the ratification process and, subsequently, four other states signed off as well. Among those ratifying the amendment were eight of the ten states whose citizens defeated referendums on this matter within the previous two years.[43] Despite this awkward predicament,

---

[40] Keyssar, 281.

[41] Kyvig, *Explicit and Authentic Acts*, 367.

[42] Ibid.

[43] Among these was Ohio, whose voters had narrowly rejected a referendum to lower their state's voting age to nineteen in 1969. Nonetheless, in 1971 the Ohio Senate ratified the amendment 30 to 2 with the House following suit by a margin of 81 to 9. In both chambers, only two legislators suggested that ratifying the amendment was contradictory to the voters' expressed wishes. Also of interest, Ohio was the critical 38th state to ratify the amendment and, thus, ensure its passage. This, despite Oklahoma giving the Buckeye State a run for its money. Following Senate approval at the other end of the state capitol, the Ohio House, aware that all the prestige of being the critical 38th state hung in the balance, called a special night session when word reached Columbus that the Oklahoma Statehouse was also working overtime for the honor. A hasty ten minute debate was ended after which the chamber held its vote. On this topic, see: "Amending the U.S. Constitution: Ratification Controversies, 1917–1971," *Ohio History* 83 (1974), 156–69.

there was virtually no controversy or protest in those states over the amendment and its apparent rebuke to public opinion. When all was said and done, the Twenty-Sixth Amendment to the U.S. Constitution was on the books in 101 days, shattering the record for fastest approval previously held by the Twelfth Amendment, which passed in 1804 after six months and six days.[44]

The Vietnam War clearly played a decisive role in lowering the voting age but, as discussed above, proposals to this end were not new. Previous attempts to allow 18 year olds the franchise were all inspired by wars and what many deemed the questionable practice of subjecting non-voting youths to the elected government's military draft. Yet these early efforts were rejected. What accounts for the issue's triumph during Vietnam after so many failures? Kyvig emphasizes the bizarre set of circumstances. As noted above, he controversially argues that there was a lack of public support for lowering the voting age, citing the multiple state-level defeats preceding the amendment. For Kyvig, the Twenty-Sixth Amendment "challenged the prevailing belief that only constitutional changes enjoying enormous popular acceptance stood any chance of being approved."[45] This assessment does not diminish Vietnam's influence, but it does suggest the amendment was an elite-driven phenomenon. Based on this interpretation, unusual circumstances ultimately led to the amendment's success. The initial rider on the Voting Rights Act renewal was only successful because major opponents like Celler were certain the Supreme Court would reject it. Then, in a surprise to everyone, Justice Black's tie-splitting opinion had the effect of holding a gun to the states' head. At that point, not passing the amendment risked a lack of standardization that could provoke major election complications. Thus, for Kyvig, Vietnam was a necessary, but not sufficient, precipitator. Only with soap-opera twists and turns did the amendment ever gain ratification.

Elite level momentum was certainly important, but at least three other factors likely played a role as well. First, Vietnam was a particularly divisive and unpopular war. Though most American wars have been controversial (with World War II as the lone exception), Vietnam was second only to the Civil War in its divisiveness. Keyssar argues that Vietnam's unpopularity led directly to a widespread anti-draft movement. "In the political climate of the mid- and late-1960s," he writes, "the issue of eighteen-, nineteen-, and twenty-year olds voting acquired an unprecedented urgency; indeed their lack of enfranchisement served . . . to underscore the absence of democratic support for the war and to legitimize resistance to the draft."[46] As such, the voting age issue probably gained more traction than it had in previous episodes. Second, voting rights broadly defined were on the national agenda in a way they had not been previously. The Civil Rights Act of 1964 and the Voting Rights Act of 1965 and other "rights" based movements may well have primed citizens and public

[44] Cultice, 215.
[45] Kyvig, 363.
[46] Keyssar, 279.

officials to be more open to teenage voting than in previous decades. Finally, constitutional amendments were a bit of a trend at the time. The Twenty-Sixth Amendment was the fourth in a ten year period – the highest concentration of amendment production since the Bill of Rights.[47] Thus, amending the Constitution appeared a less difficult hurdle in 1971 than it ever had before or than it does today.

THE FLOWER CHILDREN GO TO WASHINGTON

The Vietnam War, like other major conflicts before it, had a considerable effect on the party system. This was especially true in the battle for the Democratic Party's nomination in 1968 and 1972. And, in both cases, the combative selection process carried over into the general election. The divisive nomination battle in 1968 seriously damaged eventual nominee Hubert Humphrey's position entering the fall campaign against Republican Richard Nixon. That election spurred an important reform in the Democratic Party's method of selecting presidential candidates. Smoke-filled rooms were out and the now-familiar primary system was in. Republicans quickly followed with a primary system of their own. In 1972, operating under this new presidential candidate selection system, Democrats nominated an ideologically extreme candidate and, as a result, were severely disadvantaged in the general election.

Vietnam also upended the party system's equilibrium by producing significant changes in the Democratic Party's ideology. So-called "New Politics" Democrats rose to power through their opposition to the Vietnam War and gained control of the party. Although they successfully nominated their preferred candidate in 1972, George McGovern's decisive defeat that November weakened their position. Nonetheless, they left a significant imprint on their party's ideology that can still be seen today – especially with regard to Democratic positioning on foreign affairs, identity politics, and social (or cultural) liberalism. This key point of change in the Democrats' ideology has also contributed to the current intraparty ideological cohesion and interparty polarization.

Presidential Elections and Candidate Selection in the Vietnam Era

Like the 1952 presidential election, political scientists have written extensively about the 1968 and 1972 contests. As previously noted, foreign affairs are generally thought to have little effect on elections. The political science literature maintains this position with reference to the 1968 election, though in slightly different form. Vietnam was, according to relevant studies, electorally

---

[47] The Twenty-Third Amendment establishing presidential electors for the District of Columbia was ratified in 1961. The Twenty-Fourth, ratified three years later, banned poll taxes in federal elections. And in 1967, the Twenty-Fifth Amendment addressed presidential and vice presidential succession.

unimportant, but only because the parties offered up candidates with nearly indistinguishable views.

There is no controversy over the country's deep division over the war.[48] The 1968 Michigan election study, for instance, said Vietnam was a "towering issue," noting that voters cited the war as the most important problem facing the country.[49] Nonetheless, as Benjamin I. Page and Richard A. Brody concluded:

Despite the unusually high salience of the Vietnam war in 1968, the conventional wisdom about American electoral politics remained true; policy preferences had little effect on the major-party vote. The reason for this slight impact of a great issue lay in voters' perceptions of where the candidates stood on Vietnam. Most people saw little or no difference between Nixon's position and Humphrey's.[50]

Page and Brody further argue that this inability to perceive a difference between the two major candidates was rooted in the fact that there really was very little difference between them on Vietnam – not that the voters were simply incapable of making distinctions.[51]

One political science account reaches a different conclusion.[52] Richard W. Boyd argues that Vietnam had a striking influence on the 1968 election by using a "normal vote" analysis, an approach originally devised by Philip E. Converse.[53] This method estimates a party's expected proportion of the vote for

[48] For perhaps the best political science account of the country's division at that time, see: Sidney Verba and Richard A. Brody, "Participation, Policy Preferences, and the War in Vietnam," *American Political Science Review* 34:3 (1970), 325–32. See also: John E. Mueller, "Trends in Popular Support for the Wars in Korea and Vietnam," *American Political Science Review* 65:2 (1971), 358–75.

[49] Philip E. Converse, Warren E. Miller, Jerrold G. Rusk, and Arthur C. Wolfe, "Continuity and Change in American Politics: Parties and Issues in the 1968 Election," *American Political Science Review* 63:4 (1969), 1085, 1087.

[50] Benjamin I. Page and Richard A. Brody, "Policy Voting and the Electoral Process: The Vietnam War Issue," *American Political Science Review* 66:3 (1972), 993–4; Converse, Miller, Rusk, and Wolfe call Vietnam a "major issue influence" but do so in the context of the general setting going into the nomination battle (1088). See also: Brody and Page, "The Assessment of Policy Voting," *American Political Science Review* 66 (1972), 450–8; Verba and Norman H. Nie, *Participation in America: Political Democracy and Social Equality* (New York: Harper & Row, 1972); Verba and Nie, *Participation in America: Political Democracy and Social Equality* (New York: Harper & Row, 1972); Milton J. Rosenberg, Verba, and Converse, *Vietnam and Silent Majority* (New York: Harper & Row, 1970).

[51] Page and Brody, 994. This claim is supported by evidence that voters were able to perceive ex-Democrat and third party candidate George Wallace as favoring a hard line on Vietnam and failed Democratic nomination candidate Eugene McCarthy as an advocate for de-escalation. The authors conclude: "Americans seem to have had the capacity to vote their policy preferences."

[52] There is one other notable exception. Like his account of Korea and the 1952 election, John Kenneth White emphasizes Vietnam's effect on the 1968 and 1972 election but does not engage the political science literature. See: John Kenneth White, *Still Seeing Red: How the Cold War Shapes the New American Politics* (Boulder, CO: Westview Press, 1997), 169–78.

[53] Richard W. Boyd, "Popular Control of Public Policy: A Normal Vote Analysis of the 1968 Election," *American Political Science Review* 66:2 (1972), 429–49; Converse, "The Concept of a Normal Vote," *Elections and the Political Order*, eds., Angus Campbell, Converse, Miller, and Donald E. Stokes (New York: Wiley, 1966), 9–39. For more on the normal vote, see: Harvey

subgroups in a normal election based on party identification, typical defection rates to other parties, and turnout. Boyd notes, the "normal vote technique is a particularly useful means of relating issues to the vote by. . . . permit[ing] the analyst to separate issues from their partisan (long term) components."[54] He found that Humphrey polled 12 percentage points lower than the predicted normal vote among that portion of the public favoring a withdrawal from Vietnam. The Democratic nominee also suffered among the 34 percent of the population desiring an escalation (nearly twice as many as those seeking de-escalation) – performing 24 percentage points below his expected level. Humphrey's best segment was amongst those seeking to maintain the status quo, but even here he came in 8 points below the expected "normal" value. Though Humphrey underperformed in all areas, Boyd concludes, his liability was most profound amongst "hawks," followed by "doves," and least – but still significantly – amongst the majority advocating the status quo.[55]

The war's effect on the 1972 contest is also hazy in the elections literature. Unlike 1968, there were ostensibly unambiguous differences between the candidates on Vietnam, an issue that was of chief concern to 25 percent of voters. As a result, some scholars contend the war had more of an effect on the vote that year.[56] Yet even if this is true, the war may have been second in importance behind ideology, where Nixon had a large advantage. Paul R. Abramson, John Aldrich, and David W. Rohde demonstrate that McGovern was seen as very liberal, whereas Nixon was perceived as a moderate conservative and much more in line with the average American's thinking.[57] Moreover, Edward G. Carmines and James A. Stimson maintain that the apparently clear distinctions between the candidates on the war were actually less clear and less relevant than they appeared. The differences were only over the rate of withdrawal and were ambiguous. McGovern pledged an immediate pullout while Nixon claimed to have already resolved the situation with his hard-line approach. Carmines and Stimson conclude:

> While antiwar activists may have seen a wide gulf separating the candidates' positions, we believe most voters saw the issue in far more narrow terms, focusing mainly on the speed and conditions of withdrawal. The confusion was heightened, finally, by the fact that Democratic presidents had initiated and vigorously prosecuted the war

M. Kabaker, "Estimating the Normal Vote in Congressional Elections," *Midwest Journal of Political Science* 23 (Feb. 1969), 58–83; Barbara Hinckley, "Incumbency and the Presidential Vote in Senate Elections: Defining the Parameters of Subpresidential Voting," *American Political Science Review* 64 (Sept. 1970), 836–42; Arthur H. Miller, "Normal Vote Analysis: Sensitivity to Change Over Time," *American Journal of Political Science* 23 (1979), 406–25. Normal vote analysis later became controversial and has fallen into disuse. For unfavorable critiques of the method, see: Page and Calvin C. Jones, "Reciprocal Effects of Policy Preferences, Party Loyalties, and the Vote," *American Political Science Review* 73:4 (1979), 1078; Christopher H. Achen, "The Bias in Normal Vote Estimates," *Political Methodology* 6 (1979), 343–56.

[54] Boyd, 429–30.
[55] Ibid., 433.
[56] Paul R. Abramson, John H. Aldrich, and David W. Rohde, *Change and Continuity in the 1980 Elections* (Washington: Congressional Quarterly Press, 1982), 122, 140.
[57] Ibid., 127.

while the Republican incumbent had sharply reduced the number of U.S. troops in Vietnam.... The pace of withdrawal from Vietnam (the "choice" offered in the 1972 presidential election) was clearly a hard issue by our criteria.... [The issue] dealt with the best means of ending the war, but with nearly universal agreement on the ultimate end.[58]

In sum, Vietnam was an unusual issue in the 1972 election.

Thus, the elections literature is somewhat ambiguous about Vietnam's effect on the 1968 and 1972 general elections because these contests did not offer clear differences between the parties on Vietnam. Yet, these studies also pointedly suggest that foreign affairs had the potential to be dramatically influential in both cases. Only the difficulty in perceiving differences between the candidates mitigated the war's effect. In light of public opinion, the two parties both rushed to promise that they would bring the war to an end. Thus, even though the parties were not disagreeing with each other, these elections were very much driven by foreign policy considerations. Less ambiguously, Vietnam had a major influence on the Democratic nominations in each instance.

The 1968 Presidential Election

The Democrats had designed the 1968 party convention and campaign to bolster the prospects of President Johnson's reelection by scheduling the Chicago convention to coincide with his August 27th birthday. Yet a large segment of Democratic activists were strongly opposed to Johnson's Vietnam policies. The disapproval extended to the public as well. By February of 1968, a majority of Americans felt the U.S. made a "mistake" in entering Vietnam, and a month later 69 percent expressed a desire to phase out. At the same time, Johnson's public approval slid to 41 percent, with 47 percent disapproving of his performance. In opposition to Johnson's policies on the war and in response to this polling data, some Democrats began organizing to challenge Johnson for the nomination.[59]

Minnesota Senator Eugene McCarthy emerged as the standard-bearer for this liberal, anti-war wing of the party. He entered the race and vigorously campaigned in advance of the New Hampshire primary. Although Johnson's supporters launched a write-in campaign that succeeded, the President's scant 48.5 percent to 42 percent margin of victory was seen as a sign of weakness. This perception led New York Senator and former Attorney General Robert Kennedy to throw his hat in the ring, appealing to the same coalition that

---

[58] Edward G. Carmines and James A. Stimson, "The Two Faces of Issue Voting," *American Political Science Review* 74:1 (1980), 81.

[59] Nelson W. Polsby, *Consequences of Party Reform* (New York: Oxford University Press, 1983), 19–20. See also: Lewis Chester, Godfrey Hodgson, and Bruce Page, *An American Melodrama: The Presidential Campaign of 1968* (New York: Viking Press, 1969); Theodore H. White, *The Making of the President 1968* (New York: Atheneum Publishers, 1969).

backed McCarthy as well as those party regulars who had supported his brother but were less enthusiastic about Johnson.[60]

Two weeks later, Johnson, with a dwindling 36 percent approval rating, withdrew from contention for the Democratic nomination.[61] After a long discussion of the Vietnam War and its difficulties in a nationally televised address, the President said:

With America's sons in the fields far away, with America's future under challenge right here at home, with our hopes and the world's hopes for peace in the balance every day, I do not believe that I should devote an hour or a day of my time to any personal partisan causes or to any duties other than the awesome duties of this office – the Presidency of your country. Accordingly, I shall not seek, and I will not accept, the nomination of my party for another term as your President.[62]

As Nelson Polsby notes, Johnson's decision "gave the sizeable fraction of Democratic party activists that wanted to dump Johnson a stunning victory: Johnson had dumped himself."[63]

There is general scholarly consensus that Vietnam was pivotal in Johnson's decision to withdraw.[64] As Johnson recounted to Doris Kearns, an aide who later helped him write his memoir:

I felt that I was being chased on all sides by a giant stampede coming at me from all directions. On one side, the American people were stampeding me to do something about Vietnam. On another side, the inflationary economy was booming out of control. . . . I was being forced over the edge by rioting blacks, demonstrating students, marching welfare mothers, squawking professors, and hysterical reporters. And then the final straw. . . . Robert Kennedy had openly announced his intention to reclaim the throne in the memory of his brother. And the American people, swayed by the magic of his name, were dancing in the streets. The whole situation was unbearable to me.[65]

Were it not for the war, Johnson likely would not have sunk so far in the polls and the party would not have developed the strong anti-war faction that gave rise to McCarthy and, later, Kennedy. In short, had the focus been on Johnson's Great Society programs rather than his handling of the war, he probably would

---

[60] Ibid., 21.

[61] Jules Witcover, *Party of the People: A History of the Democrats* (New York: Random House, 2003), 544.

[62] *Public Papers of the Presidents of the United States: Lyndon B. Johnson, 1968–69*, Vol. 1, Entry 170 (Washington: Government Printing Office, 1970), 476.

[63] Polsby, *Consequences of Party Reform*, 21–2.

[64] See, for instance, Randall B. Woods, *LBJ: Architect of American Ambition* (New York: Free Press, 2006), 834–7; Johnson, *Congress and the Cold War*, 141–2; Witcover, 544; Irving Bernstein, *Guns or Butter: The Presidency of Lyndon Johnson* (New York: Oxford University Press, 1996); Doris Kearns, *Lyndon Johnson and the American Dream* (New York: Harper & Row, 1976), 343.

[65] Kearns, 343.

have remained in the race and garnered the 1968 Democratic nomination and, quite possibly, another term in the White House.[66]

With Johnson out of the picture, Vice President Humphrey quickly organized his own candidacy, announcing it publicly on April 27. Contrary to the primary-based, outsider strategy employed by McCarthy and Kennedy, Humphrey chose to fight for the nomination the old-fashioned way, as an insider and through the party apparatus at the national convention. James W. Ceaser identifies 1968 as the last nomination in the "mixed system" where candidates could attempt to win their party's nomination with an insider, outsider, or combined approach.[67] At this time, primary winners could secure delegate votes at the convention as well as momentum and credibility. But these victories were not sufficient to capture the nomination outright because many delegates were not bound by primary results. For Humphrey, the traditional approach was possible because there were still relatively few primaries, and it was necessary because of his late start in fundraising and organizing.[68]

By the time of the important California primary, polls indicated that 40 percent of Democrats supported Humphrey, 31 percent favored Kennedy, 19 percent backed McCarthy, and 10 percent were undecided. Yet the nomination was far from locked up, and Kennedy and McCarthy contrasted the several primaries they each had won with Humphrey's failure to enter any. In what Polsby calls "one of the most extraordinary and consequential events in modern American political history," Kennedy carried the California primary, along with its large total of 174 delegate votes, only to be assassinated later that night.[69]

Much has been written about what might have happened had Kennedy lived, but, despite his California victory, it seems likely Humphrey would have won the nomination based on impartial delegate counts.[70] In the end, of course, Humphrey did go on to run as the Democrats' standard bearer in the general

---

[66] There is some thinking that Johnson might have retired anyway in 1968. His health was terrible early that year, and he thought he might not survive another four year term. Indeed, he died from a heart attack almost exactly four years after leaving office. As such, his departure was overdetermined. Nonetheless, Vietnam was undoubtedly a big part of the reason. To his anti-war opposition, though, Vietnam came to exhaust the causal mix as they celebrated their efforts to force him out of office. For more on LBJ's health as one spur to his retirement, see: Robert Dallek, *Flawed Giant: Lyndon Johnson and His Times, 1961–1973* (New York: Oxford University Press, 1998), 522–3, 526–9, 602, 605, 619–22; Irwin Unger and Debi Unger, *LBJ: A Life* (New York: John Wiley, 1999), 439–41, 458–9; Woods, 767–8, 817, 882–4.

[67] James W. Ceaser, *Presidential Selection: Theory and Development* (Princeton, NJ: Princeton University Press, 1979), 227–48.

[68] Polsby, *Consequences of Party Reform*, 22–3.

[69] Ibid., 24.

[70] On delegate counts, see: Polsby, *Consequences of Party Reform*, 24–5. For speculation on what would have happened if Kennedy lived, see: Arthur M. Schlesinger, Jr., *Robert Kennedy and His Times* (Boston: Houghton Mifflin, 1978); Jack Newfield, *Robert Kennedy: A Memoir* (New York: Dutton, 1969); Witcover, *Eighty-Five Days* (New York: G.P. Putnam's Sons, 1969); David Halberstam, *The Unfinished Odyssey of Robert Kennedy* (New York: Random House, 1968).

election against Nixon – but not before he was substantially weakened. The assassination further solidified the split within the Democratic Party over the war. The McCarthy and Kennedy anti-war forces united in viewing Humphrey as an illegitimate nominee. As Polsby writes:

Finding themselves prevented by state party rules from exploiting a number of opportunities to convert their indignation about the war into solid delegate votes, McCarthy strategists called foul [and] put together a blue ribbon commission on the delegate selection process... which served as a clearing house for atrocity stories about the management of the nomination process by party leaders... [These stories] were given wide circulation and fueled resentment of Humphrey.[71]

Clearly, the Kennedy assassination inflamed the Democrats' split over Vietnam, setting the anti-war party activists even more strongly against Humphrey.

The problem was only reinforced at the Democrats' convention in Chicago. An effort to write an anti-war plank in the party's platform was overturned by Johnson (who was still in control of the convention) after Humphrey's attempts to compromise on the measure failed. The President's hostility toward McCarthy over basic procedural matters further inflamed the situation even though Humphrey received no preferential treatment. Finally, the protests and violence that accompanied the convention exacerbated the divide because, as Polsby concludes: "A significant feature of many accounts of violence at the Democratic convention was the effort to pin the blame on the Democratic nominee, Hubert Humphrey."[72]

Nixon's victory in the general election marked the first Republican triumph in twelve years. Just as notable as the GOP regaining the White House, was the dramatic plunge in Democratic support. In 1964, Lyndon Johnson won 61 percent of the popular vote while Humphrey mustered less than 43 percent in 1968, marking one of the biggest plummets in U.S. history.[73] Its only rivals are the Republicans' 1912 collapse (aided by former president Theodore Roosevelt's third party candidacy) and their 1932 disaster (following the 1929 stock market crash that initiated the Great Depression). Granted, Johnson's 1964 opponent, Barry Goldwater, was ideologically extreme. Furthermore, the 1968 election played out after Johnson signed the 1964 Civil Rights Act and the 1965 Voting Rights Act. In recent decades, political scientists and historians generally agree that, by doing so, Johnson undercut his party's support in the South, causing outrage that fueled Alabama Governor George Wallace's third party run and threw several Southern states to Nixon.[74] These domestically focused studies,

---

[71] Polsby, *Consequences of Party Reform*, 26–7.

[72] Ibid., 32.

[73] For a more extensive analysis of these kinds of short-term fluctuations (with a focus on the U.S. House), see: Gerald H. Kramer, "Short-Term Fluctuations in U.S. Voting Behavior, 1896–1964," *American Political Science Review* 65:1 (1971), 131–43.

[74] For more on the alleged racial component of growing Republican success in the South beginning in the 1960s, see, for instance: Earl and Merle Black, *The Rise of Southern Republicans* (Cambridge, MA: Harvard University Press, 2003); Dan T. Carter, *From George Wallace to*

though, often ignore the backdrop of Vietnam. In addition, accounts at the time placed much less emphasis on racism as a driving factor.[75] In any event, the Nixon and Wallace votes in 1968 certainly reflected a repudiation of the ruling Democrats. And although other things were going on, Vietnam was the major issue of the day.[76]

In sum, Vietnam had a great influence on the 1968 election. President Johnson dropped out in the face of fierce anti-war opposition within his own party. And while Humphrey eventually secured the Democratic nomination, he was weakened because, as vice president, he was closely linked with Vietnam, and he had become a source of derision for the party's anti-war faction. The nomination fight, and Humphrey's diminished position at the end of it, complements Boyd's "normal vote" analysis discussed above. Humphrey ultimately got the worst of both worlds. As Boyd shows, the Vice President was unpopular with everyone when it came to the war, coming in under his expected "normal" vote by 12 percent amongst those seeking withdrawal, by 24 percent amongst those advocating escalation, and by 8 percent amongst those favoring the status quo.[77] For those endorsing an end to the war, he was seen as Johnson's nominee and the opponent of the peace candidates, McCarthy and Kennedy. For those seeking to maintain the status quo or escalate the war, the nomination fight and the tumultuous convention cast the Democratic Party as one of withdrawal and weakness because of the strong anti-war faction within it. Finally, and as an outgrowth of many Democrats' dismay over the 1968 results, calls were issued to reevaluate the manner in which party nominees for president were selected.

Democratizing the Presidential Nominating Process

Does process determine outcome? For many Democrats in 1968, the answer was "yes." The proper mode of selecting presidential candidates has been

---

Newt Gingrich: Race in the Conservative Counterrevolution (Baton Rouge, LA: Louisiana State University Press, 1999); Carter, *The Politics of Rage: George Wallace, the Origins of the New Conservatism, and the Transformation of American Politics* (Baton Rouge, LA: Louisiana State University Press, 2000). Recently this standard view that race was behind the South's shift from the Democratic to Republican Party has been countered. This alternative view suggests that post-World War II economic development and industrialization created a new middle class in the South that was receptive to the Republicans' economic conservatism. See: Byron E. Shafer and Richard Johnston, *The End of Southern Exceptionalism: Class, Race, and Partisan Change in the Postwar South* (Cambridge, MA: Harvard University Press, 2006).

[75] The Michigan account of the 1968 election, for instance, focuses on Wallace's appeal as the "law and order" candidate. Though the authors discuss Wallace's appeal among whites, the focus on overt racism that characterizes more recent scholarship is absent. And, as stated above, the Michigan authors cite Vietnam as the number one issue in 1968. Converse, Miller, Rusk, and Wolfe, 1085–7.

[76] Converse, Miller, Rusk, and Wolfe, 993–4.

[77] Boyd, 433. See also: Converse, Miller, Rusk, and Wolfe, 1090, 1092–5; Abramson, Aldrich, and Rohde, 123.

debated since the nation's founding, and the process received a major shakeup as a result of the Vietnam War.[78] Reforms initiated by the Democratic Party following their 1968 convention made primaries the only route to a major party's presidential nomination, closing off the formerly available "insider strategy" of appealing to party leaders. According to Polsby, these reforms were important because "changing the rules of politics changes the incentives for political actors... changing incentives leads to changes in political behavior... changing behavior changes political institutions and their significance in politics."[79] In short, Vietnam played a major role in changing the presidential nominee selection process and this reform, in turn, marked a key institutional transformation in the American political system.

From 1920 to 1968 presidential candidates were selected in what James W. Ceaser calls a "mixed system." Candidates had the option of pursuing an inside, outside, or mixed strategy to gain their party's nomination. The insider approach rested on appeals to party leaders and avoidance of the relatively few primary contests. Outsiders, on the other hand, entered and tried to win as many primaries as they could in the hope of demonstrating their widespread appeal and forcing party elites to acquiesce. Other candidates chose to pursue a mixed or "entrepreneurial" approach that included some combination of insider and outsider strategies.[80] A key point here is that the importance of primaries was, at best, largely symbolic during this period. They represented a way for the public to weigh in on candidate selection before convention delegates and party elites did the real work of choosing the nominee behind closed doors.

The Democrats' 1968 nomination of Vice President Hubert Humphrey was the spark that fueled the establishment of the primary system of presidential candidate selection that remains in place today. As described earlier, Humphrey was seen as President Johnson's candidate and an opponent of the anti-war forces that rallied around New York Senator Robert Kennedy and Minnesota Senator Eugene McCarthy. The salient point is that the nomination was bitterly contested following Kennedy's assassination and the anti-war faction came to see Humphrey's victory as illegitimate because it was not in keeping with the people's wishes. McCarthy supporters railed against the lack of democracy in the delegate selection process and triggered the formation of a commission to investigate the system. In Polsby's words, "[t]he 'old' rules were 'old' politics.

---

[78] For a complete account of presidential candidate selection from the founding era through 1920 as well as the theoretical underpinnings of the debates over the process, see: Ceaser, *Presidential Selection*.

[79] Polsby, *Consequences of Party Reform*, 5. See also: Ceaser, *Reforming the Reforms: A Critical Analysis of the Presidential Nominating Process* (Cambridge, MA: Ballinger Publishing Co., 1982).

[80] Ceaser, *Presidential Selection*, 228–9. The term "entrepreneurial" comes from: Hugh Heclo, "Presidential and Prime Ministerial Selection," *Perspectives on Presidential Selection*, ed., Donald R. Matthews (Washington, DC: Brookings Institution, 1973).

'New politics' demanded new and more democratic rules."[81] In essence, the anti-war McCarthy and Kennedy supporters thought they had been cheated. As they saw it, Humphrey was the establishment candidate associated with an unpopular war and the only reason he won was because the system was rigged. As a result, liberal New Politics Democrats initiated an intraparty reform effort to ensure "the people's" candidate would fare better in 1972 and beyond.

The process was set in motion during the 1968 convention when the liberal minority report from the Committee on Rules and Order of Business called for a series of reforms and the establishment of a special committee to study delegate choice. The proposal narrowly passed with Humphrey's blessing. Many party regulars failed to realize the motion's full and potentially drastic implications.[82] As part of the reform effort, the Commission on Party Structure and Delegate Selection, or the McGovern-Fraser Commission as it was more popularly known, was formed in early 1969. This group issued its report to the Democratic National Committee in April 1970. The reformers thought that the legitimacy of the political process was at stake and that "demands for change" from underrepresented groups – especially blacks, women, and young people – and from "issue-oriented individuals," whose concerns centered on critical public policy questions not addressed in the traditional interest group system, needed attention.[83]

Revising the delegate selection system was the solution to this perceived problem. Quotas were established in the delegate selection process to, in the McGovern-Fraser Commission's words, ensure "proportional representation" in which "minority groups, young people, and women [serve as delegates] in reasonable relationship to their presence in the population of the State."[84] Although this kind of proportional representation is rare in the United States and arguably conflicts with the nation's tradition of respecting individual, rather than group, rights, the change was a way of advancing and accommodating multiculturalism. It mandated that in order to become a delegate, one had to fit into the right niche on a multidimensional demographically designed matrix. At the 1972 Democratic Convention there were three times as many female and black delegates and over seven times as many delegates

---

[81] Polsby, *Consequences of Party Reform*, 27. See also: Ceaser, "Political Parties–Declining, Stabilizing, or Resurging?," *The New American Political System*, ed., Anthony King (Washington, DC: AEI Press, 1990), 92–4.

[82] Bruce Miroff, *The Liberals' Moment: The McGovern Insurgency and the Identity Crisis of the Democratic Party* (Lawrence, KS: Kansas University Press, 2007), 20; Shafer, *Quiet Revolution: The Struggle for the Democratic Party and the Shaping of Post-Reform Politics* (New York: Russell Sage Foundation, 1983), 195–6.

[83] Ceaser, *Presidential Selection*, 279–80. See also: Miroff, 19–23; Shafer, *Quiet Revolution*; William J. Crotty, *Decision for the Democrats: Reforming the Party Structure* (Baltimore, MD: Johns Hopkins University Press, 1978).

[84] Commission of Party Structure and Delegate Selection to the Democratic National Committee, *Mandate for Reform* (Washington, DC: 1970), 34.

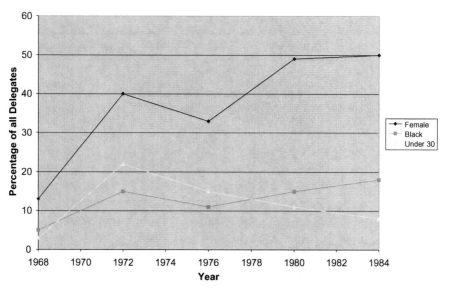

FIGURE 6.1. Sex, Race, and Age Composition of Democratic National Convention Delegates.[85]

in their twenties (see Figure 6.1). This requirement has affected the way Democratic conventions have operated ever since. Following the implementation of these reforms, Democrats have organized themselves according to group-based caucuses (Hispanic, black, women's, labor, etc.) in addition to the traditional internal organizational structure provided by state delegations.[86] While the party conventions no longer select presidential nominees, they are still symbolically important. The Democrats' adoption of proportional representation was, and remains, a clear signal that multicultural group-based considerations play a central role in the party's public philosophy.

A "plebiscitary system" was also established on the theory that mass opinion should guide presidential candidate selection rather than a group of elites hunkered down in smoke-filled rooms representing established interests. As such, the McGovern-Fraser Commission called for a completely open delegate selection process and the elimination of the practice whereby party leaders secretly selected delegates.[87] This call led most states to establish primaries, which then

[85] William Crotty and John S. Jackson III, *Presidential Primaries and Nominations* (Washington, DC: CQ Press, 1985), 108.
[86] Jo Freeman, "The Political Culture of the Democratic and Republican Parties," *Political Science Quarterly* 101:3 (1986), 327–56. See especially, pages 332–3. The Republican Party's conventions do not have caucuses, relying fully on the state delegations.
[87] The reformers' goal was not necessarily to increase the number of primaries. This approach simply proved to be the most efficient way to eliminate the party bosses. Ceaser, *Reforming the Reforms*, 123–4.

TABLE 6.2. *Number of Primaries and Delegates Selected*

Year	Democrats		Republicans	
	# of Primaries	% of Total Delegates	# of Primaries	% of Total Delegates
1952	18	48	14	45
1956	20	48	19	49
1960	18	43	16	44
1964	18	43	17	46
1968	17	41	16	43
1972	23	65	22	56
1976	29	75	28	67
1980	30	71	33	75
1984	24	54	28	63
1988	33	67	34	72
1992	35	67	38	79
1996	34	62	41	81

Source: Michael G. Hagen and William G. Mayer, "The Modern Politics of Presidential Selection: How Changing Rules Really Did Change the Game," *In Pursuit of the White House 2000*, ed., Mayer (Washington, DC: CQ Press, 2000), 11.

became the all-important basis on which delegates and, thus, presidential nominees were selected. The Republicans followed suit in short order, fearing a negative public reaction if their party's top-down status quo nomination system was retained. In this manner, the McGovern-Fraser Commission reforms fundamentally altered the presidential selection process for both parties (see Table 6.2).[88]

The reforms had the effect of enshrining the now nearly untouchable assumption that the major parties' presidential nominees should be selected in accordance with popular opinion as expressed in primary elections. Only in the event that the primaries are inconclusive (which has never happened) does the ultimate decision go to the party convention. As Ceaser argues: "The truly critical change... was not in the practices of the candidates but rather in the new institutional arrangements.... [T]he increased number of primaries meant that primaries had to be given more attention.... The principal focus of every active campaign, Republican and Democratic, now had to be on an outside strategy in the primaries. Their system is designed to produce a nominee who is a public opinion 'leader' in the sense of one who expresses the strongest current of opinion within the electorate."[89]

Despite the reformers' idealistic intentions, many scholars contend this new primary-centered nomination system produced a largely unintended and, in

[88] Ceaser, *Presidential Selection*, 276–96; Polsby, *Consequences of Party Reform*, 33–6; Shafer, *Quiet Revolution*, 197–202.
[89] Ceaser, *Presidential Selection*, 241. See also, 292.

their view, negative consequence in that it undermined the role of political parties in American government.[90] At the core of the issue is a tension between responsiveness to public opinion and responsible government. The primary system enhanced democracy, as its designers intended, and opened the process of choosing presidential candidates to the public; yet, Ceaser argues these reforms came at a steep price. Under a system with strong political parties, there is a buffer between public opinion and the government. This "'leverage' that parties possess enables them to withstand, at least temporarily, undesirable currents of opinion and extreme movements. If it is known *a priori* that the centers of power in a party are closed to certain opinions, leaders interested in higher office will be more apt to leave them alone."[91] In other words, Ceaser argues that when parties have a strong role in selecting their nominees, the dangers of demagoguery and extremism are reduced. Candidates under such a system are held to account by their party in a way that today's candidates are not. Since the primary system became entrenched, parties are more often led by, and forced to fall in line behind, their candidates rather than the reverse.

For instance, critics allege the new focus on primaries forces candidates to rely on personal campaign organizations rather than the traditional reliance on the party apparatus and currying favor with party elites. As Norman Nie, Sidney Verba, and John Petrocik argue: "Party organizations have grown weaker [and] are less relevant as electioneering institutions.... Presidential campaign organizations are created anew for each election. They represent the personal entourage of the candidate rather than a continuing partisan institution.... The individual candidates are more independent of party."[92] In short, many

---

[90] By the end of the 1970s, political scientists offered a particularly grim assessment of the state of political parties. For an overview, see: William J. Crotty and Gary C. Jacobson, *American Parties in Decline* (Boston: Little, Brown and Company, 1980). See, also: Martin P. Wattenberg, *The Decline of American Political Parties, 1952–1984* (Cambridge, MA: Harvard University Press, 1984); David E. Price, *Bringing Back the Parties* (Washington, DC: Congressional Quarterly Press, 1984). But starting in the mid-1980s, these dire evaluations were moderated, as can be seen in: Gerald Pomper, "An American Epilogue," *Parties and Democracy in Britain and America*, ed., Vernon Bogdanor (New York: Praeger, 1984); Ceaser, "Political Parties–Declining, Stabilizing, or Resurging?" For instance, writing in 1990, Ceaser maintains that parties did indeed decline during the 1970s, particularly with regard to their organizational capacities. But he also notes that it was only a partial decline because the reforms bolstered the movement aspect of parties. Thus, the political science consensus shifted from anticipating the demise of political parties to realizing that, despite the harm done by the reforms, parties would endure, albeit in a slightly different form. More recently, scholars have countered this dominant interpretation, arguing that parties experienced no meaningful decline in the 1970s. See: Marty Cohen, David Karol, Hans Noel, and John Zaller, *The Party Decides: Presidential Nominations Before and After Reform* (Chicago: University of Chicago Press, 2008).

[91] Ceaser, *Presidential Selection*, 345. See, also: Terry Sanford, *A Danger of Democracy: The Presidential Nominating Process* (Boulder, CO: Westview Press, 1981).

[92] Norman Nie, Sidney Verba, and John Petrocik, *The Changing American Voter* (Cambridge, MA: Harvard University Press, 1976), 346–7. See also: Aldrich, 266–74; James Q. Wilson, *Political Organizations* (New York: Basic Books, 1973), 115. For more on how these reforms weakened parties, see: Austin Ranney, *Curing the Mischief of Faction: Party Reform in America*

scholars maintain that the primary system has led to weaker political parties that are "distant, symbolic and noninteractive."[93]

A myriad of other charges have been leveled at the primary system. Critics argue that within parties, primaries give rise to factional rivalries instead of broad party coalitions, and there have been expanded opportunities for narrowly based single-interest groups. That is, intense minority groups have a greater role in candidate selection at the expense of moderate centrists. Post-reform candidates are said to have a more narrow appeal than the old candidates selected through compromise by party elites. The allegedly less popular candidates produced by the new primary system in turn reduce voter turnout and give rise to fewer identifying partisans and more independents in the electorate. Additionally, critics argue that the candidates produced in this process are less likely to make good presidents. Because they did not attain their position through negotiated compromise, they are insufficiently socialized in the process of brokering settlements and building coalitions – qualities these critics claim are essential to success in the Oval Office.[94] It is also said that they are likely to be less successful because the personal campaigns encouraged in the primary system reduce the number of people a president can count on for support, thus increasing the need for the chief executive to rely on direct, popular appeals to the public. Also, the mass media is alleged to have taken over the role of parties in screening candidates – a job some say it performs poorly.[95] Finally, the primary system is almost universally bemoaned for its negative effects of front-loading and financing. That is, to gain more influence in the selection process, states increasingly schedule their primaries earlier in the season.

(Berkeley, CA: University of California Press, 1975); Jeane Jordan Kirkpatrick, *Dismantling the Parties: Reflections on Party Reform and Party Decomposition* (Washington, DC: American Enterprise Institute, 1978); Everett Carll Ladd, Jr., *Where Have all the Voters Gone? The Fracturing of America's Political Parties* (New York: W. W. Norton Co., 1977). For arguments on behalf of stronger parties in the immediate post-reform era, see: *Paths to Political Reform*, ed., William J. Crotty (Lexington, MA: Lexington Books, 1980); *Party Renewal in America: Theory and Practice*, ed., Pomper (New York: Praeger Publishers, 1980).

[93] Polsby, *Consequences of Party Reform*, 141. The discussion here is focused on the national political parties, but state parties are also said to have suffered at the expense of the national parties. Again, for a different view, see: Cohen, Karol, Noel, and Zaller.

[94] Shafer, *The Two Majorities: The Issue Context of Modern American Politics* (Baltimore, MD: Johns Hopkins University Press, 1995), 23–39; Polsby, *Consequences of Party Reform*, 53–156; Ceaser, *Presidential Selection*, 254–6 and 276–353. For more on the personalization of the presidency and the arguably bad and ideologically extreme candidates produced in the primary process, see: Walter Dean Burnham, *The Current Crisis in American Politics* (New York: Oxford University Press, 1982). On the increase in independents and the electorate's "dealignment," see: Burnham, "American Politics in the 1970s: Beyond Party," *The American Party System*, eds., Chambers and Burnham (New York: Oxford University Press, 1975), 308–57.

[95] Thomas E. Patterson, *Out of Order: An Incisive and Boldly Original Critique of the News Media's Domination of America's Political Process* (New York: Vintage, 1994); Polsby, "The News Media as an Alternative to Party in the Presidential Selection Process," *Political Parties in the Eighties*, ed., Robert A. Goldwin (Washington: American Enterprise Institute, 1980).

As a result, candidates must begin campaigning and raising money much earlier than they used to, initiating an unending campaign that increases the likelihood of turning people off from politics. In addition, the primary process increases the need for money and, thus, a vast and time consuming fund-raising process.

Some of these concerns have been addressed recently by a team of political scientists led by John Zaller. Their work argues that despite the major structural change introduced with the primary system, party elites still play a critical role in selecting presidential candidates. Though less direct than before, their public endorsements narrow the field and create frontrunners far ahead of the actual election. By the time voters begin to pay attention, their choices are effectively constrained.[96] Thus, for Zaller, et al., critics of the primary system can relax a bit, while advocates of a more participatory and democratic process might justifiably feel stymied, once again, by the parties.

Regardless of where one comes down on this issue, the key point here is that this critical and seemingly enduring change to the method of presidential candidate selection is directly tied to the Vietnam War. Indeed, the war and the split it produced in the Democratic Party between the Johnson-Humphrey forces on the one hand and the anti-war faction on the other, was the driving force behind the McGovern-Fraser Commission reforms. The conclusion that this new primary process has changed American politics and the party system is uncontestable. Whether these changes have improved the health of American democracy or produced negative, unintended consequences is still being debated.

The 1972 Democratic Nomination

The most notable aspect of the 1972 Democratic presidential nomination contest was the new importance of the primary system described earlier in this chapter and its companion, the personal campaign. Just four years earlier, Hubert Humphrey captured the nomination using an insider strategy of relying on party elites and ignoring primaries. By 1972, the former Vice President wanted the nomination again but, like all candidates, was forced to seek it through primary elections. Also in the race was, among others, Humphrey's 1968 running mate, Maine Senator Edward Muskie. Initially the front-runner, Muskie failed to meet expectations by only winning the New Hampshire primary with a slim margin after the media reported that he cried when defending his wife against charges of bigotry.

Their chief competitor was South Dakota Senator George McGovern, a vocal critic of the Vietnam War.[97] The McGovern organization was the epitome of the post-reform, personal campaign operation. Marked by loyalty to the

---

[96] Cohen, Karol, Noel, and Zaller.

[97] The best and most comprehensive account of McGovern's 1972 presidential run is: Bruce Miroff, *The Liberal's Moment: The McGovern Insurgency and the Identity Crisis of the Democratic Party* (Lawrence, KS: University Press of Kansas, 2007).

candidate (as opposed to the party) and an organization with no purpose or longevity beyond the campaign, McGovern's forces focused on "get out the vote" efforts in advance of the typically low-turnout primary elections. The now commonplace aim of McGovern's campaign was to achieve victory by leading a faction, rather than through appeals to abstract ideology or by demonstrating party loyalty. This orientation is often necessary to gain the nomination in the primary-driven selection system, but can make it difficult to unite the party for the general election.[98]

Though the war was clearly drawing to a close, Vietnam was central to McGovern's 1972 campaign. Draft calls had fallen from a high of nearly 300,000 to 50,000, and almost all ground troops were out of Southeast Asia as President Nixon's "Vietnamization" policy was implemented. Nonetheless, as John Kenneth White writes, "to George McGovern and his supporters, the Vietnam War was more than a bad policy gone awry – it signaled a moral lapse."[99] Speaking to his fellow senators, McGovern said: "Every Senator in this Chamber is partly responsible for sending 50,000 young Americans to an early grave. This Chamber reeks of blood."[100] The McGovern campaign slogan, "Right from the Start," was intended to emphasize McGovern's early anti-war stance. The candidate's critique of Vietnam extended to the larger Cold War. "The war against communism is over," McGovern said. "The challenge to the free world from communism is no longer relevant. We're entering a new era. . . . There has to be an easing off of our reliance on power; too much reliance on power weakens a society."[101] Accordingly, McGovern proposed steep reductions in the defense budget.[102]

Humphrey meanwhile flailed to keep the Old Liberal order alive and emphasized McGovern's ideological distance from Democratic icons Harry Truman, John Kennedy, and Lyndon Johnson. In response to McGovern's proposals to slash defense spending, Humphrey announced his surprise that his competitor's budget cuts would come "without any similar disarmament agreements from

---

[98] Ceaser, *Presidential Selection*, 241–5. See also: Polsby, *Consequences of Party Reform*, 63–75; Xandra Kayden, "The Political Campaign as an Organization," *Public Policy* 31 (1973), 263–90.

[99] John Kenneth White, 173.

[100] George McGovern, *Grassroots: The Autobiography of George McGovern* (New York: Random House, 1977), 167.

[101] Theodore H. White, *The Making of the President, 1972* (New York: Atheneum Publishers, 1973), 116. McGovern never perceived a challenge from communism in the first place. A 1948 supporter of Henry Wallace, the Progressive Party's presidential nominee, McGovern recalled that "both the domestic health of the nation and the peace of the world would have been better served by the hopeful and compassionate views of Wallace than by the 'Get Tough' policy of the Truman administration." So, while McGovern may have proclaimed in 1972 that "the war against communism is over," it was a war he never wanted to fight to begin with. See, also: Peter Beinart, *The Good Fight* (New York: Harper Collins, 2006), 53; McGovern, 43, 45.

[102] John Kenneth White, 173–5.

the Russians. It shocks me. No responsible president would think of cutting our defense to the level of a second-class power."[103]

In the end, McGovern's organization, led by future Colorado Senator and presidential candidate Gary Hart, carried the day. After chairing the commission responsible for the development of the primary election system, McGovern was more adept at meeting the challenges and taking advantage of the opportunities associated with the new selection process. Leading a liberal faction of anti-war activists within the party, McGovern was the first nominee to emerge from this new primary system of presidential candidate selection, and his innovative primary campaign was thus instructive for future candidates from both parties.

Additionally, McGovern's 1972 campaign signaled the triumph of the party's liberal wing and set the Democrat's ideological course for many years – indeed, it still resonates today in many ways. After the disappointment of Humphrey's nomination four years before, Democratic anti-war forces established the primary system to bring more democracy to the process. The changes initiated by the McGovern-Fraser Commission paved the way for this liberal faction to get their candidate nominated in 1972. As White maintains, the 1972 Democratic nomination contest "proved to be Old Liberalism's last gasp. Henceforth, the Democratic party would be run by the New Politics types (most of them young), many enticed by McGovern into politics."[104] This assertion begs the question of how the New Politics types differed from the Old Liberals. It also raises the question of how much Vietnam had to do with this split.

A New Generation of Democrats

Political scientist John Gerring has produced the only comprehensive study of Democratic and Republican ideology spanning the full history of the party system.[105] Rejecting Hartz's conception of a liberal consensus, Gerring argues that both major parties have had coherent, identifiable, and changing ideologies from 1828 forward. "Jeffersonian" Democrats championed white supremacy, antistatism, and civic republicanism from 1828 to 1892, and then transitioned into a "Populist" era of egalitarianism, majoritarianism, and Christian humanism. Gerring argues the party entered a third phase of "Universalism" halfway into the twentieth century and is still rooted in this ideological period, which is marked by a focus on civil rights, social welfare, economic redistribution, and inclusion.

The notion of a "Universalist Epoch" stretching from 1952 to the present breaks with scholars who see Franklin Roosevelt as the father of the

---

[103] Ibid., 175.
[104] John Kenneth White, 175.
[105] John Gerring, *Party Ideologies in America, 1828–1996* (New York: Cambridge University Press, 1998).

contemporary Democratic Party.[106] The real ideological change, they contend, came with the New Deal. Gerring, on the other hand, argues that the emphasis on social justice, welfare policies, and wealth redistribution that these scholars emphasize was also present in the party of William Jennings Bryan and Woodrow Wilson. Only following World War II did Democrats' decisively shift ideological gears. Gerring argues that their class-based emphasis was replaced with an "all-embracing, none-offending character . . . that was to stamp the postwar epoch in Democratic history. Forsaking the shrill polemics of Bryan, the party now adopted a soothing tone and reassuring demeanor. The rhetoric of reconciliation replaced that of resentment. . . . The organizing theme of Democratic ideology changed from an attack against special privilege to an appeal for inclusion."[107]

While there is much to commend in Gerring's work, he overlooks a transformation in Democratic ideology between 1968 and 1972.[108] Perhaps much of the reason he sees only continuity since the late 1940s is because he exclusively focuses on domestic politics. Gerring argues that "because foreign policy has rarely played a significant role in American electoral politics, I focus primarily on domestic policies, including those policies, like immigration and trade, which responded primarily to domestic cues."[109] This approach no doubt helped keep Gerring's formidable task more manageable. However, as discussed in Chapters 1 and 4, by excluding foreign affairs, much is left out. Party platforms and candidates do devote a great deal of attention to these matters, and foreign events frequently affect domestic politics. This was clearly the case within the Democratic party from 1968 to 1972. Indeed, the party looked much different by 1973 than it had a decade before. To be sure, many of the threads

---

[106] Not all of these accounts are in lock step agreement, but all fundamentally place the birth of today's Democratic Party in the New Deal era. See, for example: Samuel Beer, "Liberalism and the National Idea," *Left, Right and Center: Essays on Liberalism and Conservatism in the U.S.,* ed., Robert A. Goldwin (Chicago: Rand McNally, 1965), 145–6; Steve Fraser and Gary Gerstle, *The Rise and Fall of the New Deal Order, 1930–1980* (Princeton, NJ: Princeton University Press, 1989); Everett Carll Ladd and Charles D. Hadley, *Political Parties and Political Issues: Patterns in Differentiation since the New Deal* (Beverly Hills, CA: Sage, 1973); Ladd and Hadley, *Transformation of the American Party System* (New York: Norton, 1975); William E. Leuchtenburg, *In the Shadow of FDR: From Harry Truman to Ronald Reagan* (Ithaca, NY: Cornell University Press, 1983); Herbert S. Parmet, *The Democrats: The Years after FDR* (New York: Oxford University Press, 1976); David R.B. Ross, "The Democratic Party, 1945–60," *History of U.S. Political Parties*, vol. 4, ed., Schlesinger (New York: Chelsea House, 1973); Theda Skocpol, "The Legacies of New Deal Liberalism," *Liberalism Reconsidered*, eds., Douglas MacLean and Claudia Mills (Totowa, NJ: Rowman & Allanheld, 1983); Richard C. Wade, "The Democratic Party, 1960–1972," *History of U.S. Political Parties*, vol. 4, ed., Schlesinger (New York: Chelsea House, 1973).

[107] Gerring, *Party Ideologies in America, 1828–1996*, 233.

[108] As discussed extensively in Chapter 1, my analysis of party ideology follows John Gerring in focusing primarily on what he calls "presidential parties" (6). For more on this approach, see the "Party Ideology" section in Chapter 1 and Gerring, *Party Ideologies in America, 1828-1996*, 6, 22–7.

[109] Gerring, *Party Ideologies in America, 1828–1996*, 7.

Gerring identifies throughout the previous six decades were more or less undisturbed by the party's Vietnam era shakeup. But, in other ways, Democratic ideology was significantly changed in an enduring manner by Vietnam.

The Rise and Fall of the New Politics Democrats

In 1978, Everett Carll Ladd noted that in the previous decade the Democratic party had split into two distinct demographic and ideological groups. The "old class Democrats" were, as their name implies, older in age. They were also more blue collar, holding economically liberal, socially conservative, and fiercely anti-communist positions. By contrast, the "new class Democrats" – also known as New Politics Democrats – were younger, educated professionals with a liberal outlook not only on economic, but also on social and foreign policy issues.[110] On their one point of commonality, left-of-center economics, the New Politics Democrats were more left than the old class Democrats. Generally speaking, the old class Democrats were Keynesians who wanted to use the state to save capitalism from its excesses. Meanwhile, and as on other matters, the New Politics wing was more radical on economics.[111] In style, they also differed from the older cohort in that they had more of an activist and reformist approach and sought to move the party in a more open and programmatic direction.[112]

The New Politics Democrats were heavily influenced by the New Left, a loose affiliation of student activists.[113] Elements of the New Left shunned the American political system as a whole – including the Democratic Party – but others worked within the organization, if only on its liberal fringes. Nonetheless, as Richard Harris and Sidney Milkis maintain, many of the ideas animating the New Politics Democrats were directly "traceable to the New Left critique" of the United States.[114]

The Vietnam War was central to the rise of the New Left. More than any other factor, the war galvanized college protesters, led to organizational

---

[110] Ladd, "The New Lines Are Drawn: Class and Ideology, Part II," *Public Opinion* 1 (Sept./Oct. 1978), 14–20. See also: James M. Carlson and Barbara Burrell, "A New Cleavage in the Democratic Party? A Comparison of Mondale and Hart Supporters at the Connecticut State Democratic Convention," *Polity* 20:1 (Autumn 1987), 101–13.

[111] With time, this generation of Democrats became more mainstream. A segment eventually produced the centrist New Democrats and the Democratic Leadership Council. At the time, though, the New Politics group was decidedly leftist on economic matters.

[112] Jeane Kirkpatrick, *The New Presidential Elite* (New York: Russell Sage, 1976).

[113] Much has been written about the New Left. See, for instance: Terry H. Anderson, *The Movement and the Sixties* (New York: Oxford University Press, 1995); Maurice Isserman and Michael Kazin, "The Failure and Success of the New Radicalism," *The Rise and Fall of the New Deal Order, 1930–1980*, eds., Steve Fraser and Gary Gerstle (Princeton, NJ: Princeton University Press, 1989), 212–42; Gitlin, *The Sixties: Years of Hope, Days of Rage*; Aaron Wildavsky, *The Revolt Against the Masses* (New York: Basic Books, 1971), especially 29–50.

[114] Richard A. Harris and Sidney M. Milkis, *The Politics of Regulatory Change: A Tale of Two Agencies*, 2nd ed., (New York: Oxford University Press, 1996), 62.

structure, and offered a common rallying cry for the disparate groups that came to comprise the New Left. In other words, opposition to the Vietnam War was perhaps the one common link holding together the diverse array of New Left causes and factions. In assessing the New Left, historian Terry H. Anderson argues that the "Vietnam War became the engine of the sixties. While the civil rights struggle began the era and introduced the moral debate, the war, more than any other issue, defined and shaped the decade."[115]

The war was similarly the driving force behind the ascendancy of the New Politics faction within the Democratic Party. While the split between the young party activists and the old liberals was not limited to war-related issues, it was Vietnam that provoked the most profound, divisive, and irreconcilable internal divide.[116] The New Politics faction shunned the older Cold Warriors who had dominated the party, rejecting their faith in American benevolence in foreign affairs. This rejection by the young activists attacked a fundamental pillar of the pre-1968 Democratic Party.[117]

The split reached its apex at the Democrat's 1972 convention in Miami. Hubert Humphrey, beloved by labor, blacks, the Jewish community, and many party regulars, represented the "old class Democrats." Meanwhile, George McGovern was the hero of the New Politics group seeking more liberal economic, social, and foreign policies. In the final primaries, as historian Richard C. Wade argues, Humphrey "raised substantive issues which reflected the party's division" and "subtly opened old Vietnam wounds" in an effort to provoke a deadlocked convention and gain the nomination. Old guard criticism centered on McGovern's proposals to drastically reduce defense spending and vastly expand welfare, and his alleged softness on drugs, abortion, and other issues. After two delegate credential disputes – including one that "involved an historical fracture of the party" in which Chicago Mayor Richard Daley and his "old class" allies were removed as delegates – McGovern eventually won the nomination. In Wade's words, "The 'new politics' had defeated the old."[118]

Beyond the New Politics Democrats' success in nominating McGovern, the 1972 convention platform also reflected key changes in line with the younger faction of the party. The Democrats' new anti-war position was evident:

We believe that war is a waste of human life. We are determined to end forthwith a war which has cost 50,000 American lives, $150 billion of our resources, that has divided us from each other, drained our national will and inflicted incalculable damage

---

[115] Anderson, 135.

[116] Other contributing factors to the rise of the New Politics faction include increases in levels of education and affluence and the model of the civil rights movement.

[117] See, for instance: Jonathan Rieder, "The Rise of the 'Silent Majority,'" *The Rise and Fall of the New Deal Order*, eds., Fraser and Gerstle, (Princeton, NJ: Princeton University Press, 1989), 244; Isserman and Kazin; Shafer, *The Two Majorities*, 87.

[118] Wade, 2851. See also, 2847–65.

to countless people. We will end that war by a simple plan that need not be kept secret: The immediate total withdrawal of all Americans from Southeast Asia.[119]

The platform went on to call for steep cuts in military spending, ending the military draft, disarmament and arms control, improved relations with the Soviet Union, and a reduction in military aid in favor of international poverty assistance.[120]

Also particularly notable was the platform's emphasis on what Gerring calls the party's theme of "inclusion." Gerring argues that inclusionary language became a staple of Democratic rhetoric beginning in the 1940s and lasting until today.[121] But while previous party platforms had called for the extension of rights to targeted groups such as racial minorities, women, children, the elderly, and the handicapped, the 1972 platform went much farther. Endorsing the "right to be different" and "rights of people who lack rights," this platform claimed "official policy too often forces people into a mold of artificial homogeneity.... We believe official policy can encourage diversity while continuing to place emphasis on equal opportunity and integration."[122] This language far exceeded the inclusionary rhetoric in previous platforms. Indeed, the 1972 Democratic platform was the first to give voice to the ideals of what came to be known as multiculturalism.

The New Politics Democrats' Legacy

The New Politics Democrats' success was, in one sense, short lived. After nominating their preferred candidate in the summer of 1972, the movement was disgraced when McGovern won only one state and 38 percent of the national popular vote. In James W. Ceaser's words, this failure so soon after the New Politics' high-water mark "discredited the movement and provided grounds for a counterattack by the proponents of the old liberalism, who came to believe they had been unjustly reformed out of their own party."[123] Tellingly, an evangelical Southerner, Jimmy Carter, gained the party's nomination four years later.

In another sense, though, the party has never been the same since the New Politics revolt. James Q. Wilson notes the transformation:

Then: The standard liberal believed in equal opportunity and a color-blind Constitution, was closely allied with and supportive of the union movement, gave unequivocal support to Israel, thought nuclear power was a blessing to mankind, opposed judicial activism because it had been used to block the New Deal, and took pride in the idea that

---

[119] "Democratic Platform 1972," *National Party Platforms, Volume II 1960–1976*, ed., Donald Bruce Johnson (Urbana, IL: University of Illinois Press, 1978), 783.

[120] Ibid., 813–8.

[121] Gerring, *Party Ideologies in America, 1828–1996*, 245–50.

[122] "Democratic Platform 1972," 791.

[123] Ceaser, "Political Parties," 93.

the United States would be the world's policeman... *Today*: Many liberals believe in affirmative action (defined as group entitlements or, sometimes, equality of outcome), ignore or actively dislike union leaders, are equivocal about Israel, oppose nuclear power, like activist judges, and think that promoting human rights abroad is more important than promoting international stability.[124]

Indeed, the New Politics left an indelible print on the Democratic Party's ideology that persists to this day. Though they failed to fully take over the party for more than several months in 1972, their legacy is still clearly felt in both foreign and domestic politics.

The major foreign policy change initiated by the New Politics Democrats' ideology was the end of the bipartisan Cold War consensus. Following World War II, both major political parties embraced essentially the same stance regarding foreign affairs and the ideological conflict against communism. Democrats and Republicans alike rejected isolationism in favor of internationalism and advocated a containment policy toward communism.[125] Differences existed but they were relatively minor and at the edges. The Vietnam War brought this consensus to an end. Initially, of course, the war was associated with the Democratic Party. Though Republican President Eisenhower sent the first American personnel to Vietnam, Democratic Presidents Kennedy and Johnson greatly increased the U.S. commitment. By the time President Nixon was elected in 1968, discussion centered on bringing the war to a close. Over the course of the next four years, however, Vietnam became a Republican burden. According to I.M. Destler, Leslie H. Gelb, and Anthony Lake, the anti-war New Politics Democrats gained control of their party with the nomination of McGovern in 1972 as a result of Vietnam.[126] Indeed, with regard to the split in the Democratic Party, it was, according to political scientist Byron Shafer, the "Vietnam War [that] gave this division its cutting edge."[127] While Democratic Cold Warriors never completely left the picture, they could no longer claim to represent the party's mainstream as they had in prior decades.

Since this shift, Democrats have had the mixed blessing of being viewed as the anti-war party. While this position has its political benefits during long, costly, unpopular wars, it has also left the party subject to charges of weakness in the face of Cold War communism and post-September 11th terrorism. Such

---

[124] Wilson, "New Politics, New Elites, Old Publics," *The New Politics of Public Policy*, eds., Marc K. Landy and Martin A. Levin (Baltimore, MD: Johns Hopkins University Press, 1995), 256. Italics in original.

[125] For an account of how Cold War liberals gained control of the Democratic Party and purged some important party members with communist sympathies, see: Peter Beinart, *The Good Fight: Why Liberals – and Only Liberals – Can Win the War on Terror and Make America Great Again* (New York: Harper Collins, 2006).

[126] I.M. Destler, Leslie H. Gelb, and Anthony Lake, *Our Own Worst Enemy: The Unmaking of American Foreign Policy* (New York: Simon and Schuster, 1984).

[127] Shafer, *The Two Majorities*, 57. See, also: John H. Aldrich, *Why Parties? The Origin and Transformation of Party Politics in America* (Chicago: University of Chicago Press, 1995), 264.

accusations were central features of the 1980, 1984, 1988, 2004, and 2008 presidential campaigns – that is, all of those elections since 1972 in which the Cold War or terrorism was a key issue, with the exception of the post-Watergate 1976 election. Only the three elections between the end of the Cold War and 9/11 (1992, 1996, and 2000) were largely devoid of foreign policy issues and, as a result, charges of Democratic weakness and capitulation in the face of foreign enemies. Perhaps it is not surprising, then, that Democrats won two of these contests and, in the third case, failed to gain the presidency despite winning the popular vote. In sum, as political scientist John Aldrich argues, "the shattering of the bipartisan consensus on foreign policy was a major and lasting realignment of the parties that was a crucial part of this critical period."[128]

This Vietnam-initiated shift in Democratic ideology also had lasting domestic ramifications. Shafer maintains that "Vietnam protest was a key route into the rest of a newly augmented set of valuational conflicts, within which foreign affairs was only one large but supporting element."[129] Many of the policy stances most associated with today's Democratic Party emanated out of the New Politics agenda. These enduring legacies can clearly be seen in the Democrats' adoption of multiculturalism, their embrace of cultural or social liberalism broadly construed, and in the party's successful efforts to democratize the political system.

The Democratic Party came to embrace their young upstarts' emphasis on identity politics in the form of multiculturalism. Although this process was partially initiated by President Johnson, it was resisted by many old class Democrats and only reached its apex with the ascendancy of the New Politics wing.[130] With their rise, rectifying past wrongs perpetrated by a sexist, racist, and patriarchal society and establishing justice for oppressed and victimized groups became an important aspect of Democratic ideology. As Maurice Isserman and Michael Kazin argue, by "the 1980s, left Democrats represented a variety of 'single-interest' movements – blacks, Chicano, feminist, environmentalist, peace, gay and lesbian, and elderly – as much as they did the party apparatus itself." These Democratic sub-groups developed professional and powerful lobbies in Washington, DC, and memberships skyrocketed in organizations like the Sierra Club and the National Organization for Women. "Liberal and radical Democratic activists helped transform Jesse Jackson into a serious

---

[128] Aldrich, 265.

[129] Shafer, *The Two Majorities*, 57. See also: Gareth Davies, *From Opportunity to Entitlement: The Transformation and Decline of Great Society Liberalism* (Lawrence, KS: University Press of Kansas, 1996).

[130] President Johnson asserted that civil rights legislation was not sufficient to fully remedy the effects of slavery and racial discrimination and articulated the concept of affirmative action in 1965 at Howard University. Lyndon Johnson, "Commencement Address at Howard University: 'To Fulfill These Rights,'" 4 Jun. 1965, *Public Papers of the Presidents: Lyndon B. Johnson*, vol. 2, 635–40.

candidate for president, promoted Geraldine Ferraro's vice-presidential nomination in 1984, and set the anti-interventionist tenor of the party's foreign policy debates." These changes endure, Isserman and Kazin suggest, largely because New Politics Democrats "increasingly supply the financial backing, political energy, and moral élan that keeps the party organization afloat."[131]

The Civil Rights Movement obviously contributed greatly to this newfound attention on identity politics. Yet Vietnam reinforced this predilection and internationalized it. Anti-war activists frequently cited racial and ethnic considerations amongst their reasons for opposition. Rhetorical denunciations of "baby killers" and the imperialistic war to kill the "yellow man" emanated out of this critique. Groups such as the Black Panthers and their allies sought solidarity with the Vietnamese people as fellow victims suffering oppression at the hands of the white, imperialist hegemon.[132] These critics asked why oppressed American blacks were being forced to go to Southeast Asia to kill other oppressed minorities. Black leader Stokely Carmichael, for example, wrote:

The colonies of the United States – and this includes the black ghettoes within its borders, north and south – must be liberated. For a century, this nation has been like an octopus of exploitation, its tentacles stretching from Mississippi and Harlem to South America, the Middle East, southern Africa, and Vietnam; the form of exploitation varies from area to area but the essential result has been the same – a powerful few have been maintained and enriched at the expense of the poor and voiceless colored masses.[133]

As such, the Democrats' enduring attention to identity politics is not just an outgrowth of the New Politics faction's broader ideology relating to domestic politics, but is also uniquely associated with the war.

This multicultural focus has been evident in the Democratic Party since the Vietnam era. For instance, in contrast to the traditional American notions of the "melting pot," assimilation, individual rights, and equality of opportunity, Democrats frequently came to favor what former New York City Mayor David Dinkins referred to as the "gorgeous mosaic" model whereby each race, ethnicity, sexual orientation, and religious group maintains its distinct identity, and whereby group rights are valued and elevated, often over those of the

---

[131] Isserman and Kazin, 235.

[132] See, for instance: Stokely Carmichael, "Power and Racism," *The Rhetoric of the Civil-Rights Movement*, eds., Haig A. Bosmajian and Hamida Bosmajian, (New York: Random House, 1969), 101–8; Carmichael, "Speech at Morgan State College," *The Rhetoric of the Civil-Rights Movement*, eds., Bosmajian and Bosmajian (New York: Random House, 1969), 109–25; Floyd B. McKissick, "Speech at the National Conference on Black Power," *The Rhetoric of the Civil-Rights Movement*, eds., Bosmajian and Bosmajian (New York: Random House, 1969), 127–42; Curtis J. Austin, *Up Against the Wall: Violence in the Making and Unmaking of the Black Panther Party* (Fayetteville, AR: University of Arkansas Press, 2006), 99–104, 336; Gitlin, 184–92, 261–82.

[133] Carmichael, "Power and Racism," 103–4.

individual.[134] In the policy realm, this shift was most clearly seen in the party's eventual full support for affirmative action, at times in the form of racial or other ascriptive quotas.

The New Politics brand of social or cultural liberalism has also endured. Conservation and environmentalism, for example, had once been the province of Republicans, while Democrats traditionally emphasized economic redistribution and tangible benefits. But the New Politics legion embraced environmentalism and the issue has since been associated with the Democratic Party.[135] Indeed, environmentalism has arguably never been more important to the party than today amidst growing concerns over global warming.[136] Additionally, old-style liberal Democrats tended to be economically left of center but socially conservative. Today, Democrats, following the New Politics cohort, are almost universally liberal on social issues. Pro-life Democrats, for instance, are exceedingly rare, whereas in the late 1960s and 1970s they comprised a majority, including many party leaders and luminaries such as Humphrey, Jesse Jackson, and Gore.[137] The rise of the New Politics group also led the party toward secularism.[138] Although Democrats are loathe to vocally embrace secularism, many in the party struggle with, and appear uncomfortable addressing, personal religious faith, as was particularly evident in the 2004 presidential campaigns of John Kerry and Howard Dean. In response to the Democrats' relative liberalism on these and other cultural issues, Republicans have frequently painted Democrats as far-left, hedonistic, and morally vacant. This strategy has often been electorally and politically successful. Indeed, many see the rise of the "religious right" as a response to the social liberalism emerging out of the late 1960s and early 1970s.[139]

---

[134] Fred Siegel, *The Prince of the City: Giuliani, New York and the Genius of American Life* (New York: Encounter Books, 2005), 16, 32, 37, 80.

[135] Shafer, *The Two Majorities*, 18–9.

[136] See, for instance: Harris and Milkis, *The Politics of Regulatory Change*; Michael J. Lacey, ed., *Government and Environmental Politics: Essays on Historical Developments Since World War Two* (Washington: Wilson Center Press, 1993); Samuel P. Hays, *Beauty, Health and Permanence: Environmental Politics in the United States, 1955–1985* (New York: Cambridge University Press, 1990); Al Gore, *The Assault on Reason* (New York: Penguin Press, 2007); Gore, *Earth in the Balance: Ecology and the Human Spirit* (New York: Rodale, 1992). Gore's documentary film about global warming received significant attention, garnering an Academy Award: *An Inconvenient Truth* (2006).

[137] Shafer, *The Two Majorities*, 30–8. The nation as a whole became more pro-choice since the emergence of the New Politics Democrats. Nonetheless, the shift within the Democratic party from a largely pro-life organization to the standard bearer for the pro-choice movement is remarkable. During this time the Republican Party has become nearly as uniform in its adherence to the pro-life movement.

[138] Louis Bolce and Gerald De Maio, "Our Secularist Democratic Party," *The Public Interest* 149 (Fall 2002).

[139] See, for instance: Geoffrey Layman, *The Great Divide: Religious and Cultural Conflict in American Party Politics* (New York: Columbia University Press, 2001); Gary Wills, *Under God: Religion and American Politics* (New York: Simon and Schuster, 1990); Erling Jorstad, *Holding Fast/Pressing On: Religion in America in the 1980s* (Westport, CT: Greenwood,

A final strong example of the New Politics faction's ideology leading to lasting domestic change can be seen in the democratization of the larger Democratic Party and the American political process as a whole. The idea here was to open up the political system for broader participation and public oversight. In place of backroom deals outside of public view, New Politics Democrats wanted to decentralize policy making by creating a participatory process overseen by public interest groups, bureaucratic experts, the court system, and the media.[140] In addition to reforming the presidential nomination system, the New Politics faction succeeded in instituting democratizing changes in Congress. These included a more powerful role for party caucuses in relation to committee chairs, a decrease in secrecy, televised proceedings, and a more centralized budget process.[141] As noted earlier, critics allege these changes had the controversial effect of weakening political parties.[142]

This shift in Democratic ideology is a major factor in Aldrich's assessment of the 1960s (which he defines as the period lasting through 1972) as a "critical era in American politics." Though it does not constitute a realignment in the strictest sense, the changes were profound, occurred quickly, and were lasting. "Traumatic events were associated with a critical era that led to fundamental changes in the institutional bases of political parties." Vietnam, according to Aldrich, was critical to this transformation because it had such a demonstrable influence at the elite level.[143]

The changes in Democratic ideology described above made the two major parties more internally ideologically coherent.[144] In response to the Democrats' increasing liberalism, many traditionalists and conservatives left for the GOP,

1990); Jon A. Shields, *The Democratic Virtues of the Christian Right* (Princeton, NJ: Princeton University Press, 2008).

[140] Julian E. Zelizer, *On Capitol Hill: The Struggle to Reform Congress, 1948–2000* (New York: Cambridge University Press, 2004); Jeffrey M. Berry, *The New Liberalism: The Rising Power of Citizen Groups* (Washington, DC: Brookings Institution Press, 1999); Harris and Milkis, *The Politics of Regulatory Change*; Thomas Byrne Edsall, "The Changing Shape of Power: A Realignment in Public Policy," *The Rise and Fall of the New Deal Order*, eds., Fraser and Gerstle (Princeton, NJ: Princeton University Press, 1989); Berry, *Lobbying for the People: The Political Behavior of Public Interest Groups* (Princeton, NJ: Princeton University Press, 1977).

[141] Zelizer, 125–55. See also: Walter J. Oleszek, *Congressional Procedure and the Policy Process* (Washington, DC: CQ Press, 1978).

[142] See, for instance: Milkis, *Political Parties and Constitutional Government: Remaking American Democracy* (Baltimore, MD: Johns Hopkins University Press, 1999), 103–36 and 174–86; Milkis, *The President and the Parties: The Transformation of the American Party System Since the New Deal* (New York: Oxford University Press, 1993); Polsby, *Consequences of Party Reform*.

[143] Aldrich, 260–6. See also: Aldrich and Richard G. Niemi, "The Sixth American Party System: 1952–1992," *Broken Contract: Changing Relationships Between Americans and Their Government*, ed., Stephen C. Craig, (Boulder, CO: Westview, 1996).

[144] George Rabinowitz, Paul-Henri Gurian, and Stuart MacDonald, "The Structure of Presidential Elections and the Process of Realignment, 1944 to 1980," *American Journal of Political Science* 28 (Nov. 1984), 611–35.

especially in the South – a region once nearly totally dominated by Democrats but now largely controlled by Republicans.[145] Advocacy on behalf of multi-culturalism and the environment further strained the Democratic Party's relationship with labor unions because the emphasis on diversity and environmental protection often directly conflicted with labor's defense of jobs and the blue collar worker. The Democratic Party has also struggled to woo white males, arguably because elements of the party's base – emanating out of the New Politics cohort – appear to loathe, or at best disregard, middle class aspirations.[146] As a result, the white working class, and especially males, have drifted toward the GOP. This change became strikingly clear in the 2000 election when George W. Bush bested Al Gore by 17 percentage points among the white working class as a whole and by 34 percentage points among males in that group.[147]

Although the rise of "New Democrats" in the 1990s has partially blunted the effects of the New Politics faction, the group's legacy lives on and is arguably expanding.[148] The "net-roots" liberal base has become an important part of the party. In addition, it remains true that the party's financial base of contributors is largely tied to its liberal wing, which still embraces much of the New Politics agenda. (Of course, the same must be said of the Republican Party and its conservative base.)[149] The New Politics Democrats rose to power behind their opposition to the Vietnam War and led the party system toward a more ideologically consistent, if more polarized, status.

[145] Isserman and Kazin, 236; Earl Black and Merle Black, *The Rise of Southern Republicans* (Cambridge, MA: Belknap Press, 2003); Shafer and Johnston.
[146] See, for instance: Thomas Frank, *What's the Matter with Kansas? How Conservatives Won the Heart of America* (New York: Metropolitan Books, 2003). For a parody, see: Walter Shapiro, "What's the Matter with Central Park West?," *The Atlantic Monthly* 295:2 (Mar. 2005), 46.
[147] William A. Galston, "Democrats Adrift?," *The Public Interest* 157 (Fall 2004), 21.
[148] On the rise of New Democrats, see, for instance: Jon F. Hale, "The Making of New Democrats," *Political Science Quarterly* 110 (Summer 1995); Kenneth Baer, *Reinventing Democrats* (Lawrence, KS: University Press of Kansas, 2000); Philip Klinkner, "Democratic Party Ideology in the 1990s: New Democrats or Modern Republicans?," *The Politics of Ideas: Intellectual Challenges Facing the American Political Parties*, eds., John K. White and John C. Green (Albany, NY: State University of New York Press, 1999); Franklin Foer, "Center Forward? The Fate of the New Democrats," *Varieties of Progressivism*, ed., Peter Berkowitz (Stanford, CA: Hoover Institution Press, 2005).
[149] On the Democratic party's liberal base, the Republicans' conservative base, and their financial influence, see, for instance: Clifford W. Brown, Jr., Lynda W. Powell, and Clyde Wilcox, *Serious Money: Fundraising and Contributing in Presidential Nomination Campaigns* (New York: Cambridge University Press, 1995), Chapter 3; Morris P. Fiorina, Paul E. Peterson, Bertram Johnson, and D. Stephen Voss, *The New American Democracy*, 4th ed. (New York: Pearson, 2005), 261; Isserman and Kazin, 235; Pietro S. Nivola and David W. Brady, eds., *Red and Blue Nation? Characteristics and Causes of America's Polarized Politics* (Washington, DC: Brookings Institution Press, 2006); Nolan McCarty, Keith T. Poole, and Howard Rosenthal, *Polarized America: The Dance of Ideology and Unequal Riches* (Cambridge, MA: MIT Press, 2006).

CONCLUSION

In many respects, Vietnam was an atypical American war. It was never declared, did not have a clearly defined beginning or end, and was an obvious defeat. In addition, and unlike other wars, which have tended to build the American state and enhance the power of the federal government, the Vietnam War did not produce significant state expansions. On the contrary, the war's major influence on the state was the termination of the military draft, along with the infrastructure and societal regimentation it produced.

In other ways, though, Vietnam was typical of major American wars. It led to an important expansion of democratic rights. This time 18–20 year olds were the beneficiaries. This extension, the most recent of its kind, raises the question of which groups might benefit from this pattern of service-for-rights in the future – a topic that will be explored in the following chapter. Finally, the political party system was upended by the intrusion of this controversial war on the national agenda. Vietnam played a key role in the 1968 and 1972 elections, heavily influencing the Democratic Party's nominees in each contest and setting the stage for the general elections. It also led to the now-familiar primary system of selecting presidential nominees. Additionally, the war elevated the New Politics faction within the Democratic Party. Though this cohort's reign was brief, it had lasting effects on Democratic ideology in ways that are still evident today in the party's perceived weakness in foreign affairs, its embrace of identity politics, and its social liberalism. This internal shift also produced greater democratization of the American political system, increased ideological cohesion in both parties, and heightened polarization. Indeed, Vietnam arguably did more to shape the last thirty years of American politics than any other event.

7

Conclusion

American involvement in foreign affairs, and particularly major wars, has had a significant and often even dominating influence on the state and domestic politics. It is surprising, then, that these major wars and conflicts are so frequently left out of analyses of U.S. politics. This project has been an effort to systematically explore this relationship in a broad context.

Disciplinary boundaries likely account for much of the underappreciation of war's influence on domestic American politics. Political science departments are split into subfields that often do not speak to one another (sometimes literally as well as metaphorically). With few exceptions, political scientists studying the United States focus solely on the domestic realm, leaving foreign affairs and wars to international relations specialists. As such, the role wars play in U.S. domestic politics has often fallen through the cracks and been lost amidst the acronyms and jargon separating American politics and international relations scholars. Other factors might also help to explain the frequent absence of international influences in the American politics literature. For example, the professional norms that reward building on already accumulated knowledge and the formation of sub-subfields might serve to reinforce and perpetuate the domestic focus. Additionally, the notion of American exceptionalism may have subtly and inadvertently pushed scholars studying the United States to turn inward.

Whatever the reason, and with a full appreciation of the plentiful knowledge this domestic orientation has yielded, the failure to adequately account for the role of foreign affairs in American politics is glaring and creates a serious barrier to a full understanding of U.S. politics for two reasons. First, recognizing the influence wars have had on domestic politics is critical for achieving a fuller understanding of America's political development. The United States has been blessed with relatively few debilitating and transformative wars as compared to, say, France or Germany. Yet even for the relatively sheltered United States, its major conflicts have changed the face of the country in important ways. The Vietnam War is a case in point. It was a war of choice and was fought thousands of miles away, with a relatively low tally of 58,000 U.S. deaths. The Vietnam-era U.S. homeland never experienced the World War II horror of Pearl Harbor, London, Dresden, or Hiroshima or, for that matter, the contemporary devastation of bombed out North Vietnam. But even in these comparatively sheltered conditions, the United States's Vietnam experience had demonstrable and enduring effects on American politics and society. The country simply looked different after this war – perhaps not in terms of how citizens lived their everyday lives – but, nonetheless, in significant ways. America's other major foreign entanglements have dramatically influenced domestic politics as well. This influence has manifested itself in certain identifiable and consistent patterns: The state's role in society has been altered, key aspects of citizens' relationships with one another and with their government have changed, and parties have been forced to adjust to, and compete in, an altered political environment.

Second, appreciating how wars have affected American political development is important for understanding the contemporary period and in looking toward the future. Although political leaders (including each of the presidents presiding over the wars examined here) frequently, and probably sincerely, view wars as a means to achieve some kind a peaceful utopia, history suggests that human nature does not change very much. War has always been a part of human society and, even while seeking to learn from the past and avoid future violence at all reasonable costs, it seems unlikely that it will go away. It is important, then, to understand how war has shaped American political development both for a more complete understanding of history, and because the future will almost certainly bring similar situations in which this knowledge might be instructive.

WAR AND AMERICAN POLITICAL DEVELOPMENT: 1898–1975

The Spanish-American War, World War I, World War II, the Korean War, and the Vietnam War have all left their mark on U.S. domestic politics. Three particularly important aspects of wartime American political development have been addressed here: the American state, democratic rights policy, and the party system.

War and the American State

State building is more difficult in the United States than in many other countries because, as has long been observed, Americans are protective of individual liberty and skeptical of centralized power and authority. Europeans, by contrast, are less ideologically resistant to strong, centralized government. As such, it is not surprising that Europeans tend to live in more fully developed welfare states. Many countries have developed state capacities because the polity decides that the economic and social benefits outweigh the costs. State development has occurred in the United States, too; it has just had to overcome a higher threshold. Frequently, a crisis is necessary for major American state building to occur. Necessity, rather than preference, has typically driven U.S. state building.

The development of the American state has received extensive scholarly attention. Accounts generally focus on particular periods such as the decades between Reconstruction and the Great Depression or the New Deal era. This body of work has shed considerable light on the growth of American state capacities, but has been largely episodic in its focus and, thus, risks overlooking key connections that have played out over the course of American history. Much of this literature ignores the role wars play in influencing the American state. By and large, this scholarship offers a peacetime, domestically oriented account. At times, there is an attempt to justify the omission of international origins of American political development on the grounds that foreign affairs only infrequently impinge on domestic politics. At other times, the domestic focus is simply accepted as a matter of course.

This study has found some limited evidence to vindicate Aaron Friedberg's "rollback effect" argument.[1] Certain war-induced state expansions have been rescinded. American colonial flirtations following the Spanish-American War came to a comparatively quick end in the Philippines. The World War I-aided Prohibition Era went bad after less than fifteen years. Tax rates dropped dramatically after the world wars. Vietnam forced the end of the draft. In short, war has not been the one-way, fast-track route to state expansion that Bruce Porter and others have observed in many other countries.[2]

Nonetheless, to consider the American state and war, is to see an overall process in which both government capacities and reach have seen profound growth. Friedberg's antistatist argument certainly has comparative merit. In relation to European states, U.S. wartime state expansion appears mild. Yet when considered on its own terms and in comparison to other major episodes of American state growth, wars have clearly exerted a dramatic influence. Focusing too much on American antistatism risks losing this more important and fundamental point.

The present work argues that international events in the form of foreign wars have played a role in state development from the outside in and constitute a connective theme running throughout American history. This treatment of the wartime American state is not meant to be exhaustive. Rather, it is intended to link a shared phenomenon at several observation points and to identify the kind of changes in the state that wars frequently provoke.

The account presented here, like the New Deal literature, examines the American state in crisis. Major wars make for major crises and, as such, demand massive amounts of personnel, money, and logistical coordination. The magnitude of these problems tends to mean that the easiest way to address

[1] Aaron L. Friedberg, *In the Shadow of the Garrison State: America's Anti-Statism and Its Cold War Grand Strategy* (Princeton, NJ: Princeton University Press, 2000).
[2] Bruce D. Porter, *War and the Rise of the State: The Military Foundations of Modern Politics* (New York: Free Press, 1994).

them is by increasing state capacities. International conflicts also tend to affect such change because of their unpredictability. Such unpredictability often casts a spotlight on deficiencies that might otherwise be ignored. Wars are inherently messy affairs that generally go off script. Even in those rare cases where they initially appear to proceed according to plan, unanticipated problems tend to arise, as seen, for example, in the insurgencies that followed the quick and successful Spanish-American War and the 2003 overthrow of Saddam Hussein in Iraq. An additional complication of prosecuting a war is that, because each situation is unique, the wheel needs to be reinvented each time. Waging a war is much more complicated than the routine and relative predictability of, say, plowing snowy streets in the winter. In sum, wars are intense, chaotic, resource-depleting events marked by new and often unanticipated problems. The easiest and quickest way to address these problems has typically been by increasing state capacities and creating new institutions.

The most common manner in which wars have influenced the state is as an accelerant. Frequently, the newly adopted policies or state expansions associated with war did not emerge out of thin air. On the contrary, they were typically on the backburner for years as proponents toiled to convince others that certain policies should be pursued. When their efforts proved unsuccessful, these advocates were confined to disgruntled minority status – at least until the outbreak of a "hot war." Wars change calculations and place new considerations on the agenda. In this manner, major American wars have pushed previously proposed, but marginalized, policies forward; they have provided the final and pivotal push from minority proposal to popular endorsement and enactment.

These war-induced policy changes that have strengthened Washington's hand have often come at the expense of the states. In this manner, the system of federalism has also been fundamentally altered by major wars. The Spanish-American War saw states lose control over the military. World Wars I and II placed the federal government in the role of primary tax recipient, a position previously held by the states. The Eighteenth Amendment mandating Prohibition usurped what had been a state prerogative. Expansions of democratic rights also generally nationalized previously state-based realms of influence.

Wars provide unique "windows of opportunity" for such change.[3] Centralization of power runs counter to traditional American liberalism. But because wars are such intense events, they frequently compel the kind of centralizing activity that would otherwise be highly controversial. They have the unique ability to move elite and public opinion toward consensus, an unusual occurrence in American democracy. Although this process plays out through sheer necessity and a realization that no other options are available, the fact remains that wars have a tendency to compel state responses that are rare in the absence of major crises and that generally have a lasting effect on the American political

---

[3] John W. Kingdon, *Agendas, Alternatives, and Public Policies* (Boston: Little, Brown, 1984).

system. The state's increased influence typically remains even after the precipitating crisis has subsided. In this sense, wartime state building turns into a story of path dependence. Wars force the government's hand; responsive action is taken; and, once taken, is usually not reversed even after resolution of the instigating problem is achieved.

As mentioned above, wars do not *always* induce enduring state building. In some of the cases examined here, state expansions have only been temporary in nature. The acquisition of the Philippines lasted for several decades, but ultimately proved to be impermanent. Prohibition came to the same fate: a vast, but temporary, expansion of state authority. And the draft, institutionalized by Korea, was undone by Vietnam. Additionally, Vietnam did not produce any significant state expansions. These cases suggest that although wars can normally be expected to induce enduring growth in the American state, the process is not uniform. In some cases, the new policies are subsequently seen as having been enacted in haste, come to be regretted, and are ultimately abandoned. And Vietnam suggests that, at least in certain conditions, wars do not expand the state at all.

Nonetheless, America's modern wars have led to numerous significant alterations to the state. The Spanish-American War highlighted the inefficiency and ineptitude of the decentralized, state-based militia system. In response, a professional army was created. Proposals for such reform were not new on the policy agenda, but the war with Spain created the political consensus necessary for substantive change. This war also thrust the country into the role of an imperial power with new holdings in the Philippines. Again, some in the U.S. had been advocating for American expansion abroad, but it took the war to actually push President William McKinley into formally taking an international possession.

The federal revenue system and the institutions overseeing it are also intricately tied to foreign wars. World War I's financing crisis compelled the full adoption of an income tax. Although revenue had been generated in this manner during previous crises, these earlier incarnations of the tax were dismissed when peace returned. The World War I income tax, by contrast, stayed in place and has ultimately come to constitute the core source of government financing. World War II added on by making the income tax mass-based; that is to say, applicable to the vast majority of income-earning Americans. Earlier versions affected only the wealthy. Predictably, new ways of spending the money were discovered once these wars ended. This basic tax structure has remained in place.

World War I also had the idiosyncratic effect of bolstering the Prohibition movement, largely because of the anti-German sentiment the conflict generated and the association that ethnic group had with the alcohol industry. The Temperance movement was not new. Anti-alcohol crusaders had been working to reduce or eliminate spirits in America well before the United States was founded, particularly in the decades following the Civil War. Yet Prohibition only came about when World War I mixed compelling new factors into the rhetorical cocktail of the Dry Movement and added a shot of urgency to boot. Though only in existence for thirteen years and widely regarded as a failure, Prohibition points to the wide range of possible effects wars can spawn. In addition, it highlights a consistent theme concerning the wartime American state: The growth of the national government's capacities during wartime often comes at the expense of the states.

Like the Spanish-American War, Korea provoked major changes in the national security state. These changes had been rejected on many previous occasions. Only with the outbreak of Korean hostilities was the political consensus achieved to provide the massive military spending that had been called for by fringe elements within the State Department and Pentagon for years. The Korean War also had the effect of instituting the first and only peacetime draft in the United States, which in turn, regimented American society for some twenty-five years until another war brought about conscription's demise.

In this area of state expansion, Vietnam is an anomaly. Whereas other conflicts have seen at least some increase in state capacities, this war saw no state growth. Another key difference between Vietnam and other major American wars, of course, is that it was a clear defeat. This consideration points to an important aspect of wartime state building. With this one exception (as of this writing), the United States has not experienced clear military defeats. The outcome of military ventures, then, may have much to do with wartime state building and institutional development. Vietnam was, like the other wars examined here, a major event with its share of crises; however, it was more divisive than those that came before it. The bitterness of this division was likely exacerbated by the defeat. Accordingly, wartime state building may get bogged down or even reversed if a war is unsuccessful. The demise of the draft offers a case in point. This important state resource became increasingly untenable politically as the war became increasingly unsuccessful. It should be noted, though, that the end of the military draft – despite depleting a state resource – may have had the unintended consequence of actually making it easier for presidents to enter into wars. Relying on a volunteer army partially mitigates the steep political costs of compelling young people to serve in dangerous situations abroad.

In sum, the political science literature has largely failed to observe how major wars have influenced the American state. Because they are such transformative events, the strains on resources and institutions that seem to inevitably accompany wars cannot be ignored. The response to these problems has usually involved strengthening the state. Frequently, the expanded state capacities in question had been previously advocated by a vocal but marginalized minority whose efforts were unsuccessful until the outbreak of war introduced new considerations that produced a consensus for state expansion. Traditional American attachments to decentralization and federalism fall victim to urgency and efficiency at such times. Conflicts of this sort have a tendency to focus attention on problems, produce consensus, and, in this manner, offer opportunities to effect change that are rare in American democracy.

War and Democratic Rights Policy

Wars have had the unintended effect of enhancing and improving democracy for women, African Americans, and youths after these marginalized groups contributed to a war effort. Major wars place an enormous strain on state capacities and institutions, requiring personnel. Outreach efforts to underutilized segments of the population have been used to satisfy these needs. Often, the tasks called for by the state involve putting one's life on the line. Accepting these challenges with bravery and honor is regarded as the supreme and unassailable claim to full citizenship. This moral claim trumps practically all else in political life and has for a long time, as evidenced in the writings of Thucydides and Aristotle.[4] In the most basic terms, wars recast the relationship between citizens and their government.

Another factor at work in the extension of democratic rights is the national unity and cohesion that is often a byproduct of foreign wars. As John Jay noted in *The Federalist Papers*, the American Revolution required citizens to come together in a shared enterprise and, as a result, strengthened the bond between the former colonies.[5] This process played out in ensuing American wars as well. The team effort inherent in wartime national service frequently undercuts stereotypes supporting a group's marginalized status. Additionally, the state has an incentive to undertake initiatives to promote cohesion. The resulting unity makes it even more likely that new rights will be extended to marginalized groups that contribute to a shared project.

In all of the cases explored here, efforts were already under way to bring about the rights extensions in question. But critically, the war introduced new considerations and new reasons to offer new rights. Advocates had been pushing for rights expansions in each of these instances, but they only succeeded when there was a war. Put simply, in each of the episodes detailed here, policy changes would not have occurred when they did without the new wartime considerations being added to the debate. It is true that – with the possible exception of 18–20-year-olds voting – the rights extensions explored here almost certainly would have materialized at some point even without the contributing war. However, it is far from clear *when* these advances would have been made. It could well have been decades before a similarly conducive environment for change appeared. It is also not clear *how* the changes would have been implemented in the absence of these wars. Maybe the policy shifts could somehow have been more fully or more efficiently implemented. But they undoubtedly could have also been more poorly done and consisted of half measures. Finally, it is uncertain how delays in implementing these policies would have influenced future rights extensions. To the extent gains embodied in, for example,

---

[4] Thucydides, *History of the Peloponnesian War*, 3.27. Aristotle, *The Politics*, Book 6, Chapters 6–7.

[5] John Jay, "No. 2: Concerning Dangers from Foreign Force and Influence," *The Federalist Papers*, ed., Clinton Rossiter (New York: Mentor, 1999), 6.

the Soldier Voting Act and *Smith v. Allwright* were building blocks for future advances, it is certainly plausible that there would have been an extensive and compounding cost to inaction.

This pattern of wartime military service bringing about democratic gains can be seen in World War II, Korea, and Vietnam. Tangible voting rights gains for African Americans were made during, and largely because of, World War II by way of the Soldier Voting Act of 1942 and the Supreme Court's *Smith v. Allwright* decision in 1944. During the Korean War, African American military service spurred the Army's desegregation. Similarly, wartime service in Vietnam by 18–20-year-olds who were eligible for the draft but not the franchise created the necessary momentum for reducing the voting age. Yet the kind of wartime service required for an extension of democratic rights need not take place solely in the military. The women's suffrage movement received a boost and succeeded in gaining voting rights for females with the Nineteenth Amendment when women *en masse* replaced men leaving their jobs to fight in Europe during World War I. Notably, all of these democratic rights expansions came by way of nationalizing what had previously been state prerogatives. The wartime influence on rights expansions, then, is similar to the wartime influence on the state, in that changes in both realms have had deep ramifications for federalism. In all of these cases, state powers have been appropriated or superseded by the national government.

The Spanish-American War is unique in that it is the one conflict examined here that did not produce such democratic gains for a marginalized minority group. Unlike the other cases, the "splendid little war" was only a few months long and never taxed state capacities in the way most wars have. This difference points to a crucial prerequisite for war to have the effect of expanding democratic rights. Extensions of democratic rights do not inherently accompany war; they have to be earned through service. Moreover, this service has to be required by a depleted and weary state – the desire to contribute is insufficient. While women, blacks, and other groups may well have been more than willing to pay this price during the Spanish-American War, they did not have the opportunity to do so.

As emphasized throughout, this argument is not intended to overlook or minimize the civil rights and civil liberties abuses that have all too often accompanied American wars. Every war involves some degree of rights retraction. Curtailment of rights is a perennial issue when wars are being fought, and the well- known catalogue of wartime injustice includes the forced relocation of Native Americans, Civil War suspensions of *habeas corpus*, imprisoning dissenters in World War I, and Japanese internment during World War II. This tradition of wartime rights abuses has been extensively explored and, unfortunately, these retractions seem to go with the territory. It is also a fact that aspects of these retractions endure. Later presidents, for example, are able to cite previous wartime rights restrictions as a precedent for their own. These miscarriages of justice are hardly unique to the United States, but they are particularly disgraceful for a nation espousing liberal, humanitarian ideals. Nonetheless, advances made by marginalized groups that contribute to a war effort constitute a less well-known story, and one that is arguably more important because it involves far more people and its effects have been more enduring – rights retractions, for the most part, have been temporary whereas rights expansions have endured. This book has been, in part, an effort to better understand how this long recognized, but frequently overlooked, process has played out in the American case.

War and the American Party System

Political parties and political actors must respond to the hands they are dealt and take stock of both domestic and international considerations – including contingent events. Wars and the financial, personnel, and societal crises they provoke demand attention, often reshaping the political landscape and supplanting other policy issues. Accordingly, parties and political actors adjust their public philosophies or electoral appeals in light of the altered political terrain. This phenomenon can be seen both in the parties' electoral competition and in their ideological development.

Elections. By and large, the American politics literature assigns foreign affairs a minimal role in elections. Much attention has been devoted to long-term factors such as party identification or social characteristics as vote determinants. The only issue that is consistently said to be relevant in the voting booth is the economy. Lost in all this is any significant role for international influences. As a result, the elections literature is incomplete. Much of this oversight is due to the purpose of this flagship political science subfield. In its effort to identify ongoing patterns that can routinely be expected to explain electoral outcomes, the critical role of events has been obscured. In general, foreign affairs constitute an afterthought in election studies.

Given the body of knowledge available in the political science literature, then, it might seem surprising that real-world politicians seeking federal office, especially presidential candidates, spend so much time talking about foreign affairs. An approach more firmly rooted in the academic literature might involve dispensing with non-economic issues altogether – especially international issues. The political scientist-cum-campaign advisor might suggest doing only three things: manipulating data to paint an appropriately dire or robust picture of the nation's economic health, rallying the candidate's fellow partisans, and mobilizing voters possessing certain demographic attributes. Alas, few political scientists direct campaigns. And although politicos certainly do engage in the three activities scholars might recommend, they also spend an inordinate amount of time discussing all kinds of issues, including foreign affairs, as if these things mattered. Perhaps there is an explanation for their behavior.

Although the argument presented here does not speak to all elections, it does suggest that ongoing or recently concluded wars recast the political landscape and, as a result, are pivotal factors in many elections, shaping both elite and mass behavior. Wars alter expectations, values, beliefs, and aspirations, thus forging the psychological state of a people. It is not surprising that in a democratic political system, this effect finds expression in the voting booth. This conclusion suggests that the elections literature is overly deterministic in its assertion that party identification, social characteristics, or the state of the economy are the be-all, end-all factors driving elections. Events matter too.

America's major wars have almost always had electoral ramifications. Throughout American history wars have been highly contentious and part of partisan rancor. Yet to a striking degree, this was not the case in World War II. Although the conflict was a key factor in Franklin Roosevelt's election to third and fourth terms, the war had overwhelming and unquestioned support from both Republicans and Democrats, and did not produce the kind of electoral fireworks other major wars have generated. If the United States engages in a similarly popular war in the future, it is reasonable to expect that elections surrounding those conflicts would also not be greatly influenced. But World War II was an anomaly in this respect. All of America's other major wars have been controversial, and in that more common climate, they are often pivotal election issues.

The Spanish-American War and World War I were major forces in the 1898 and 1900 elections and in the 1918 and 1920 elections, respectively. In the first case, the GOP rode a wave of patriotism and, bolstered by President William McKinley's victory tour, made a strong showing in the 1898 midterm election in what otherwise would almost certainly have been a rough political climate. Two years later, the war-spurred issue of imperialism played a central role in the campaign. Similarly, World War I was the primary issue in 1918 and 1920. In the first of these elections, the ruling Democrats lost both houses of Congress. Critically, the Midwest – home to most of the German-Americans who were heavily repressed during the war – was the only region of the country to have a dramatic swing toward the GOP. In 1920, the war and its lingering effects led voters to give the Republicans unified control in Washington.

Taken together, these four elections surrounding the Spanish-American War and World War I pose a serious problem for realignment theory's sacrosanct "System of 1896." That body of scholarship suggests that Republican victories in 1898 and 1900 were inevitable. Yet the GOP was likely poised for a major rebuke in 1898 had the war not saved the party. Those crucial issues that allegedly infused American politics for a generation beginning in 1896 were decidedly subordinate to the war and its offspring issue, imperialism, in 1900. The "System of 1896" also suggests that the twelve years of Republican dominance after World War I (1920–1932) were a continuation of the McKinley era. But this assertion ignores a ten-year stretch of Democratic control prior to 1920 that has the awkward effect of splitting this golden era of the GOP into two pieces with a big chunk missing in the middle. Adding to realignment theory's problems at this juncture, the key Republican victory in 1920 that swept the party back into control was beholden to World War I rather than the issues associated with the "System of 1896."

The Cold War conflicts in Korea and Vietnam also had a demonstrable electoral influence. Dwight Eisenhower's victory in 1952 offers a prime case study demonstrating how foreign affairs can play a defining role in an election. The war was the campaign's primary issue, and public opinion polling indicates that Eisenhower benefited at those points in the campaign when other issues were obscured.

In 1968, the Vietnam War was the major influence in President Lyndon Johnson's decision to abandon his hopes for reelection and in weakening the Democrat's eventual nominee, Vice President Hubert Humphrey, who was seen as an opponent of what had become the substantial anti-war wing of the party. In a political season overshadowed by Vietnam, Republican Richard Nixon won a general election that saw the Democratic Party take a massive plunge in its popular support relative to the previous presidential election that can only be compared to the GOP's 1912 and 1932 debacles. Four years later, in the first nomination contest under the new primary system, Democrats selected the ideologically extreme George McGovern after the anti-war New Politics faction took control of the party.

The foregoing analysis raises further doubts about the usefulness of realignment theory's explanation of the party system. Like much of the American politics literature, it is plagued by a kind of tunnel vision that only acknowledges domestic factors. In addition, the argument by some of the theory's most fervent practitioners that the party system experiences a realigning or "critical" election on a generational basis omits any role for contingent events that do not operate according to a fixed schedule. Even the theory's less ardent advocates endorse a relatively rigid framework that risks reducing American political history to multi-decade units that obscure as much as they enlighten. As such, realignment theory needs to be permanently discarded. Periodization schemes, like that proposed by realignment theory, are a natural pursuit, but deterministic claims that ignore foreign affairs and the political reality of contingent events must be avoided. One reason partisan regimes have difficulty dominating for very long is because of random, unforeseen events. Luck plays an important role in political fortunes. This reality is one reason why efforts to periodize are difficult. A new theory to replace the realignment paradigm would need to make room for the profound influence of international events and contingency in general. Any such theory would, like realignment theory, necessitate identifying those elections that achieve a certain level of significance. A more nuanced and qualified theory would likely yield a wider set of "critical elections." Such demarcations are inevitably controversial and subject to some of the same kinds of objections that plague the realignment model. But a more humble, less deterministic, and contextual theory would at least have the virtue of not attempting to explain or account for more than it can. A new theory on this order would have to sacrifice the realignment genre's most grandiose assertions, but it would benefit from increased potency and accuracy.

In sum, the elections explored here suggest that under the right circumstances – namely, a controversial major war – foreign affairs can play a pivotal role in elections. And such an influence occurs frequently. Of the nineteen presidential elections held during this study's span (1900–1972), five, or 26 percent,

TABLE 7.1. *War-Influenced Presidential Elections, 1900–1972*

1900	X	1940[*]	
1904		1944[*]	
1908		1948	
1912		1952	X
1916		1956	
1920	X	1960	
1924		1964	
1928		1968	X
1932		1972	X
1936			

X indicates the elections in which a hot war had a major influence.

[*] denotes the two elections in which World War II did not play a major role, but was a pivotal factor in Franklin Roosevelt's decision to run for reelection.

were heavily influenced by a hot war (see Table 7.1). Two others – 1940 and 1944 – were not marked by war in this manner, although World War II was the decisive factor in President Franklin Roosevelt's decision to seek reelection. As important as party identification, demography, and the state of the economy are, they do not tell the whole story of political party competition. With the relative frequency in which the United States is engaged in foreign conflicts, the political science elections literature should recognize the influence foreign affairs have in the ballot box.

Party Ideology. The ideological component of American political parties has received increased attention in recent decades. Scholars have posited various sources of party ideology, including class-based economics, ethnicity and culture, critical elections, and various elite driven initiatives. Left out of these accounts, once again, is a role for international events.

Major wars shape and change party ideologies by resetting the political landscape and, as a result, forcing political parties to alter their governing philosophies. In other words, wars drive the element of international relations into political parties' public philosophies. The focus of this study has not been to promote an overarching theory to explain all changes in party ideology, but to isolate and explain a key source of party ideology that has often been inappropriately overlooked.[6]

Two shifts in the Democratic Party's post-World War II ideology highlight the way in which war influences this important aspect of domestic politics. The first occurred in the late 1940s. Before the war, Democrats were rooted in a class-based populist rhetoric pitting "the people" against powerful and

---

[6] As discussed extensively in Chapter 1, my analysis of party ideology follows John Gerring in focusing primarily on what he calls "presidential parties" (6). For more on this approach, see the "Party Ideology" section in Chapter 1 and Gerring, *Party Ideologies in America, 1828–1996* (New York: Cambridge University Press, 1998), 6, 22–7.

entrenched elites; following World War II, the party's ideology has been characterized by inclusion. The war was a key contributing factor in this major shift. Most importantly, the war effort required national solidarity, which undermined and negated the often fierce and divisive prewar Democratic rhetoric. Accordingly, the party adopted a more unifying and inclusive public philosophy as is evident in the party's platforms and President Roosevelt's speeches. In addition, World War II contributed to and reinforced the economic prosperity that made the Democrats' "people versus the powerful" rhetoric less resonant with the newly expanded middle class. The humming economy was also linked to the ruling Democrats and, thus, led them to embrace the success of their Keynesian-style capitalism even more fully and in a way they previously had not. The war was also intertwined and played a reinforcing role with several other factors that simultaneously pushed Democrats toward this ideological shift, including the emergence of racial politics, the lack of a challenge from the left, and the new era of Cold War anticommunism.

The second hinge point in post-World War II Democratic ideology occurred as a result of the Vietnam War. Influenced by the New Left, the so-called "New Politics" or "new class" Democrats emerged in the 1960s as a young, educated, anti-war faction within the party that stood in contrast to the blue collar, socially conservative, anti-communist, and pro-Vietnam "old class Democrats." The New Politics cohort was delighted in 1968 when President Johnson announced that he would not run for reelection, but was sorely disappointed when neither of its favored anti-war candidates, Senators Robert Kennedy and Eugene McCarthy, became the party's presidential nominee. Four years later, the New Politics faction reached its apex with the nomination of anti-war Senator George McGovern. Although Richard Nixon's landslide reelection undermined the New Politics group, its influence on the party's ideology has endured. In foreign policy, the Cold War consensus that emerged between the parties following World War II was shattered and Democrats have, for better or worse, been viewed as the anti-war party ever since. In the domestic realm, the full Democratic Party came to embrace, and continues to embrace, identity politics and multiculturalism – a legacy not only of the Civil Rights Movement, but also of Vietnam, which reinforced and internationalized this predilection. Additionally, the New Politics faction succeeded in making the Democratic Party home to social and cultural liberalism. Finally, the young cohort's legacy endures in the democratization they imposed on their party and the American political system as a whole. This shift in Democratic ideology had the side effect of making each party more ideologically coherent.

As with other sections of this project, this analysis of the Democratic Party's ideology following World War II and Vietnam is not intended to be fully exhaustive of war-induced ideological change. Smaller shifts were certainly present in the other wars explored here, and wars prior to 1898 had ideological implications too. Because wars are such major events with the frequently realized capacity to fundamentally shift the country's political landscape, it is natural for political parties to adjust their ideologies to the new terrain. Other instances of war-induced shifts in party ideology could be explored in future research. The two cases presented here were highlighted because they are the most important and enduring shifts and because they so clearly display the way in which wars can alter a party's ideology. In addition, they present two kinds of ideological effects war can induce. The successful and uncontroversial World War II brought a unifying and inclusive shift in Democratic ideology, whereas the unsuccessful and controversial Vietnam led to a bitter and divisive shift to a new Democratic order.

More research that encompasses both foreign and domestic policy is needed in order to gain a complete picture of party ideology. Ideally, such work should be comprehensive and address party ideology on both of these fronts – as parties themselves are forced to do – rather than isolate a domestic ideology and a foreign affairs ideology. In the real world of politics, these arenas influence one another and cannot be divorced. Scholarly attempts to do so will yield only a partial and distorted picture of parties and their ideological makeup.

THE "WAR ON TERROR," AFGHANISTAN, AND IRAQ

For the most part, America's wars have taken place on foreign soil. But they have nonetheless brought significant domestic ramifications. Any thorough understanding of American politics must grapple with these and other international events. As of this writing, the United States is in the midst of hot wars in Afghanistan and Iraq, as well as a broader "war on terror." For the Bush Administration, these three initiatives were linked. Critics, including President Barack Obama, on the other hand, argued that Iraq was a tragic diversion from the more important fight against Al-Qaida. In any event, the current wars in Afghanistan and Iraq, and the larger conflict they are arguably a part of, will likely leave their own lasting legacies for domestic American politics. However, as most historians would caution, it is far too early to draw definitive conclusions, not only because the distance and perspective afforded by the passage of time sharpens our assessments of the past, but also because, with troops still on the ground in Afghanistan and Iraq, these conflicts have not yet even entered the past. But in the years to come, scholars of American politics will clearly have much to grapple with in the decade following the attacks of September 11, 2001.

Index

Note: Page numbers in **bold** represent main discussions of the topic.

CPSIA information can be obtained
at www.ICGtesting.com
Printed in the USA
LVOW12s1117130816

500251LV00005B/202/P